Land, Law and People in Medieval Scotland

For Stephen
with love and thanks

Land, Law and People in Medieval Scotland

Cynthia J. Neville

EDINBURGH
University Press

© Cynthia J. Neville, 2010, 2012

First published in 2010 by
Edinburgh University Press Ltd
22 George Square, Edinburgh EH8 9LF
www.euppublishing.com

The paperback edition 2012

Typeset in Minion and Gill Sans
by Servis Filmsetting Ltd, Stockport, Cheshire

A CIP record for this book is available from the British Library

ISBN 978 0 7486 3958 8 (hardback)
ISBN 978 0 7486 5438 3 (paperback)
ISBN 978 0 7486 6463 4 (epub)
ISBN 978 0 7486 6462 7 (Amazon ebook)

The right of Cynthia J. Neville to be identified as author of this work
has been asserted in accordance with the Copyright, Designs
and Patents Act 1988

Contents

Acknowledgments — vi

Introduction — 1

Part I Land and law

1. Baronial courts in Scotland, 1150–1350 — 13
2. The perambulation of land — 41
3. The development of 'trust in writing': written documents and seals in Scotland, 1100–1300 — 72

Part II Land and people

4. Managing the Strathearn estates: the Muschamp inheritance, 1243–1322 — 113
5. Peasants, servitude and unfreedom in Scotland, 1100–1350 — 147
6. The social space of Scottish lordship: finding friendship in written source materials, 1100–1400 — 186

Conclusion — 206

Bibliography — 212

Index — 240

Maps

Scottish earldoms and major lordships, c. 1100–c. 1400 — viii
The Strathearn–Muschamp inheritance in the late thirteenth century — 114

Acknowledgments

In the course of writing this book I incurred a number of debts, some professional, some personal, all meriting recognition. A generous research grant from the Social Sciences and Humanities Research Council of Canada made it possible for me to undertake several visits to UK archives between 2005 and 2008. I received financial support also from the Society of Antiquaries of Scotland. In the fall of 2006 a month as a Mayers Research Fellow at the Huntington Library in San Marino, California offered me access to an important collection of hard-to-find printed source materials. I spent the late winter and spring of 2007, while on sabbatical leave from Dalhousie, at University College Durham as the Leonard Slater Research Fellow. The Master, Maurice Tucker, the College Fellows, and members of the Department of History more generally went out of their way to make me a part of a vibrant community of scholars and students. Versions of some of the chapters in this book were first presented at conferences held in Canada, the United States, England and Scotland, and I benefited immensely from the helpful suggestions that a host of colleagues offered me in all these venues. I wish to thank Keith Stringer especially for allowing me to read pre-publication versions of some of his forthcoming work and for the generous support that he has consistently given me over the course of my career. I would be negligent indeed if I were to omit thanking the staff of the many libraries and archives that I visited in the last four years. The people who work in the Document Delivery Department at Dalhousie University's Killam Memorial Library dealt with my (never-ending!) requests for interlibrary loan materials with diligence and unflagging patience. I very much appreciate the assistance of the archivists and members of the Reading Room staff at the National Library of Scotland and the National Archives of Scotland, who have welcomed me back to Edinburgh warmly every summer for as long as I can remember. In particular, I wish to mention Kenneth Dunn at the NLS, who went out of his way to help me navigate a series of intractable inventories and to locate important charter materials. Linda Amichand, from Archival and Special Collections at the University of Guelph Library, offered enthusiastic assistance in helping me to secure a copy of a charter of Duncan IV earl of Fife. Thanks, too, to Esmé Watson

ACKNOWLEDGMENTS

at EUP and to Eliza Wright for her editing. Last, but by no means least, I wish to acknowledge the love and support of my husband, Stephen. Over the years he has always demonstrated a keen interest in my research, and his good humour has done much to carry us through the frequent absences from home that my work requires.

Scottish earldoms and major lordships, c. 1100–c. 1400

Introduction

In January 2007 Scottish historians, archaeologists and literary scholars gathered to mark the fiftieth annual meeting of the organisation known as The Scottish Medievalists. The theme of the conference was that of 'renaissances', and several papers explored the ways in which research on the kingdom's past has changed over the previous half century. One of the developments identified as most significant in recent years is the welcome reception that the field of Scottish studies has given to new theoretical paradigms through which to interpret the comparatively limited range of primary source materials that survives from the medieval period. Among the most important of these new perspectives has been the model of thick description, an analytical approach that first animated studies in cultural anthropology and ethnography in the 1970s, then was applied (though not always to acclaim) by other social scientists and humanists.[1] In the last two decades especially the fluidity of disciplinary boundaries within the field of Scottish studies has borne rich and varied fruit. It has opened the way, among other things, to a new kind of 'Celtic' history, one that neither laments a vanished Celtic past, nor celebrates a mythical pan-Celtic British experience. Drawing heavily on the methodologies that inform the 'new' British history, moreover, recent work has sought to compare, contrast and juxtapose the experiences of Scotland with those of Ireland and Wales in the three centuries after 1066, a period that, as Professor Rees Davies argued some years ago, was critical in the construction of the British polity.[2] The efforts of the team that Donald Watt assembled in the mid-1980s to produce a new edition of Walter Bower's *Scotichronicon* have been particularly important in shedding new light on the intricacies of national and historical identity-making in the medieval period,[3] and have in turn made possible a highly sophisticated understanding of the encounter that took place between Gaels and Europeans in the two to three centuries after the death of King Mael Coluim III in 1093.

The 'new' Scottish history has not, however, proven uncontroversial. If there is, by now, some consensus among historians that the settlement of a European aristocracy in Scotland in the twelfth and thirteenth centuries effected profound change to the social, political and religious landscapes of the kingdom, there is much less agreement about the ways in which the cultures of the native Gaels and the incoming Europeans interacted with and influenced each other. In their efforts to challenge the nineteenth-century paradigm that contrasted Celtic 'barbarism' with European 'civilisation', Scottish historians have formulated several contesting perspectives from which to analyse the interaction of indigenous Gaelic and innovative continental customs, mores and laws. One particularly effective model, that of periphery and core, was first developed in the Scottish context by Keith Stringer as a vehicle through which to understand relations between the crown and its great territorial lords.[4] Another approach has argued for a conceptualisation of the medieval kingdom as a series of interacting 'power centres' from which great lords, including the king himself, actualised political, legal and economic authority in a series of constantly mutating spheres of influence. Although they have examined the topic from different perspectives, scholars interested in this approach have done much to illuminate the complex process by which the multiple estates, thanages and mormaerships of ancient Alba coalesced into the kingdom about which chroniclers such as the authors of the *Gesta Annalia I* and *II*, John of Fordun and Walter Bower could later write so confidently.[5] The work of archaeologists on the material remains of such power centres, moreover, has added breadth and depth to the portrayal of the medieval Scottish state as the culmination of a series of stages that, between the ninth and the thirteenth centuries, profoundly altered 'ideological structures' linking 'the powerful and the subservient'.[6] A firmer grasp of the power structures of the kingdom in this period has led scholars to examine the negotiation, on a regional level, of royal and lordly authority, and detailed examinations of great lordships have highlighted the ways in which medieval aristocrats perceived, conceived and experienced the exercise of political power in territories as far apart as Galloway, the western isles and Moray.[7]

Common to most of these studies is the recognition of the aristocratic household as the nexus between the local world of the lordship and the wider political space of the kingdom. Historians have therefore devoted considerable attention also to the reconstruction of noble affinities, particularly during the period that Geoffrey Barrow long ago dubbed the 'Anglo-Norman era',[8] when the settlement of new families from England and the continent transformed the cultural landscape of Scotland and initiated within the kingdom a rich commingling of the languages and customs of people of Gaelic, Norse, Brittonic, Anglian, English, French and Flemish descent. At the level of the aristocracy the mechanics of these myriad encounters left traces in new patterns of marriage and inheritance, structures of land holding, the exploitation of peasant labour, and practices of generating and preserving the collective memory of events. All these topics are examined in this volume.

Despite the vigour with which they sometimes delimit, define and defend their theoretical positions, almost all scholars are in agreement in viewing the two and a half centuries after the accession of David I in 1124 as a formative period in the history of Scotland. Most are also of the opinion that the outbreak of war with England in 1296 marked a watershed within this phase of the nation's development, signalling not merely a dislocation of the course of Scottish politics at home and in the wider European sphere, but also a shift in the configuration of the kingdom's legal institutions and in popular and elite manifestations of its cultural heritage. By the year 1400 Scotland had developed a distinct identity within the British Isles, a sense of a past that was neither wholly Gaelic nor self-consciously European.[9] Yet, if there is broad agreement among scholars about the period during which the late medieval Scottish polity took shape, there is still scope for discussion about the relationships among the several ethnic groups that populated the kingdom in the early 'Anglo-Norman era'. Recent arguments aimed at emphasising the uniformity that characterised the political aspirations, economic ambitions and spiritual beliefs of Gaels, Norse, English and Europeans in twelfth- and thirteenth-century Scotland have offered timely warnings against reducing the complexity of the cultural encounter of the period to such simple diachronic models as native 'barbarism' versus European 'civility', conquest versus submission, and active resistance versus passive accommodation.[10]

Too strong an emphasis on cultural harmony none the less runs the risk of effacing the very real and profound linguistic, religious and cultural differences that distinguished the native Gaelic population of Scotland in particular from that of the English and continental newcomers after 1124. Despite the allure of Angevin notions of legal, jurisdictional and political authority, the Scottish crown never lost touch with the Irish past of the kingdom of Alba; indeed, in the thirteenth century literate scholars came to deploy the unique history of the Scottish people as a potent weapon in defence of the independence and sovereignty of the realm.[11] The great Gaelic magnates had even less inclination to divest themselves entirely of their native antecedents and powerful reasons to champion their ethnic identities. Most obviously, their status as mormaers endowed them with incontestable claims to distinction and high honour within their own lands and in the entourage of the Mac Malcolm court. After 1124, moreover, the readiness of the crown itself to accommodate their customs, language and territorial claims promised (and delivered) them an ongoing share in the governance of the realm.[12] Alexander Grant's observation that in Clydesdale the continuities associated with Scotland's twelfth- and thirteenth-century 'Normanisation' were as significant as the changes, may aptly be applied to the whole kingdom.[13]

In many respects, then, the Scotland of the late fourteenth-century king Robert III was a unique kingdom, with 'hybrid institutions, hybrid law, a hybrid Church, and an increasingly hybrid landowning class'.[14] The chapters in this volume explore, from a variety of perspectives, the encounter between Gaels and Europeans in the kingdom, and the ways in which this hybridisation took shape as the customs and practices of both groups found expression in Scottish legal and social contexts. These studies are based on a close reading of several hundred charters, brieves and other written deeds that survive from the period between 1100 and 1400 from across the length and breadth of the kingdom. Many of these documents have long been available in print in the volumes published by historical and antiquarian societies such as the Maitland, Bannatyne and Spalding Clubs and the Scottish History Society. Others (though far fewer) remain in manuscript form, housed in the collections of the National Archives and the National Library of Scotland. Where it has been deemed appropriate, that is, where the published documents offer reliable transcriptions of the original charter texts, references in this book are made to printed versions. In several chapters the use of Gaelic forms of personal names – or the choice to eschew them – is deliberate, signalling an intention to draw the reader's attention to the different perspectives that native Gaels and European newcomers brought to processes as varied as dispute resolution, boundary marching, estate management and social categorisation.

Twelfth-, thirteenth- and fourteenth-century Scotland was a rich blend of native Gaelic and European influences, where the customs and practices of two very distinct cultures interacted and worked together to shape a unique kind of lordly authority. Part I of this book examines aspects of the relationship between land and law in this period. One of the more interesting manifestations of the blend of 'old' and 'new' is the system of courts that developed in the course of the thirteenth century. Unlike contemporary England, where justice and dispute settlement came under the increasing control of the Norman, and especially the Angevin period crown, the Scottish medieval legal system saw the kings continue to share responsibility for punishing misdeeds and misdoers with their more important subjects, including the great Gaelic magnates who had once enjoyed exclusive responsibility for dispensing justice in the territories of the old mormaerships as heads of extensive kinship networks. The native lords none the less found much to attract them in the broad spectrum of lordly prerogatives of justice that incoming barons introduced to the kingdom from England and northern France. The first chapter of the book examines the early evidence relating to lordly courts in the late twelfth and the thirteenth centuries, both those of the Anglo-Norman and European newcomers and, more particularly, those of the great native dignitaries. It then explores, compares and contrasts the ways in which native aristocrats adopted and adapted English and European concepts of justice within these courts down to the mid-fourteenth century. A chief focus of the chapter is on the ways in which Gaelic lords used the ceremony and ritual associated with the dispensation of justice to perpetuate – and enhance – uniquely native concepts of lordly authority.

The formal marching of boundaries – perambulation – remained for many years after the accession of King David I in 1124 one of the most important legal procedures at Scottish common law. While the practice eventually declined in importance in England, it retained in Scotland a variety of social and political dimensions, yet it has been the subject of relatively little close scholarly scrutiny.[15] Chapter 2 explores the significance of perambulation in medieval Scottish society. It begins with a brief review of the work that legal historians have done on the origins of the royal brieve that, as early as the reign of David I, initiated as a matter of routine the act of perambulating the marches of an estate. It examines also the steadily increasing popularity of the procedure after 1124, the ways in which it was carried out, and the identity both of the litigants who sought to settle disputes with recourse to perambulation and the witnesses upon whose expertise they depended. Finally, the chapter discusses the act of perambulation within the wider context of the social and cultural history of 'Anglo-Norman era' Scotland, and emphasises the usefulness of treating the process as a lens through which to explore the ways in which the intermingling of Gaelic and European customs shaped the early development of Scottish law.

By the early thirteenth century throughout lowland Scotland, letters, charters, indentures and notifications authenticated with waxen seals had acquired an evidentiary authority that was effecting a profound transformation of legal practice in royal and baronial courts. Increasing reliance on written deeds and personal seals as 'credible media' is symptomatic of a profound shift within medieval culture and the development of what scholars now generally refer to, *pace* Michael Clanchy, as 'trust in writing'.[16] Scottish historians have only recently begun to explore in depth the mechanics of that process as it occurred in Scotland.[17] The first section of Chapter 3 examines the ways in which lay persons became accustomed to using written documents in the important business of acquiring and conveying estates of land and their perquisites. A second section traces the proliferation of seal usage in Scotland. The chronological focus in this chapter is on the century or so between the accession to the throne in 1124 of David I and c. 1250, by which time there is discernible in Scotland a 'community bound together by a common attitude towards the uses of documents and a shared interpretation of certain texts'.[18] Within the mere century and a quarter between these dates, title to property (and its revenues) had become so closely tied to possession of some kind of sealed instrument that in almost all regions of the kingdom there can have been few landholders who were not thoroughly acquainted with the evidentiary value of written charters. The stages by which medieval Scottish people came to 'develop trust' in documents and in the images impressed on waxen seals offer a unique vehicle through which to trace changing notions of personal and family identity among the landholding ranks.

In Part II of this book the focus shifts to the twin themes of land and people. Chapter 4 offers a study of medieval Scottish landownership at the level of the aristocracy in the context of a single lordship, examined over the *longue durée* of the years 1240 to 1322. Around 1243 the Scottish magnate Malise II earl of Strathearn married Marjory, daughter of Robert de Muschamp, baron of Wooler in Northumberland. The match typifies the social currency that marriage represented to high-ranking families throughout Britain in the mid-thirteenth century, in that it allowed Muschamp to associate himself on equal terms with one of the most ancient and respected Gaelic families in the kingdom, and made it possible for Malise to join the exclusive ranks of the Anglo-Scottish border aristocracy. This chapter reviews the links, familial, social and political, that Earl Malise II (d. 1271) and his son, Malise III (d. c. 1317) forged with the barony of Wooler in Northumberland from the middle years of the thirteenth century down to the severance of that link in the opening decades of the fourteenth. Of especial interest here are the strategies that the father devised for preserving the benefits of English-held property for his kindred as a consequence, and in spite, of the challenges posed by the outbreak of war in 1296. The chapter is grounded in the new (and thoroughly appropriate) emphasis on the wide lens of the aristocratic gaze that scholars such as Robin Frame, Keith Stringer and others have shown is essential to an understanding of the nobility of the period.[19] Medieval magnates were above all driven by a profound preoccupation with the advancement of the family; as one scholar has trenchantly put it: '[k]in solidarities were central in shaping patterns of property, power and violence'.[20] So, too, were they the guiding spirit behind the formulation of noble strategies designed to protect and preserve landed wealth at virtually all costs. The late thirteenth-century wars of independence generated political crises at every level of Scottish society; arguably, nowhere was the uncertainty of these years more acute than among men and women who had the most to lose. Malise II proved surprisingly successful in planning and implementing strategies for managing his Northumberland estates on behalf of his extended family; his sound work is evident in the relative success of his heirs in navigating the troubled waters of the post-1296 crisis. The achievements of the Strathearn kindred in holding on to their English property stands in vivid contrast to the disasters that befell Earl Malise III and his son in Scotland at the height of the conflict.[21]

Chapter 5 examines the other end of the social spectrum. Current scholarship sheds comparatively little light on the ways in which people who occupied the lowest ranks of Scottish society experienced unfreedom and servility in the period between roughly 1100 and the middle years of the fourteenth century. The precarious nature of surviving source materials has long obscured the meaning of slavery and serfdom in this period and has made it difficult for historians to paint a clear picture of the lot of the poor folk of Scotland. This chapter revisits some of the evidence that scholars have already explored, and several of its arguments echo the conclusions of earlier historians, but it seeks primarily to understand the ways in which the changing economic, political and social landscapes that marked the 'Anglo-Norman era' in Scotland affected people of low social rank, especially native Gaels. Although Archibald Duncan has issued a stern warning against close comparison of any kind between Scotland and Ireland,[22] the argument is made here that the conditions which transformed the social and legal status of a broad spectrum of the indigenous population in Ireland after 1171 were in many respects similar to those which affected peasants in the course of the 'Normanisation' of Scotland. The methodologies and findings of Irish historians are applied to Scottish charter texts in an effort to detect the otherwise muted voices of the tillers of the soil.

Chapter 6 explores the ways in which the methodological and theoretical perspectives of recent scholarship in the humanities and social sciences may be applied to the large body of charter and charter-related source materials that survives from the medieval period. Scottish historians, particularly those interested in the years between 1100 and 1400, have long acknowledged the centrality of written title deeds to the study of the medieval landed elite, and have learned to mine the technical language of these documents to uncover information 'which they were not in the first place designed to provide'.[23] The study offered here examines the concept of friendship (*amicitia*) among the landholding ranks of Scottish society, and shows that despite their limitations charter texts are rich sources for the study of personal relationships in the medieval kingdom. It begins with a brief review of historiographical trends, notably the concept of 'social space', that have deeply influenced recent studies of the European world or Europe and discusses how scholars have used this paradigm to uncover the complex nature of friendship in the medieval period. The chapter then turns to a study of *amicitia* as it is expressed in extant charter texts from the period 1100–1400. It argues that the *literati* who drafted charters, indentures, notifications and other kinds of written instruments on behalf of noble patrons were very much up to date with, and receptive to, concepts of friendship then current in Europe. Scottish clerks used the terms associated with *amicitia* in a wide range of contexts; chiefly, but by no means exclusively, in the curial setting; moreover, they deployed the language of friendship in thoughtful, articulate and meaningful fashion. In seeking to understand the circumstances in which medieval Scottish clerks, the landholders who employed them, and the people who interacted with them thought about and identified 'friends', the chapter offers still another model by which to analyse the cultural encounter that took place between Gaels and Europeans and a different conceptual framework for evaluating the role that both peoples played in the genesis of a uniquely Scottish, hybrid, society.

The Conclusion, finally, reviews the several themes that run through this book. The particular perspective here is once again that of the British Isles as a whole, the aim being an effort to situate Scottish evidence about land, law and people within a broader geographical context.

Notes

1. C. Geertz, *The Interpretation of Cultures* (New York, 1973), pp. 3–30.
2. R. R. Davies, 'In praise of British history', in R. R. Davies (ed.), *The British Isles, 1100–1500: Comparisons, Contrasts and Connections* (Edinburgh, 1988), pp. 10–17 and, more recently, R. R. Davies, *The First English Empire: Power and Identities in the British Isles, 1093–1343* (Oxford, 2000), pp. 2–3.
3. B. E. Crawford, 'Introduction', in *Church, Chronicle and Learning in Medieval Scotland: Essays presented to Donald Watt on the Occasion of the Completion of the Publication of Bower's* Scotichronicon (Edinburgh, 1999), pp. 7–8.
4. K. J. Stringer, 'Periphery and core in thirteenth-century Scotland: Alan, son of Roland, lord of Galloway and constable of Scotland', in A. Grant and K. J. Stringer (eds), *Medieval Scotland: Crown, Lordship and Community – Essays presented to G. W. S. Barrow* (Edinburgh, 1993), pp. 82–113; studies applying this model include R. Oram, *The Lordship of Galloway* (Edinburgh, 2000), and R. A. McDonald, 'Matrimonial politics and core-periphery interactions in twelfth- and early thirteenth-century Scotland', *Journal of Medieval History*, 21 (1995), pp. 227–47.
5. Alexander Grant and Dauvit Broun in particular have written at considerable length about the subject; see especially A. Grant, 'The construction of the early Scottish state', in J. R. Maddicott and D. M. Palliser (eds), *The Medieval State:*

Essays presented to James Campbell (London, 2000), pp. 47–71; D. Broun, 'The property records in the Book of Deer as a source for early Scottish society', in K. Forsyth (ed.), *Studies on the Book of Deer* (Dublin, 2008), pp. 309–60; and D. Broun, *Scottish Independence and the Idea of Britain from the Picts to Alexander III* (Edinburgh, 2007).

6. S. T. Driscoll, 'Formalising the mechanisms of state power: early Scottish lordship from the ninth to the thirteenth centuries', in S. M. Foster, A. Macinnes and R. MacInnes (eds), *Scottish Power Centres from the Early Middle Ages to the Twentieth Century* (Glasgow, 1998), pp. 33–58 and, in the same volume, the essays by Foster and Watson. For a brief commentary on the contribution of some of this literature to concepts of space and political community in the medieval European context, see W. Davies, 'Introduction', in W. Davies, G. Halsall and A. Reynolds (eds), *People and Space in the Middle Ages, 300–1300* (Turnhout, 2006), esp. pp. 4–7, and W. Davies, 'Populations, territory and community membership: contrasts and conclusions', ibid. pp. 299–303.
7. See here the items listed in the Bibliography under the following authors' names: Beam (Balliol family), Blakely (Bruce family), Boardman and Ross (various families), R. A. McDonald (lordship of Argyll), Neville (families of Strathearn and Lennox), Oram (Moray and the lords of Galloway), Simpson (family of de Quincy), Stringer (lords of Galloway and Lauderdale, David earl of Huntingdon), A. Young (Comyn family).
8. G. W. S. Barrow, *The Anglo-Norman Era in Scottish History* (Oxford, 1980).
9. See the recent discussions in C. J. Neville, *Native Lordship in Medieval Scotland: The Earldoms of Strathearn and Lennox, c. 1140–1365* (Dublin, 2005), pp. 2–9; K. Stringer, 'The emergence of a nation-state, 1100–1300', in J. Wormald (ed.), *Scotland: A History* (Oxford, 2005), pp. 39–76. Emphasis on the importance of this period also lies at the heart of the discussion in K. Stringer, 'States, liberties and communities in medieval Britain and Ireland (c.1100–1400)', in M. Prestwich (ed.), *Liberties and Identities in the Medieval British Isles* (Woodbridge, 2008), pp. 5–36.
10. See, most recently M. Hammond, 'Ethnicity and the writing of medieval Scottish historiography', *Scottish Historical Review*, 85 (2006), pp. 1–27; and M. Hammond, 'Ethnicity, personal names and the nature of Scottish Europeanization', in B. K. U. Weiler et al. (eds), *Thirteenth Century England, XI: Proceedings of the Gregynog Conference, 2003* (Woodbridge, 2007), pp. 82–94.
11. D. Broun, *The Irish Identity of the Kingdom of the Scots* (Woodbridge, 1999), passim.
12. See here the arguments offered in Neville, *Native Lordship*, passim.
13. A. Grant, 'Lordship and society in twelfth-century Clydesdale', in H. Pryce and J. Watts (eds), *Power and Identity in the Middle Ages: Essays in Memory of Rees Davies* (Oxford, 2007), pp. 122–3. Dauvit Broun offers equally convincing arguments for viewing the early encounter between Gaels and Europeans as a process of accommodation in which the customs and practices of both groups

contributed in significant fashion to the development of Scottish political and social identity; 'Anglo-French acculturation and the Irish element in Scottish identity', in B. Smith (ed.), *Britain and Ireland, 900–1300: Insular Responses to Medieval European Change* (Cambridge, 1999), pp. 135–53.
14. A. Grant, 'Scotland's 'Celtic fringe' in the late middle ages: the MacDonald lords of the Isles and the kingdom of Scotland', in Davies (ed.), *The British Isles, 1100–1500*, p. 119.
15. See, however, I. D. Willock, *The Origins and Development of the Jury in Scotland* (Edinburgh, 1966), pp. 9–14, 126–9.
16. P. Schulte, M. Mostert and I. van Renswoude (eds), *Strategies of Writing: Studies on Text and Trust in the Middle Ages* (Turnhout, 2008), p xii; M. T. Clanchy, *From Memory to Written Record: England, 1066–1307*, 2nd edn (Oxford, 1993).
17. A notable exception here is D. Broun, *The Charters of Gaelic Scotland and Ireland in the Early and Central Middle Ages* (Cambridge, 1995).
18. C. F. Briggs, 'Literacy, reading and writing in the medieval west', *Journal of Medieval History*, 26 (2000), p. 418.
19. R. Frame, 'Aristocracies and the political configuration of the British Isles', in Davies (ed.), *The British Isles, 1100–1500*, pp. 142–59; K. J. Stringer, 'Identities in thirteenth-century England: frontier society in the far north', in C. Björn, A. Grant and K. J. Stringer (eds), *Social and Political Identities in Western History* (Copenhagen, 1994), pp. 28–66; R. Blakely, *The Brus Family in England and Scotland, 1100–1295* (Woodbridge, 2005), pp. 2–6; A. Beam, *The Balliol Dynasty, 1210–1364* (East Linton, 2008), pp. 7–8, 273; A. King, 'Best of enemies: were the fourteenth-century Anglo-Scottish marches a "frontier society"?', in A. King and M. A. Penman (eds), *England and Scotland in the Fourteenth Century: New Perspectives* (Woodbridge, 2007), pp. 116–35.
20. R. Bartlett, 'Medieval and modern concepts of race and ethnicity', *Journal of Medieval and Early Modern Studies*, 31 (2001), p. 44.
21. See here the detailed study of Malise III's wartime misfortunes in C. J. Neville, 'The political allegiance of the earls of Strathearn during the War of Independence', *Scottish Historical Review*, 65 (1986), pp. 133–53.
22. A. A. M. Duncan, *Scotland: The Making of the Kingdom* (Edinburgh, 1975), p. 106.
23. B. Webster, *Scotland from the Eleventh Century to 1603* (Cambridge, 1975), p. 62.

PART I

LAND AND LAW

CHAPTER 1

Baronial courts in Scotland, 1150–1350

INTRODUCTION

Writing the early history of the common law in medieval Scotland is an exercise fraught with difficulty. Scholarly discussions of this topic almost always begin with a lament about the challenges that extant source materials pose to a clear understanding of the business of medieval courtrooms, royal and baronial, and invidious comparisons with the plentiful records that survive from England. Sixty years ago, for example, Lord Cooper remarked sadly that 'of Plea Rolls and Year Books we have none'.[1] More recently, in a study that remains authoritative, Hector MacQueen reminded his readers that, but for the work of William Croft Dickinson, we would know precious little about the procedures used in the Scottish courts even as late as the sixteenth century.[2]

The picture, however, is improving. Thanks to the efforts of Geoffrey Barrow, the role and responsibilities of the two most important officers of the Scottish crown, the justiciar and the sheriff, are now better understood; so, too, is the extraordinary resilience, well into the thirteenth century in the region north of Forth, of the *breitheamh*, whom the Latin charter-writers called the *iudex*.[3] Barrow's work on onomastics has also identified several dozen sites where local communities gathered to hear the judgments of dempsters and other Gaelic officials such as mairs and, presumably, the public proclamations of royal officials.[4] The research of MacQueen and Alan Harding on early Scottish brieves has highlighted the critical importance of English legal principles to the development of several aspects of Scots law in the fourteenth and fifteenth centuries, the same period that Lord Cooper once dismally dubbed the 'dark age' of Scottish legal history.[5] Perhaps most important, the combined scholarship of a handful of historians on mechanisms of dispute settlement within the wider contexts of Britain and Europe has finally put to rest the assumption that the survival of seigniorial jurisdiction in later medieval Scotland was symptomatic of the inability of the crown to provide its subjects with effective or satisfactory justice.[6] In the twelfth century and for long thereafter, the Scottish judicial system was far more accommodating of lordly justice than post-Angevin England ever was; in Scotland, unlike its neighbour, kings and magnates shared responsibility for maintaining law and order and for overseeing the business of dispute settlement. Flexibility, recognition of the central importance of the kin group, and the existence of a series of 'extremely regionalized power structures': all have been identified as hallmarks of a uniquely Scottish form of common law.[7]

Positing the effectiveness of the Scottish medieval legal system and arguing for its distinctiveness are one thing; understanding the ways in which this accommodation between local and royal justice actually operated on the ground is quite another. Here, the nature of surviving legal materials has more seriously circumscribed attempts to uncover seigniorial authority at work, especially in the period before the reign of Robert Bruce. This chapter offers a morphology of the secular lordly court in Scotland in the two centuries between 1150 and 1350. It explores a range of topics relating to the operation of baronial justice, among them fundamental questions concerning contemporary understandings of the function of lordly courts, the kind of business that lords and litigants alike considered appropriate to baronial justice and, perhaps most elusive of all in surviving records, the rituals and ceremonies that governed the conduct of people who went to court. The use of charter materials as a window into medieval baronial courts in medieval Britain is hardly new, but recent work has demonstrated just how essential is this body of record to an understanding of the Scottish legal system.[8] Formulaic though the texts may be, their minutiae are of great value to the historian of the law. Of especial interest here are the courts over which members of the Gaelic-speaking aristocracy presided. If the absence of plea rolls, year books, lists of fines and similar materials has discouraged scholars interested in the extent to which the 'feudal' institutions of post-Conquest England were transplanted into southern Scotland, greater frustrations still attend those who have sought to understand how the courts of native magnates functioned within the great territorial lordships north of Forth. Surviving written sources here are not merely meagre; they are all but non-existent. This study seeks also, therefore, to uncover new evidence from oft-cited record materials to shed fresh light on the exercise of lordly authority within the Gaelicised regions of the kingdom.

The origins of lordly courts in Scotland

Historians are in general agreement that the extent to which Scottish magnates exercised jurisdiction over their tenants varied from place to place, and reflected in turn the degree to which the relationship between the king and individual magnates was set out in written charters of infeftment.

Often noted in this context is a confirmation of King William I to Robert Bruce II of the lands of Annandale, in which Bruce was given extensive rights of jurisdiction, excluding only 'the causes that the king has reserved to himself', later known as the pleas of the crown.[9] Although its text is now lost, another royal charter, this one dated c. 1138, granting the earldom of Fife to Donnchadh I, appears to have conferred on a native dignitary similarly broad legal authority, an impression that is clarified and confirmed in a later act.[10] But not all magnates had such charters. One of the many unusual aspects of the twelfth- and thirteenth-century political landscape of Scotland is the significant number of noblemen (and women), most of them of native extraction, who held their lands without benefit of written deeds, chief among them the Gaelic earls of Lennox, Strathearn, Buchan, Atholl, Mar and Angus, and many other men of less exalted rank. In the late twelfth century, and for a considerable period before this, these lords, too, enjoyed comprehensive jurisdiction over quarrels between their tenants and cognisance of all but the most serious criminal offences that the latter committed.[11] Such prerogatives were often expressed in the jingle 'sake, soke, toll, team and infangenthief' so familiar to historians of late Anglo-Saxon and Norman England.[12] Scottish charters frequently add to the phrase the words 'with gallows and pit', that is, provision for the execution of condemned criminals and the staging of ordeals. Surviving charters make it clear that virtually all the great baronial families who first came to Scotland in the twelfth century – Bruces, Stewarts, Morvilles, Comyns and their ilk – enjoyed such authority as a matter of course in the portions of Scotland in which they settled in the opening phases of the 'Anglo-Norman era'.[13] So, too, however, did the great Gaelic aristocratic kindreds, descendants of the mormaers of old who, designated as 'earls' (*comites*) by the Latin-writing charter scribes of their day, had enjoyed extensive rights over their men long before David I came on the scene. Although few of these great Gaelic lords thought it necessary – or, indeed, wise – to define the authority that they exercised in formal, written title deeds,[14] there is little doubt that, perhaps even more than the newcomers, they were powerful figures in the judicial landscape of their day. It was, for example, in their capacity as mormaers that in 1240 Eoghan son of Donnchadh of Argyll summoned a gathering of his kinsmen to bear witness to his grant of lands in Lismore to the bishop of Argyll and that, a decade or so earlier, Margaret, countess of Buchan in her own right, required that an assembly of her tenants attest a series of gifts to the church of St Andrews.[15]

By the early years of the fourteenth century the right to maintain pit and gallows and the powers of life and limb implicit in this prerogative had become 'the distinguishing mark and test' of tenure *in baroniam*.[16]

The term was a loan from earlier English and, ultimately, Norman usage, and although it appeared late in Scotland, it spoke to a distinction already more than a century old between magnates of great stature and landholders of less exalted rank.[17] In the early fourteenth century, moreover, tenure in barony is found throughout the kingdom, both in the region south of Forth where English and continental newcomers had first put down roots, as well as in the great provincial lordships north of Forth, many still under the control of Gaelic-speaking noblemen. Discussion of the antecedents of these broad jurisdictional powers, however, has given rise to considerable debate and disagreement. As far back as 1920, Rachel Reid argued that the ancient judicial authority exercised by native mormaers and thanes, including powers of life and limb, merged seamlessly with those enjoyed by Anglo-Norman barons under the benign influence of King David I.[18] Barrow is not convinced that the transition occurred so smoothly, and has drawn a distinction between lords who wielded authority by virtue of their status as agents of the crown (that is, as thanes, justiciars and sheriffs), and those who exercised what he called 'mediated', or private, justice, acquired by means of a royal grant, as did Robert Bruce II in Annandale.[19] More recently, Alexander Grant has refined this argument, positing a pre-twelfth-century legal structure in which the great provincial lords and their thanes (Gaelic *tòiseachean*) enjoyed the prerogative of high justice, administering the law within their territories subject only to the general oversight of the crown.[20] Their authority, he has shown compellingly, was 'public', arising as it did from their status as mormaers, 'great stewards', an office that they held, implicitly at least, by royal appointment. Beyond the territorial lordships, in those parts of the kingdom controlled directly by the king, royal thanes operated in much the same fashion. The continuing exercise of public justice at the behest of the crown distinguishes the early history of Scottish common law from that of contemporary England;[21] more important still, it set earls and royal thanes apart from the great barons of the period and the power that they wielded over their tenants by royal gift. The complex political and cultural changes that occurred in Scotland in the first century of the 'Anglo-Norman era' saw the transformation of some royal thanages into sheriffdoms, and others into knights' feus that resembled in many respect those that were being created afresh for incoming English and continental magnates. The landholders established in all these instances had the responsibility to administer justice on behalf of the king, though each derived his legal authority from different foundations. Over time, however, and particularly in the reigns of Alexander II and Alexander III, the distinction between 'public' and 'private' justice faded in practice.[22]

In the one hundred and fifty-odd years before the reign of Robert Bruce, then, native lords and incoming barons alike convened courts of various kinds in which decisions of weight and significance were made. Precisely how these tribunals were conducted is extremely difficult to trace other than in the charter texts that survive from this period. An untold number of parchment sheets recording decisions made in baronial courts found their way into the rolls of 'recognitions', 'inquests', 'perambulations', 'extents' and the records of 'plaints', 'pleas' and 'settlements' that Edward I carried off to England between 1291 and 1296, then systematically destroyed.[23] Nevertheless, it is pertinent to bear in mind here the injunction that Lord Cooper voiced sixty years ago against attributing all the archival shortcomings of the thirteenth century to Edward's depredations. In his opinion, there is compelling evidence to suggest that records of the sort generated by baronial courts were never written in the first place.[24] Precisely because justice was a cooperative effort in medieval Scotland, and the business of the baronial courts was the purview of local communities and 'amateur judges', most disputes could be settled either informally, out of court, or with the assistance of lordly arbitration.[25] Tantalising allusions in extant charter texts to the presence of friends and kinsmen in curial settings show that arbitration and mediation might play vital roles in the judicial process,[26] but they also suggest that in many of these instances there was no need to record judgments, whether these were delivered orally by native *breitheamhnan* or noble arbitrators.[27] The question for the historian of the medieval legal system in Scotland should not, then, be, 'Where are the missing legal records?', but rather, 'What evidence is there of magnates acting in their capacities as dispensers of justice?'

The answer here, fortunately, is encouraging. For most of the period between 1150 and 1350, while the king and his justiciars and sheriffs generated formularies, brieves and other ephemera in the work they performed on behalf of the crown, secular lords and ecclesiastical prelates acting in their capacity as barons of the realm left ample traces of their judicial activity in the texts of charters, notifications, chirographs and indentures. If, in 1150, medieval landholders and lawmen did not yet accord such instruments full dispositive or evidentiary authority, less than one hundred years later written documents had become deeply embedded within the legal culture of Scotland and, as discussed below, had acquired intrinsic, probative value in the curial setting. Moreover, the variety of uses to which the charter form might be directed made it an ideal medium in which to preserve written accounts of actions done, promises offered and decisions effected in the courtroom.

Historians of early Scots law have already made fruitful use of written *acta* to sketch the contours of the baronial court in the regions of the kingdom that saw intensive Anglo-Norman and continental settlement, an area still sometimes referred to as the 'feudalised' portions of the realm.[28] Chief among their concerns has been the need to distinguish the baronial court as a predominantly social space in which magnates interacted with clients from the court as a site in which these lords negotiated power by means of the exercise of jurisdiction.[29] The two were by no means exclusive. The social world of the European noblemen who now called Scotland their home revolved around the Christian calendar, and the great feast days of Christmas, Easter and Pentecost saw regular gatherings in great halls across the kingdom of the kinsmen, tenants, clients and friends of important noblemen. These events were primarily occasions for celebration, but also opportunities to conduct business relating to landownership. Such, most notably, were the three 'head courts' of Yule, Easter and Michaelmas, mention of which is frequent in the charters that survive from across Scotland beginning in the thirteenth century. Assemblies of magnates and their followers, however, did not take place only in response to the demands of the Christian calendar. Other gatherings reflected more specifically the events associated with the life cycle of the feu and the important business of estate management. Among the Anglo-Norman and continental incomers, for example, it was customary for great lords to summon their tenants on special occasions such as the knighting of an eldest son, the marriage of a daughter, the coming of age of an heir. These events combined the obligations of social convention with the duty of all vassals to lend aid and counsel to their lords in matters relating to the governance of the barony. The most prestigious and best recorded of such occasions were those that took place in the presence of the king. Such, for example, were the knightings of John Comyn in 1267 and of Nicholas de Soules in 1271, performed by King Alexander III himself.[30] The Gaelic year was similarly marked with ceremonies, also revolving around holy days, in which tenants met formally with their lords. Native society attached profound significance to the twin obligations of guesting and feasting, the former manifested in the requirement of tenants to render conveth (hospitality and wayting) to their overlords, and the latter in the duty of a head of kindred to offer his followers opportunities to eat, drink and revel at his table.[31] The constant movement of Gaelic magnates across the length and breadth of their provinces made gatherings such as these ideal venues for the conduct of business. It was on the occasion of his coming of age, for example, that around 1220 Robert, son and heir of Gille Brigte earl of Strathearn, made a solemn pledge before witnesses to protect his family's religious foundation at Inchaffray, and at the same time took advantage of the assembled crowd to issue to the canons his confirmation of several earlier deeds.[32] Similarly, in 1248 the healing of a rift between

Mael Coluim son of Earl Maoldomhnaich of Lennox and another comital tenant took place in a formal gathering that may well have marked some celebration; certainly, Mael Coluim and his father together issued a series of charters at this time.[33]

Distinct from these occasions, however, were the more routine, business-like gatherings the principal purpose of which was the exercise of lordly authority. The scribes who drafted charters on behalf of secular and ecclesiastical donors and beneficiaries who lived in portions of the realm where lords were replicating English-style feu holdings were in no doubt that these were baronial 'courts' proper. From the late twelfth century on references abound to the discussion and settlement within such settings of matters arising from the claims of tenants and lords to estates of land and lucrative franchisal privileges, as well as to the sometimes fraught business of conveyance. Thus, a 'full court' (*plena curia*) convened in Annandale sometime between 1194 and 1211 was the forum for the resignation of an estate of land into the hands of William Bruce.[34] In the mid-thirteenth century Alan Durward presided over a *curia* located at Urquhart; nearby, his rival William Comyn earl of Mar did the same at Lochindorb.[35]

Surviving evidence suggests that north of Forth the terminology associated with the baronial court in England gained ground rather more slowly over the course of the thirteenth century. An unusually early charter of 1212, executed in what has been described as 'strict feudal form', mentions the *curia* that Feargus earl of Buchan was accustomed to convene at Ellon.[36] A dozen years later in distant Carrick, Alan son of Roland supervised the resignation of a widow's terce in an assembly that an attending scribe identified as his *curia*,[37] and his contemporary, Gille Brigte of Strathearn, set down – in duplicate deeds – the forfeitures from his comital court that he was prepared to share with the canons of Inchaffray.[38] It is only in mid-century, however, that Maoldomhnaich of Lennox is on record conducting business with his tenants in assemblies that he described as 'my court'.[39] Thereafter, mentions of such venues begin to occur more frequently in written *acta* originating in this part of the realm, as well as in other areas north of Forth.

The more measured spread of the terminology of the seigniorial court into the Gaelicised portions of the realm reveals a degree of uncertainty among the scribes whose task it was to describe formal assemblies. Here, as is the case with other aspects of the contemporary Scottish tenurial landscape, it is probable that the formal language of written charters attests changes that may be more apparent than real. In Lennox, for example, the knight's feu does not make its appearance in written record until the 1240s; when it does, it is confined, significantly, to the portion of the earldom that lay hard by the Stewart lordship of Strathgryfe. In Strathearn, likewise, the lands held by knight service lay well beyond the highland core of the earls' power base.[40] This pattern of creating new, European-style tenures in carefully designated pockets of territory has been traced in other native lordships as far apart as Buchan, Mar, Fife and Galloway, as has the uneven spread of the terminology associated with the classical 'feudal' holding.[41] Likewise, the specific obligation of a tenant to perform suit of court as a condition of landownership, widely considered a hallmark of Anglo-Norman 'feudalism' both in England and Scotland, appears only later in the thirteenth century in some of the Gaelic provinces: in Strathearn, for example, not until the time of Earl Malise III in the 1280s.[42]

A glance at other tenant obligations in the lands north of Forth reinforces the impression of a uniformity of charter terminology that masks considerable variety on the ground. Among the responsibilities that historians have traditionally associated with tenure was the 'feudal' obligation of all who held knights' feus to perform mounted military service or its concomitant, castle guard. Yet, scholars are now well aware that thirteenth-century Scottish armies were not assembled by the cobbling together of the renders of half, third, eighth or thirty-second parts of knights, obligations that were already by the mid-thirteenth century normal throughout the kingdom. By the time of Alexander II, rather, the king's general musters were highly sophisticated affairs, bringing together a small body of 'genuine' knights, fully armed and trained in combat on horseback, with reinforcements in the shape of lightly equipped mounted sergeants and other specialised units. These 'feudal' hosts fought alongside the much larger infantry corps comprised of the army in which all free men had traditionally served in the pre-'feudal' period.[43] Of castle guard there is precious little notice in surviving documents, a reflection, perhaps, of the lack of interest that many native magnates demonstrated in constructing European-style strongholds.[44]

Much as the written charters of the thirteenth century obscure the vitality of the common army of ancient Alba, so does the increasingly formal terminology of the baronial *curia* mask the resilience of assemblies of mormaers and the men of their provinces, such as the '*curia* of Fife and Fothrif' that gathered to witness a perambulation in 1252.[45] 'Law courts', it has been shown in the context of native Wales, 'only emerge as specialised assemblies when their status and functions are delimited, their methods regularized and their proceedings formalized'.[46] This process of transformation aptly describes the state of affairs in early thirteenth-century Scotia; here, too, native assemblies became the baronial *curiae* familiar to the Latin-trained scribes who observed them rather more gradually than charter materials might suggest. In some thirteenth-century documents, then, magnate courts in Buchan, Strathearn, Fife, Mar and elsewhere sometimes look very much like gatherings of suitors that historians traditionally associate with tenure by knight's feu (though there appears to have been in Scotland little of the contention that troubled landholders in contemporary England in respect of the obligation).[47] By and large, the business conducted there may have differed little from the matters that were deliberated in courts convened in lordships governed by Bruces, Stewarts and Comyns. The evolution of old assemblies into baronial *curiae* is well illustrated in the examples of two native courts that met almost exactly one hundred years apart. In 1128, a solemn assembly of Gaelic worthies gathered in Fife under the watchful eye of Earl Causantin of Fife, who appeared complete with 'satraps', 'satellites', 'the men of the army', thanes, 'high-ranking men' (*premicerios*), 'governors' (*duces*) and other 'officials' (*lumnarcas*).[48] This gathering has an unmistakably Gaelic feel to it, and indeed its indigenous peculiarities have been the subject of comment by scholars.[49] Barely one hundred years later, Alan son of Roland, lord of Galloway, was treating his own version of gatherings of satraps and satellites as an appropriate venue in which to conduct a very European-looking act of quitclaim, complete with a ceremony that featured the handing over of 'rod and staff'.[50] In the mid-thirteenth century, likewise, Maoldomhnaich of Lennox confirmed the written deeds that had transferred an estate from one tenant to another in an open assembly before men who were clearly suitors; some of the witnesses to these deeds, in fact, held land of the earl under the specific condition that they perform suit of court.[51] A generation later still, the bishop of Glasgow issued instructions to the dean of Lennox regarding the 'bailies and suitors' of the court of Earl Malcolm.[52] In 1284 Earl Malise III of Strathearn summoned a 'full court' (*plena curia*) of his tenants, Gaelic and European, in order to formalise the transfer of an estate of land from one native family to another.[53] By the end of this same century, it has been suggested, the perquisites arising from the routine business of baronial courts both north and south of Forth were contributing to the development of a rich and varied money economy;[54] certainly, the revenues generated by the earl of Fife's baronial courts were substantial enough to merit separate entries in Exchequer audits ordered by King Edward I of England.[55] From Ellon in Buchan to Doune in Menteith, the thirteenth century in Scotland witnessed a period of accommodation between the institutions of the Gaelic past and those of the contemporary European world, not least in the very heart of the old provinces of Scotia. The process was not played out at the same pace in all parts of the kingdom: the Gaelic lords of Argyll and the western isles adopted only gradually the practice of using charters and the tenurial customs associated with the knight's feu. Yet here, too, native and European practices eventually merged. The *barones totius Ergadie et Ynchgalle* appeared in the parliament held at St Andrews in 1309, and a jury of *barones* appeared again in the record of an inquest summoned in 1355.[56] In both instances, scribes used the term to designate men who attended court in their capacities as suitors of high status.[57]

The concept of accommodation rather than assimilation is none the less key here. There did not occur north of Forth the eclipse of the old by the new, or the retreat of the traditional before a rising tide of the novel, and there is no longer any reason to doubt the significant contribution that Gaelic legal elements made to the development of Scottish common law in its formative years.[58] Native magnates continued to count among their tenants a significant number of Gaels, who held their lands on terms that were remarkably different from those that characterised the tenure of incoming Europeans. The transfer of the earldom of Buchan from a native family to that of the Comyns, effected by marriage around 1212, brought an influx of new families to north-eastern Scotland, but it did not see the displacement of sitting tenantry, whose members looked on the new earl, foreign or not, as a mormaer in the old style.[59] Comyn himself clearly saw advantages in behaving as one. Thus, he continued to welcome in his court the doom-saying of a provincial *breitheamh* and, in deference to Gaelic custom, acknowledged his wife's prerogative to make grants of earldom land under her own authority.[60] In nearby Badenoch and Strathspey, native dynasties of thanes appear to have survived unscathed the political upheavals of the later twelfth and the early thirteenth centuries,[61] and here, too, despite the introduction into lordly courts of new ideas, practices and modes of expression, in many respects the customs of these assemblies probably changed very little.[62] In 1232 a very public gathering of kinsmen and tenants (including her dowager mother) assembled to bear witness to Countess Isabella of Atholl's grant of lands to Coupar Angus abbey;[63] her sister Farbhlaidh confirmed in a *curia* of her own the acts of one of her vassals.[64] Recent research on the enduring influence of native culture in the earldoms of Lennox, Strathearn and Mar only strengthens the impression of continuity underneath an appearance of conformity to European practice.[65] Here, too, in assemblies that Latin-trained scribes almost invariably referred to as *curiae*, thirteenth-century Gaelic magnates played out before assembled kinsmen, clients, tenants and friends the myriad tasks that had always been associated with the governance of their considerable territories: ordering the perambulation of newly created estates,[66] arranging for the reassessment of the value of an estate in the event of war,[67] presiding over ceremonies of quitclaim,[68] granting the patronage of a church,[69] confirming transactions made between tenants. Examples of grants (or reservations) of the fines, forfeitures and escheats levied in the courts of Gaelic lords also attest the involvement of heads of kindred in the affairs of their tenants and clients.[70] Collectively, the sources reveal that magnates were keenly aware of the valuable profits, social and political as well as financial, that accrued to lords who learned to exploit new practices governing tenure and new ways of expressing old prerogatives.

On rare occasions it is possible to glimpse in extant records the work of distinctively native assemblies, behind the scenes, as it were, of the more specifically 'feudal' *curiae* that brought suitors into the presence of their lords. Few though these insights may be, they lend weight to the oft-expressed view that justice in medieval Scotland was ultimately 'the community's', and that 'quarrels were often settled through the efforts of local magnates and heads of kin'.[71] Around 1240, for example, Earl Maoldomhnaich of Lennox summoned a number of the 'new' men of Anglo-Norman and continental stock whom he had recently settled in his territories to witness his grant of an annual rent to Sir David de Graham. The monies came from an estate once held by the native tenant Farquhar Mac Gille Martain, who had forfeited them when the earl ruled against him in an earlier forum, this one comprised of local recognitors.[72] Native tenants, kinsmen and clients also came together to march the bounds of newly created estates, then reported their findings in a formally constituted court. This is what happened in 1219, when the earl of Angus summoned Gaelic worthies from Kinblethmont to determine the bounds of two adjacent estates, who later appeared before a royal *curia* to deliver their verdict, and again in 1231 in Fife.[73] It occurred again around 1252, when the resolution of a dispute concerning the marches of an estate was announced before 'the court of Fife, Fothrif and Kinross',[74] reminiscent of the gathering of 1128 noted earlier. The responsibility of sergeants to pursue and apprehend thieves and other miscreants is well attested in regions such as Carrick and Lennox and, if scholarly conjecture is correct, in most of the provinces north of Forth,[75] as are the Gaelic terms *sorryn*, *frithalos* and *calumpnie*, associated with their activities.[76] Behind each of these written references there lie countless sessions of the mormaers' courts where, by arbitration or fiat, decisions were made, settlements devised and verdicts delivered. Some were perhaps summoned on an ad hoc basis, for example, to provide a public setting for the handing over of cows and sheep awarded at the conclusion of litigation in Aberdeenshire,[77] to oversee the transfer of sasine from one Lennox man who had forfeited his estate to a new tenant,[78] to assess the value of stolen animals,[79] to hear allegations concerning a theft of coin in Perth.[80] Others resembled more closely the baronial *curiae* familiar to historians of Anglo-Norman England, venues at which all who held feus in return for rendering suit of court were obliged to appear on pain of censure. The most infamous of these were the sessions that Edward I convened at Berwick in 1296, where the oaths of suitors were carefully recorded in the Ragman Roll.[81] The hundreds of resignations performed *per fustum et baculum in plena curia* that are so fully attested in records originating both north and south of Forth, the giving and taking of homage, and the making and confirmation of grants all took place in such formal venues.

In the mid-thirteenth century, then, Gaelic magnates presided over different kinds of assemblies, before tenants and suitors of varying stripes. Moreover, they appear to have responded to changes that were taking place in the legal landscape around them with varying enthusiasm. As noted above, at least one of the scribes employed by Feargus of Buchan was distinguishing his head courts from other venues as early as 1212, but those of the native earls of Lennox did not do so until 1240,[82] those of the earls of Atholl not until the end of the thirteenth century,[83] and those of the lords of Strathearn not until later still, in the 1320s.[84] At the most fundamental level, none the less, the spread across the kingdom of written charters themselves, with their references to *curiae*, fines, escheats and forfeitures, attests the incorporation into the native legal system of new kinds of curial debate, discussion and decision making in power centers such as Migvie, Balloch and Kenmore. Yet, the adoption of novel practices by no means signalled the demise of older styles of Gaelic assembly. Native men continued to play prominent roles in the legal world of the thirteenth and fourteenth centuries as recognitors, witnesses and oath helpers.[85]

The siting of lordly courts

While Latin-language charters yield useful information about the early growth of baronial courts, they also have much to reveal about other aspects of these assemblies in the thirteenth and fourteenth centuries. There is much cause, here again, to rehearse the traditional lament about the paucity of extant, pre-1400 legal sources, particularly from the 'land of earls' north of Forth. Even more regrettable is the absence in Scotland of materials comparable to the lawbooks of Ireland and Wales that have made it possible for historians to reconstruct so vividly the courtroom procedures of the medieval past in those realms. Scottish charter texts seldom permit more than a glimpse inside the baronial court, but close scrutiny of the documents that do survive suggests that the drama and ceremony of lordly courts in this realm were as richly textured as they were elsewhere in the British Isles.

Latin-trained scribes almost invariably use the term *curiae* to describe meetings of barons and their suitors, but magnate 'courtrooms' were as likely to be located outdoors as they were within the confines of a fortified residence or a monastic precinct. An abundant scholarly literature on British assembly sites in the Middle Ages, combining the methodologies and theoretical approaches of historians, archaeologists and ethnologists, has uncovered evidence of dozens of such sites and has shed important new light on the range of physical, topographical and monumental features that characterised meeting places from the earliest times through the late medieval period.[86] In Scotland, as in England, Wales and Ireland, the word *curia* itself always had a double meaning, designating both a grouping of persons around the central figure of a king or baron, as well as a physical setting – a hall, a church, a moot hill – in which great men gave ritual and symbolic expression to their authority over other persons. Scribes in Scotland elided the two meanings as frequently as they did elsewhere, and it is often difficult to uncover information about the locations that magnates considered most appropriate as venues for their courts. Judicial sessions over which the king presided took place in a variety of places, and sometimes in unusual circumstances: in 1234, for example, within the precincts of Balmerino abbey, where Alexander II was celebrating the obsequies of his mother, Queen Ermengarde; in 1261, 'in the larger tower of Jedburgh castle, on the west side', where Alexander III, his wife and several barons had taken up residence;[87] and in 1263, in the refectory at Melrose abbey.[88]

Surviving evidence, while not abundant, leaves little doubt that suitors to Scottish magnate courts regularly assembled at the lord's *caput* or chief residence.[89] In the thirteenth century clerics included mention of such mundane information only when so inclined, but by the early years of the fourteenth administrative efficiency made the practice of including a place name in the final clause of charters more common. Scribal whim, or perhaps disapproval, accounts for the reference in a document of 1382 to the *curia* that Sir John Ramsay held before 'a concourse of people gathered for a tournament' on the West Sands near St Andrews.[90] Courts held in venues such as these may have been particularly attractive to Scottish lords anxious to appropriate the customs of the native Gaels, which accorded reverence to the liminal area between the sea and the land.[91]

That native assemblies were sometimes elaborate gatherings held in the open air – in other words, Scottish versions of the well documented meetings known in Ireland as *óenaig* and Welsh *cymanfa*[92] – is implied in the Fife document of 1128, cited above, when 'a multitude of men' came together at the command of the king and under the presidency of Earl Causantin.[93] In 1264 a court was held near Dull, in Atholl, 'next to the large stone on the west side of the house of Thomas the vicar',[94] while in 1268, the parish church of Errol was the site of a large assembly of men and women.[95] In 1281, a justiciar's court, summoned to hear the findings of a perambulation, met in an open moor at Nigg, Aberdeenshire, perhaps at the site later known as Baron's Cairn.[96] Later thirteenth-century documents show the men of Menteith witnessing a quitclaim performed on the very site of the estate in question, and those of Buchan gathering 'next to the castle of Aberdeen, in the place known as Castleside'.[97] The open air remained, in the fourteenth century, an appropriate setting for occasions that brought together large numbers of suitors, litigants and observers. In 1240, for example, a dispute about the marches of the moor lands of Fordell was settled *super dictam moram*.[98] In 1306, a group of Fife jurors assembled 'on the hill at Largo', while in 1313, Roger de Mowbray, lord of Methven, chose the site he called 'le Farnyhill' as a suitable venue for the holding of a session of his baronial court.[99]

The practice of hosting open air meetings was certainly not unknown to the Anglo-Norman and continental lords who settled in Scotland in the thirteenth century, but it had particular resonance among the native aristocracy. Studies of Finlaggan in Argyllshire and Tynwald on the Isle of Man have emphasised the central significance of these outdoor sites to the expression of the social, political and legal authority of the Lords of the Isles and the rulers of Man, respectively. In both places, moreover, magnates convened annual assemblies that were 'not just gatherings of the great and good, but of all and sundry'.[100] Much as Scone fulfilled a variety of functions in the royal context,[101] Finlaggan and Tynwald were closely associated with the exercise of quasi-royal lordship: they were used simultaneously as places of inauguration and sites for council meetings, courts of law, fairs and games.[102] Other topographically distinct sites scattered across the kingdom, especially places identified in written record as moot hills, performed similarly varied functions within the provincial lordships of the 'land of earls' as well as in the new baronies created by the Scottish crown.[103] In Strathearn and Lennox several such locations (Kenmore, Castelton, Tom-na-Chaisteal, Catter) have been identified on the basis of archaeological, documentary and onomastic evidence.[104] Similar work has brought to light other multipurpose power centres at Migvie and the Doune of Invernochty in Mar; Ellon and Kelly in Buchan; and Coupar in Fife;[105] and the study of lordship in Galloway over several centuries has identified the near continuous use, throughout the entire later medieval period, of early power centres such as Cruggelton.[106] Barrow's research into the geographical distribution of *comhdhail* place names offers compelling evidence of the existence of well known sites for popular courts in each of the shires that were the main administrative units of pre-twelfth-century Scotland.[107] Charter evidence confirms, moreover, that magnates sometimes deliberately chose – or reserved for themselves – a setting in recognition of its symbolic, traditional or emotive significance. Settlements achieved in such places acquired special status, and were both destined and intended to endure well beyond the lifetime of the suitors who witnessed them. In 1249, for example, a bitter and long-simmering dispute concerning the moor of Fordell in Fife ended on the very site of the contested boundary line.[108] A century later, in nearby Perthshire, David Stewart earl of Strathearn exempted from his grant of the lands of Findony the 'earl's seat' and the parcel of land next to it, each obviously a potent locus of local lordship.[109] Sites such as these were not abandoned or alienated carelessly, particularly by canny magnates such as the Stewarts, whose lordship over Strathearn had only recently supplanted that of a long-lived Gaelic lineage.

Ritual and ceremony in the baronial courts

Irrespective of whether they convened their courts indoors or out, the magnates who summoned suitors, tenants, clients and friends to court encoded in the business that was conducted there a highly complex series of symbols, rituals and performances: manifestations both overt and covert of their lordship in action. Medieval gesture, it has been noted, 'gave legal actions a living image';[110] in a world in which few people had the ability to read or to comprehend the Latin language of newfangled charters, 'commitment had to be made through ritual gestures, formal words, and symbolic objects'. Close study of extant deeds from Scotia of the twelfth and thirteenth centuries reveals the importance of these elements. Pronouncements made in court were much more than words spoken; they acquired the status of the 'speech acts' familiar to ethnologists and anthropologists, which a host of recent studies has shown gave performative procedures their authority in the communities within which they were enacted.[111] Consisting as they did of words, gestures and sounds, and indeed in seeking as they did to appeal to all five senses of the assembled witnesses,[112] speech acts fulfilled a crucial mnemonic function among audiences that, like those of thirteenth- and fourteenth-century Gaelic Scotland, were only just making the transition to written culture. The scholars who have so carefully studied the Welsh and Irish lawbooks have shown that sight, sound, touch and smell were the tools with which rulers in those realms gave concrete expression to their control over subordinates.[113] The ceremonies that scribes recorded in Scottish charters reveal that such markers fulfilled similar functions in the baronial courtrooms of this kingdom, too. Most intriguing of all are the glimpses that these documents afford of the ways in which the performances enacted in Gaelic courtrooms came to incorporate, accommodate and ultimately appropriate the written deeds that European newcomers had made popular in the kingdom in the twelfth century.

Speech alone was a powerful medium in the context of the medieval court. There are occasional references to testimony delivered aloud, such as occurred at an inquest convened around 1259 in Dumfries, where the court heard, and a scribe recorded, the words of insult that one man hurled at another, and those that the defendant himself allegedly uttered as he stabbed his attacker.[114] An early thirteenth-century charter recounts how one landholder confirmed his father's grant to Paisley abbey by addressing the assembled suitors, whose names the scribe then carefully recorded.[115] In a highly unusual document of this period a Melrose clerk set down verbatim the solemn words that Sir Robert de Muschamp spoke to the men who gathered to witness his promise to protect the abbey.[116] The use of repetitive verbal formulae, one of the characteristic features of the oral literature of Gaeldom, is sometimes discernible as well, for example in the record of the oral testimony that no fewer than a dozen Gaelic notables from Lennox proffered in 1233, and in the description of the testimony of an Argyll jury, whose members responded to a question 'with one voice'.[117] Such records, incidentally – although unfortunately all too rare – attest the bilingual or multilingual skills of some of the Gaelic *literati* who officiated in native courts in thirteenth-century Scotland.[118]

When accompanied by performance, speech acquired greater dimension, deeper meaning and longer-lasting significance. The linking of aural and visual cues is readily observable in Scottish courtrooms in a host of contexts across the length and breadth of the kingdom throughout the twelfth, thirteenth and fourteenth centuries. References abound, for example, to the practice of touching the 'holy evangels' which accompanied the swearing of oaths. The act was still as powerful in 1361, when Colin 'Iongantach' Campbell made a promise to Gilbert of Glassary, as it had been almost 200 years earlier, when Isabel the wife of William of Riddell confirmed the gift of an oxgang that her father had made to the monks of Melrose.[119] The potency of spoken utterances reinforced by the totemic power of relics and other objects of religious significance is apparent in the account of a struggle for control of a parish church that occurred around the year 1180, when several canons of Inchcolm, seeking to prevent the intrusion of a client of William de Mortimer, 'stood before the door of the church with their cross and many relics', and called upon the protection of the pope.[120] It is more evident still in charters that preserve, sometimes well into the late medieval period, the ritualistic warnings intoned by donors anxious to ensure the integrity of their grants among their descendants. When Raonall son of Somhairle of the Isles, for example, made a gift of money to the Cluniacs of Paisley, he invoked the protection of no less a saint than Columba, and threatened with his 'eternal curse' anyone who might in future seek to challenge the monastery's title.[121] Raonall's ringing words, no doubt accompanied by elaborate gesture and perhaps reinforced by the proximity of gospel books and other holy objects, constituted a carefully staged performance, one that cannot have failed to impress the occasion firmly in the memory of its witnesses. Relics and bibles were, in fact, considered to be such integral props in the drama of the courtroom that lords who owned these precious and expensive objects were none the less willing to carry them out of the security of the castle to fields, hilltops and other venues, as required.[122] Queen Margaret herself apparently lost her lovely gospel book in such circumstances, when she loaned it to '[c]ertain folk who wanted to swear an oath among themselves'.[123] In the thirteenth century the royal family of Scotland kept a substantial collection of relics and other holy objects in the Treasury in Edinburgh castle; these were presumably in regular use in court ceremonies and on other solemn occasions.[124]

In Scotland, as in England, the formal conveyance of title to land occurred not as a consequence of a charter being written or sealed, but rather when 'witnesses "heard" the donor utter the words of the grant and "saw" him make the transfer by a solemn object'.[125] The ceremonies associated with delivery of sasine and its opposite, quitclaim, were already in the mid-twelfth century so commonplace in parts of the kingdom that they merited little attention by the clerics who drafted charters. References to the resignation of title to land almost always include only brief mentions of the handing over of staff and rod (quitclaim *per fustum et baculum*), but in some regions the enactment of these little dramas caught the fancy of scribes well into the thirteenth century. Thus, a document of 1235 describing the collective resignation by Constantine of Lochore, his heir David, and his brother Philip, of title to lands in Fife notes that Constantine and David each uttered the words of surrender as they laid their hands on the high altar of the church of Dunfermline.[126] The ceremony of homage that invariably accompanied delivery of sasine was likewise so routine that it lies for the most part hidden in the laconic terminology of vast numbers of extant title deeds. Only occasionally did its enactment inspire a scribe to write about it, but when this did happen the scene described is highly evocative. In 1279, for example, at St Andrews, a native landholder performed homage to his lord 'on bended knee, placing his hands between the hands of the prior'.[127] In 1316, again in Fife, a panel of jurors recalled the day on which the late Earl Malcolm performed homage to the abbot of Dunfermline for the lands of Clunie before the high altar of the church, as well as another occasion on which his son did the same in the chapter house of the monastery.[128]

In the mid-thirteenth century the use of charters as evidence of deeds done and grants made had yet to become routine in many parts of Scotland.[129] This was particularly the case in the regions still controlled by Gaelic-speaking magnates, where oral testimony remained of central importance. In 1259 a Lennox jury, questioned about the conveyance of an estate, swore that the claimant to the land had a valid title, because 'they knew, and they saw, when Somerled alienated that land . . . and assigned it to his son Thomas, in the presence of the earl'.[130] The inquest convened in Fife in 1316, noted above, heard the sworn testimony of men who 'knew' that the earl and his kinsmen had performed homage for the lands of Clunie, because they had seen the ceremonies 'with their own eyes'.[131] After losing a bitter contest over title to some lands to the abbot of Paisley, Earl Maoldomhnaich of Lennox surrendered his claims in a full court. His charter of quitclaim begins with the observation that, in his day, 'it has become useful and desirable for actions to be set down in writing for the sake of posterity'. He went on to add rather less graciously: 'lest the fact of [this restoration of lands] to the abbey in true and pious devotion sink into the blind oblivion of the future, I command that my grant be written down and the impression of my seal be appended to it'.[132]

As the century wore on, however, in Lennox and elsewhere claims to land or privilege were increasingly associated with written instruments. Earl Malcolm of Lennox confirmed a grant to one of his tenants after he had 'inspected and diligently heard' the text of the original charter.[133] Alexander of the Isles confirmed to the monks of Crossraguel a gift that his father had made, first by 'inspecting' the original title deed, then by reading it aloud; on another occasion, he both 'inspected and touched' his father's charter.[134] The actions recorded in these documents are redolent of the symbolism that characterised the court of a great lord, consisting as they did of visual cues as the original parchment deed was produced, aural cues as the document was recited aloud, and perhaps even olfactory cues in the odour of hot wax that may have wafted through the air as Alexander set his seal to his deeds of confirmation.[135] Other examples of the assimilation of written materials into the speech acts of medieval Scottish courtrooms may be found in increasingly frequent references to the handing over of charters from one landholder to another as a regular feature of conveyance ceremonies,[136] and in the occasional reference to the 'enchartering' of a tenant, found in a document from Eskdale dating from the reign of King Alexander II.[137]

Conclusion

There can be little doubt that in the period between 1150 and 1350, Scottish baronial courts experienced the kind of profound change in 'literate mentality' that Michael Clanchy has written about so eloquently.[138] Charters became one of an array of symbolic artefacts in the courtrooms of medieval Scotland, to be deployed – as were daggers and gospel books, rings and relics – as props incorporated into performances that lent authenticity and permanence to the actions done there.[139] Written deeds, however, acquired their potency at least in some measure from the settings in which they were deployed. The courts of the barons of Scotland, native or newcomer, secular or ecclesiastical, became essential and enduring features of the medieval political, legal and social landscapes because they functioned as a vital nexus of both lordly authority and vassalic expectation and, equally vitally, as a site in which both native Gaels and newly established aristocrats negotiated relations with their tenants. In the written deeds that the business of these tribunals generated scholars have a unique opportunity to study at first hand not just the business of medieval courts, but also the encounter between the culture of the Gaels and that of the Europeans.

Notes

1. T. M. Cooper, 'The general development of Scots law', in *Introduction to Scottish Legal History* (Edinburgh, 1958), p. 5. See also G. W. S. Barrow, 'Popular courts', in G. W. S. Barrow, *Scotland and its Neighbours in the Middle Ages* (London, 1992), p. 219.
2. H. L. MacQueen, *Common Law and Feudal Society in Medieval Scotland* (Edinburgh, 1993), p. 57. For similar remarks about the legal customs of Galloway, see H. L. MacQueen, 'The laws of Galloway: a preliminary survey', in R. D. Oram and G. P. Stell (eds), *Galloway: Land and Lordship* (Edinburgh, 1991), p. 131.
3. G. W. S. Barrow, *The Kingdom of the Scots: Government, Church and Society from the Eleventh to the Fourteenth Century*, 2nd edn (Edinburgh, 2003), pp. 57–67; *The Sheriff Court Book of Fife, 1512–1522*, ed. W. C. Dickinson (Edinburgh, 1928), pp. xiii–lxxxvi.
4. Barrow, 'Popular courts', pp. 217–46.
5. H. L. MacQueen, 'Tears of a legal historian: Scottish feudalism and the *ius commune*', *Juridical Review*, New Series (no vol.) (2003), pp. 1–28; A. Harding, 'The medieval brieves of protection and the development of the common law', *Juridical Review*, New Series, 11 (1966), pp. 115–49; T. M. Cooper, *The Dark Age of Scottish Legal History, 1350–1650* (Glasgow, 1952). See also MacQueen's recent study of the nature of trespass jurisdiction, in 'Some notes on wrang and unlaw', in H. L. MacQueen (ed.), *Stair Society Miscellany Five* (Edinburgh, 2006), pp. 13–26.
6. See here the remarks of M. Brown, 'Scotland tamed? Kings and magnates in late medieval Scotland: a review of recent work', *Innes Review*, 45 (1994), pp. 123–6.
7. W. C. Dickinson, 'The administration of justice in medieval Scotland',

Aberdeen University Review, 34 (1952), pp. 338–51; A. Grant, 'Crown and nobility in late medieval Britain', in R. Mason (ed.), *Scotland and England, 1286–1815* (Edinburgh, 1987), pp. 34–59; A. Grant, *Independence and Nationhood: Scotland, 1306–1469* (London, 1984), pp. 156–61; MacQueen, *Common Law*, pp. 50–7, 66; A. A. M. Duncan, *Scotland: The Making of the Kingdom* (Edinburgh, 1975), pp. 202–3; B. Webster, *Scotland from the Eleventh Century to 1603* (Cambridge, 1975), p. 159; J. Wormald, 'The blood feud in early modern Scotland', in J. Bossy (ed.), *Disputes and Settlements: Law and Human Relations in the West* (Cambridge, 1983), pp. 101–44 ; J. Wormald, 'An early modern postscript: the Sandlaw dispute, 1546', in W. Davies and P. Fouracre (eds), *The Settlement of Disputes in Early Medieval Europe* (Cambridge, 1986), p. 202.

8. A. Grant, 'Franchises north of the border: baronies and regalities in medieval Scotland', in M. Prestwich (ed.), *Liberties and Identities in the Medieval British Isles* (Woodbridge, 2008), pp. 155–99; J. Hudson, 'Legal aspects of charter diplomatic in the twelfth century: a comparative approach', *Anglo-Norman Studies*, 25 (2003), pp. 121–38.
9. *Charters of David I*, no. 16; *RRS*, ii, no. 80; Duncan, *Making of the Kingdom*, p. 202.
10. *Charters of David I*, no. 267; NAS, RH 6/29.
11. MacQueen, 'Tears of a legal historian', pp. 12, 20.
12. *RRS*, ii, p. 49.
13. G. W. S. Barrow, *The Anglo-Norman Era in Scottish History* (Oxford, 1980). See here also Grant, 'Franchises', pp. 189–90 and MacQueen, 'Tears of a legal historian', p. 12.
14. C. J. Neville, 'Charter writing and the exercise of lordship in thirteenth-century Celtic Scotland', in A. Musson (ed.), *Expectations of the Law in the Middle Ages* (Woodbridge, 2001), pp. 76–86.
15. NAS, RH 1/2/49; *St. Andrews Liber*, pp. 252–4.
16. *RRS*, ii, p. 49.
17. R. R. Reid, 'Barony and thanage', *English Historical Review*, 35 (1920), pp. 161–99; Barrow, *Anglo-Norman Era*, p. 136.
18. Reid, 'Barony and thanage', pp. 179–86. See also J. Ferguson, 'The barony in Scotland', *Juridical Review*, 24 (1912–13), pp. 99–121.
19. *RRS*, ii, pp. 48–50.
20. A. Grant, 'The construction of the early Scottish state', in J. R. Maddicott and D. M. Palliser (eds), *The Medieval State: Essays presented to James Campbell* (London, 2000), pp. 55–6; A. Grant, 'Scotland: politics, government and law', in S. H. Rigby (ed.), *A Companion to Britain in the Later Middle Ages* (Oxford, 2003), pp. 293–4.
21. MacQueen, 'Tears of a legal historian', pp. 13, 20; Hudson, 'Legal aspects of charter diplomatic', p. 133.
22. H. L. MacQueen, 'Canon law, custom and legislation: law in the reign of Alexander II', in R. Oram (ed.), *The Reign of Alexander II, 1214–49* (Leiden,

2005), pp. 232-51; H. L. MacQueen, 'Scots law under Alexander III', in N. H. Reid (ed.), *Scotland in the Reign of Alexander III, 1249-1286* (Edinburgh, 1990), pp. 92-5.
23. *APS*, i, p. 114.
24. T. M. Cooper, *Select Scottish Cases of the Thirteenth Century* (Edinburgh, 1914), p. xlvi.
25. Grant, 'Politics, government and law', p. 303; Grant, *Independence and Nationhood*, p. 161.
26. See, for example, the text of a charter of 1270 x 1289, in which Sir Reginald Cheyne made provision for lordly arbitration should litigation arise with the monks of Newbattle over damage to crops in his lands of Strathbrock. NAS, GD 40/1/2.
27. See, for example, the agreements reached in 1240 between William, lord of Fordell and the monks of Inchcolm, and in 1268 between Christine, lady of Maule and Alexander de Inchmartin. Each notes that settlements were reached 'in the presence of friends of both parties'. *Inchcolm Chrs*, no. 19; BL, Harl. Ch. 52. B.16. A Melrose charter of the later thirteenth century mentions the mediation of 'good men'; *Melrose Liber*, no. 334.
28. See, for example, G. W. S. Barrow, *Kingship and Unity: Scotland, 1000-1306*, 2nd edn (Edinburgh, 2003), p. 51; MacQueen, 'Tears of a legal historian', pp. 1-28; K. J. Stringer, *Earl David of Huntingdon, 1152-1219: A Study in Anglo-Scottish History* (Edinburgh, 1985), pp. 68-103; Hudson, 'Legal aspects of charter diplomatic', pp. 121-38.
29. See, for example, G. G. Simpson, 'The *familia* of Roger de Quincy, earl of Winchester and constable of Scotland', in K. J. Stringer (ed.), *Essays on the Nobility of Medieval Scotland* (Edinburgh, 1985), esp. pp. 121-2; Stringer, *Earl David of Huntingdon*, pp. 155-76.
30. *Scotichronicon*, v, pp. 366-7, 382-3. For an example from 1261, see W. W. Scott (ed.), 'Eight thirteenth-century texts', in *Scottish History Society Miscellany, vol. XIII* (Edinburgh, 2004), Text 3.
31. K. Simms, 'Guesting and feasting in Gaelic Ireland', *Journal of the Royal Society of Antiquaries of Ireland*, 108 (1978), pp. 67-100; Duncan, *Making of the Kingdom*, p. 154. Reference to a man responsible for collecting substantial food rents on behalf of the earl of Strathearn suggest that such traditions were still meaningful in the thirteenth century; *Inchaffray Chrs*, no. 9.
32. *Inchaffray Liber*, no. 16.
33. NAS, GD 220/2/8, 220/2/9, 220/2/10; NAS, RH 6/32.
34. TNA, DL 25/90. For the dating of this charter, see R. M. Blakely, *The Brus Family in England and Scotland, 1100-1295* (Woodbridge, 2005), p. 224. For other thirteenth-century examples, see BL, MS Harl. 4693, fo. 34v, which describes a *plena curia* held by Gilbert de Hay lord of Errol; *Melrose Liber*, no. 269, the court of Earl Patrick II of Dunbar; and *Paisley Reg.*, p. 204, a court of Earl Malcolm I of Lennox.
35. Fraser, *Grant*, iii, pp. 4-5; NLS, Adv. MS. 15.1.18, no. 18.

36. Barrow, *Anglo-Norman Era*, p. 140; A. Young, 'The earls and earldom of Buchan in the thirteenth century', in A. Grant and K. J. Stringer (eds), *Medieval Scotland: Crown, Lordship and Community – Essays presented to G. W. S. Barrow* (Edinburgh, 1993), p. 179.
37. K. J. Stringer, 'Periphery and core in thirteenth-century Scotland: Alan, son of Roland, lord of Galloway and constable of Scotland', in Grant and Stringer (eds), *Medieval Scotland*, p. 110.
38. *Inchaffray Chrs*, nos. 43, 44.
39. NAS, GD 220/1/A1/2/2, GD 220/1/A1/2/3.
40. C. J. Neville, *Native Lordship in Medieval Scotland: The Earldoms of Strathearn and Lennox, c. 1140–1365* (Dublin, 2005), pp. 44, 50, 55–7; C. J. Neville, 'A Celtic enclave in Norman Scotland: Earl Gilbert and the earldom of Strathearn, 1171–1223', in T. Brotherstone and D. Ditchburn (eds), *Freedom and Authority: Scotland c. 1050–c. 1650: Historical and Historiographical Essays presented to Grant G. Simpson* (East Linton, 2000), pp. 89–91.
41. R. Oram, *The Lordship of Galloway* (Edinburgh, 2000), pp. 191–233. For Mar, see R. D. Oram, 'Continuity, adaptation and integration: the earls and earldom of Mar, c.1150–c.1300', in S. Boardman and A. Ross (eds), *The Exercise of Power in Medieval Scotland, c. 1200–1500* (Dublin, 2003), pp. 46–66; Buchan: Young, 'The earls and earldom of Buchan', pp. 174–202; Fife: Barrow, *Anglo-Norman Era*, pp. 84–90, 129–30; Galloway: Oram, *Lordship of Galloway*, pp. 191–217. There are now several studies on the encounter between the culture of the Gaels and that of the Europeans. See, for example, R. D. Oram, 'David I and the Scottish conquest and colonisation of Moray', *Northern Scotland*, 19 (1999), pp. 1–20; R. D. Oram, 'A family business?: colonization and settlement in twelfth- and thirteenth-century Galloway', *Scottish Historical Review*, 72 (1993), pp. 111–45; R. A. McDonald, 'Rebels without a cause? The relations of Fergus of Galloway and Somerled of Argyll with the Scottish kings, 1153–1164', in E. J. Cowan and R. A. McDonald (eds), *Alba: Celtic Scotland in the Medieval Era* (East Linton, 2000), pp. 166–87; R. A. McDonald, 'Matrimonial politics and core-periphery interactions in twelfth- and early thirteenth-century Scotland', *Journal of Medieval History*, 21 (1995), pp. 227–41; Stringer, 'Periphery and core', pp. 82–113; G. W. S. Barrow, 'Badenoch and Strathspey, 1130–1312. 1. Secular and political', *Northern Scotland*, 8 (1988), pp. 1–15; G. W. S. Barrow, 'Badenoch and Strathspey, 1130–1312. 2. The church', *Northern Scotland*, 9 (1989), pp. 1–16; C. J. Neville and R. A. McDonald, 'Knights, knighthood and chivalric culture in Gaelic Scotland, c.1050–1300', *Studies in Medieval and Renaissance History*, 3rd Series, 4 (2007), pp. 57–106. For Ireland, see, for example, M.-T. Flanagan, 'Strategies of lordship in pre-Norman and post-Norman Leinster', *Anglo-Norman Studies*, 20 (1997), pp. 107–26 and, more generally, the essays collected in B. Smith (ed.), *Britain and Ireland, 900–1300: Insular Responses to Medieval European Change* (Cambridge, 1999). For Wales, see, R. R. Davies,

The Age of Conquest: Wales, 1063–1415 (Oxford, 1991); R. R. Davies, *Lordship and Society in the March of Wales, 1282–1400* (Oxford, 1978).
42. Fraser, *Grandtully*, i, App., no. 69.
43. Duncan, *Making of the Kingdom*, pp. 386–7; G. W. S. Barrow, 'The army of Alexander III's Scotland', in N. H. Reid (ed.), *Scotland in the Reign of Alexander III, 1249–1286* (Edinburgh, 1990), pp. 132–47.
44. See here F. Watson, 'The expression of power in a medieval kingdom: thirteenth-century Scottish castles', in S. Foster, A. Macinnes and R. MacInnes (eds), *Scottish Power Centres from the Early Middle Ages to the Twentieth Century* (Glasgow, 1998), pp. 59–78; and F. J. Watson, 'Adapting tradition? The earldom of Strathearn, 1114–1296', in R. Oram and G. Stell (eds), *Lordship and Architecture in Medieval and Renaissance Scotland* (Edinburgh, 2005), pp. 26–43.
45. NAS, GD 254/1. For a reference to the several *barones* of Fife, who look very much like the *curia* of c. 1252, see *Balmerino Liber*, nos. 42, 43.
46. R. R. Davies, 'The administration of law in medieval Wales: the role of the *Ynad Cwmwd (Judex Patrie)*', in T. M. Charles-Edwards, M. E. Owen and D. B. Walters (eds), *Lawyers and Laymen: Studies in the History of Law presented to Professor Dafydd Jenkins on his Seventy-fifth Birthday, Gŵyl Ddewi 1986* (Cardiff, 1986), p. 260.
47. See here especially the recent discussion of the problems that attended the enforcement of suit of court, in P. Brand, *Kings, Barons and Justices: The Making and Enforcement of Legislation in Thirteenth-century England* (Cambridge, 2003), esp. pp. 43–53.
48. *St Andrews Liber*, pp. 117–18
49. Duncan, *Making of the Kingdom*, p. 167. For a discussion of similar terminology in an earlier Welsh context, see W. Davies, 'Land and power in early medieval Wales', *Past and Present*, 78 (1978), pp. 14–15.
50. Stringer, 'Periphery and core', p. 110.
51. Fraser, *Lennox*, ii, nos. 6, 9. For an example from Buchan, see *Aberdeen-Banff Collections*, pp. 407–9.
52. *Paisley Reg.*, p. 204. For other references to attendance at Earl Malcolm's *curia*, see ibid. pp. 180–3, 189, 192, 195, 198, 201.
53. *Inchaffray Liber*, p. xxxvi.
54. W. W. Scott, 'The use of money in Scotland, 1124–1230', *Scottish Historical Review*, 58 (1979), p. 109.
55. *Documents Illustrative of the History of Scotland from the Death of King Alexander the Third to the Accession of Robert Bruce*, ed. J. Stevenson, 2 vols (Edinburgh, 1870), i, nos. 317, 319, 320; ii, no. 345.
56. *APS*, i, p. 459; *Highland Papers*, ed. J. R. N. MacPhail, 4 vols (Edinburgh, 1914–34), ii, p. 138. The resilience of Gaelic custom and practice in the region is discussed in J. Bannerman, 'The Scots language and the kin-based society', in D. S. Thomson (ed.), *Gaelic and Scots in Harmony: Proceedings of the Second International Conference on the Languages of Scotland (University*

of Glasgow, 1988) (Glasgow, 1988), pp. 1–19, and J. Bannerman, 'The lordship of the Isles', in J. M. Brown (ed.), *Scottish Society in the Fifteenth century* (London, 1977), pp. 209–40. For the spread of charter usage, see S. Boardman, 'The Campbells and charter lordship in medieval Argyll', in Boardman and Ross (eds), *Exercise of Power*, pp. 95–117.

57. NAS, RH 5/21. For other examples, see NAS, RH 5/22, RH 5/23; *Dunfermline Reg.*, no. 85.
58. W. D. H. Sellar, 'Celtic law and Scots law: survival and integration', *Scottish Studies*, 29 (1989), pp. 1–27; W. D. H. Sellar, 'Law and institutions, Gaelic', in M. Lynch (ed.), *The Oxford Companion to Scottish History* (Oxford, 2001), pp. 381–2.
59. Young, 'Earls and earldom of Buchan', pp. 179–85. See also BL, MS Harl. 4693, fo. 33, where Comyn decribes himself holding by the 'tenure of Buchan'.
60. *Aberdeen Reg.*, i, p. 15; *Arbroath Liber*, i, nos. 227, 247; *Lindores Cart.*, no. 124; NLS, Adv. MS. 15.1.18, no. 18; C. J. Neville, 'Women, charters and land ownership in Scotland, 1150–1350', *Journal of Legal History*, 26 (2005), p. 32. Comyn referred specifically to the landholding customs of native Buchan in a charter in favour of Sir Gilbert de Hay; NAS, RH 1/2/31.
61. Barrow, 'Badenoch and Strathspey, secular and political', pp. 1–15. For the disturbances in Moray at this time, see, most recently, R. A. McDonald, *Outlaws of Medieval Scotland: Challenges to the Canmore Kings, 1058–1266* (East Linton, 2003), and Oram, 'David I and the Scottish conquest and colonisation of Moray', 1–20.
62. In Strathspey alone in the early thirteenth century four lordships were in the hands of native earls or their kinsmen; see A. Ross, 'The lords and lordship of Glencarnie', in Boardman and Ross (eds), *Exercise of Power*, p. 164.
63. *Coupar Angus Rental*, i, pp. 331, 333.
64. NAS, GD 83/2, GD 83/3.
65. Neville, *Native Lordship*; Oram, 'Continuity, adaptation and integration', pp. 46–66.
66. *Paisley Reg.*, pp. 171–2; *Arbroath Liber*, i, no. 227.
67. Fraser, *Grant*, iii, p. 4.
68. E.g. Fraser, *Douglas*, iii, pp. 4–5; *Cambuskenneth Reg.*, no. 49; *Beauly Chrs*, p. 60; *Paisley Reg.*, pp. 183–4.
69. NLS, Adv. MS. 15.1.18, no. 58.
70. NLS, Adv. MS. 15.1.18, no. 65; Blair Atholl, Muniments of the Duke of Atholl, Athole Charters, Box 1, Parcel i, nos. 3–6; NAS, GD 220/1/A1/3/8; *Inchaffray Chrs*, no. 25.
71. Grant, *Independence and Nationhood*, pp. 157, 158. For similar statements, see MacQueen, *Common Law*, p. 37, and Duncan, *Making of the Kingdom*, pp. 168, 206–7.
72. Fraser, *Lennox*, ii, no. 6.
73. *Arbroath Liber*, i, no. 228; *Dunfermline Reg.*, p. 111.
74. NAS, GD 254/1.

75. MacQueen, 'Laws of Galloway, pp. 134-7; Neville, *Native Lordship*, pp. 103-4, 108.
76. NAS, RH 1/2/49; NAS, GD 212/2/33, pp. 3-4; *RMS*, i, no. 508; H. L. MacQueen, 'The kin of Kennedy, "kenkynnol" and the common law', in Grant and Stringer (eds), *Medieval Scotland*, p. 281; W. C. Dickinson, 'Surdit de sergaunt', *Scottish Historical Review*, 39 (1960), pp. 170-5.
77. *Aberdeen-Banff Collections*, p. 523.
78. *Paisley Reg.*, pp. 178-80.
79. NAS, RH 6/28.
80. TNA, SC 1/31/19.
81. A. A. M. Duncan, 'William, son of Alan Wallace: the documents', in E. J. Cowan (ed.), *The Wallace Book* (Edinburgh, 2007), pp. 51-2.
82. NAS, GD 220/1/A1/2/2.
83. NAS, RH 6/67.
84. *Inchaffray Liber*, App., no. 24.
85. The participation of native recognitors was particularly marked in the practice of perambulation. See below, Chapter 2, 'The perambulation of land'.
86. The literature here is now considerable, but see especially N. Johnstone, 'Cae Llys, Rhosyr: a court of the princes of Gwynedd', *Studia Celtica*, 33 (1999), pp. 251-95; T. M. Charles-Edwards, M. E. Owen and P. Russell (eds), *The Welsh King and his Court* (Cardiff, 2000); P. J. Duffy, D. Edwards and E. FitzPatrick (eds), *Gaelic Ireland, c. 1250-c. 1650: Land, Lordship and Settlement* (Dublin, 2001); Foster, Macinnes and MacInnes (eds), *Scottish Power Centres*; R. Welander, D. J. Breeze and T. O. Clancy (eds), *The Stone of Destiny: Artefact and Icon* (Edinburgh, 2003); A. Pantos and S. Semple (eds), *Assembly Places and Practices in Medieval Europe* (Dublin, 2004); E. FitzPatrick, *Royal Inauguration in Ireland, c. 1100-c. 1600: A Cultural Landscape* (Woodbridge, 2004).
87. *Arbroath Liber*, i, no. 102; SCA, MS JB 1, no. 3, fo. 61v; Scott (ed.), 'Eight thirteenth-century texts', Text 3.
88. *Melrose Liber*, no. 243.
89. For some examples, see *Cambuskenneth Reg.*, no. 104; *Beauly Chrs*, no. 3; *Selectus diplomatum et numismatum Scotiae thesaurus*, ed. J. Anderson (Edinburgh, 1739), no. 80; BL, MS Harl. 4693, fo. 34v; BL, Campbell Chr. xxx.13.
90. NAS, GD 82/6.
91. H. McKay and R. F. Wolf, 'Pictland and its symbols stones', in P. O'Neill (ed.), *Exile and Homecoming: Papers from the Fifth Australian Conference of Celtic Studies* (Sydney, 2005), pp. 306-7; see also the arguments in favour of regarding rivers as important cultic sites offered in W. F. H. Nicolaisen, 'On Pictish rivers and their confluences', in D. Henry (ed.), *The Worm, the Germ and the Thorn: Pictish and Related Studies presented to Isabel Henderson* (Balgavies, 1997), pp. 116-17.
92. The contemporary literature relating to both is discussed briefly in R. Davies,

'Kinsmen, neighbours and communities in Wales and the western British Isles, c.1100–c.1400', in P. Stafford, J. Nelson and J. Martindale (eds), *Law, Laity and Solidarities: Essays in Honour of Susan Reynolds* (Manchester, 2001), pp. 183–5; and R. Sharpe, 'Dispute settlement in medieval Ireland: a preliminary inquiry', in W. Davies and P. Fouracre (eds), *The Settlement of Disputes in Early Medieval Europe* (Cambridge, 1986), pp. 186–7.

93. *St Andrews Liber*, p. 117.
94. *Arbroath Liber*, i, p. 349.
95. BL, Harl. Ch. 52. B.16.
96. *Arbroath Liber*, i, p. 114; RCAHMS, CANMORE Database, site number NJ90SE6.
97. *Cambuskenneth Reg.*, no. 49; *Arbroath Liber*, i, no. 231; Scott (ed.), 'Eight thirteenth-century texts', Text 4.
98. *Inchcolm Chrs*, no. 19.
99. *Dunfermline Reg.*, no. 590; NAS, GD 212/1/17, p. 39.
100. D. H. Caldwell, 'Finlaggan, Islay – stones and inauguration ceremonies', in Welander, Breeze and Clancy (eds), *The Stone of Destiny*, p. 70; R. A. McDonald, *Manx Kingship in its Irish Sea Setting, 1187–1229: King Ragnvaldr and the Crovan Dynasty* (Dublin, 2007), pp. 173–84.
101. S. T. Driscoll, 'The archaeological context of assembly in early medieval Scotland – Scone and its comparanda', in Pantos and Semple (eds), *Assembly Places*, pp. 81–91; S. T. Driscoll, 'Govan: an early medieval royal centre on the Clyde', in Welander, Breeze and Clancy (eds), *The Stone of Destiny*, pp. 82–3.
102. Caldwell, 'Finlaggan, Islay', pp. 69–72; B. Megaw, 'Norseman and native in the kingdom of the Isles: a re-assessment of the Manx evidence', *Scottish Studies*, 20 (1976), pp. 24–5. The significance of open air meetings is reviewed also in R. Davies, 'Kinsmen, neighbours and communities', pp. 183–5; see also below, Chapter 6 'The social space of Scottish lordship'.
103. See, for example, the discussion of moot hills in RCAHMS, *Eleventh Report with Inventory of Monuments and Construction in the Counties of Fife, Kinross and Clackmannan* (Edinburgh, 1933), pp. 6, 22, 197–8, 209, 212, 270–1.
104. Neville, *Native Lordship*, pp. 117–23.
105. Oram, 'Continuity, adaptation and integration', pp. 57–9; Young, 'Earls and earldom of Buchan', p. 185; G. W. S. Barrow, 'The earls of Fife in the 12th century', *Proceedings of the Society of Antiquaries of Scotland*, 87 (1955), p. 56; G. W. S. Barrow, *Anglo-Norman Era*, pp. 85–6.
106. Oram, *Lordship of Galloway*, pp. 223–4. For the re-use of early medieval sites in the later Middle Ages, see S. T. Driscoll, 'Picts and prehistory: cultural resource management in early medieval Scotland', *World Archaeology*, 30 (1998), pp. 142–58.
107. Barrow, 'Popular courts', p. 227; Barrow, 'Pre-feudal Scotland: shires and thanes', in *Kingdom of the Scots*, pp. 7–56.
108. *Inchcolm Chrs*, no. 19.

109. BL, Campbell Chr. xxx. 19.
110. J.-C. Schmitt, 'The rationale of gestures in the west: third to thirteenth centuries', in J. Bremmer and H. Roodenburg (eds), *A Cultural History of Gesture* (Ithaca, 1991), p. 60.
111. R. C. Stacey, *Dark Speech: The Performance of Law in Early Ireland* (Philadelphia, 2007), esp. pp. 15–52; R. Finnegan, *Oral Traditions and the Verbal Arts* (London, 1992), pp. 13, 19; B. Stock, *The Implications of Literacy: Written Language and Models of Interpretation in the Eleventh and Twelfth Centuries* (Princeton, 1983), pp. 91, 472.
112. See here P. Stoller, *The Taste of Ethnographic Things: The Senses in Anthropology* (Philadelphia, 1989).
113. On this theme more generally, see M. Bloch, 'Introduction', in M. Bloch (ed.), *Political Language and Oratory in Traditional Societies* (London, 1975), pp. 5, 12, 16, 20–5 and, for the medieval period in Britain, C. M. Woolgar, *The Senses in Late Medieval England* (New Haven and London, 2006).
114. NAS, RH 5/22. See also *APS*, i, p. 87.
115. *Paisley Reg.*, p. 50.
116. *Melrose Liber*, no. 306.
117. *Paisley Reg.*, pp. 166–8; *Highland Papers*, ii, p. 138.
118. J. Bannerman, 'The king's poet and the inauguration of Alexander III', *Scottish Historical Review*, 68 (1989), p. 148.
119. *Highland Papers*, i. p. 143; *Melrose Liber*, no. 163. For other noteworthy ceremonies at which the gospels were both invoked and touched, see *Inchcolm Chrs*, no. 19 and *Paisley Reg.*, p. 50. Colin's identity and the context of this deed are discussed in S. Boardman, *The Campbells, 1250–1513* (Edinburgh, 2006), pp. 68–70.
120. *Inchcolm Chrs*, no. 5.
121. *Paisley Reg.*, p. 125. For an example from 1304, see NAS, RH 1/2/79.
122. See, for example, the relics used in a Fife ceremony of c. 1128, and the 'holy evangels' carried to the moor of Fordell more than a century later, in *St Andrews Liber*, pp. 117–18; *Inchcolm Chrs*, no. 19.
123. R. Gameson, 'The gospels of Margaret of Scotland and the literacy of an eleventh-century queen', in L. Smith and J. H. M. Taylor (eds), *Women and the Book: Assessing the Visual Evidence* (London, 1997), p. 165, citing Oxford, Bodleian Library, MS Lat. liturg. fo. 5, fo. 2; R. Rushforth, *St. Margaret's Gospel-book: The Favourite Book of an Eleventh-century Queen of Scots* (Oxford, 2007), p. 55.
124. *APS*, i, pp. 5–6; *CDS*, ii, no. 840. See also Mary Bateson (ed.), 'The Scottish king's household and other fragments, from a 14th century manuscript in the library of Corpus Christi College, Cambridge', in *Scottish History Society Miscellany*, vol. II (Edinburgh, 1904), pp. 35–6, for mention of the obligations of the clerk of the wardrobe to keep securely the 'relics' belonging to the crown.
125. M. T. Clanchy, *From Memory to Written Record: England, 1066–1307*, 2nd

edn (Oxford, 1993), p. 254; more generally, see S. E. Thorne, 'Livery of seisin', *Law Quarterly Review*, 52 (1936), pp. 345–56.

126. *Dunfermline Reg.*, no. 179; see ibid. no. 178. When Robert de Vere made a gift of land to the monks of Melrose he did so by laying a wand on the altar of the monastic church; *Melrose Liber*, no. 259.
127. *St Andrews Liber*, p. 349. For another example from c. 1270, see Fraser, *Douglas*, iii, p. 4.
128. *Dunfermline Reg.*, nos. 348, 349.
129. See here the recent discussion of the relationship between charters and delivery of sasine in G. Donaldson, 'Aspects of early Scottish conveyancing', in P. Gouldesbrough (ed.), *Formulary of Old Scots Legal Documents* (Edinburgh, 1985), p. 165.
130. NAS, RH 5/19.
131. *Dunfermline Reg.*, no. 348.
132. *Lennox Cart.*, pp. 12–13; *Paisley Reg.*, pp. 160–1. For similar statements, all interestingly from Lennox, see Fraser, *Colquhoun*, ii, 273–4; *Lennox Cart.*, pp. 75–6.
133. *Lennox Cart.*, pp. 23–4.
134. *Crossraguel Chrs*, i, no. 7 (c. 1286); *Paisley Reg.*, p. 128 (1274 x 1292).
135. See here Woolgar's comment that 'smell, like all other aspects of sensory perception in the Middle Ages, was charged with moral and spiritual dimensions'. Woolgar, *The Senses in Late Medieval England*, p. 118.
136. See, for example, Fraser, *Carlaverock*, ii, pp. 404–5; *Morton Reg.*, ii, no. 11; *Cambuskenneth Reg.*, no. 49; *Spalding Misc.*, ii, p. 310.
137. *Melrose Liber*, no. 196. Written instruments in the curial setting are discussed below, Chapter 3, 'The development of "trust in writing"'.
138. Clanchy, *From Memory to Written Record*, esp. pp. 254–78.
139. In this respect, the treatment of parchment charters in Scotland closely resembled that found in Anglo-Saxon England and Ireland. See S. Kelly, 'Anglo-Saxon lay society and the written word', in R. McKitterick (ed.), *The Uses of Literacy in Early Medieval Europe* (Cambridge, 1990), pp. 44–7; *Irish Royal Charters: Texts and Contexts*, ed. M. T. Flanagan (Oxford, 2005), p. 25.

CHAPTER 2

The perambulation of land

Introduction

Early in the year 1272, in a letter directed to his father-in-law, Henry III, King Alexander III complained that an English baron had ridden roughshod over the jurisdiction of the Scottish crown within the liberty of Tynedale.[1] The king of Scots had good reason to suspect that a jury composed of the men of Northumberland might be prejudicial to him should the matter come to trial,[2] but the requirements of diplomatic correspondence and respect for Henry's advanced years compelled Alexander to defend his rights in circumspect language. In a typical combination of tact and critical acumen, he proposed that no dispute resolution process would better preserve 'peace and tranquility' between the realms than a formal perambulation of the marches of the property in question by a panel of recognitors drawn equally from the liberty itself and the neighbouring county of Northumberland.

In 1272 recourse to the marching of boundaries as a mechanism of dispute resolution was a well established process in Scotland. In contrast to England, in fact, where it was fast disappearing from regular common law procedure, it was destined to enjoy a rich and long history. This chapter explores the significance of perambulation in the kingdom in the period between the accession of David I in the twelfth century and the legal reforms effected by Robert I in the early fourteenth. It begins with a brief review of the work that legal historians have done on the origins of the royal brieve that, from David's reign,[3] regularly initiated the act of perambulating the marches of an estate. It explores the circumstances under which the procedure first became popular in the kingdom, the identity of the litigants who sought to settle disputes with recourse to the customs and practices associated with it, and the problems associated with the marching of boundaries. Finally, the chapter discusses the act of perambulation within the wider context of the social and cultural milieux of Scotland. Viewed in this broad perspective, the process of perambulation becomes a novel way through which to examine the encounter between Gaelic and European customs and mores that so deeply shaped the history of Scottish law and Scottish society in this early period.

Historians have long been aware of the links between the early development of the royal inquest in Scotland and the prominent place of the brieve of perambulation in the history of disputes about title to land. In seeking to reconcile the sometimes conflicting arguments of a previous generation of scholars, notably Lord Cooper of Culross and Sheriff Hector McKechnie, Ian Willock and Hector MacQueen have shed valuable light on both these topics. Willock's study has demonstrated that panels of jurors were actively engaged in the process of perambulation long before the fourteenth century, and that already in the late twelfth and the thirteenth Scottish kings were closely involved in litigation about boundary lines,[4] while MacQueen has clarified the judicial process that followed the request for perambulation.[5] Together, Willock and MacQueen have placed the practice of formally marching the bounds of estates firmly within the maturation and elaboration of a judicial system that prized title to land and its pertinents as 'the most important single source of wealth and economic activity' in the kingdom.[6] By 1250 it was becoming common scribal practice to embed within the body of written charters elaborate descriptions of the marches of an estate, as well as the text of the royal or baronial precept that had initiated the process. When, therefore, Robert I's chancery officials set themselves the task of assembling the earliest extant 'registers' of Scottish brieves and compiling the wording of a typical brieve of perambulation, they had available to them dozens of exemplars.[7]

Perambulation as a legal process

As Willock has argued, the earliest recorded royal perambulations reflect the pragmatic function of ensuring that all who gathered to witness a new ceremony of endowment or infeftment were in agreement about the boundaries of the estate in question.[8] The medieval cartulary of St Andrews, for example, includes notice of a late eleventh-century grant to the Céli Dé of the land of Kirkness, by Mac Beatha son of Findlaech and his wife Gruoch, in which the extent of the property was carefully described and recorded.[9] Some of the Gaelic charter texts in the Book of Deer also refer to donors walking the metes of the properties they granted.[10] From an early period, then, there developed the custom 'by which the granter of lands personally pointed out the boundaries of the subject of his grant in the presence of witnesses'.[11]

There survive sufficient references in extant sources from the years between 1124 and the early thirteenth century to reconstruct with some confidence the ways in which the Scottish crown first became, then remained, actively involved in the process of perambulation. A charter of David I, dating to the early 1140s, for example, notes that the king sent 'ministers and honest men' to perambulate the land around the parish church of Airth when this was first established.[12] Similarly, when, towards mid-century, the king made a grant of land to the priory of May he referred not merely to the estate itself, but also specifically to the common pasture located nearby that was associated with it.[13] In a comprehensive charter of confirmation to Holyrood abbey, Malcolm IV mentioned a command issued to his officials to 'view' and 'perambulate' the land attached to the church of Bathgate.[14] Another royal precept of 1162 sent the sheriffs of Lanark, Edinburgh, Linlithgow and a group of other men to perambulate the estate of Drumpellier in Lanarkshire, and to 'show' its marches to the monks of Newbattle.[15] From the reign of William I on, royal scribes began the practice of noting within the texts of their charters the occasions when the king ordered a perambulation. A royal deed of 1184, for example, records that such a procedure took place at Moorfoot 'at my command'.[16] From this same period, moreover, come the earliest suggestions that the crown was beginning to treat the ritual marching of bounds as an essential feature of the act of giving. A charter of 1205 made this conceptual link explicit: at the command of King William, a group of local landholders confirmed Newbattle abbey in possession of Peffer only after they had perambulated it.[17] The large crowd assembled to witness the event heard the recognitors declare aloud the marches of the property, revealing that the *viva voce* description was part and parcel of the monastery's title.

That the reign of David I should have been of critical importance to the early history of perambulation is hardly surprising. This was the period in which many of the parish churches of the kingdom were first laid out and provision made for priests in endowments of lands, teinds, revenues and other perquisites. Alexander Grant has offered compelling evidence of 'barony-parish correspondence' in pre-1300 Clydesdale boundaries,[18] confirming a relationship between ecclesiastical and secular estate formation that scholars have long posited.[19] Both kinds of reorganisation required an initial marching of boundaries and together, both played a crucial role in securing an important place for the practice of perambulation in the development of legal custom in Scotland.

There is a good deal of scholarly agreement that the period of David I's reign was equally significant in cementing the reputation of perambulation as a promising and highly effective mechanism for resolving disputed title to property. Many years ago, Geoffrey Barrow noted that the practice of marching the boundaries in such circumstances 'was a substitute for the petty assizes, grand assizes and final concords familiar in the courts of Angevin England'.[20] That this was the case even before the twelfth century is apparent in the record of a bitter dispute that erupted around 1128 between the Céli Dé of the church of St Serf on the island of Loch Leven and Sir Robert of Burgundy.[21] The document has long been of interest to historians for the rare glimpse it affords of relations between the native Gaels of Fife and the European aristocrats who settled in their midst in the twelfth century, but it is valuable also because it preserves one of the earliest comprehensive descriptions of a legal tradition the details of which have, for the most part, been lost to historians. The litigants reached a satisfactory compromise when King David I ordered a group of local worthies, including two 'venerable and old' men, to submit sworn testimony regarding their knowledge of the boundaries of the lands at Kirkness. The presiding justices, members of the legal order of *breitheamhnan*, eventually ruled in favour of the Céli Dé, but the argument was resolved only after these local recognitors had physically marched the territory and reported their findings before the assembled men of the province. The frequency with which the charters of David I's reign note the process of perambulation lends convincing support to the claims of Lord Cooper and his commentators that by the mid-twelfth century there existed a specific royal assize the purpose of which was to make the process available to all who wished to use it. Thereafter, interested parties lodged a record of inquest findings in the king's writing office.[22]

References drawn from the length and breadth of the kingdom leave little doubt that the reign of William I saw continuing interest on the part of the crown in providing, by means of ceremonies of perambulation, a reliable royal remedy to landholders involved in disputes concerning their estates. Indications of this development are found in the increasingly precise language with which scribes in the king's employ described requests for his assistance in conducting formal marches and in their readiness to link the formal marching of bounds with the act of delivering or confirming sasine.[23] Many of William's charters specifically state that a tenant acquired title to property only after royal officials had travelled to a locality to lay out its boundaries.[24] Descriptions of the physical act of boundary walking also became more formulaic in this period. David I's clerks drew on a rich and varied array of terms when they wrote about the procedure: royal agents perambulated,[25] measured,[26] traversed,[27] augmented[28] and pointed out[29] the marches of estates. Those of his grandson, Malcolm IV, measured,[30] went around,[31] viewed,[32] traversed[33] and laid out new metes,[34] but even before William's reign the king's scribes were tending to choose the simple verb *perambulare* to describe the process.[35] Variety in terminology became much more circumscribed after 1165. Ploughgates were still occasionally 'measured' by royal precept,[36] but early in the reign of William I the clerks of the king's chapel were demonstrating a notable preference for clarity and simplicity in legal language.[37] Such sophistication has been noted in other aspects of chancery practice as well.[38]

The association of perambulations undertaken by royal precept with the giving of sasine is evidence of still another development in the nascent common law of real property. Only one of Malcolm's surviving acts links the two actions unambiguously.[39] It may be significant that the charter in question dates from the end of the reign and the period during which Walter de Bidun was chancellor. After a hiatus of nine years, the latter resumed office in 1171.[40] Two of King William I's early charters, issued under de Bidun's supervision, included the reference. Admittedly, the double verbs *perambulare et tradidere* appear in only a handful of documents from the reign.[41] To these references, however, may be added another unusual royal act of 1184, a notification that, in response to a precept from the king, the sheriffs of Haddington and Traquair and others had convened to hear the sworn testimony of men who had perambulated the marches of Moorfoot. As a consequence of the inquest, the royal scribe noted, the king was now able to confirm title to the property to the monks of Newbattle.[42]

Another indication that the king and his chapel were developing a more sophisticated understanding of perambulation was the changing role of the figure of the king in the acts associated with the procedure. In the twelfth century it was by no means uncommon for the king himself to participate in, or at least to preside over, the formal marching of boundaries. David I did the former in May 1142, for example, when he augmented an earlier grant to Melrose abbey by adding to the property a portion of his forest lands in Gatton.[43] His presence is explicitly recorded on a number of other occasions,[44] and it may be inferred in still other contexts, notably when, together with his son, Earl Henry, he issued solemn charters of foundation or confirmation, as well as when his name appears in the witness lists of Henry's *acta*.[45] Charter materials from the period of Malcolm IV's rule make no reference to the king's presence at ceremonies of perambulation. The explanation for this may lie in the early history of the reign, part of which Malcolm spent abroad, and during which the government of the realm lay not in the hands of the boy king, but in those of friends and relations.[46] It was, thus, *in loco regis* that the king's mother, Ada de Warenne countess of Northumberland presided over the resolution of a dispute between two tenants in Huntingdon, which the young king visited on his way to France in 1159,[47] and it may have been in a similar capacity that Malcolm's constable, Richard de Morville, marched the bounds of an estate located within the royal forest of Selkirk.[48] There may have been other occasions solemn enough to warrant the king's attendance, written records of which have now perished.

Extant documents from William's reign none the less suggest that learned opinion about the appropriateness of the royal presence at the marching of boundaries was beginning to change, and that it was coming now to be regarded with some scepticism. William considered at least two occasions worthy of his attendance but very few more. In 1180, when a dispute arose between Richard de Morville and Melrose abbey concerning pasturage rights in the royal forests of Gala and Leader, the king sought to make peace between the parties by personally leading a group of prelates, earls and other worthies around the newly settled boundary line.[49] William again oversaw a perambulation in 1184, when the monks of Melrose quarrelled with royal tenants at Stow over the limits of another area lying within Ettrick Forest;[50] later, when Pope Celestine III directed him to intervene in person, he took part in the settlement of a more contentious dispute between the abbeys of Melrose and Kelso.[51] William's carefully cultivated image as a devout son of the Scottish church may explain why he considered it important to take an active part in disputes involving the greatest and richest of his ecclesiastical vassals,[52] but it is noteworthy that the matter at issue in each of these cases was the delineation of land designated as forest. Fresh grants made out of such land were invariably preceded by a formal perambulation, if not in William's presence, then before his constables, justiciars, sheriffs or *iudices*, or some combination of these officials.[53] The late twelfth century was an important period in the development of forest law in Scotland, during which native customs were steadily giving way before novel practices introduced by English and continental incomers.[54] William's varied contacts with the English court acquainted him with the leading role that his contemporaries, Henry II, Richard and John, were playing in the shaping of forest law there. He can hardly have failed to be impressed, moreover, with the lucrative returns that were a consequence of the Angevins' skilful exploitation of royal jurisdiction in the forest.[55] A wish to emulate Angevin authority in the resolution of forest-related litigation lay at the heart of the Scottish crown's claims to an equally comprehensive jurisdiction north of the border.

It is none the less apparent from surviving record materials that William considered the act of tramping around woods and fields rather less appropriate than had his grandfather, David I. Barrow's extensive studies have shown that the closing years of the twelfth century were an important period in the development of the offices of justiciar, *iudex* and sheriff. The increasingly visible activities of these officers is symptomatic of a change of policy at the heart of Scottish government, a readiness to delegate business that was becoming routine to specially empowered officials. The move towards a standardised terminology in royal commands relating to perambulations and the withdrawal of the figure of the king from all but the most important ceremonies of boundary marching were further manifestations of this increased sophistication. All are also features of a wider process that Scottish scholars, like their English counterparts, have long associated with the 'routinisation' of central government.[56]

Alexander II and Alexander III imitated William's policy of limiting their attendance at ceremonies of perambulation to rare and especially solemn occasions. Both also began to use the process as a means of safeguarding royal property. Already in the opening decades of the thirteenth century there is evidence that the crown was becoming concerned about the extent to which the generosity of David I and his grandsons had eroded the financial and material resources available from the forest. A royal precept of 1219 ordering an inquest to determine whether there had been encroachments on royal pasture in Innerleithen was but the first of a series of perambulations designed to arrest the continued attenuation of royal lands.[57] There were several more such demands for the marching of crown estates, both within and beyond the forest, in regions as far apart as Dumbarton, Banff and the Carse of Gowrie,[58] with each ceremony recording, sometimes down to the smallest stone marker, the extent of arable, pasture or moor land that remained to the king. Royal clerks prudently enrolled in chancery the testimony of local jurors about these possessions, usually under the rubric of a *recognitio perambulacionis*.[59] The care with which they did so speaks of the early chancery's awareness of the probative value of a properly constituted perambulation. It suggests also that officials in the royal employ were consulting these documents in regular fashion. When, for example, William I was asked to settle a dispute between the cathedral church of Glasgow and one of its tenants concerning rights to pasture in Ashkirk, Selkirkshire, he sent his constable, armed with a copy of King Malcolm IV's original grant, to perambulate the estate.[60] By the late thirteenth century the royal chancery had assigned to one cleric responsibility for all the king's 'charters and muniments',[61] and among the documents that Edward I so infamously carried off in 1296 was a bag said to have held several dozen 'little rolls, schedules and memorials' relating to a variety of inquests and perambulations.[62] Quite what these consisted of is as much a mystery as are the contents of so many other materials listed in the inventories of the period, but they do suggest that before the end of Alexander III's reign landholders were taking advantage, as a matter of routine, of the chancery's reputation for careful record keeping.

Already in the late twelfth century it is apparent that the crown was invoking the process of perambulation as a political weapon. There were many occasions in which the findings of one group of boundary marchers were at odds with those of another. Such dilemmas afforded the king a valuable opportunity to act as arbitrator and, as MacQueen has shown, these rulings 'could of course have the effect of putting someone out of land' as much as it could award a litigant secure title.[63] This is what happened in 1184, when David Uviat tried to defend his title to an estate that the abbot of Newbattle claimed as monastic property. The matter was put to the test by means of a royal precept of perambulation, which found in favour of the monks.[64] Sometimes even the threat of a perambulation was sufficient cause for quarrelling parties to come to an agreement. Around 1205, William de Vaux lost hope of winning a claim against Newbattle abbey after the monks secured permission to conduct a formal marching of boundaries, and a group of their *fideles homines* gathered for this purpose.[65] In the later twelfth century the Cistercians of Melrose, the Premonstratensians of Dryburgh and the Tironensians of Kelso were all engaged in aggressive programmes designed to augment their control over the rich grazing country of Wedale and Lauderdale and their environs. On more than one occasion they 'came to blows' with a handful of powerful secular landholders in the border region.[66] Repeated appeals for royal mediation of such disputes permitted William I not merely to exercise a highly valued prerogative, but also to reap the political benefits attendant on championing the interests of the monastic orders in Scotland. Such manoeuvres were powerful assets in the crown's ongoing struggle with neighbouring England for control over the border region and the *ecclesia Scoticana* itself.

Charter evidence from the reigns of Alexander II and Alexander III attests the widespread use of royally mandated perambulations in virtually all parts of the realm. References abound to ceremonies of boundary marching undertaken prior to delivery of sasine and as a regular feature of dispute resolution, with royal scribes taking care in each of these cases to inscribe into the texts of charters detailed descriptions of the estates at issue.[67] Extant documents also bear witness to the growing awareness among landholders that the process might be put to good use in contexts other than the creation of new estates. In 1171, for example, Robert de Quincy made an arrangement to lease some land to Newbattle abbey in return for a sum of cash. The indenture that records the agreement notes that the transfer was considered complete only after the land had been perambulated.[68] Thus, when Gilbert de Bara made provision for his widowed mother by assigning to her a portion of his estate he did so by means of a formal perambulation, which was in turn witnessed by a group of local men.[69] The litigiousness of thirteenth-century landholders was fuelled in large part by growing competition to control the rich revenues generated by a vigorous agrarian economy, and quarrels about common land in particular grew noticeably more rancorous.[70] Yet, the readiness of litigants to go to court speaks also of the confidence – and the ease – with which they were now able to invoke the process of perambulation as a dependable mechanism of dispute resolution. Alexander II and Alexander III continued to receive a steady stream of requests to issue royal precepts for the formal marching of boundaries, and to respond to these by ordering their justiciars and sheriffs to convene inquests of local recognitors.[71]

In the opening decades of the thirteenth century, moreover, perambulation was no longer the exclusive business of the king and his designated representatives. Secular and ecclesiastical landholders, great and small, were making increasing use of the process, both when they created estates *de novo* and as a means of protecting their possessions from would-be intruders. As far back as the reign of David I, the beneficiaries of private grants had required that the metes of new estates be properly delineated at the time of the infeftment. In a period when the use of maps was still many years in the future, the ceremonies that attended the formal marching of boundaries before assembled witnesses had the effect of generating a public record. Wise lords – and none were wiser than the monastic corporations recently established in the kingdom – anticipated disputes about their lands by ensuring that the testimony of recognitors was included within the body of a charter. Similarly, the circumstances that gave rise to requests begin to show greater variation. The marching of newly created estates continued apace,[72] but the procedure was now invoked, for example, when a landholder surrendered title to one estate in exchange for another.[73] Perambulations such as these were almost certainly carried out at the urging of tenants anxious to ensure that the exchange to which they had agreed was fair. At the commencement of a new reign, moreover, it was common for the heads of the great Scottish religious houses to seek confirmation of their possessions. On some occasions they requested that the king include in his confirmation charter explicit reference to earlier perambulations or to the bounds that an earlier ceremony had established. The priors of St Andrews, Holyrood, Newbattle and Dryburgh, as well as the prioress of Manuel, for example, all secured new charters from William I that recited estate boundaries which had been laid out in previous years.[74] The canons of Glasgow cathedral similarly requested, and were granted, a hearing at which the record of a perambulation made in the reign of Malcolm IV was recited aloud.[75]

In the closing decades of the twelfth century requests for perambulations were being made not only of the king, but also of his magnates. The terminology of extant charters reveals that donors were sometimes the active agents here. When he measured out a single acre from his holding in East Haven for the monks of Coupar Angus, for example, Philip de Valognes was concerned above all to protect the portion of the modest property that remained to him.[76] For much the same reason, Henry de Revel, too, preceded his grant of a parcel of land to the priory of St Andrews by walking its boundaries in the company of his son and heir, Richard.[77] Walter the Steward, his son, Alan, and other *probi homines* likewise measured out and perambulated three carucates of land that Walter wished to gift to Paisley abbey; in the late twelfth century Alan himself measured out and 'demonstrated' the metes of a new estate to a favoured tenant.[78] More frequently, however, requests for perambulations came from beneficiaries. When the monks of Paisley expressed concern that a charter of Walter's wife, Eschina, had failed to cite clearly the bounds of a new estate, they sought, and received, from her a new charter that specified the marches in question.[79] Towards the end of the twelfth century, Robert de Kent indicated his intention of gifting some arable and pasture land to the monks of Melrose. They shrewdly insisted that he organise a perambulation of the estate and that the witnesses to the procedure include monks from Kelso abbey, which owned an adjacent parcel of land.[80] Similarly, around the year 1200 the monks of Cambuskenneth requested of the grandson of a long dead benefactor confirmation of the original gift of land, complete with a fresh perambulation of its metes in the presence of the chief men of the nearby town of Stirling.[81] Such caution was not confined to ecclesiastical beneficiaries. Sometime between 1189 and 1195 Odo son of Simon secured from King William I confirmation of a grant in which the prior of St Andrews had given him 'the whole shire of Kinninmonth'. When Odo's son in turn inherited the land he requested a new charter of the prior, one that specified the names of the estates that comprised the 'whole shire'.[82] Transactions such as these took place not in the king's court, but rather before suitors attending tribunals summoned by secular and ecclesiastical barons. Most often they were the courts of the beneficiaries of a new grant or of a party who had won title to land as a consequence of litigation, but occasionally the outcome of a perambulation was announced elsewhere. A final concord between Thomas de Restalrig and the parson of Hailes resolving a question about the boundaries of the mill pool of Hailes, for example, was sealed in Restalrig's court before the men who owed suit there.[83] In the 1230s John earl of Huntingdon effected a settlement with the monks of Lindores abbey before the suitors of his court.[84] Like his contemporary, Feargus of Strathearn, he had attempted to encroach on territory that the monks claimed should be held in common; as in Feargus's case, too, the matter was settled after the land had been marched at the earl's command by *probi homines* of the district.[85] Around the same time, Ingram de Balliol also conceded defeat in a dispute with Holyrood abbey, agreeing with the findings of a body of local recognitors specially summoned to hold an inquest and to perambulate the estate that was the subject of the litigation.[86] After losing his case, Earl John of Huntingdon was made to promise that in future he would not seek to dispute the boundaries of common land by means of the procedure of perambulation. A similar concession to the same house from Sir Reginald Cheyne made later in the century reveals that land-hungry lords were making effective use of the legal procedure at the expense of unwary neighbours.[87]

That perambulation was a convenient legal weapon in the armouries of both complainants and respondents is apparent also in the demands that litigants sometimes made for second or third ceremonies, or for a confirmation of pre-existing boundaries. Soon after 1220, for example, Earl Patrick I of Dunbar was involved in a dispute with Dryburgh abbey over the boundaries of Earlston and Caddesley. The abbot successfully contested the claim after securing royal letters of perambulation, but the settlement of the quarrel was announced in the earl's own court, after Patrick had agreed to 'certify' the findings of the men whom he had sent to perambulate the properties. The monks later secured from the earl's son and heir written confirmation of these same marches.[88] The monks of Melrose, ever vigilant against the dangers of encroachments on their properties, demanded that John de Normanville's confirmation of a grant of his father include a considerably more detailed description of the marches of the estate than had appeared in the father's document.[89] They requested that another benefactor perambulate afresh the marches of lands that they had received, and they made sure to include in the new charter a clear statement that the lands comprised 'eight acres of arable'.[90] David de Lindsay was made to do the same in 1244, when the monks of Holyrood abbey asked him to confirm their title to lands that Richard Comyn, a former lord of Slipperfield, had made them some seventy years earlier. The boundary clause inserted into the later charter repeated almost verbatim that which Comyn had included in his original grant.[91]

A late medieval popular song held that when Alexander III plunged to his death at Kinghorn in 1286, he left his kingdom in a state of 'perplexyte'.[92] Members of the hastily assembled provisional government grappled with a series of unprecedented constitutional and political consequences of the king's demise, but his chancery clerks set about conducting their daily business with hardly a pause. The creation of a special seal endowed the Guardians with the royal dignity that they required to initiate precepts and letters patent, and throughout the period 1286-92 warrants to disburse payments and gifts to a variety of creditors and beneficiaries, for example, issued forth in a steady stream.[93] The degree to which the production of brieves had become thoroughly routine is also demonstrated by the professionalism with which the Guardians' chancery coped with sometimes complex matters at issue in litigation. Thus, within just months of the king's death, letters patent directed four men to convene an inquest to disentangle, by the oaths of 'honest and faithful men', the extent of Christina de Maule's titles to pasture in Panmure from those of her neighbour, and to retour their findings to the royal chapel.[94] Original documents survive in disappointingly few numbers from this fraught period in Scottish history, but extant materials convey the clear impression that the absence of an adult ruler did not adversely affect the judicial process upon brieves. The treatise known as 'The Scottish king's household', which has been dated to the early 1290s, devotes considerable discussion to the chancellor's office, and shows that by then it had become routine for contesting parties to settle a host of disputes concerning title to land by recourse to perambulation.[95] Certainly, the confidence of landholders themselves in the efficacy of the procedure did not diminish. Many of Robert I's earliest acts, it is true, were confirmations of grants made by his predecessors, recent and of old, but there was no willy-nilly clamour at the new king's court on the part of anxious landholders for a review of settlements effected as a consequence of perambulation, or for the confirmation of new estates recently marched. Continuing confidence in the procedure, moreover, is apparent in the years after 1306, when the chancery resumed almost immediately its function of issuing precepts ordering perambulations as a matter of course.[96] The programme of legal reform initiated by Robert I and continued by his successors made the fourteenth century a period 'fertile in judicial brieves', and none was more frequently sought than that which initiated perambulation.[97] The procedure retained its popularity after 1329 because litigants continued to see in it a tool that was at once simple, efficient and trustworthy and, not least, because it generally worked in favour of the pursuer. Yet, it was not for legal reasons alone that the formal marching of boundaries remained popular in the kingdom for as long as it did. The rituals and ceremonies associated with the act also had a profound resonance among the people of medieval Scotland. The twelfth and thirteenth centuries are rich in charter texts that include boundary clauses. Some describe the carving out of new estates in the landscape; others are found in royal, baronial or episcopal charters of confirmation. Still others were embedded in written instruments because the perambulations that they recount were undertaken in the resolution of boundary-related disputes. In all these cases, donors, beneficiaries and pursuers looked to the sworn testimony of 'honest' or 'honest and faithful' recognitors, and the charter texts that preserve the names of these persons offer valuable glimpses into the world of estate making in medieval Scotland.

Perambulation in a Broader Context

The practice of marching the bounds of new estates is found not only in the regions of the kingdom that were heavily influence by the arrival of Anglo-Norman and European settlers, but also in the Gaelicised heartland of the realm. When, soon after 1200, Phillip de Melville married, he had his new father-in-law set down in writing the boundaries of the estate of Mondynes in the Mearns that his bride brought to him as tocher.[98] On another occasion, arable acreage assigned to Arbroath abbey from estates in Angus and the Mearns was similarly measured out and its marches carefully recorded on behalf of the monks.[99] A short time later Earl Mael Coluim of Fife established a new Cistercian house at Culross. He marked the solemnity of the occasion by organising before a large and distinguished assembly a perambulation of 'the whole land of the shire' of Culross that comprised the monks' endowment.[100] Extant charter materials originating north of Forth none the less suggest that recourse to perambulation in this part of the kingdom served different needs and purposes than it did elsewhere. The most extensive perambulations were those of Prince David through the lands of Glasgow, carried out in the early 1120s,[101] and the survey of the boundaries of the lordship of Garioch that David of Huntingdon set in motion in the late 1180s or early 1190s. The earl, however, had pressing reasons to establish clearly the physical extent of his territory, because it 'was not an ancient integral land-division'.[102] Within Garioch, however, his infeftments were made out of estates that required no perambulation; most of the tenancies here were centred on lands the marches of which 'were unlikely to be disputed'. A similar pattern pointing to the re-infeftment of estates already well delineated appears in extant charters relating to Strathearn. Here, the grants of the thirteenth-century descendants of the mormaers of old usually referred to estates bounded simply 'by their right marches'.[103] In Strathearn, moreover, recourse to perambulation was invoked in specific circumstances; chiefly when disputes arose about the boundaries of adjoining lands or entirely new properties carved out of existing field patterns.[104] The early twelfth-century charters of neighbouring Lennox likewise refer to grants of land simply 'by their rightful marches'.[105] Here, too, detailed boundary clauses were included in deeds only under unusual circumstances, most notoriously when, after a long quarrel, Earl Maoldomhnaich surrendered to the monks of Paisley abbey the several estates traditionally attached to the ancient church of Kilpatrick, but also when he divided a bloc of land between co-parceners and sought to remedy a defect of title that troubled one of his important tenant families.[106]

Earl Mael Coluim of Fife's grant of the 'shire' of Culross serves as a reminder of the existence, across the length and breadth of the kingdom, of a territorial framework that was already ancient in the twelfth century. Former multiple estates, abthanages and, in the highland zone, the lands governed by large kindred groups all offered to benefactors anxious to endow the church and lords looking to acquire new tenants a host of pre-existing territorial blocs, the boundaries of which had long been fixed in time.[107] Such ancient divisions, combining as they often did regions of arable and pasture, upland and moor, had been the focus of a rigorous and thoughtful process of boundary drawing in the period before 1100.[108] They were features of the landscape that many, if not most, land lords of the thirteenth century were content to leave unaltered.

The names of the men (and women) who tramped the fields, valleys and woodlands of the Scottish countryside in the course of performing perambulations bear witness to the multicultural kingdom over which David I and his grandson ruled. A royal perambulation of c. 1140 in East Lothian, for example, brought together both Anglo-Norman tenants newly settled in the region and Anglian locals.[109] When King William offered a new estate near Stirling to the monks of Dunfermline abbey in exchange for lands that he intended to empark, he entrusted the task of perambulation to a very distinguished group consisting of the constable, the justiciar of Scotia, the sheriff of Stirling and an experienced clerk of the royal chamber, who walked the new bounds in the company of a jury of men recently settled in the region.[110] Recognitors drawn from newly established Flemish families performed the task of perambulating for the same king in distant Forres.[111] Some early ceremonies resembled the 'especially solemn and responsible' events that characterised the act in the twelfth century,[112] notably the royal perambulation of Melrose estates that occurred in 1184, when twelve recognitors returned their findings 'tremblingly and reverently, and upon the relics of the church'.[113] The 'perambulation' of the entire Scottish kingdom said to have been undertaken in 1218 by papal envoys was an even more momentous affair, even if it came to an undignified end when the pope's men nearly lost their lives in a conflagration when they lodged one night at Lindores abbey.[114] More often than not, however, the work of marching the fields fell to persons of less exalted status. David earl of Huntingdon, for example, called on men of his household to measure a ploughgate of arable land in Ardlair that he wished to gift to the monks of Arbroath.[115] Alexander II commanded a group of seven Gaelic tenants living in Kinblethmont to confirm the boundary line between two estates in Angus, which they did before an assembly consisting of men of mixed ethnic background.[116] The great religious houses employed a variety of monastic officials as perambulators, including cellarers, terrars and, on one occasion, the cantor of

Glasgow cathedral.¹¹⁷ Until the mid-thirteenth century it was not unusual for women to participate in boundary marching, or even to take a leading part in it. Early in the reign of William I, Eschina de Maule, the wife of Walter the Steward, ordered a perambulation of an estate she intended to gift to Paisley abbey.¹¹⁸ Some time before 1205, the king's mother made a similar request of tenants who held property in Fife.¹¹⁹ A generation later, Iseulte of Strathearn summoned tenants from her own land of Abercairney and led them herself around the five-acre parcel that she intended to gift to the canons of Inchaffray.¹²⁰ The presence of both husband and wife at the marching of newly created estates shows that women retained considerable control over their tocher lands, a feature of early Scottish common law that has been noted in other contexts.¹²¹

Scholars have long debated the extent to which Anglo-Norman and European newcomers to Scotland displaced a sitting population in the regions where they settled in large numbers. Charter texts that preserve detailed boundary clauses offer a fresh perspective from which to explore this question. Documents relating to the zone of intensive new settlement, chiefly the region south of Forth, as well as Moray, convey an initial impression that new lordships were created at the expense of native freeholders. Keith Stringer's study of Earl David of Huntingdon's Garioch, for example, led him to conclude that Gaelic landholders here lost both land and status to incoming settlers, and testing clauses of his charters bear witness to a lordly court that had very little place for men of Scottish birth.¹²² The following of another great Anglo-Norman family, the Stewarts, suggests a similar displacement of Gaels in the lordship that the crown created for its hereditary stewards in Clydesdale.¹²³ Alexander Grant's recent examination of twelfth-century settlement in this same region has none the less offered compelling evidence that a handful of 'high status' Gaelic landholders survived relatively unscathed the 'Normanisation' of the area that David I effected; they were not, however, a conspicuous element in the tenurial landscape after 1174.¹²⁴ At first glance, the texts of some charters from other 'Normanised' regions of the realm convey a similar impression of a native Gaelic landholding order roughly excluded from the enjoyment of social and political prestige accorded the incoming aristocratic population. Scribes in the employ of some of the great monastic houses, for example, tended to identify by name only the men of high status who undertook the work of perambulation.¹²⁵ Lower fry they relegated to the anonymous category of *probi homines* or *probi et fideles homines*, or to the still more obscure ranks of *alii quamplures*.¹²⁶

Fortunately, clerics often did preserve in writing the circumstances under which new estates were carved out of the landscape or title to disputed territories examined afresh. The perambulation clauses that they embedded in their charters reveal with unmistakable clarity that the work involved in marching and meting fell overwhelmingly to the native freeholders of Scotland, whose familiarity with their own localities lent them an expertise far greater than that of the newcomers. Such local knowledge counted far more than social status in the weighty business of estate planning. In Fife, for example, King David I assigned the task of perambulating a new estate to the Gaelic men Gille Coluim, Mac Beatha Mac Torphin and Maol Muire the thane of Kellie.[127] In East Lothian, the earls of Dunbar called upon the experience of men such as Ness of Walton, Norman son of Eduf and Ketel de Letham.[128] In neighbouring Peeblesshire, a scribe trained in the customs and practices of Anglo-Norman diplomatics dutifully included at the head of a list of perambulators the names of two knights recently settled in the region, but also those of several men whose names unmistakably attest their native origins.[129] As Geoffrey Barrow long ago pointed out, some of the latter attended ceremonies of perambulation in their capacity as *breitheamhnan*, that is, as members of the learned legal orders. Brice the king's *iudex*, for example, presided over a series of such ceremonies in Angus and the Mearns for a period extending over more than thirty years in the late twelfth and early thirteenth centuries.[130] Within the great lordships governed by the earls of Strathearn, Fife, Buchan and Lennox, the *breitheamhnan* fulfilled vital functions in the perambulation of lands. Some, like Brice, Donnchadh and Boli Mac Gillerachcah, *iudices* of Mearns, attended by side with the king's justiciars, and in doing so lent these ceremonies the full weight of Gaelic tradition.[131] A rare letter written by Brice in 1221 describes how he assembled the 'good men' of the locality, all Gaels and all 'well versed about the boundaries between the lands' then in dispute, and required each in turn to swear on a relic that he would speak truthfully.[132] Others, like Gille Crìosd the *breitheamh* of Lennox, Mac Beatha the *breitheamh* of Strathearn, and Gille Moire the *breitheamh* of Atholl appear in the testing clauses of charters that record, or implicitly refer to, perambulations.[133] Here, inclusion of their names served the specific purpose of legitimising their mormaers' acts of lordship. Mention of the presence of provincial *iudices* in some ceremonies of boundary marching offer rare and precious glimpses of a period when the native legal system was first coming into contact with written texts. A dispute in 1236 between Marjory countess of Buchan and the abbot of Arbroath concerning the land of Tarves was amicably resolved when the *breitheamhnan* of Buchan and neighbouring lordships assembled the men of the province specifically to listen to the testimony of local jurors who had marched the bounds of the estate.[134] In many parts of twelfth- and early thirteenth-century Scotland the spoken testimony of eye witnesses still mattered more than possession of a charter written in Latin.

The presence of the native lawmen at ceremonies of perambulation was, moreover, something of a necessity. The boundary clauses of later twelfth- and thirteenth-century charters sometimes describe in exhaustive detail the ritual march of local recognitors up hills, down valleys, along the banks of rivers and across substantial obstacles, natural and man-made, all the while identifying markers of different sorts. At each stage of the procession the assembled jurors, and the suitors who had been summoned to witness their actions, must have engaged in considerable discussion and perhaps debate. Native *breitheamhnan*, whose linguistic skills are well attested,[135] acted as indispensable agents in the process of perambulation as they translated the findings of Gaelic-speaking recognitors for English or European witnesses. Such were the perambulations undertaken in 1224 and 1231, for example, when in response to a royal precept, William Comyn justiciar of Scotia assembled a dozen Perthshire freeholders, all Gaels, and set them the task of marching the boundary between two estates. Their findings might well have been incomprehensible but for the attendance at the ceremony of Angus the *iudex*.[136] A bitter dispute between the family of the Gaelic earls of Lennox and Paisley abbey over control of the rich lands of Kilpatrick could never have been resolved without the testimony of a dozen men, who dutifully appeared before royal, episcopal and papal justices to recall and recite, in their own tongue, the local history of the church.[137] Similarly, Alexander II's failure in 1236 to describe in detail the 'marches of Fedale in the thanage of Auchterarder' caused the monks of Lindores no end of trouble when, a decade later, Feargus brother of Earl Robert of Strathearn attempted to exert his control over neighbouring lands. His efforts were frustrated thanks only to the readiness of local men to clarify what Alexander's charter had left vague.[138] Episodes such as these serve as salutary reminders that the encounter between the legal cultures of Gaels and Europeans was not everywhere, or even necessarily, contentious in nature. Walking the grounds of an estate and agreeing on the features that delimited its metes required a cooperative effort, and must have generated a great deal of rough and ready camaraderie between perambulators and the men who, in their capacity as suitors to the lordly courts of complainants and respondents, dutifully followed them to bear witness to their findings. The boundaries of the parishes of Stobo and Campsie, in the diocese of Glasgow, were laid out by two such gatherings,[139] and there is no indication that either event was anything but cordial. It might even be argued that ultimately, the fellowship required of perambulation inquests contributed in modest but significant fashion to the larger process that marked the integration of Gaels and Europeans within the kingdom of Scotland.

The minutiae attendant on individual ceremonies of perambulation are shrouded in mystery because few of the scribes considered it worth the effort to describe such mundane matters. The clerk who was responsible for compiling the thirteenth-century portion of the Dunfermline register, however, may be an exception. A series of entries inserted near the end of the manuscript records the genealogies of several neyfs belonging to the abbey; it is followed by a detailed description of the boundaries of four of the monks' estates.[140] (Both entries probably represent the concluding phases of actions initiated by royal precept, perhaps even by the specific brieves *de nativis* and *de perambulacione*.) The first of the boundary descriptions concerns the marches of estates that bordered royal lands. It includes two lists, one of the ten men who witnessed the ceremony, most of them minor freeholders, but one identified as the mair (cain collector) of Glasgow;[141] the second of the men who performed the task of formally walking the bounds. The latter is of especial interest. The persons named there are consistently described in groups of three: the *sector* of a place and two others associated with him, almost invariably Gaels, thus, the 'suitor of Auchtergaven and with him Donnchadh the Small or the Younger and Cailean Mackindoyr'; 'Robert de Caputh the suitor of Murthly and with him William Callendar and the servant of Murthly'; 'Cristin the *sector* of Strathardle and with him Cailean Megdubyl and Mac Beatha Mac Banhyl', and so on. The *sectores* were presumably the suitors to the royal and baronial courts of the district, their partners the otherwise anonymous *probi homines quamplures* who populate so many records of perambulation in the twelfth and thirteenth centuries. Assemblies such as these would not have been possible without the presence of officials armed with the linguistic skills needed to communicate in a bilingual setting. The formal laying out of new estate boundaries or the re-marching of existing ones, bringing together the *viva voce* testimony of local men and *breitheamhnan* alike such as occurred near Dunfermline must have had the effect of fixing the event in the collective memory of a community more powerfully and in more enduring fashion than any written instrument. That was certainly the intent behind a ceremony of perambulation staged in Fife in 1240. On this occasion representatives of two parties in dispute together walked the newly agreed metes of an estate, reciting their movements aloud as they progressed and marking their reference points with stones and crosses.[142]

Deeds originating in the Gaelicised parts of Scotland offer a valuable glimpse of the conceptual framework within which native magnates of the thirteenth century understood boundaries and their functions. The adoption of written instruments in general, it has been shown, added a new dimension to the relations between the native aristocracy and their secular and ecclesiastical clients.[143] The mormaers' authority to create new estates out of earldom land likewise bore eloquent witness to the prestige of great lords within the territories they governed. The early thirteenth century was a period during which 'a lord enjoyed real powers and normally chose his own tenants, and where lord-man relations had genuine meaning'.[144] When Gaelic magnates such as the earls of Fife, Lennox, Mar and Strathearn set native friends and kinsmen the task of describing the bounds of new estates, they accomplished several purposes, simultaneously attesting their parity with Anglo-Norman and European aristocrats who were creating new lordships elsewhere in the kingdom; reinforcing their supremacy within the tenurial structure of their own kindred; and delimiting, in the placement of physical markers, the social space within which they gave expression to lordly influence.[145] Thus, Gaelic magnates viewed control over the circumstances in which perambulations were staged as a potent expression of power and authority in a world in which native ideas about lordship and its perquisites were being challenged by novel, foreign, concepts.

The boundary clauses of extant charters are rich in topographic details; they also have much to reveal about the mental world of perambulators, Gaelic, Anglian or European. These men knew that the practice of including a clause that described boundaries was important to the recipients of charters and realised that the written word represented, for all time to come, a perpetuation of the original act of marching.[146] They were equally aware that such records offered beneficiaries a reliable means of preventing future disputes relating to title. They knew that their goal in tramping up hill and down dale was the drawing of a speculative map that would endure well beyond the time when everyone involved in the act – donor, beneficiary, perambulators and witnesses – had 'gone the way of all flesh', as contemporaries often referred to death. To Gaelic speakers in particular, the very act of declaring aloud the marches of an estate must have represented a powerful affirmation of linguistic and ethnic identity in a period when both were being challenged. The *viva voce* recitation of the names of hills, valleys, rivers and streams offered them a royally sanctioned context in which to assert the equality of their spoken tongue with the English, French and Flemish of the incoming nobility. Moreover, written records of testimony delivered orally gave concrete expression to the legitimacy of the Gaelic language in a world in which learned men privileged writing over the spoken word. The identification of natural sites with Gaelic place names must have been especially evocative to people who lived in the parts of the kingdom where, by the end of the period under examination here, the Gaelic tongue had vanished or was in retreat. The oral description of long-established boundaries, finally, generated a powerful link between assembled witnesses, suitors and perambulators and the long dead ancestors, neighbours and kinsmen who had first delineated them. For all these reasons, the formal marching of estates fulfilled vital functions not merely among the newcomers to the realm, but among its long-established native population.

Whenever possible, perambulators used natural linear features to describe boundaries: rivers, lakes, burns and springs. The course of waterways might alter over time, as King Alexander II found in 1237, when revenues from his share of the River Leven near Dumbarton came under threat,[147] but other features of the landscape, including hills, crags, wells, springs and, where they were known, compass directions served as reference points against which to monitor such changes. The landscape of the more remote reaches of Scotland offered a series of natural referents on a monumental scale, among them the numerous islands scattered the length and breadth of Loch Lomond, the slopes of Glen Fruin and the Corrie of Balglass (all in Lennox),[148] but here, too, the passage of small rivers, streams and rivulets offered plenty of scope for detail. When lords carved new estates out of sparsely settled regions, however, plain features of the landscape generally sufficed as points of reference for the delineation of boundaries. Thus, the bounds of the substantial lordships that Earl Maoldomhnaich of Lennox created for his brother Gille Crìosd around Arrochar and for a favoured native tenant at Luss were both described in relatively simple terms.[149]

The impact of human exploitation of the environment that historians have so comprehensively documented in the period between 1100 and 1300 is echoed in the larger repertoire of names for boundary markers available to perambulators in the thirteenth century, a list that now came to include footpaths, roads, named fields, quarries, wood lots, yares and saltpans, as well as fermtouns and crofts, newly reclaimed marsh lands and even, in one case, a recently erected gallows.[150] Among the many consequences of increased pressure on the land throughout the arable regions of the kingdom was greater precision in clauses that record the boundaries of contiguous estates or those carved *de novo* out of existing properties. When in the mid-thirteenth century, for example, Ness son of Ness gifted ten acres of arable to the monks of Melrose out of his own relatively modest holdings, he made sure to march the edges of the field in person and to point out the layout of the acres in question before assembled witnesses.[151] A generation later, Luke son of Theobald of Pitlandy ordered his men to measure out equally carefully a toft of four acres lying within the field that he called 'Fitheleres Flat', so that he might make a gift of it to the canons of Inchaffray abbey.[152] In circumstances such as these, donors, beneficiaries and perambulators all required the use of an expanded and more precise vocabulary with which to describe physical markers. Charters drafted in favour of Newbattle abbey, for example, refer to 'the stones that were deposited to attest' a change of direction of a boundary line, to mark the division between adjacent fields, to represent the four corners of an estate, to distinguish one ditch from another.[153] Stones were in plentiful supply, and landholders all over the kingdom emulated the monks of Newbattle in making use of them in ceremonies of perambulation.[154] Stones might also, however, be moved, and countless boundary disputes must have had their origins in the attempts of landholders anxious to augment yields from their small acreage at the expense of a neighbour. The ease with which boundaries marked with stones might be compromised may be the reason why some lords preferred to erect crosses. In the late twelfth century, for example, Abbot William of Melrose planted three of them along the boundary of his newly acquired land of Mauchline, perhaps believing that no one (least of all his benefactor, Walter son of Alan the Steward) would dare to violate such holy symbols.[155] Crosses, moreover, had long been used to mark the boundary lines of religious property and at sites set apart as sanctuaries, notably at St Andrews. Here, an entirely fictitious foundation legend held that Hungus king of the Picts had commemorated his perambulation of the priory's lands with the placement of twelve stone crosses.[156] Much earlier still, the monks of Deer had made efficient use of the symbol stones that littered the countryside of Buchan to delineate the boundaries of some of their estates.[157]

The problems associated with movable markers led some landholders to separate their fields from adjacent properties by more durable means. The footpaths and rivers that crisscrossed the rural landscape made suitable boundary lines, and these are mentioned frequently in extant charters. So did the lines demarcating properties that were already under lordly exploitation as woodlands, peat bogs or quarries. The advantage of using such features lay in both their durability and their visibility. In the early years of the thirteenth century the Augustinian canons living on the Isle of Masses used trenches to delimit their arable fields, not merely because the marshy land on which the house was built made these necessary, but also because the precious acres of arable that they had acquired in the narrow valley of the Pow Water were hedged about by those of other tenants.[158] Towards the end of the same century, a rancorous dispute erupted between Paisley abbey and its neighbour, William de Sanquhar, concerning the boundaries of the lands of Sanquhar. William's father had granted the monks a parcel of arable land, the marches of which he had ordered marked with crosses and a trench. Despite the fact that these were erected and dug in considerable numbers, William claimed that the monks had encroached on his portion of the estate. The argument was resolved after a group of local recognitors carried out a new perambulation, and careful provision was made for the digging of two new trenches, one on William's property, the other on the abbey's, 'each', the parties stipulated, 'to be six feet wide'.[159] Just how much these actions cost them in wasted effort and money is not known, but neither William's descendants nor the fourteenth-century abbots of Paisley had subsequent need to revisit these boundaries.

Conclusion

A fifteenth-century compilation of early Scottish laws includes the text of a 'statute' concerning perambulation said to have been enacted by King William I. It reads as follows:

> The lord king, on the advice of [the men of] his shires, has ordained that if he grants land within his domains to anyone by extent on an oath of the same [as sworn] by the country, or at his pleasure without any [such] oath, and assigns him [i.e., the grantee] lands with established boundaries, he shall hold them according to their boundaries and without restriction in perpetuity; and in time coming he shall not lose any part of that land through [process by] a brieve of perambulation or on any other brieve, unless [it be] the lord king's letter of right. In the latter event, the king must make fitting substitution for the said land, or else provide him with warranty.[160]

Few of the so-called *Assise Regis Willelmi* are genuinely attributable to his reign. Many date from the period of Alexander II, still others from that of his successor,[161] and this reference to the judicial process on brieves of perambulation and brieves of right attests a date of composition much later than the early thirteenth century. Nevertheless, it seems clear that long before 1214, landholders great and small were aware of the implications of vaguely worded charter texts which left the precise boundaries of an estate to the memory of recognitors who might all too easily take their local knowledge with them to the grave. Why else would the monks of Melrose have pestered Affrica, daughter of Edgar de Dunscore, for no fewer than three separate charters, each describing in increasingly elaborate detail the marches of the parcel of land she had granted them, then have sought royal confirmation of these same bounds?[162] How else, moreover, to explain the confidence with which litigants appeared in royal and baronial courts with sealed charters in hand, prepared to challenge the claims of an opponent with the written boundary clauses penned into them?

The increasingly vigorous economy of the thirteenth century and concomitant activity in the land market generated a host of new questions relating to the tenure and conveyance of estates, to which the crown was in many cases able to respond speedily and satisfactorily. The carefully stage-managed ceremonies associated with perambulation met the challenges of the period in highly effective fashion. The practice of embedding boundary descriptions within the texts of the charters that commemorated the creation of new estates served a pre-emptive function for beneficiaries by actively discouraging would-be encroachers. The inclusion of such a clause proved salutary when, around 1205, William de Valognes sought to wrest from the monks of Newbattle abbey control of a small estate in East Lothian. The abbot secured royal permission to organise a perambulation *secundum assisam terre*, whereupon William 'seeing and understanding by the counsel of his friends that he had no case to pursue', abandoned his attempt and renounced forever all claims to the land.[163] Elaborate descriptions of new estates served an equally important, if rather different, purpose among donors, permitting lords to demonstrate by action, deed and word that their authority encompassed the power to raise ordinary men to the status of the noble tenantry. Finally, by the late thirteenth century, the probative value of written records of perambulation became increasingly weighty in cases in which oral testimony could no longer be invoked or was deemed insufficiently weighty. Disputes that might in one generation have been resolved by summoning the *probi et fideles homines* of the neighbourhood left both pursuers and respondents in the next at the mercy of opponents who knew that such witnesses were no longer living. The collective memory of the locality certainly played a central role in the resolution of such disagreements, but written boundary clauses endowed title to land with greater permanence and security than fragile human recollection could ever offer.

Perambulation became, and remained for several centuries, a popular procedure at Scottish common law because it offered something to everyone involved in litigation. Surviving charter materials suggest that Ian Willock's argument that the summoning of solemn inquests 'met with a certain resistance' because people resented their use for 'merely administrative purpose' is in need of revision.[164] Perambulation became the legal procedure of choice because, across the length and breadth of the kingdom, it gave a meaningful voice to tenants great and small, Gaelic-, English- and French-speaking, male and female, in the great sharing out of land that marked the 'Anglo-Norman era'. The royal command that initiated the procedure and the jurisdiction of royal courts over a considerable proportion of cases involving conveyance and title positioned the king at the very heart of the dispute-resolution mechanism, and so allowed him to play the role that all landed subjects expected of a wise ruler. Ultimately, perambulation retained its importance at the heart of the legal system for as long as it did because it permitted the crown and the aristocracy to exercise the kind of cooperative government that was so distinctive a feature of the medieval kingdom of Scotland.

NOTES

1. TNA, SC 1/5/37; see also SC 1/5/52. The liberty was then in Scottish hands.
2. The case is discussed in some detail in M. Holford and K. Stringer, *Border Liberties and Loyalties: North-east England, 1200–1400* (Edinburgh, forthcoming).
3. G. W. S. Barrow, *The Kingdom of the Scots: Government, Church and Society from the Eleventh to the Fourteenth Century*, 2nd edn (Edinburgh, 2003), p. 60n; H. L. MacQueen, *Common Law and Feudal Society in Medieval Scotland* (Edinburgh, 1993), pp. 86–7. Both cite *APS*, i, p. 53. See also below, pp. 43–4.
4. I. D. Willock, *The Origins and Development of the Jury in Scotland* (Edinburgh, 1966), pp. 122–3.
5. H. L. MacQueen, 'Pleadable brieves, pleading and the development of Scots law', *Law and History Review*, 4 (1986), 416–17.
6. MacQueen, *Common Law and Feudal Society*, p. 3.
7. The Ayr MS, now NAS, PA 5/2, discussed in *The Register of Brieves as contained in the Ayr MS., the Bute MS., and Quoniam Attachiamenta*, ed. T. M. Cooper (Edinburgh, 1946), pp. 1–52 and *Formulary E: Scottish Letters and Brieves, 1286–1424*, ed. A. A. M. Duncan (Glasgow, 1976), pp. 1–2.
8. Willock, *Jury in Scotland*, pp. 10–11.
9. *St Andrews Liber*, p. 114.
10. K. H. Jackson, *The Gaelic Notes in the Book of Deer* (Cambridge, 1972), pp. 33–66. See also the discussion at pp. 88, 117–18.
11. T. M. Cooper, *Select Scottish Cases of the Thirteenth Century* (Edinburgh, 1914), p. 22.
12. *Charters of David I*, no. 147; see also no. 41.
13. Ibid. no. 165.
14. *RRS*, i, no. 199.
15. Ibid. no. 198.
16. *RRS*, ii, no. 252; see also nos. 222, 262, 277, 286, 291, 344, 345, 513.
17. *Newbattle Reg.*, no. 119. Another early reference to assizes of the land is found in *Arbroath Liber*, i., no. 189. See also below, pp. 62–3.
18. A. Grant, 'Lordship and society in twelfth-century Clydesdale', in H. Pryce and J. L. Watt (eds), *Power and Identity in the Middle Ages: Essays in Memory of Rees Davies* (Oxford, 2007), pp. 98–124; see especially table 1. See also A. Grant, 'Franchises north of the border: baronies and regalities in medieval Scotland', in M. Prestwich (ed.), *Liberties and Identities in the Medieval British Isles* (Woodbridge, 2008), pp. 160–6, and R. Richens, 'Ancient land divisions in the parish of Lesmahagow', *Scottish Geographical Magazine*, 108 (1992), pp. 184–9.

19. G. W. S. Barrow, *Kingdom of the Scots*, pp. 261–2; G. W. S. Barrow, *The Anglo-Norman Era in Scottish History* (Oxford, 1980), pp. 30–60; S. Taylor and J. M. Henderson, 'The medieval marches of Wester Kinnear, Kilmany parish, Fife', *Tayside and Fife Archaeological Journal*, 4 (1998), pp. 232–47.
20. Barrow, *Kingdom of the Scots*, p. 91.
21. *St Andrews Liber*, pp. 117–18.
22. Cooper, *Select Cases*, p. 22; *APS*, i, p. 53 and references at n. 3 above.
23. Barrow, *Kingdom of the Scots*, p. 59 notes the latter briefly; see also *Formulary of Old Scots Legal Documents*, ed. P. Gouldesbrough (Edinburgh, 1985), pp. 167–70.
24. *RRS*, ii, nos. 39, 48, 61, 75, 130, 222, 233, 236, 277, 286, 392, 378.
25. *Charters of David I*, nos. 41, 86, 87, 120, 147, 165, 166, 174, 175, 216.
26. Ibid. nos. 86, 87, 216.
27. Ibid. no. 98.
28. Ibid. nos. 115, 147.
29. Ibid. nos. 174, 175.
30. *RRS*, i, nos. 234, 266.
31. Ibid. no. 41.
32. Ibid. no. 199.
33. Ibid. nos. 29, 168.
34. Ibid. no. 29.
35. Ibid. nos. 138, 198, 199, 259, 270, 284.
36. *RRS*, ii, nos. 184, 222, 277.
37. Ibid. nos. 28, 39, 48, 61, 75, 130, 170, 184, 215, 233, 236, 252, 262, 286, 291, 342, 344, 377, 392, 402, 469, 524, 540; *Newbattle Reg.*, nos. 25–7.
38. *RRS*, ii, nos. 70–4; G. W. S. Barrow, 'The Scots charter', in G. W. S. Barrow, *Scotland and its Neighbours in the Middle Ages* (London, 1992), pp. 102–4.
39. *RRS*, i, no. 198.
40. Ibid. no. 28; *RRS*, ii, nos. 29–30.
41. *RRS*, ii, nos. 39, 61, 262, 291.
42. *RRS*, i, no. 252.
43. *Charters of David I*, nos. 120, 121.
44. Ibid. nos. 98, 164, 174, 175.
45. Ibid. pp. 5–8.
46. *RRS*, ii, nos. 6–7, 114–15.
47. Ibid. nos. 105–06. See also Edinburgh University Library, Laing Charters, no. 67, which describes another perambulation ordered by Countess Ada.
48. *Glasgow Reg.*, i, no. 30.
49. *RRS*, ii, no. 236.
50. Ibid. nos. 288–9; *The Chronicle of Melrose from the Cottonian Manuscript, Faustina B. IX in the British Museum*, ed. A. O. Anderson and M. O. Anderson (London, 1936), p. 44.
51. *RRS*, ii, no. 440.

52. On this subject, see G. W. S. Barrow, *Kingship and Unity: Scotland, 1000–1306* (Edinburgh, 2003), pp. 57, 66; A. A. M. Duncan, *The Kingship of the Scots* (Edinburgh, 2002), p. 114.
53. The references here are numerous, but see, for example, *RRS*, ii, nos. 130, 215, possibly 345. Nos. 402 and 409 did not concern forest, but rather royal moor land.
54. J. M. Gilbert, *Hunting and Hunting Reserves in Medieval Scotland* (Edinburgh, 1979), pp. 9–12, 22–8.
55. C. R. Young, *The Royal Forests of Medieval England* (Leicester, 1979), pp. 18–73.
56. MacQueen, *Common Law and Feudal Society*, pp. 34–5, 47–50; MacQueen, 'Canon law, custom and legislation: law in the reign of Alexander II', in R. D. Oram (ed.), *The Reign of Alexander II, 1214–49* (Leiden, 2005), pp. 224–35; *RRS*, ii, nos. 28–67.
57. *Newbattle Reg.*, no. 121.
58. See, for example, *Newbattle Reg.*, no. 165; NLS, Adv. Ch. B 1356; *Paisley Reg.*, p. 218; *Aberdeen-Banff Antiquities*, ii, p. 109; *Lindores Cart.*, no. 23.
59. See, for example, *Arbroath Liber*, i, nos. 227–9; *Dunfermline Reg.*, nos. 192–3; BL, Add MS 33245, fos. 157v–158r, 158r–167v.
60. *RRS*, ii, nos. 215, 284.
61. M. Bateson (ed.), 'The Scottish king's household and other fragments, from a 14th century manuscript', in *Miscellany of the Scottish History Society, ii* (Edinburgh, 1904), p. 32.
62. *APS*, i, p. 114.
63. H. L. MacQueen, 'The brieve of right in Scots law', *Journal of Legal History*, 3 (1982), p. 62.
64. *RRS*, ii, no. 252; see also NAS, GD 45/27/67 for a similar case.
65. *Newbattle Reg.*, no. 119.
66. R. Fawcett and R. D. Oram, *Dryburgh Abbey* (Stroud, 2005), p. 150; T. M. Cooper, 'Melrose abbey *versus* the earl of Dunbar', *Juridical Review*, 55 (1943), pp. 1–5.
67. Examples may be found in *Dunfermline Reg.*, no. 181; *Holyrood Liber*, no. 72; *Cambuskenneth Reg.*, p. 104; *Panmure Reg.*, ii, pp. 125–6; *Dryburgh Liber*, nos. 73, 104, 105, 165, 216, 288; *Lindores Cart.*, nos. 16, 71, 140; *Inchaffray Chrs*, no. 46; *Kelso Liber*, i, no. 245; *May Records*, no. 26; *Melrose Liber*, nos. 232, 233, 249, 302; *Newbattle Reg.*, no. 34; NAS, RH 1/2/51.
68. NAS, GD 40/1/6. See also G. W. S. Barrow, 'A twelfth century Newbattle document', *Scottish Historical Review*, 30 (1951), pp. 41–9.
69. *May Records*, nos. 33, 34. For a brief discussion of the related brieves of division and terce, see MacQueen, *Common Law and Feudal Society*, p. 123, and Willock, *Jury in Scotland*, p. 122.
70. See, for example, NAS, GD 254/1; *Lindores Cart.*, no. 24; C. J. Neville, 'Native lords and the church in thirteenth-century Strathearn, Scotland', *Journal of Ecclesiastical History*, 53 (2002), pp. 467–9.

71. The examples here are numerous; see, among others, NLS, Adv. MS. 29.4.2(x), fos. 22r–23r; NLS, Adv. MS. 34.4.3, fo. 27; *Arbroath Liber*, i, nos. 107, 229; *Paisley Reg.*, pp. 88, 227–8; *Melrose Liber*, no. 268; *Holyrood Liber*, no. 70; NAS, GD 220/1/1, RH 5/31; *RRS*, v, nos. 141, 346; *Dunfermline Reg.*, no. 193; *Midlothian Chrs, Soutra*, no. 32; *Newbattle Reg.*, nos. 119, 121; J. Raine, *The History and Antiquities of North Durham* (London, 1852), App., no. 62; *Panmure Reg.*, ii, pp. 138–40; NAS, GD 254/1; G. G. Simpson, *Handlist of the Acts of Alexander III, the Guardians, John, 1249–1296* (Edinburgh, 1960), no. 251.
72. See, for example, *RRS*, ii, nos. 222, 233, 286, 345, 392, 469.
73. Ibid. nos. 130, 277, 291, 344. For a late example, see NAS, GD 93/1.
74. *RRS*, ii, nos. 28, 39, 61, 75, 262.
75. Ibid. no. 215.
76. NAS, RH 6/20.
77. NLS, Adv. MS. 15.1.18, no. 46.
78. *Paisley Reg.*, pp. 5–6; NAS, GD 220/2/1, no. 16.
79. *Paisley Reg.*, pp. 74–5.
80. *Melrose Liber*, no. 59. For the interests of Kelso abbey, see *Kelso Liber*, i, nos. 248, 253, 255, 256, 258, 260, 261. For similar examples, see ibid. nos. 82, 85–7.
81. *Cambuskenneth Reg.*, no. 104.
82. G. W. S. Barrow, 'The early charters of the family of Kinninmonth of that ilk', in D. A. Bullough and R. L. Storey (eds), *The Study of Medieval Records: Essays in Honour of Kathleen Major* (Oxford, 1971), pp. 121, 124.
83. *Dunfermline Reg.*, no. 218.
84. *Lindores Cart.*, no. 19.
85. See below, p. 57. For another example from Strathearn, when a panel of arbitrators decided that a stretch of territory was in fact common land between two tenancies, see *Inchaffray Liber*, nos. 47, 48.
86. *Holyrood Liber*, no. 70. For a discussion of other cases likely to have been settled in baronial courts, see H. L. MacQueen, 'The brieve of right re-visited', in R. Eales and D. Sullivan (eds), *The Political Context of Law: Proceedings of the Seventh British Legal History Conference, Canterbury 1985* (London, 1987), pp. 22–3.
87. *Lindores Cart.*, no. 130.
88. *Dryburgh Liber*, nos. 114, 115.
89. *Melrose Liber*, no. 249.
90. Ibid. no. 252.
91. NLS, Acc. 9769, Scottish Deeds, Add. 545, 546.
92. 'Scotland after Alexander (*c*.1300)', in *The Triumph Tree*, ed. T. O. Clancy (Edinburgh, 1998), p. 297, later recorded in *The Original Chronicle of Andrew of Wyntoun*, ed. F. J. Amours, 6 vols (Edinburgh, 1903–14), v, p. 145.
93. Simpson, *Handlist of the Acts of Alexander III*, pp. 44–55. The early months of the provisional government are discussed in Barrow, *Robert Bruce and the*

Community of the Realm of Scotland (Edinburgh, 2005), pp. 23–6; Duncan, *Making of the Kingdom*, pp. 604–7.
94. BL, Harley Ch. 43.B.9.
95. Bateson (ed.), 'The Scottish king's household', pp. 31–2; for the dating of this manuscript, see Duncan, *Making of the Kingdom*, pp. 595–6.
96. See the extensive discussion in *RRS*, v, pp. 3–126 and an example in *Dunfermline Reg.*, no. 352.
97. H. McKechnie, *Judicial Process upon Brieves, 1219–1532* (Glasgow, 1956), pp. 18–28; see also MacQueen, *Common Law and Feudal Society*, passim; *APS*, i, pp. 470, 731.
98. *Arbroath Liber*, i, no. 93.
99. Ibid. nos. 63, 67, 83.
100. *Chron. Melrose*, ed. Anderson and Anderson, p. 67.
101. *Charters of David I*, no. 15.
102. K. J. Stringer, *Earl David of Huntingdon, 1152–1219: A Study in Anglo-Scottish History* (Edinburgh, 1985), p. 66; see also pp. 240–1.
103. See, for example, *Inchaffray Chrs*, nos. 4, 11, 12, 13, 27, 33; *Inchaffray Liber*, App., no. 2.
104. *Inchaffray Chrs*, nos. 2, 19, 26, 34, 37, 46.
105. For some examples, see *Lennox Cart.*, pp. 26–7, 30–1; Fraser, *Lennox*, ii, nos. 4, 7, 11, 202, 203.
106. *Paisley Reg.*, pp. 160–2; *Lennox Cart.*, pp. 25–7; Fraser, *Lennox*, ii, no. 207.
107. A. Grant, 'Thanes and thanages, from the eleventh to the fourteenth centuries', in A. Grant and K. J. Stringer (eds), *Medieval Scotland: Crown, Lordship and Community – Essays presented to G. W. S. Barrow* (Edinburgh, 1993), pp. 39–81; Barrow, *Kingdom of the Scots*, pp. 7–56; Barrow, 'The pattern of lordship and feudal settlement in Cumbria', *Journal of Medieval History*, 1 (1975), pp. 117–38; R. A. Dodgshon, *Land and Society in Early Scotland* (Oxford, 1981), pp. 58–9. For abthanages, see G. W. S. Barrow, 'The lost Gàidhealtachd of medieval Scotland', in G. W. S. Barrow, *Scotland and its Neighbours in the Middle Ages* (London, 1992), pp. 121–3, and A. Macdonald, 'Major early monasteries: some procedural problems for field archaeologists', in D. J. Breeze (ed.), *Studies in Scottish Antiquity presented to Stewart Cruden* (Edinburgh, 1984), pp. 74–5.
108. A. L. Winchester, 'The multiple estate: a framework for the evolution of settlement in Anglo-Saxon and Scandinavian Cumbria', in J. R. Baldwin and I. D. Whyte (eds), *The Scandinavians in Cumbria* (Edinburgh, 1985), pp. 89, 92–5.
109. BL, Campbell Chrs, xxx. 1.
110. *RRS*, ii, no. 130.
111. Ibid. no. 543.
112. *RRS*, i, pp. 49–50.
113. *Chron. Melrose*, ed. Anderson and Anderson, p. 44.
114. Ibid. p. 70.
115. *Arbroath Liber*, i, no. 83.

116. Ibid. nos. 227, 228; BL, Add MS 33245, fo. 158v.
117. *Melrose Liber*, nos. 108, 109, 116, 135, 169, 249, 252; *Dunfermline Reg.*, nos. 180, 181; *Newbattle Reg.*, no. 3.
118. *Paisley Reg.*, pp. 74–5.
119. *RRS*, ii., no. 469.
120. NAS, GD 24/5/1/1. For an early fourteenth-century example of a woman ordering a perambulation, see *Lindores Cart.*, no. 136.
121. C. J. Neville, 'Women, charters, and land ownership in Scotland, 1150–1350', *Journal of Legal History*, 26 (2005), pp. 21–45.
122. Stringer, *Earl David of Huntingdon*, pp. 81, 86, 160–1.
123. Barrow, *Kingdom of the Scots*, pp. 312–31.
124. Grant, 'Lordship and society', pp. 101–13.
125. See, for example, *Arbroath Liber*, i, nos. 83, 81, 124; *Melrose Liber*, no. 118; *Newbattle Reg.*, no. 119, *Dunfermline Reg.*, no. 196.
126. *Melrose Liber*, no. 118.
127. *Charters of David I*, no. 165.
128. *Coldstream Chrs*, nos. 3, 4, 7, 24, 26–8.
129. *Glasgow Reg.*, no. 104; Barrow, *Kingdom of the Scots*, p. 66; *Dunfermline Reg.*, no. 332; *Arbroath Liber*, i, nos. 89, 227, 228.
130. Barrow, *Kingdom of the Scots*, p. 62.
131. Ibid. p. 60.
132. BL, MS Add. 33245, fos. 162v–163r, printed in Barrow, *Kingdom of the Scots*, pp. 66–7.
133. *Paisley Reg.*, pp. 174–5, 178; *Inchaffray Chrs*, nos. 46, 47, 52; I. R. Milne, 'An extent of Carrick in 1260', *Scottish Historical Review*, 34 (1955), 48–9; NAS, GD 212/1/6, pp. 19–20.
134. *Arbroath Liber*, i, no. 227.
135. J. Bannerman, 'The Scots language and the kin-based society', in D. S. Thomson (ed.), *Gaelic and Scots in Harmony: Proceedings of the Second International Conference on the Languages of Scotland (University of Glasgow, 1988)* (Glasgow, 1988), pp. 11–12.
136. NAS, GD 1/828/1/1. For a similar ceremony held in 1231, over which David de Lindsay justiciar of Lothian presided, see *Dunfermline Reg.*, no. 196. See also another mixed panel of recognitors in *Lindores Cart.*, no. 23.
137. *Paisley Reg.*, pp. 166–8.
138. *Lindores Cart.*, nos. 22, 23.
139. *Glasgow Reg.*, nos. 103, 104.
140. NLS, Adv. MS. 34.1.3A, fos. 3–3v, 16v, 27, 69, printed in *Dunfermline Reg.*, nos. 325–31 (genealogies), 332–5 (boundary descriptions).
141. For the office of mair, see Barrow, *Kingdom of the Scots*, pp. 55–6, and *The Sheriff Court Book of Fife, 1515–1522*, ed. W. C. Dickinson (Edinburgh, 1928), p. lxii.
142. *Inchcolm Chrs*, no. 19.
143. C. J. Neville, *Native Lordship in Medieval Scotland: The Earldoms of Strathearn and Lennox, c. 1140–1365* (Dublin, 2005), pp. 188–95.

144. K. J. Stringer, 'The charters of David earl of Huntingdon and lord of Garioch: a study in Anglo-Scottish diplomatic', in K. J. Stringer (ed.), *Essays on the Nobility of Medieval Scotland* (Edinburgh, 1985), p. 76.
145. C. J. Neville, 'Charter writing and the exercise of lordship in thirteenth-century Celtic Scotland', in A. Musson (ed.), *Expectations of the Law in the Middle Ages* (Woodbridge, 2001), pp. 83–4.
146. A. Alexander, 'Perambulations and boundary descriptions', in H. E. J. Le Patourel, M. H. Long and M. F. Pickles (eds), *Yorkshire Boundaries* (Leeds, 1993), p. 39.
147. *Paisley Reg.*, p. 218.
148. *Lennox Cart.*, pp. 25–6, 34–5; Fraser, *Lennox*, ii, no. 204.
149. Royal Faculty of Procurators, Glasgow, Hill Collection of MSS, Macfarlane Muniments, ii no. 3; Fraser, *Lennox*, ii, nos. 204, 207.
150. K. J. Stringer, 'Acts of lordship: the records of the lords of Galloway to 1234', in T. Brotherstone and D. Ditchburn (eds), *Freedom and Authority: Scotland c. 1050–c. 1650: Historical and Historiographical Essays presented to Grant G. Simpson* (East Linton, 2000), p. 228; *Dunfermline Reg.*, no. 165; Neville, *Native Lordship*, pp. 97–8; *Newbattle Reg.*, no. 125; *Inchaffray Chrs*, no. 57.
151. *Melrose Liber*, no. 302. William son of Bernard showed a similar concern to delimit carefully the boundaries of a seven-acre property that he gave to the monks of Arbroath; *Arbroath Liber*, i, no. 124; for still another example, see *Inchcolm Chrs*, no. 19.
152. *Inchaffray Chrs*, no. 103. For another example, see BL, Cotton Ch. xviii, 25.
153. *Newbattle Reg.*, nos. 28, 29, 31, 32, 79, 91, 97, 100, 106, 107, 111, 275.
154. See, for example, *Melrose Liber*, nos. 48, 77, 87, 90, 232, 233, 249, 252, 256; *Lindores Cart.*, nos. 90, 91; *Arbroath Liber*, i, no. 353; *Kelso Liber*, i, nos. 118, 119; *Cambuskenneth Reg.*, no. 104.
155. *Melrose Liber*, no. *72.
156. S. Taylor, 'The coming of the Augustinians to St Andrews and Version B of the St Andrews foundation legend', in S. Taylor (ed.), *Kings, Clerics and Chronicles in Scotland, 500–1297: Essays in Honour of Margaret Ogilvie Anderson on the Occasion of her Ninetieth Birthday* (Dublin, 2000), p. 116; H. L. MacQueen, 'Girth: society and the law of sanctuary in Scotland', in J. W. Cairns and O. F. Robinson (eds), *Critical Studies in Ancient Law, Comparative Law and Legal History* (Oxford, 2001), pp. 340–3.
157. K. Forsyth, 'The stones of Deer', in K. Forsyth (ed.), *Studies on the Book of Deer* (Dublin, 2008), pp. 398–402. For the use of both stones and crosses, see *Inchcolm Chrs*, no. 19.
158. Neville, *Native Lordship*, pp. xii–xiii, 81–3, 96–9, 135–8. For other references to trenches, see also *Melrose Liber*, no. 109; *May Records*, nos. 33, 34; *Kelso Liber*, i, nos. 122–4, 129.
159. *Paisley Reg.*, pp. 227–9.
160. *Quoniam Attachiamenta*, ed. T. D. Fergus (Edinburgh, 1996), p. 325; *APS*, i, p. 379, cap. xxiv.

161. *Quoniam Attachiamenta*, ed. Fergus, p. 90; MacQueen, *Common Law and Feudal Society*, pp. 87–9; MacQueen, 'Scots law under Alexander III', in N. H. Reid (ed.), *Scotland in the Reign of Alexander III, 1249–1286* (Edinburgh, 1990), pp. 75–80; Duncan, *Making of the Kingdom*, pp. 185–6, 200–3; *RRS*, ii, pp. 42, 45–6, 69; Barrow, *Kingdom of the Scots*, p. 105.
162. *Melrose Liber*, nos. 199–202.
163. *Newbattle Reg.*, no.119.
164. Willock, *Jury in Scotland*, p. 10.

CHAPTER 3

The development of 'trust in writing': written documents and seals in Scotland, 1100–1300

INTRODUCTION

In 1231 Patrick, eldest son of Earl Patrick I of Dunbar, wrote to Thomas prior of Coldingham to report that he would be unable to attend in person a meeting in which Thomas had undertaken to remit payment on an outstanding debt. In his stead, Patrick proposed to send two knights of his affinity and, unusually, a notary, to whom, he noted, he had entrusted custody of his seal.[1] Patrick must have felt confident that the prior would acknowledge his vassals as appropriate spokesmen for him and, more important, his seal as a valid attestation of their authority to accept payment of the monies on his behalf. Thomas's reply, if he wrote one, has not survived, but he appears to have concurred. The seal that Patrick sent to the monastic precincts was probably the same one that he appended to a series of other documents issued around the same time: measuring just over 5 cm in diameter, of natural, undyed wax, it depicted a knight on horseback, in armour, with a raised sword in his right hand, and on his left arm a kite-shaped shield, devoid of any markings.[2] In appearance it resembled closely hundreds of other equestrian seals found throughout the British Isles in the early to mid-thirteenth century. Its authority as a legally valid expression of Patrick's will lay specifically in the legend inscribed around the outer edge of its face, SIGILL' PATRICII FILII COMITIS PATRICII, and in the image of the cross, the symbol of the divine, stamped into the wax at the head of these words. Prior Thomas's clerical education will have enabled him to read the inscription, and he will certainly have understood the significance of the cross. He will also have known that if Patrick later tried to claim that the debt had not been discharged the seal, together with the letter that it authenticated, would constitute compelling evidence that the payment had indeed been made. Nevertheless, in order to ensure that future generations did not forget the substance of the transaction, Thomas carefully stored the document in the priory archives, from where it was later sent on to the mother house of Durham.

Patrick's simple letter to Coldingham reveals the extent to which the closely related technologies of writing and sealing had become embedded in the conduct of everyday business in East Lothian in the early thirteenth century. By 1231, secular and ecclesiastical lords throughout lowland Scotland were imitating him, and sealed letters, charters, indentures and notifications had acquired an evidentiary authority that was effecting a transformation of customs relating to debt, landownership and other property-related concerns negotiated in royal and baronial courts the length and breadth of the kingdom. Patrick's use of a written letter and a personal seal are symptomatic of a profound shift within medieval culture, a process that scholars have variously described in the European context more generally as the emergence of 'textual communities', the development of 'pragmatic literacy', and the growth of a 'literate mentality'.[3] Historians have only recently begun to understand the mechanics of that process as it occurred in Scotland.[4] This chapter explores the use that lay persons made of written documents and seals in Scotland in the period between the accession to the throne in 1124 of David I and the year 1300, by which time documents had acquired near undisputed authority as records of actions done and promises made. It examines, more particularly, the process by which these artefacts were first deployed in the curial setting in the twelfth century, and the ways in which they subsequently became steadily more popular with the landholding nobility. Understanding the talismanic value that Scottish men – and women – attached to documents and seals, and the layers of meaning with which they invested these objects, offers scholars the chance to trace the interaction of orality and literacy in a realm that may have lain on the periphery of western Europe but which was none the less closely in tune with cultural developments there.

The political development of the Scottish kingdom after 1124 offers a unique opportunity for historians to examine the introduction and early impact of the twin technologies of writing and sealing. The realm to which David I succeeded was still very much a kingdom in the making, consisting of several regions, each with distinctive linguistic and ethnic cultures. Probably the most important divide was that between the parts of the kingdom which lay north of the Forth–Clyde rivers, the heartland of the ancient land of Alba, and those which lay to the south, where noblemen from Anglo-Norman England and the continent first settled in considerable numbers at the king's invitation. By 1250, the Mac Malcolm kings had succeeded in bringing much of the turbulent north under their political control by defeating a series of rebellions and establishing in the area a handful of new lordships loyal to the crown. The land benorth Forth retained much of its distinctly non-European linguistic and cultural identity; nevertheless, with few exceptions, the Gaelic magnates who were the king's chief tenants there considered themselves as much subjects of Alexander III and members of a single Scottish realm as did the great 'feudal' lords of the south. One of the central themes of the history of Scotland in the century or so after the reign of David I is the encounter between two very different cultures, one that brought with it from abroad familiarity with written instruments and the waxen seals so closely associated with them, and another, which vested individual and collective authority in the oral testimony of eye-witnesses and the memory of a specially trained order of learned poets, historians, doomsmen and genealogists. The spread of written documents and waxen seals from the 'Anglo-Norman' south into the 'land of earls' north of Forth has much to reveal about the nature of this encounter.

The development of Scottish 'trust in writing'

Among the more famous stories associated with the life of St Margaret of Scotland is the miraculous recovery of the queen's illuminated bible from the bottom of a river, where a servant had dropped it. Despite its immersion, the book survived 'so perfect, so uninjured, so free from damage that it looked as if it had not been touched by the water'.[5] The story inspired a later owner of the manuscript to add to its leaves an explanation of how such a rare and valuable object should have suffered such careless treatment. The gospel book was lost, the cleric wrote, after the queen had permitted 'certain folk who wanted to swear an oath among themselves' to borrow it. The inscription, one historian has remarked, bears eloquent testimony to the 'variety of ways in which people could interact with books and writing besides reading them personally'.[6]

Books of scripture, crucifixes and relics were integral to the celebration of the medieval mass. In twelfth-century Britain they also served more pragmatic purposes in the environment of royal and baronial courts, as divine pledges that guaranteed undertakings made before witnesses and, ultimately, as instruments of God's vengeance when human beings disavowed their promises. Sermon *exempla*, chronicles and hagiographies abound with tales of the terrible fate that awaited persons who dared to violate the sanctity of these objects. The supernatural powers of holy books and relics lay also at the heart of the sanction clauses found in twelfth-century Scottish charters, like that written on behalf of Thor Longus, on the occasion of his grant of the land of Ednam to the church of St Cuthbert of Durham. Its concluding clause made the uncompromising statement that 'if any one shall presume, by any violence or device, to take away this my grant from the saint aforesaid and the monks serving him, may God Almighty take away from him the life of the kingdom of heaven and may he undergo everlasting punishment with the devil and his angels'.[7]

The ground-breaking research of Michael Clanchy on the introduction of charters and other written instruments to the legal and administrative business of medieval England has shown how complex was the transition there from an 'oral' to a 'written' culture. Until well into the twelfth century, Clanchy has nevertheless argued, 'contemporaries continued with their pre-literate habits'.[8] The value of documents lay in their potent status as symbolic objects; their purpose was to reinforce, but not yet to replace, the physical actions that effected delivery of seisin, the acknowledgment of debt, and any number of other formal undertakings. For this reason, different forms of ratification – seals, witness lists, crosses – existed alongside each other for the period that it took medieval English people to develop what Clanchy has called 'trust in writing'.[9] A similar distinction between the symbolic and dispositive functions of written deeds characterised the business of secular courts elsewhere in the British Isles. Thus, in formal gatherings in Ireland and Wales, charters were long regarded as 'optional records' of past events, useful for supplying reliable corroborative evidence of a deed done or a promise made, the absence of which, however, did not constitute adequate grounds for challenging a donor's intentions.[10]

In Scotland, the introduction of written deeds to the business of landholding reflects a similar pattern. Pre-twelfth century references to the use of writing in the curial setting are rare, though the impression they convey is that here, as elsewhere, the power of writing lay more in the novel technology that it represented than in the words that made up written records. The production of a document at a ceremony of conveyance normally occurred at an important, but by no means defining, moment in the business of giving. In the years before his succession as king, Prince David made skilled use of the stage-managed deployment of written instruments; for example confirming his brother Edgar's grant of lands in Swinton to the monks of Durham by laying the latter's charter on the altar of the church of Coldingham. Another of Edgar's deeds served an equally symbolic purpose when David despatched it to the household of Bishop John of Glasgow as a visible attestation of his brother's intentions with respect to the lands of Horndean.[11] In the early twelfth century, none the less, transactions involving land acquired legal status only when witnesses saw and heard a grantor make a symbolic act and a recipient in turn acknowledge a gift in a gesture of his own.[12] A deed issued at the command of David in his capacity as prince of Cumbria makes this clear. In 1123–4, the findings of an inquest into the possessions of the cathedral church of St Kentigern, Glasgow, achieved the status of legal fact when a panel of carefully chosen recognitors 'heard and saw' the proceedings.[13] Their findings were set down in writing, but it was the oaths that they swore, rather than the act of recording their actions on parchment, that gave the bishop and his see secure title to a rich array of properties.

In the later part of the twelfth century, the chronicler Jordan Fantosme described Henry II's enfeoffment of a new tenant. The king, he stated, 'picked up a little stick and handed it to Brien, thus investing him with ten square leagues of land as a reward for his efforts'.[14] Although he wrote of an English ceremony, Fantosme was in close contact with the Scottish royal court, and must have believed that the actions he described would be familiar to readers there. The author of a mid-twelfth-century history of St Andrews certainly would have done so: in his – altogether fanciful – account of the foundation of the priory he imagined the legendary Pictish king Hungus placing a clod of earth on the high altar of the new church as a symbol marking his act of establishment.[15] Another ceremony of sasine, this one occurring in Angus in the later 1220s, nevertheless affirms the continued primacy of symbolic objects other than written instruments in the conveyance of land. On this occasion, the parson of the church of Melginch formally relinquished possession of his office by placing in the hands of the abbot of Holyrood the lock and key that belonged to the main door of the building as well as the chalice from its altar.[16]

In Scotland, as in Ireland and Wales, rulers in the later eleventh and the twelfth centuries appropriated the new clerical emphasis on the authority of the written word and transformed it into a powerful tool for expressing the royal will. They did so in myriad ways, and with a subtlety that is sometimes overlooked by modern observers. In their charters and brieves, the purpose of which was to give effect to royal commands in regions where the crown's authority was contested, the ambitious Mac Malcolm kings exploited the new technology much as did their contemporaries in Leinster and Gwynedd 'as a literary vehicle for furthering their own agenda'.[17] David I and his successors, moreover, provided tenants newly infeft in such areas with handsomely written deeds, solemnly authenticated with a seal that invoked the majesty of the crown. They intended that these be displayed in the great halls where barons convened their courts and entertained visitors; in short, that the documents function as parchment counterparts of the powerful new castles erected as visible expressions of the crown's colonising efforts in the countryside where rebels and other troublemakers contested royal authority. Such, for example, were the acts issued under the great seal that gave away vast tracts of Moray to ecclesiastical and secular beneficiaries after the collapse of uprisings there led by Mael Coluim Mac Aeda and his associates.[18] The encoding of royal charters with carefully crafted political messages accomplished a similar purpose when kings instructed their scribes to make creative use of other features of the written deed. The illuminated initial of Malcolm IV's charter of 1159 to Kelso abbey, most notably, depicts an elderly David I and his youthful grandson side by side in a potent image of authority that served to emphasise the majesty of the Mac Malcolm kings.[19] Likewise, visual cues linking David I's dynasty to the governance of the realm were repeated time and time again on the face of the great seal that graced all royal charters and the coins that circulated in the king's name in most parts of the realm.

David I's adoption of diplomas, charters and brieves as regular vehicles for disseminating the will of the Scottish royal administration reveals both a keen appreciation of the ways in which his kinsman and contemporary, King Henry I of England, used writing as an instrument of royal power and a shrewd grasp of its potential in the realm to which he had succeeded. The vague terminology of his earliest charters, such as that of the oft-cited grant to Robert I Bruce of Annandale, which specified only that the lands were to be held 'with all those customs which Ranulf le Meschin ever had in Carlisle and his land of Cumberland', gave way within a generation to documents that set out in more careful language both lordly prerogatives and vassalic obligations.[20] By the later twelfth century, moreover, the king's clerks were drafting royal *acta* in a recognisably standardised form, which, in its substance, was to endure until the end of the Middle Ages and beyond.[21] The issue of a written instrument under the great seal came to follow the act of granting itself as a matter of course, with royal, episcopal and monastic chanceries regularly enrolling these documents in their archives should future generations need to revisit their terms.

From the royal court, the practice of committing grants of estates and other privileges to parchment spread to 'a wider pool of individual landholders', first to the Anglo-Norman and continental aristocracy newly settled in the region south of Forth and the far north and, later, to the great Gaelic lordships of the kingdom.[22] Extant records from the century and a half or so after 1124 bear witness to an increasing familiarity with the usefulness of written deeds in the earliest baronial courts of Scotland and a growing confidence in their deployment. In the Europeanised parts of the kingdom, within a generation of David's death, charters were fast acquiring intrinsic value as the legitimate expression of their authors' intentions, alongside older, more traditional acts of sasine, quitclaim, excambium and sale. By the later thirteenth century, landlords in the Gaelicised regions were likewise moving towards the literate modes of thought and were developing the 'trust in writing' that Clanchy has studied in England. Like David I, Malcolm IV and William I, the bishops, abbots and the heads of religious houses who were such avid consumers of royal deeds understood the difference between sasine lawfully given before witnesses and the purely commemorative purpose of the charter that recorded the act. The monastic houses of the reformed religious orders were in the vanguard of the movement to establish formal chanceries and archives, where the records of grants, quitclaims and other land-related matters were carefully stored, copied and consulted as circumstances required. The collection of Melrose abbey charters currently housed in the National Archives of Scotland constitutes the richest examples of this kind of scrupulous record keeping, but the new and newly restored episcopal sees of the kingdom were equally meticulous in their preservation of written deeds.[23] The cartulary of the cathedral church of Glasgow known as the *Registrum vetus*, for example, portions of which belong to the thirteenth century, brought together what must already been a considerable corpus of royal and baronial deeds;[24] similarly, the clerics in the employ of the bishop of Moray began to assemble a register in the mid-thirteenth century, mindful of the consequences of the periodic upheavals that troubled the region during the protracted rebellion of Mac Uilleim kindred.[25] Nor was such monkish caution misplaced. In 1215 papal judges delegate had to revisit afresh a quarrel between the abbots of Dunfermline and Cambuskenneth because an agreement on the issue made in the reign of King William 'had not been committed to writing as it should have been'.[26]

The charter texts inscribed into the Book of Deer a century earlier still reveal how the power of the written word had captured the imagination of Gaelic-speaking clerics in a distant corner of the kingdom. Analysis of the entries demonstrates a concerted effort to 'use writing more effectively' in the new European-style courts that had recently been established in Banff and Aberdeen.[27] Commemorating and preserving gifts of land and privilege in the 'protective and inviolate' milieu of sacred writings such as gospel books, moreover, bestowed on such writings a solemnity unmatched by other records.[28]

The secular noblemen of the day were not quite as sophisticated. For them, the relationship between ceremony and record was a great deal more ambiguous. For this reason, donors and beneficiaries alike invested charters and other written documents with a range of different meanings. Like the gospel book of Queen Margaret, these instruments in turn performed a variety of functions within the context of landownership. In the later twelfth and the thirteenth centuries the words inscribed on parchment sheets had the power to persuade merely by being seen and heard. Thus, acts of

THE DEVELOPMENT OF 'TRUST IN WRITING', 1100–1300

confirmation frequently began with a *viva voce* recitation of the text that recorded an original grant, and not merely its dispositive clauses, but also the phrases that described dedication, corroboration, sanction and attestation. Such recitations had the power to recall for witnesses, even many years after the event in question, the circumstances under which an act of endowment had first been made, and to conjure into their presence the ghosts of persons who had seen it at first hand. Around 1180, for example, in their capacity as papal judges, the abbots of Melrose and Dryburgh summoned before them members of the Riddell family, and began an investigation into Hugh's claims to the church of Cranston in Midlothian by reading aloud the contents of three different documents authenticated by the seals of Hugh and his father Richard.[29] Hugh's oath was not the only issue at stake here: so, too, was the reputation of all his noble predecessors. Ambivalence about the capacity of written documents to embody facts relevant to a case lay at the heart of a request, made two hundred years after this, that the contents of two charters be 'expounded in the vernacular' before a specially summoned audience.[30] Growing confidence in the use of writing is discernible, if only distantly, in the terminology of charter texts themselves. Transfer of sasine might well be legally accomplished only when an act of infeftment had been publicly performed, but the ambiguity of dispositive clauses encouraged donors to endow written instruments with the powers to 'attest', 'confirm' and 'corroborate' their actions. A beneficiary of Dryburgh abbey confirmed that the monks had firm title to previous gifts because, he said, '*plures cartas feotestantur*'.[31] A Melrose charter of the reign of William I 'expressed more clearly' and made 'stronger provision for' the rights they enjoyed in the forest of Ayr than had an earlier deed.[32] The act of 'enchartering' a beneficiary, consisting as it did of both visual and written cues, offered the recipient good reason to consider his title unassailable.[33] The permeability of the conceptual space between what was spoken aloud and what was subsequently recorded in writing is especially evident on occasions when a scribe enshrined in a charter the very words of a donor, as did a cleric who was present when Richenda daughter of Winfred de Berkeley infeft a new tenant in Laurencekirk.[34]

In some parts of the kingdom, landholders great and small associated ownership of a written instrument and title to property so closely that from the late twelfth century onwards the surrender of title deeds became a condition of quitclaim and sale.[35] So important was this aspect of the transfer of title that wives, children and any other family member who might later lay claim to a property often appeared together to take part in the handing over of title deeds.[36] Quitclaims and excambia touched also on the prerogatives of a donor's lord, and, as Peter de Asseby did around 1200, persons involved in such transactions asked that the lord, members of his family or the suitors of his court attend the ceremony of quitclaim in order to witness the transfer of charters with their own eyes.[37] When noblemen like Constantine and David de Lochore relinquished their hold on estates of land by placing the relevant deeds on the high altar of a church,[38] or, as William Comyn of Kilbride did in 1261, when he handed over to a new owner the indentured instrument by which the king had infeft him,[39] the documents they surrendered assumed especially weighty status, as both visual props intended to symbolise an act performed before witnesses and divinely sworn guarantees of the donor's intentions.

Just as landholders became increasingly familiar with the practice of handling written instruments, so did they come to accord them, if sometimes grudgingly, weightier probative value. By the later years of the thirteenth century, even in the Gaelicised portions of the kingdom, the validity of claims backed up by the evidence of documents could no longer easily be challenged. In 1273 Earl Malcolm of Lennox was forced to concede his indebtedness to the monks of Arbroath abbey when the abbot confronted him with the evidence of various 'muniments and writings' that recorded his predecessors' obligations.[40] A decade and a half later a dispute between Earl Malise III of Strathearn and Inchaffray abbey concerning the right of presentation to the parish church of Strageath was resolved not only after 'trustworthy men' had testified on behalf of the canons, but when Abbot Hugh exhibited in the earl's own court 'public instruments bearing various authoritative seals'.[41] In related fashion, refusal to acknowledge the evidence of the written word could have dire consequences. Thus, in 1293, John Balliol's unwillingness to uphold the terms of a charter of Alexander III was instrumental in losing him the support of the important nobleman MacDuff of Fife.[42]

Belief in the power and authority inherent in the written word was also expressed in the preoccupation of medieval Scottish landholders with the misuse or abuse of written documents. A late thirteenth-century assize enjoined severe penalties on anyone caught trafficking in 'false charters'.[43] For at least a century before this, members of the ecclesiastical and secular nobility alike had been aware that unscrupulous persons might attempt to mount challenges to lawful title on the basis of written documents, not all of which were necessarily spurious. Around 1190, for example, the abbot of Kelso demanded that Robert de Kent and his father Ralph explain why they had granted to Melrose abbey a charter granting access to valuable pasture land in the Lammermuir hills when he had in his possession a similar document limiting these privileges to the monks of Kelso.[44] It became increasingly common for recipients of lands that had been quitclaimed to require not only a clear statement that any written instruments pertaining to the donor's property had been dutifully surrendered into the hands of the new owner, but also another, disavowing the contents of any charters 'that might appear' in future.[45] In related fashion, the loss of title deeds and other muniments was a matter of grave concern, especially to the churchmen who were such avid collectors of archival materials. In 1305 the abbot of Kelso petitioned Edward I for advice about how he might enforce the monastery's claims to its vast properties, because the monks' charters had been destroyed in recent campaigns. The king's answer is instructive: he suggested that the abbot should be able to make successful use of the 'common law of those parts' in order to re-establish title.[46] More famously, in 1291–2 investigation of the claim of Count Florence of Holland to the throne of Scotland stalled when he proved unable to produce authentic documents in support of his cause.[47]

Despite a demand for properly executed charters on the part of both clerical and secular beneficiaries, Gaelic magnates were much slower than most of their Anglo-Norman and European contemporaries to incorporate the technology of writing fully and firmly into the business associated with lordship, and in many parts of the kingdom there is abundant evidence of the survival of Clanchy's 'pre-literate habits'. Scholars have discussed at length why this should have been the case,[48] but more difficult to trace in extant source materials are the stages by which Gaelic lords and their tenants gained trust in the power of the written word. No doubt some lords used charters in much the same way and for similar reasons as did their kings, to give tangible force to their claims to control lands that had not previously been subject to their kindred. Richard Oram's examination of Galloway, for example, has shown how adept were successive rulers there in using written *acta* to consolidate their hold over the district of Desnes Ioan, beyond the patrimonial lands bounded by the River Urr.[49] The division of the earldom of Mar in the 1220s thrust Thomas Durward into the upper ranks of regional society, a position that he entrenched by issuing charters intended to foster a 'sense of continuity' with the tenants of his mother's Gaelic progenitors;[50] in nearby Kinveachy, a recently established lord issued charters in his name in order to forge new relationships with the local tenantry.[51] Two hundred year later, the Campbell chiefs of Argyll were still employing these tried and proven methods to attract – and to control – new members of their affinities.[52]

The lesser nobility of thirteenth-century Gaelic Scotland had less aspiration, imperative or opportunity to use writing in this kind of tactical fashion. Most confined their handling of documents to their contacts with the church. Clerical beneficiaries throughout the British Isles insisted on making formal records of the gifts of land and privilege that they received from men and women of lesser ranks, and they demanded no less of the Gaels who inhabited the great territorial lordships north of Forth. The charters transcribed into the registers of monastic houses and episcopal sees from across the region reveal that, to this extent at least, lesser Gaelic noblemen actively partook of the 'literate mentality' of the day. This was the case even in the most remote corners of lordships, such as that of Lennox. The handful of charter texts issued under the authority of lesser lords here none the less suggests an ambivalence towards the evidentiary function and authority of written documents. In the later 1230s, for example, the Cluniac monks of Paisley successfully challenged the earls' kindred for title to the valuable lands attached to the ancient church of Kilpatrick. While Earl Maoldomhnaich conceded defeat by dutifully agreeing to the terms of a charter that confirmed the abbey's claim, his brother Dùghall, rector of the parish church, simply set about procuring for himself forged deeds assigning him a portion of the disputed lands, on the basis of which he infeft several new tenants. The monks were eventually able to prove that Dùghall's charters were 'adulterine and illicit' and, under threat of excommunication, he and his men surrendered them into the hands of papal judges delegate.[53] It would be fascinating to know which features of the documents so quickly alerted the church's agents to Dùghall's deception and, more intriguing still, to identify the cleric who dared to draft them. Such details, alas, do not appear in the otherwise abundant records relating to the case.

Some Lennox noblemen used their own bodies as pledges of the commitments they undertook. Earl Maoldomhnaich and his brother Amhlaibh, for example, promised that in commemoration of their death and burial at Arbroath abbey, the Lennox family would forever provide the monks with four oxen annually;[54] in neighbouring Kintyre, Dùghall Mac Suibhne made a gift of the advowson of the parish church of St Colban to the monks of Paisley in return for burial in the abbey's precincts.[55] Despite the fact that their grants were subsequently recorded in writing, all these donors expressed in these arrangements a deep-seated belief in the power of their physical presence, even beyond the grave itself, to bear witness to, as well as to compel, observance of, their earthly actions.

Other Lennox landholders demonstrated a similarly simplistic understanding of written instruments. Around 1234 poverty drove another Dùghall, the son of the provincial *iudex*, and his wife to resign into the hands of Abbot William of Paisley a small estate at Cochno. They held, they said, no charters relating to the land. Instead, they gave legal weight to the resignation by placing their hands on a bible at the high altar of the abbey church and speaking oaths, but they also foreswore the validity of any charters that might somehow be found (where?) at some vague time in the future.⁵⁶ When Maurice of Luss, the representative of a very old native Lennox family, sought to ensure that the cathedral church of Glasgow would always have access to his gift of timber for its bell tower, he solemnly enjoined his heirs to honour his promise on the mere word of the abbey's servants. Bishop Wishart was not inclined to trust such pious imprecations. He had his chancery clerks draw up a written record of the gifting ceremony, and, 'for weightier evidence still', requested that the Official of the see append his seal to the document.⁵⁷ Despite the preference of clerics for written instruments, until well into the thirteenth century and indeed beyond, the people of Lennox continued to privilege the oral testimony of eye-witnesses and of local men with deep roots in the community over the evidence of written acts. So, too, must countless other landholders living elsewhere in Gaelic Scotland.

In Scotland, as elsewhere in the medieval west, the appearance of written documents introduced a new dynamic to the business of landholding and estate management. Here, too, however, the diffusion of the new technology of writing had implications beyond the merely pragmatic. Documents became fixtures in the baronial courts of the kingdom not only because the ecclesiastical beneficiaries of lordly generosity sought to protect title to their gifts, but because the deployment of parchment sheets inscribed with Latin words served an important purpose in the drama and ceremony associated with the conveyance of land. It is no accident that in Scotland so many more charters issued by lay donors to lay recipients should survive from the period after c. 1250 than from before that date. Written documents remained the near exclusive preserve of kings and *literati* because until then they functioned within the limited sphere of royal and ecclesiastical government. From the mid-thirteenth century onwards charters became more numerous because people everywhere now endowed them with a much broader range of powers, meanings and functions in the conduct of their everyday lives.

SEALS AND THE REPRESENTATION OF INDIVIDUAL AND FAMILY IDENTITY

In 1401 a statute of the Scottish parliament required that 'each baron and others holding of the king should have his own seal to serve the king as he is bound by law', and further, 'that these should be seals and not signets or signatures as has been customary before this time'.⁵⁸ Such legislation was possible in the early fifteenth century because for a long time already seals had become a common currency in royal, baronial and urban environments. A century earlier, indeed, the treatise known as *Regiam Majestatem* had devoted considerable attention to the matter, in a discussion of the ways in which a creditor might establish valid claim to payment of a debt. The author of these chapters suggested that special importance be paid to the seal appended to the document in question,

> viz. by comparison of several seals and other writs attested by the same seal. If on this being done it is found that the seals coincide and that there is no suspicion of difference... then, the point is usually regarded as concluded... But if any seal is challenged and cannot be verified by comparison or recognised in court, then the matter must go to combat because it pertains to the crime of falsehood.[59]

This passage was borrowed, almost verbatim, from the late twelfth-century English treatise known as *Glanvill*.[60] The extent to which *Regiam Majestatem* reflects the state of legal practice in fourteenth-century Scotland is still a matter of scholarly debate,[61] yet the inclusion of this discussion in the treatise is noteworthy because it speaks clearly to the strong link that contemporaries drew between a seal marked with specific armorial symbols and the person whom it purported to represent. The texts of hundreds of charters that survive from the period, originating from Moray to East Lothian and Fife to Lennox, drafted on behalf of persons great and small, male and female, offer further corroboration of the evidentiary value of seals: by 1300, and indeed considerably earlier, a sealing clause which set out the donor's intent in making a gift of land or some other privilege had become a standard feature of almost all written *acta*. In the early fourteenth century, however, there were probably a few Scots men and women old enough to recall a time when seals had been very simple objects, and perhaps even a handful of persons who remembered when seals had been altogether rare. Extant evidence suggests that seals and the armorial bearings that historians associate so closely with them spread across the length and breadth of Scotland only in stages and, compared with England and the continent, in some parts of the kingdom at a comparatively late date.[62] Jordan Fantosme, for example, who devoted scrupulous attention to the arms, equipment and knightly accoutrements of many of the Scottish lords who invaded England in the wars of 1173–4, makes no mention of shields embossed with armorial bearings.[63] By the early fourteenth century, moreover, heraldic seals were no longer the exclusive preserve of the higher aristocracy, secular and ecclesiastical: they were becoming increasingly popular, too, among townsmen and urban corporations, lairds great and modest, men and women, even common folk.

It is only recently that the study of seals and their usage in medieval

Scotland has moved beyond its infancy. Historians have shown that by the later medieval period Scottish landholders had enthusiastically adopted these and other aspects of European material culture,[64] and seal designs have long been the subject of close scrutiny by genealogists, professional and amateur. With some exceptions, however, the authors of even the most extensive of these studies have asked few more penetrating questions of their medieval source materials than did the antiquarians who first compiled comprehensive catalogues of seals and their heraldry, notably Henry Laing, Walter Birch, Joseph Horne Stevenson and Marguerite Wood,[65] and there remain unanswered crucial questions about sigillographic practice in Scotland. For example, scholars still know little about why and how, in the twelfth and early thirteenth centuries, Gaelic landholders in particular adopted the continental-style armorial seal as a potent representation of individual and family identity, or about the ways in which impressions in wax reveal the interaction of native belief systems and European concepts of self and representation. Using the evidence of several hundred surviving charter texts and seals, the second part of this chapter explores these questions and offers tentative conclusions about the development of the link between identity and imagery in the first century after the accession of David I.

The research of sigillographers has shown that almost everywhere in western Europe seal usage spread from the crown downward through the ranks of society, with ecclesiastical lords the first to imitate royal practice, followed by secular magnates, then lesser landholders and, eventually, townsfolk and common people. The dissemination of seal usage occurred only over several centuries, beginning in the heartland of post-Carolingian Europe, but picking up pace in England after 1066, where aristocrats were adopting personal seals as early as the third decade of the twelfth century.[66] In some respects this pattern was repeated in Scotland. Around 1094 Duncan II was the first to use a seal that identified him as king, though his differed from contemporary English models in being only one-sided,[67] and the document to which it was appended was further authenticated by the addition of signatories' crosses.[68] Almost a century after Edward the Confessor, Alexander I (1107–24) was the first king of Scots to use a double-sided seal depicting the king in majesty; his immediate successors, David I, Malcolm IV (1153–65) and William I (1165–1214) each used a device almost identical to his, with the inscriptions appropriately altered to represent their respective names.[69] By the mid-twelfth century, bishops and monastic houses had begun to generate a steady demand for written instruments issued under the royal seal; they had also begun to authenticate their own *acta* with devices that symbolised their spiritual and political authority.[70] The earliest seals of the secular nobility date from slightly later. Among the devices catalogued by Laing and Stevenson and Wood were those of Robert Bruce lord of Annandale and his son Robert II (d. 1194);[71] Eustace de Vescy,[72] Robert de London,[73] Robert and William Avenel,[74] Walter son of Alan the steward and his son Alan,[75] Saer de Quincy,[76] William de Lindsay,[77] David earl of Huntingdon[78] and Richard and William de Morville.[79] More surprising, men of non-magnate status, some of quite modest standing, were also using seals at almost the same time. The examples here are numerous, but they include persons such as Thor son of Sweyn and Robert son of Fulbert, of East Lothian;[80] Patrick de Whitton, John son of Orm, and Patrick, Robert and Walter de Corbet, all of Roxburghshire,[81] Edward de Restalrig, from the environs of Edinburgh;[82] Roger de Scalebroc from Ayrshire,[83] and Peter de Curry from Kyle in Dumfriesshire,[84] all of whom employed the devices between c. 1150 and 1180.[85] Persons who had no seal, or who claimed that 'my seal is not well known' or 'not authoritative' simply borrowed one from their lord or a wealthier neighbour.[86] Although he claimed to own a 'large seal', on one occasion Ralph de Clere resorted to using his signet and the seals of several other knights to authenticate a charter granting an estate of land to the monks of Kelso.[87]

Several observations arise from this very brief survey, all of which have implications with respect to sigillographic practice in twelfth-century Scotland. In the first place, notably absent from the first group of extant seals are examples belonging to the Gaelic magnates who were such prominent members of the ruling aristocracy of the period. The single exception is Donnchadh son of Gille Brigte lord of Carrick, whose seal is affixed to grants of land to Melrose abbey and the nunnery of North Berwick.[88] Seal usage among the great territorial lords who lived north of Forth was, in fact, highly unusual, and in many cases rare, until well into the thirteenth century. The earliest examples to survive from Angus date to 1225; from Atholl to c. 1230, the period of Thomas of Galloway's tenure of the title of earl; from Buchan not until after the title had been assumed by William Comyn in 1212; from Lennox not until c. 1250;[89] from Caithness and Ross not until the very end of the thirteenth century; and from Mar, Menteith and Sutherland later still, not until the fourteenth century.[90] Waxen seals are friable, and the preservation of some and the loss of others owing to purely accidental conditions undeniable. Some of the great lordships, moreover, notably those in the northern reaches of the kingdom, did not achieve recognisable status as units of baronial administration until the reign of Alexander II (1214–49). Nevertheless, the impression that Gaelic magnates were slow to adopt waxen seals as valid expressions of their authority and identity is noteworthy. More striking still are the exceptions to this general rule. The native earls of Fife, for example, began to use seals during the rule of Donnchadh II (d. 1204). There survives a fine example appended to one of his documents, as well as two that belonged to his son Mael Coluim, from both before and after his succession to the earldom.[91] Gille Brigte of Strathearn (d. 1223) was affixing seals to his written acts as early as 1198, and used them consistently thereafter.[92] Although not Gaels, Gospatrick I earl of Dunbar I (d. 1138) and his sons were using seals with considerable familiarity from the reign of David I, and with regularity thereafter.[93] In the far west, Raonall son of Somhairle lord of Argyll and Ragnvald king of Man, too, appended seals elaborately decorated with images of galleys to their written grants.[94] The divide between magnates who used seals and those who did not cannot be explained as a simple distinction between 'foreigners' – Anglo-Norman and European incomers – and 'natives', Gaels or Anglian. Rather, seal usage reflected other, more profound influences at work in the multicultural environment of twelfth-century Scotland.

One of these was exposure to the royal court and its practices. Historians have long been aware of the close relationship that bound the earls of Fife to the king. The proximity was based in part on ties of kinship, but found expression also in the extensive political and judicial authority that they exercised by royal fiat from the time of David I. Through much of the twelfth and early thirteenth centuries Donnchadh I, Donnchadh II and Mael Coluim I were frequently in attendance on the king as witnesses to royal *acta*, and in his capacity as justiciar of Scotia, Donnchadh II came into regular contact with the European barons who regularly served the crown. The earls of Dunbar also claimed kinship with the Mac Malcolm rulers, and emulated royal practices in expression of that relationship. Like these men, the earls of Strathearn, too, moved in the exclusive circle of the Scottish court. Gille Brigte's first wife was Maud D'Aubigny, the daughter of the prominent English knight Sir William D'Aubigny and his wife Maud de Senlis, cousin to Kings Malcolm IV and William I.[95] The earl's prominent family connections kept him close to the royal court; for many years William, for his part, made good use of this proximity to cultivate the friendship and service of one of the most important and deeply respected Gaelic magnates in the realm.[96] As justiciar of Scotia and a frequent witness to the king's charters, Gille Brigte was introduced to the use of seals at an early date.

The lords of Carrick shared the earl of Strathearn's familiarity with the growing authority that the royal court associated with seal usage. Donnchadh son of Gille Brigte, whose mother was almost certainly related to the earls of Fife, owed his elevation to the status of earl to William I's attempts to settle a bitter feud between rival factions of the rulers of Galloway.[97] Like the earls of Dunbar, Donnchadh's predecessors had cultivated close links with the nobility of neighbouring Cumbria, and through them with the sigillographic culture of late twelfth-century England. Despite royal efforts to integrate Galloway more fully into the kingdom of Scotland, moreover, the earls of Carrick retained pretensions to princely authority, and may have used seals much as did the lords of Argyll and Man, to give concrete visual expression to their claims.[98] In the later years of the twelfth century, then, exposure to the significance of sealing was not unknown in Gaelic Scotland, but in some contrast to the English and European nobility it had yet to appeal to a wide segment of the Gaelic aristocracy of the realm.

A similar reluctance to adopt wholesale new and foreign aspects of European culture is apparent among the native tenantry and kinsmen who made up the second tier of the native landholding ranks. Men like Sir Robert de Croc and Sir Ralph de Kent, both well endowed vassals of Walter son of Alan, lord of Strathgryfe,[99] set great store by the honorific title of *miles*, and indeed built their political, social and dynastic aspirations on the basis of a firm commitment to the 'sophisticated, international' appeal of chivalry and knighthood, one feature of which was the equestrian seal that so clearly symbolised membership in this 'exhilarating international world'.[100] In the late twelfth century, however, they had few obvious imitators among their Gaelic contemporaries, who did not begin to adopt the title and its associations until considerably later.[101] In like fashion, the seals that men like Sir Robert and Sir Ralph appended to written documents as tangible representations of their authority were all but unknown among their native fellows. Of the many tenants of Earl Gille Brigte of Strathearn, only one appears to have possessed such a device. Tristram de Gorthy was, significantly, a newcomer to the earldom, who settled in Strathearn in the entourage of Gille Brigte's wife, Maud D'Aubigny.[102] The earl's brother, Maol Iosa son of Ferchad, was a tenant in chief of King William, and also held land of Gille Brigte, but he did not identify himself as a *miles*, and may not have had a seal of his own.[103] Maol Iosa's heir, his nephew Fergus son of Gille Brigte, did not use a seal regularly until the 1240s although the earl's youngest son, Gille Brigte, to whom the earl granted a series of far-distant possessions in Inverness-shire, appears to have had one a decade earlier.[104] Beyond the comital family, very few native noblemen considered it necessary, or even expedient, to own a seal.[105]

The Strathearn evidence is admittedly impressionistic but it approximates that of nearby Lennox in the same period. Here, too, Earl Maoldomhnaich (d. c. 1250) was lord of tenants both native and newcomer, among whom were his ten brothers and their followers.[106] In the 1220s, only one of the former, Amhlaibh, appears to have had the use of a personal seal.[107] It is significant that in Lennox, as in Strathearn, moreover, early mentions of seals among the landed nobility occur exclusively in documents that were issued in favour of the church. The charters from both lordships reinforce the impression that the early catalogues of Scottish seals convey of a paucity of personal seal devices among the native landholding ranks. Just as religious houses were a powerful force in promoting the use of written instruments in the kingdom, lords great and small may have invested in the purchase of a seal matrix only under pressure from ecclesiastical beneficiaries anxious to ensure that their charters conformed to the legal standards then current in England and on the continent. Many, like Gille Mícheil Mac Edolf and his son Donnchadh, men of the earls of Lennox, and Gille Moire, a tenant of St Andrews, simply did without them; others, including a panel of Lennox jurors assembled in 1259, resorted to borrowing the seals of presiding judges or suitors to lordly courts.[108] In the twelfth and thirteenth centuries women, in particular, made use of men's seals, often claiming that even if they owned them, theirs were 'not well known'.[109] Gaelic seal owners were sometimes uncertain about the power and authority believed to be inherent in seals; they were, in other words, slow to develop 'trust in seals'. Oengus son of Donnchadh son of Ferchad, a modest Lennox lord, set his seal to a confirmation of his father's grant to the monks of Paisley but, concerned that his word and his device might not carry sufficient weight, added to the document the seals of the bishop of Argyll, the dean of Glasgow and the treasurer of the cathedral church of St Kentigern.[110]

A charter of Gille Brigte of Glencarnie, son of Gille Brigte of Strathearn, offers a further glimpse of the measured pace at which waxen seals penetrated the Gaelic environment of the 'land of earls'. A later medieval portion of the register of the see of Moray preserves the text of an indenture of 1232 that he made with Bishop Andrew.[111] To the part of the document that remained with Gille Brigte the bishop affixed his seal and that of the chapter of Moray, but Gille Brigte added to the other part both his seal and his *signum*. Precisely what comprised the latter remains uncertain, because the original document is no longer extant, but it was perhaps a cross, an authenticating mark that is found elsewhere in the kingdom in the period before seals became widely used.[112] In Scotland, as in England, the practice of validating documents with both crosses and seals bears witness to an early stage in the development of Clanchy's 'trust in writing'. The rate of survival of single sheet charters in Scotland, however, is relatively low, and it is difficult to ascertain the extent to which crosses preceded, or coexisted with, waxen seals in the twelfth and early thirteenth centuries.

By c. 1250 seal usage among the baronage of Scotland had begun to spread from the areas first settled by incomers into most of the Gaelicised regions of the kingdom. A similar pattern of slow but steady progression is apparent in the development of heraldic images and armorial bearings on the faces of waxen seals. Here again, there is much evidence to suggest that Gaelic noblemen were reluctant to absorb, willy-nilly, European ideas about the seal as a signifier of individual and family identity. Heraldic symbols and devices did eventually spread across the length and breadth of Scotland, but only after native aristocrats had made a series of adaptations to the medium which reflected their own traditions, circumstances and needs.

English scholars have explored in minute detail the introduction of heraldry to that kingdom and the several stages by which the great variety of 'pre-' and 'proto-heraldic' symbols came to stand as symbols associated with specific noble families. Adrian Ailes, for example, has discussed the ways in which the 'random and unsystematic designs' depicted on the Bayeux Tapestry, used here for purely decorative purposes, found more standardised expression in the early twelfth century on the shields that were integral to the equipment of mounted fighting men. By the second quarter of that century, he has shown, the principles of 'heraldry proper' had taken firm root among the English aristocracy.[113] More recently still, Michael Clanchy and Brigitte Bedos-Rezak have emphasised the power and authority of a 'language of signs' among noblemen who were still, in the twelfth century, 'on the threshold of literacy', and the key role that armorial devices depicted on seals played in the transition towards acceptance of written documents as the 'authentic voices' of a donor.[114]

The several stages marking the increasing sophistication of armorial bearings that these scholars have so carefully traced are apparent also in Scotland, though their origins date to a slightly later period and their cultural antecedents are more complex. The newcomers who settled in Scotland in the second half of the twelfth century brought with them some familiarity with the function of seals, but for some years yet the insignia and designs that they impressed on them varied widely. By 1190 alone among their contemporaries, Alan and Walter, the king's stewards, and Saer de Quincy had begun to use hereditary symbols; the former the pattern of a fess chequy, a visible link to its members' continental associations, and the family's chosen armorial bearings for centuries to come;[115] the latter a fess and label also denoting his ties to FitzWalter.[116] The design and markings of other magnate seals of the period 1150–1200 show that the use of these devices among foreigners was still something of a novelty in Scotland. Many were of the generic equestrian type typical of twelfth-century English and continental design, stamped on one side only, portraying a knight on horseback. In their depictions of a mounted warrior carrying a shield and pennon, the seals of Walter son of Alan the steward and Saer de Quincy were something of a throwback, for this style was already giving way elsewhere to more up-to-date images of sword and shield. The equestrian seals of their contemporaries, David earl of Huntingdon, Robert de London and Robert Avenel, for example, showed knights on horseback equipped in this fashion.[117] This style of seal was already in wide use beyond the confines of Scotland, and its growing popularity there after 1165 owed much to the influence of the royal family.

King William was an ardent devotee of the chivalric culture of the day, and in 1166 his passion took him to the tournament fields of France, where he is said to have won renown.[118] The many contacts that he maintained with the English court were not always amicable, but they kept him abreast of the latest fashions in chivalric conduct. Earl David of Huntingdon's landed interests south of the border also brought him, as well as the Scotsmen in his affinity, into close touch with changing sigillographic styles. All were aware that equestrian seals decorated with armorial bearings were fast replacing earlier seal designs, notably the antique gem. Yet, some Scottish noblemen continued to use gems in addition, and sometimes in preference, to the former. Around 1160, for example, Eustace de Vescy authenticated a grant to Melrose abbey with a seal that was stamped on both sides with the impressions of finely crafted gems.[119] Although his father had used an equestrian seal, William Avenel also preferred a gem,[120] as did Simon de Lindsay of Roxburghshire.[121] Well into the thirteenth century, the earls of Ross and Mar and members of the Dunbar family were still using finely wrought antique gems as counter-seals.[122] The nineteenth-century cataloguer, Henry Laing, suggested that Scotsmen became collectors of these precious objects after encountering them in the crusading states of the east,[123] but there is little need to attribute their preferences to such exotic influences. Gems like those favoured by Vescy, Avenel and Lindsay were not used merely, or even primarily, as seals; set into pendants or rings, they were worn as jewellery and were much valued for their magical or curative properties.[124] Eustace, for example, set each of the two highly decorated gems that he used as a seal and counter-seal into a ring and a locket, which he wore as extravagant displays of his wealth and status.[125] The document to which he appended these symbols describes a grant of the lands of Whitton to Melrose abbey. The monks might have preferred that he authenticate his charter with the kind of equestrian seal that had become *de rigueur* elsewhere in western Europe as a symbol of magnate identity, and which Vescy himself used both on later Scottish documents and on his English *acta*.[126] The monks of Kelso abbey may have been expressing a similar concern for conformity with convention when they asked a beneficiary to fortify the evidentiary weight of his privy seal with the full-sized equestrian seals of several bystanders.[127]

Vescy's preference for a gem at this early date attests the variety of sigillographic practices current in the Scotland of his day. A generation later, most of the Anglo-Norman and continental newcomers to the kingdom had begun to use waxen seals on a regular basis. Initially, they employed a range of images on the devices, much as noblemen elsewhere had done in the 'proto-' or 'quasi-heraldic' periods.[128] The generic symbols used in Scotland included fleurs-de-lys, birds of prey and lions.[129] In England the transition from this phase to the use of inherited heraldic devices occurred rapidly, over the course of only one or two generations, partly in response to the growing pageantry associated with the public display of the tournament, but also as a visual expression of increasing noble preoccupation with the links that bound individuals both horizontally and vertically to members of their greater families, ties that David Crouch has distinguished as those of *parage* and *linéage*.[130] In Scotland, the origins of heraldic display similarly owed much to the circumstances under which the kingdom was first colonised by newcomers.

Many of the noblemen who made their fortunes in this 'land of opportunity'[131] were the junior members of landed families from England and the continent, 'younger sons with no patrimony to inherit' south of the border or in France.[132] FitzAlans, Bruces, Morvilles and others who joined them in the first century of Barrow's 'Anglo-Norman era' were very much aware that they were setting down the roots of new noble dynasties in Scotland, and many chose wholly new armorial bearings in an effort to give visual expression to their status as pioneers. Henry Laing thought that the wyverns, dragons and eagles of this early period were 'non-heraldic' and entirely fanciful. They should more appropriately be regarded as representing a phase in the development of Scottish armorial bearings akin to that which scholars have traced in early post-Conquest England.

In Scotland, moreover, the pace of change was more measured. In the first half of the thirteenth century the spectacle of the tournament had no indigenous history in the kingdom. Although the Picts had once decorated their shields with simple designs intended to assist warriors to identify their leaders and fellows on the battlefield,[133] the little-known tactics of thirteenth-century European-style warfare made the acquisition of armorial devices for similar purposes much less urgent.[134] Nevertheless, by c. 1250, some Scottish landholders could lay claim to several generations' descent from great English or continental families. These magnates were among the earliest to demonstrate a sensibility to the dynastic implications of deploying heraldic symbols. Around 1204, for example, Saer de Quincy changed his seal to portray the arms of the earl of Leicester, whose sister and co-heiress he had married; thereafter, the Leicester mascles passed to his sons, legitimate and illegitimate.[135] The lions and wyverns that graced the first seals of the earls of Dunbar were standard features of the family's armorial bearings from 1200 down to the end of the Middle Ages and beyond;[136] so were the saltire, which the Bruces of Annandale used from the late twelfth century onwards, and the three crescents, deployed in Oliphant seals well into the fourteenth century.[137] Over the course of the thirteenth century up-and-coming members of the aristocracy similarly staked their claims to heraldic devices: the men of the family of de Moravia, for example, a star of six points, the Grahams the scallop shell.[138] Just as lesser noblemen and hangers-on scrambled for favour and advancement in the baronial affinities of the day, so too did they seek to align themselves with their betters by adopting the armorial symbols of their lords. In this fashion the Dunbar lion found its way onto the seals of members of the families of Riddell, de Penshiels and de Horndean,[139] the Graham scallops onto a device of Thomas Alneto,[140] the Quincy mascles onto that of Alan de Kinloch,[141] the Oliphant crescents onto Seton seals[142] and Mar cross-crosslets onto devices of other northern Perthshire landholders.[143] By mid-century, the fashion for displaying arms had become so widespread among Scottish noblemen that the earliest compilers of rolls of arms considered it appropriate to list them alongside those of English families.[144]

The enthusiasm with which noblemen who were in close contact with continental culture embraced the latest fashions in heraldic display stands in some contrast to the more muted reception that native magnates accorded conventions governing the use of armorial bearings. Few among this group were quick to follow the examples set by Comyns, Bruces, Lindsays and Grahams. The heraldic symbols that the great colonising families of the early to mid-thirteenth century chose as visual representations of their dynastic origins are distinguished by their range and variety. Such diversity is strikingly absent from the earliest armorial seals of the Gaelic nobility; absent as well is the tendency for certain devices to become hereditary within families. When the religious houses to which he intended to make gifts of land required that he append a seal to his charters, Donnchadh of Carrick chose a fairly simple design of a wyvern, probably not because it had specific associations with his family, but more likely because the imaginary heraldic beast had become by the late twelfth century a commonplace feature of English heraldic practice, and as such was bound to be familiar to the clerical beneficiaries of his charter.[145] Mael Coluim earl of Angus opted for an equally simple lion, perhaps in emulation of his more sophisticated contemporary, Patrick I earl of Dunbar,[146] but when title to his lordship passed to his only daughter's husband, the new earl's arms changed.

The early seals of the earls of Strathearn suggest a similar ambivalence towards heraldic fashion. In the late twelfth century Gille Brigte (d. 1223) was a frequent visitor to the court of William I, where he became familiar with the practice of decorating waxen seals with family coats of arms. Like other Gaelic magnates, he appears to have settled on a design that was at once simple and widely identifiable as of noble bearing. His early equestrian seals depict a knight on horseback, the animal's caparisons only slightly ornamented with small points. A second seal repeats this design on its obverse; the reverse is impressed with a plain design of nine billets. Gille Brigte's successor, however, abandoned these designs and changed altogether the appearance of his seal, choosing the commonplace lion rampant. It was not until the time of Malise II (d. 1271) that the earls adopted the chevrons that remained associated with the family until the later medieval period.[147]

More generally, the thirteenth century was drawing to a close before the lesser nobility in the great native lordships north of Forth began to deploy heraldic imagery in the systematic way familiar to noblemen elsewhere in the kingdom and in England. They did so, moreover, in singular circumstances. The proceedings held between May 1291 and November 1292 to determine the legitimate succession to the Scottish throne (the Great Cause) required, on more than one occasion, that landed persons great and small affix their seals to written documents in formal acknowledgment of their compliance with decisions made at each stage of the proceedings. Similarly, in 1296 Edward I concluded his rapid conquest of the kingdom by demanding that several hundred landholders provide him with written and sealed instruments attesting their fealty.[148] Edward's commands must have had as one of their consequences the sudden enrichment of countless skilled metalworkers able to produce brass and copper matrices,[149] but they also took by surprise a very large number of persons who had managed to date to conduct their business without benefit of seals.[150] The sigillography of the so-called Ragman Roll has been the subject of close study[151] and one recent scholar has noted in passing the frequency with which 'arms of dependence' appear on it.[152] A hundred years ago Stevenson termed such heraldic devices 'arms of vassalage', and explained that their purpose 'was to announce the existence of a feudal bond between vassal and overlord'.[153] Examples of such armorial borrowings in the Ragman Roll are numerous, but they are especially so among tenants and kinsmen of the great native magnates of Gaelic Scotland. In parts of Strathearn, Lennox and Fife written documents themselves were still something of a novelty in 1296. Seals and the heraldic imagery imprinted on them were even more exotic, and it is perhaps no wonder that people unfamiliar with them should have resorted to the simple but effective expedient of borrowing the symbols of their lords. Thus Alan FitzAvelyn and Walter Sproull, for example, tenants of Lennox, adopted the roses of Earl Malcolm of Lennox and Sir William de Moravia of Tullibardine the chevrons of his lord Malise III of Strathearn.[154] In 1296 the widespread adoption by persons of modest rank of the heraldic devices of great Scottish baronial houses may also have accomplished another, entirely different, purpose. Edward I's claims to have conquered the kingdom generated a new sense of solidarity among the landed orders, and accelerated the development of their role and function within the 'community of the realm' of Scotland.[155] The deliberate alignment of several hundred lesser families with armorial devices associated with their own lords gave concrete expression to this new sense of identity, in a 'language of signs' that would have been thoroughly familiar to Edward himself, as well as to his European contemporaries.

The records of the Great Cause and its aftermath saw a large number of minor landholders take up seals for the first time. Men of relatively modest means, like John Avesans, John de Kintore and Robert Solet did not move among the rarefied ranks of aristocrats whose acts of generosity to the church had well acquainted them with charters and seals, and few can have had much reason (or time) to ponder how best to give expression to their identity through the medium of sigillographic imagery. The documents that Edward collected are notable above all for the astonishing variety of devices that they display, few of which may be considered genuinely heraldic. There is an abundance of wheels and fleurs-de-lys, the stock-in-trade of skilled artisans who were accustomed to embellishing everyday objects from bowls to cups to jewellery with decorations of this type. A few people gave free rein to their imaginations, commissioning matrices that they hoped would evoke their names in pictures: such, for example, were the devices of Robert Falconer, which depicted a falcon preying on a smaller bird,[156] of William de Herez, whose hedgehog device was a visual representation of the animal with which he shared his name, and of John and Fergus Marshall, whose seals showed horseshoes.[157] Forest creatures such as stags, boars, hares, foxes and squirrels; domesticated dogs; birds of different kinds; and a variety of flowers attest the otherwise difficult-to-document awareness of Scottish men and women of the natural world with which they came into contact in both rural and urban settings. There are echoes in devices like those of Roger de Fotheringham and William de Arlesay of the dissemination downward through the ranks of landed society of the devotional and romantic literature of the late thirteenth century, a phenomenon that archaeologists have shown left its mark elsewhere in the material culture of the period.[158] Edward's heavy-handed administration had the fortunate consequence for historians of fostering the creative impulses of a segment of society whose aesthetic sensibilities are otherwise almost impossible to recapture.

The significance of seal usage

The evidence relating to aristocratic landholders reviewed here suggests that until very late in the thirteenth century Gaelic magnates and their wealthier tenants found little in the traditions associated with European-style heraldry to appeal to their individual or family identities. The extent to which surviving seals are genuinely representative of armorial trends among the Gaels is difficult to estimate, but the nature of the sigillographic materials, the limited imagery that they deploy, and the late date at which armorial devices become indelibly linked to specific kindred all speak to a marked ambivalence in respect of the iconographic, semiotic, dynastic and, perhaps most important, the social implications of armorial symbols and the language of heraldry among this segment of the Scottish nobility.[159] A remarkably similar pattern of sigillographic and armorial usage in Gaelic Ireland, however, offers compelling support for the argument that the development of 'trust in seals' among the native aristocracy of Scotland reflected a phenomenon common to the British Isles more generally.[160] The reasons why this should have been the case are varied and complex, but collectively they offer valuable glimpses into deeply rooted cultural differences between Gaels and Europeans in the 'Anglo-Norman era'.

The newcomers who settled in Scotland in the two or three generations after 1124 brought with them not merely familiarity with the use of seals, but an understanding of their function freighted with sophisticated beliefs about sign theory. Prescholastic schoolmen of the late eleventh and the twelfth centuries were much preoccupied with conceptualising problems of representation in the service of Christian theology. Their efforts to explain fundamental notions of the image as imprint, mirror and replica frequently led them to use waxen seals as metaphors and similes in order to explain the significance of mediation, representation and signification in the context of such tenets of the faith as the Trinity and the Eucharist.[161] The spread of seal usage among the aristocracy of western Europe gave concrete expression to the arguments of the schoolmen, and seals acquired profound importance within noble society both as legal 'objects denoting both identity and authority' and everyday signifiers of 'both person and personal identity'.[162]

The Anglo-Norman and European adventurers who looked to Scotland as a 'land of opportunity' were unlettered and unable to grasp the theological subtleties of Anselm of Laon, Hugh of St Victor or Gilbert of Poitiers, but the implications of the prescholastic philosophical enquiry that Bedos-Rezak has described so eloquently resonated with them as much as it did their brothers and cousins in England, Normandy, Picardy and Flanders, and found visible expression in their seals. In the early twelfth century, however, humanist influences had yet to have a noticeable impact on the secular aristocracy of Gaelic Scotland. The physical structure of the seal itself must have served further to discourage native landholders to use it as a means of expressing their sense of self. In England, as on the continent, the symbols impressed on seals in the pre- or proto-heraldic period drew freely on the texts of bestiaries and romance stories that were so integral a feature of the chivalric culture of western Europe. Although such manuscripts were not unknown in Scotland in the later twelfth and the thirteenth centuries, they did not circulate widely, especially among Gaelic speakers.[163] The language of the inscriptions carved onto seal matrices also made them of limited appeal to native lords. Seal impressions derived their power as authentic voices of their bearers only in part from the symbols they depicted. A second, equally essential component of their authority to represent what Bedos-Rezak has termed 'the ego of diplomatic discourse' was the legend, the inscription carved around the outer edge of the seal matrix that identified its owner by name.[164] In the medieval period the language of universal authority was Latin, and diplomatic practice in Scotland, as elsewhere, meant that inscriptions appear in this language alone. Prejudice against Gaelic as an uncouth and barbarous tongue militated against its suitability for use on waxen seals. Indeed, the shift from Gaelicised to Latinised spellings of personal names, apparent on seal legends as early as the reign of William I,[165] speaks in compelling fashion of the contempt with which cultured clerics regarded the language of native people. The dogged efforts of charter scribes to transform the likes of Gille Brigte, Maoldomhnaich and Mael Coluim into intelligible Latinate forms was a constant reminder of the social exclusion that attended the Gaelic language in the world of the *literati*.

In the final analysis, Gaelic noblemen found little in English and European sigillographic practice to engage their sense of personal and family identities because their own cultural mores offered them rich and satisfactory avenues through which to express these solidarities. The work of scholars such as John Bannerman and Derick Thomson has emphasised the crucial role that the native poetic orders played in preserving the conceptual identity of the Gaels in the 'Anglo-Norman era' of Scottish history.[166] While there is compelling evidence to suggest that the Gaelic language began its retreat into the Highlands as early as the thirteenth century, there was still plenty of scope in the Scotland of the Mac Malcolm kings for native musicians, historians, genealogists and poets to reap the rewards of noble patronage. Moreover, 'membership of a kinship group', it has been aptly observed, 'literally identified the individual',[167] and the centrality of the family pervaded the oral and written literature of Gaelic Scotland. It found tangible expression in the context of native lordship, among other things, in the practice of assigning choice estates within earldom lands to the brothers, sons and nephews of heads of kindred, and in the prominent role that native magnates accorded their relatives in the conduct of the business relating to lordship.[168] In short, the preoccupation with fashioning images of family identity, solidarity and social status that animated developments in heraldic display among the Anglo-Norman and European newcomers of the twelfth and thirteenth centuries had for a long time already found creative expression in other aspects of Gaelic culture. Magnates like Gille Brigte earl of Strathearn and Mael Coluim earl of Angus, as well as the Gaels who held land of them, used waxen seals displaying armorial bearings in circumstances in which these were required, notably when the recipients of their charters insisted on them as evidence of authentication. Just as they accommodated the concerns of their beneficiaries by affixing seals to their written instruments, so did they become steadily more accustomed to including clauses of corroboration in their charters. Gille Brigte's early deeds, for example, only rarely make reference to the act of sealing, suggesting that he had not yet fully grasped the significance of the avowal of identity and authority implicit in the words that constituted the clause. Nevertheless, in the decade before his death in 1223 sealing clauses became standard in his *acta*, even if they demonstrated considerable variety in their wording.[169] Strathearn kinsmen and tenants did not use seals and sealing clauses until the middle years of the thirteenth century;[170] indeed, Gille Brigte's own wife had to borrow her husband's matrix when she sought to authenticate a grant to Inchaffray abbey because she did not have one of her own.[171] In nearby Lennox, the texts of the earls' written acts similarly began to include clauses of corroboration on a regular basis only around the year 1250.[172] The witness lists of Maoldomhnaich's charters, however, were heavily dominated by the names of his ten brothers and their sons.[173] While some thirteenth-century Scottish noblemen looked to waxen seals to give concrete expression to identity, status and lineage, Gaelic lords found other ways to use the new technology of the written instrument to achieve similar ends. In the multicultural environment of mid-thirteenth century Scotland, such diversity was still possible.

Conclusion

In Scotland, as elsewhere in Britain and western Europe more generally, the growth of trust in the power of documents and seals to represent the intentions of donors took root only gradually, and in response to a variety of stimuli. Recent discussions of the shift from 'orality' to a 'literate mentality' have quite appropriately emphasised the dangers of portraying the change as either abrupt or dislocating, as did some early scholarly treatments of the subject. The evidence of media as varied as king lists, gospel books and minted coins militates against a view of the period before c. 1050 as a kind of prelapsarian phase in which the great mass of Scottish people went about the business of living, managing property and remembering in innocent ignorance of the benefit of charters or sealed instruments, only to have these technologies thrust upon them thereafter by a 'civilised' and well-meaning Mac Malcolm monarchy. Robert Bartlett has aptly noted that charters (and coins) 'are not simply artefacts, like pots of a certain style, or tools of a certain shape, whose spread can be taken as evidence of migration, trade or influence' [174] and whose dissemination can be traced and recreated systematically. The developments that have been examined in this chapter attest, rather, a combination of cultural conditions and specific circumstances that made it not only possible, but also expedient, for men and women to think about the twin technologies of writing and sealing in novel ways. The growth of trust did not occur everywhere in the kingdom at the same time or at the same pace. In the closing years of the reign of Alexander II seal usage was fast becoming *de rigueur* in the prosperous urban centres, yet even in Perth, the most cosmopolitan of Scottish towns, a wealthy goldsmith could still be so worried about the 'authenticity' of his personal seal that he reinforced a grant to the monks of Scone with the full weight of the burgh's corporate seal.[175]

Trust in the power of charters and seals to 'speak' on behalf of their owners long after death was generally slower to develop in the Gaelicised 'land of earls' than it was south of Forth. This was not because native landholders lacked sophistication, but because here, the customs that comprised good lordship offered other, equally effective avenues for expressing favour and commemorating the act of gift giving. But adopt these artefacts they eventually did. When the biographer of Queen Margaret looked back with amusement at the wonder, reverence and awe with which her husband regarded her books,[176] he did so with some justification, for already in the time of Mael Coluim III the written word was fast becoming an integral part of the everyday business of native Gaelic lordship in Scotland.

Notes

1. Durham, Dean and Chapter Muniments (DCD), Misc. Ch. no. 738.
2. J. H. Stevenson and M. Wood, *Scottish Heraldic Seals: Royal, Official, Ecclesiastical, Collegiate, Burghal, Personal*, 3 vols (Glasgow, 1940), iii, p. 334; DCD, Misc. Chrs nos. 733, 734*, 735, 736, 739, 741, 742.
3. The literature here is now considerable, but see, for example, B. Stock, *The Implications of Literacy: Written Language and Models of Interpretation in the*

Eleventh and Twelfth Centuries (Princeton, 1983); R. Britnell (ed.), *Pragmatic Literacy, East and West, 1200–1330* (Woodbridge, 1997); F.-J. Arlinghaus et al. (eds), *Transforming the Medieval World: Uses of Pragmatic Literacy in the Middle Ages* (Turnhout, 2006); M. T. Clanchy, *From Memory to Written Record: England, 1066–1307*, 2nd edn (Oxford, 1993), pp. 24–33. B. V. Street, *Literacy in Theory and Practice* (Cambridge, 1984) offers a useful starting point for discussions of the theoretical and methodological approaches that dominate scholarly discussions of the transition between orality and literacy.

4. D. Broun, *The Charters of Gaelic Scotland and Ireland in the Early and Central Middle Ages* (Cambridge, 1995); C. J. Neville, 'Charter writing and the exercise of lordship in thirteenth-century Celtic Scotland', in A. Musson (ed.), *Expectations of the Law in the Middle Ages* (Woodbridge, 2001), pp. 67–89; G. W. S. Barrow, 'The Scots charter', in G. W. S. Barrow, *Scotland and its Neighbours in the Middle Ages* (London, 1992), pp. 91–104.
5. *Life of St. Margaret Queen of Scotland by Turgot Bishop of St Andrews*, ed. W. Forbes-Leith (Edinburgh, 1884), p. 67.
6. R. Gameson, 'The gospels of Margaret of Scotland and the literacy of an eleventh-century queen', in L. Smith and J. H. M. Taylor (eds), *Women and the Book: Assessing the Visual Evidence* (London, 1997), p. 162.
7. *Early Scottish Charters Prior to A.D. 1153*, ed. A. C. Lawrie (Glasgow, 1905), no. 24.
8. Clanchy, *From Memory to Written Record*, p. 256.
9. Ibid. pp. 294–5.
10. M. T. Flanagan, 'The context and uses of the Latin charter in twelfth-century Ireland', in H. Pryce (ed.), *Literacy in Medieval Celtic Societies* (Cambridge, 1998), p. 120. See also W. Davies, 'Charter-writing and its uses in early medieval Celtic societies', in ibid. p. 101.
11. *Charters of David I*, nos. 9–11.
12. S. E. Thorne, 'Livery of seisin', *Law Quarterly Review*, 52 (1936), pp. 345–64.
13. Ibid. no. 15.
14. *Jordan Fantosme's chronicle*, ed. R. C. Johnston (Oxford, 1981), pp. 150–1.
15. *Chronicles of the Picts, Chronicles of the Scots, and Other Early Memorials of Scottish History*, ed. W. F. Skene (Edinburgh, 1867), p. 187.
16. *Holyrood Liber*, App. ii, no. 3.
17. Flanagan, 'The context and uses of the Latin charter', pp. 17–19; *The Acts of the Welsh Rulers, 1120–1283*, ed. H. Pryce (Cardiff, 2005), pp. 50, 55–7, 141–2.
18. *Charters of David I*, no. 185; *RRS*, ii, no. 116; R. D. Oram, 'David I and the Scottish conquest and colonisation of Moray', *Northern Scotland*, 19 (1999), pp. 5–7.
19. *Kelso Liber*, iii–vii, and Plate 1, discussed in G. W. S. Barrow, *Kingship and Unity: Scotland, 1000–1306*, 2nd edn (Edinburgh, 2003), p. 48, and R. D. Oram, *David I: The King Who Made Scotland* (Stroud, 2004), p. 205.

20. *Charters of David I*, no. 16. See also no. 54, which granted lands in Swinton to Ernulf de Morwick, to be held 'by the same customs by which Liulf son of Eadulf and his son Udard held'.
21. Barrow, 'The Scots charter', pp. 91–104.
22. D. Broun, 'The writing of charters in Scotland and Ireland in the twelfth century', in K. Heidecker (ed.), *Charters and the Use of the Written Word in Medieval Society* (Turnhout, 2000), p. 112; C. J. Neville, *Native Lordship in Medieval Scotland: The Earldoms of Strathearn and Lennox, c. 1140-1365* (Dublin, 2005), pp. 188–95; and, more generally, the Introductions to *RRS*, i and *RRS*, ii.
23. NAS, GD 55.
24. G. G. Simpson and B. Webster, 'The archives of the medieval church of Glasgow: an introductory survey', *Bibliotheck*, 3 (1962), p. 198; G. R. C. Davis, *Medieval Cartularies of Great Britain* (London, 1958), no. 1150.
25. For an examination of the codicology of the cartulary of Moray, see A. Ross, 'The Bannatyne Club and the publication of Scottish ecclesiastical cartularies', *Scottish Historical Review*, 85 (2006), pp. 217–22. The Mac Uilleim insurrections of the thirteenth century and their antecedents are discussed in R. A. McDonald, *Outlaws of Medieval Scotland: Challenges to the Canmore Kings, 1058-1266* (East Linton, 2003), pp. 36–47.
26. *Cambuskenneth Reg.*, no. 188, discussed in T. M. Cooper, *Select Scottish Cases of the Thirteenth Century* (Edinburgh, 1914), pp. 13–17.
27. D. Broun, 'The property records in the Book of Deer as a source for early Scottish society', in K. Forsyth (ed.), *Studies on the Book of Deer* (Dublin, 2008), pp. 313, 356; Broun, 'The writing of charters', p. 117; K. Jackson, *The Gaelic Notes in the Book of Deer* (Cambridge, 1972), pp. 89–91, 94–7.
28. M. Herbert, 'Charter materials from Kells', in F. O'Mahoney (ed.), *The Book of Kells: Proceedings of a Conference at Trinity College Dublin, 6-9 September 1992* (Aldershot, 1994), p. 67.
29. *Kelso Liber*, i, nos. 316–17; ii, no. 318.
30. NAS, GD 82/6.
31. *Dryburgh Liber*, no. 140.
32. *Melrose Liber*, no. 73.
33. Ibid. nos. 39, 41, 196.
34. NLS, Adv. MS. 15.1.18, no. 61. Richenda's words do not, however, appear in the version of the original charter that a later clerk copied into the cartulary of St Andrews priory; *St Andrews Liber*, pp. 285–6.
35. The examples here are too numerous to list comprehensively, but for three examples from 1233, c. 1250 and 1281, see Fraser, *Carlaverock*, ii, p. 405; *Calendar of Writs preserved at Yester House 1166-1503*, ed. C. C. H. Harvey and J. Macleod (Edinburgh, 1930), no. 15; *Morton Reg.*, ii, no. 11.
36. See, for example, *Dunfermline Reg.*, nos. 194, 195; see also C. J. Neville, 'Finding the family in the charters of medieval Scotland, 1150-1350', in E. Ewan and J. Nugent (eds), *Finding the Family in Medieval and Early Modern Scotland* (Aldershot, 2008), pp. 13–14.

37. *Dryburgh Liber*, no. 221; *Balmerino Liber*, nos. 4, 5. For another occasion, where the donor's brother was also his lord, see *Lindores Cart.*, no 25.
38. *Dunfermline Reg.*, no. 179. For another example, see ibid. no. 171.
39. W. W. Scott (ed.), 'Eight thirteenth-century texts', *Scottish History Society Miscellany, vol. XIII* (Edinburgh, 2004), Text 3.
40. *Arbroath Liber*, no. 342.
41. *Inchaffray Chrs*, no. 118.
42. *APS*, i, p. 445.
43. Ibid. p. 373.
44. *Kelso Liber*, i, no. 258.
45. Here again, the examples are numerous, e.g. *Kelso Liber*, i, no, 50; ii, no. 524; *Yester Writs*, ed. Harvey and Macleod, no. 15; *Beauly Chrs*, no. 6.
46. P. Brand (ed.), 'Parliament of autumn 1305, text and translation', in C. Given-Wilson et al. (eds), *The Parliament Rolls of Medieval England. CD-ROM.* (Leicester, 2005), item 323. The monks of Culross abbey and the canons of Restenneth likewise worried about the danger of losing valuable charters as a consequence of the Anglo-Scottish conflict. In the early fourteenth century, they requested that the earl of Fife make specific provision for such an eventuality. See W. Douglas, 'Culross abbey and its charters, with notes on a fifteenth-century transumpt', *Proceedings of the Society of Antiquaries of Scotland*, 60 (1925–6), p. 75; NLS, Adv. MS. 34.2.1b, fo. 127. In 1290 the abbot of Lindores sought from Pope Nicholas IV a confirmation of a papal bull of 1195 which, he wrote, was deteriorating with age. *Vetera monumenta Hibernorum et Scotorum historiam illustrantia*, ed. A. Theiner (Rome, 1864), no. 335. For a late fourteenth-century example of similar concern over the loss of written muniments owing to wartime conditions, see *Inchcolm Chrs*, no. 38.
47. G. G. Simpson, 'The claim of Florence, Count of Holland, to the Scottish throne, 1291–2', *Scottish Historical Review*, 36 (1957), pp. 113–14, 117, 120.
48. Broun, *Charters of Gaelic Scotland*; Neville, 'Charter writing', pp. 73–6; Neville, *Native Lordship*, pp. 188–95.
49. R. Oram, *The Lordship of Galloway* (Edinburgh, 2000), pp. 191–217. See also K. J. Stringer, 'Acts of lordship: the records of the lords of Galloway to 1234', in T. Brotherstone and D. Ditchburn (eds), *Freedom and Authority: Scotland c. 1050–c. 1650: Historical and Historiographical Essays presented to Grant G. Simpson* (East Linton, 2000), pp. 204–5.
50. M. H. Hammond, '*Hostiarii regis Scotie*: the Durward family in the thirteenth century', in S. Boardman and A. Ross (eds), *The Exercise of Power in Medieval Scotland, c. 1200–1500* (Dublin, 2003), pp. 124–7.
51. *Moray Reg.*, no. 80; *Fraser, Grant*, iii, nos. 6, 11; C. J. Neville, 'The earls of Strathearn from the twelfth to the mid-fourteenth century, with an edition of their written acts', 2 vols, unpublished PhD dissertation (University of Aberdeen, 1983), i, pp. 76–7.
52. S. Boardman, 'The Campbells and charter lordship in medieval Argyll', in Boardman and Ross (eds), *Exercise of Power*, pp. 5–117.

53. The incident is reviewed at length in Neville, *Native Lordship*, pp. 145-8.
54. *Arbroath Liber*, i, no. 133.
55. *Paisley Reg.*, pp.120-1.
56. Ibid. pp. 178-80.
57. *Glasgow Reg.*, no. 229.
58. *The Records of the Parliaments of Scotland to 1707*, ed. K. M. Brown et al, http:// www.rps.ac.uk, 1401/2/4 (date accessed: 2 May 2008); *APS*, i, p. 575.
59. *Regiam Majestatem and Quoniam Attachiamenta*, T. M. Cooper (Edinburgh, 1947), pp. 199-200.
60. *Tractatus de legibus et consuetudinibus Angliae qui Glanvilla vocatur*, ed. G. D. G. Hall (London, 1965), pp. 126-7.
61. See the extensive discussion and the sources cited in H. L. MacQueen, *Common Law and Feudal Society in Medieval Scotland* (Edinburgh, 1993), pp. 89-98.
62. In the western isles, however, seals and charters remained uncommon until c. 1400. See. Boardman, 'The Campbells and charter Lordship', p. 116 and, more generally, J. Bannerman, 'The Scots language and the kin-based society', in D. S. Thomson (ed.), *Gaelic and Scots in Harmony: Proceedings of the Second International Conference on the Languages of Scotland (University of Glasgow, 1988)* (Glasgow, 1988), pp. 1-19, and J. Bannerman, 'Literacy in the Highlands', in I. B. Cowan and D. Shaw (eds), *The Renaissance and Reformation in Scotland: Essays in Honour of Gordon Donaldson* (Edinburgh, 1983), pp. 214-35.
63. Fantosme alludes to 'finely coloured' and 'bossed' shields, ' silken pennon' borne on fine lances, and 'gay' and 'gleaming' banners, but does not otherwise describe heraldic arms. *Jordan Fantosme's Chronicle*, ed. R. C. Johnston (Oxford, 1981), pp. 44-5, 66-7, 82-3, 90-1, 100-1, 102-3.
64. See, for example, the information on individuals' seals provided in the several volumes of J. B. Paul (ed.), *The Scots Peerage*, 9 vols (Edinburgh, 1904-14); J. H. Stevenson, *Heraldry in Scotland*, 2 vols (Glasgow, 1914); T. Innes, *Scots Heraldry: A Practical Handbook* (Edinburgh, 1934).
65. H. Laing, *Descriptive Catalogue of Impressions from Ancient Scottish Seals* (Edinburgh, 1850); H. Laing, *Supplemental Descriptive Catalogue of Ancient Scottish Seals, Royal, Baronial, Ecclesiastical, and Municipal, embracing the period from A.D. 1150 to the Eighteenth Century* (Edinburgh, 1866); W. de G. Birch, *Catalogue of Seals in the Department of Manuscripts in the British Museum*, 6 vols (London, 1887-1900); Stevenson and Wood, *Scottish Heraldic Seals*. For recent studies in heraldry, see C. Campbell, *The Scots Roll: A Study of a Fifteenth Century Roll of Arms* (Kinross, 1995); C. J. Burnett and M. D. Dennis, *Scotland's Heraldic Heritage: The Lion Rejoicing* (Edinburgh, 1997), pp. 9-15. See now B. A. McAndrew, *The Historic Heraldry of Scotland* (Woodbridge, 2006), and B. A. McAndrew, 'The Sigillography of the Ragman Roll', *Proceedings of the Society of Antiquaries of Scotland* 129 (1999), 663-752.

66. B. Bedos-Rezak, 'Medieval seals and the structure of chivalric society', in H. Chickering and T. H. Seller (eds), *The Study of Chivalry: Resources and Approaches* (Kalamazoo, 1988), pp. 317-18; B. Bedos-Rezak, 'The king enthroned, a new theme in Anglo-Saxon royal iconography: the seal of Edward the Confessor and its political implications', in B. M. Bedos-Rezak, *Form and Order in Medieval France: Studies in Social and Quantitative Sigillography* (Aldershot, 2003), Article IV; T. A. Heslop, 'English seals from the mid-ninth century to 1100', *Journal of the British Archaeological Association*, 133 (1980), pp. 1-16; D. Crouch, *The Image of Aristocracy in Britain, 1100-1300* (London, 1992), pp. 226-40; P. D. A. Harvey, 'Personal seals in thirteenth-century England', in I. Wood and G. A. Loud (eds), *Church and Chronicle in the Middle Ages: Essays presented to John Taylor* (London, 1991), pp. 117-27; A. F. McGuinness, 'Non-armigerous seals and seal-usage in thirteenth-century England', in P. R. Coss and S. D. Lloyd (eds), *Thirteenth Century England V: Proceedings of the Newcastle upon Tyne Conference 1993* (Woodbridge, 1995), pp. 165-77.
67. A. A. M. Duncan, 'The earliest Scottish charters', *Scottish Historical Review*, 37 (1958), pp. 121-3.
68. A. A. M. Duncan, 'Yes, the earliest Scottish charters', *Scottish Historical Review*, 78 (1999), pp. 6-7.
69. B. Bedos-Rezak, 'The king enthroned', IV, p. 53; Heslop, 'English seals', p. 9; *Charters of David I*, p. 30; *RRS*, i, p. 87; *RRS*, ii, p. 91.
70. Broun, 'The writing of charters', pp. 119-24; *Charters of David I*, p. 3.
71. DCD, 4.8 Spec. 1; Stevenson and Wood, *Scottish Heraldic Seals*, ii, p. 265; R. M. Blakely, *The Brus Family in England and Scotland, 1100-1295* (Woodbridge, 2005), p. 220, no. 119 (1170 x 1190).
72. NAS, GD 55/168; Stevenson and Wood, *Scottish Heraldic Seals*, iii, p. 638 (c. 1160).
73. NAS, GD 55/88; Stevenson and Wood, *Scottish Heraldic Seals*, ii, p. 479.
74. NAS, GD 55/40, 140; Stevenson and Wood, *Scottish Heraldic Seals*, ii, p. 233.
75. NAS, GD 55/66, 97; Stevenson and Wood, *Scottish Heraldic Seals*, iii, p. 600.
76. NAS, GD 45/13/241; Stevenson and Wood, *Scottish Heraldic Seals*, iii, p. 551.
77. DCD, Misc. Ch. no. 713; Laing, *Ancient Scottish Seals*, p. 87, no. 503.
78. NAS, GD 28/4; Stevenson and Wood, *Scottish Heraldic Seals*, i, p. 40; K. J. Stringer, *Earl David of Huntingdon, 1152-1219: A Study in Anglo-Scottish History* (Edinburgh, 1985), pp. 215-16, 234, no. 27 (1173 x 1174).
79. NAS, GD 55/95, 106, 108; Stevenson and Wood, *Scottish Heraldic Seals*, iii, p. 516.
80. NAS, GD 45/13/223; NAS, GD 55/63; Laing, *Ancient Scottish Seals*, p. 116, no. 697; p. 137, no. 822.
81. NAS, GD 55/58, 113, 114, 127; Stevenson and Wood, *Scottish Heraldic Seals*, ii, p. 294.

82. NAS, RH 6/11; Stevenson and Wood, *Scottish Heraldic Seals*, ii, p. 458. The unusual features of this seal are discussed in G. D. S. Henderson, 'Romance and politics on some medieval English seals', *Art History*, 1 (1978), pp. 27–8.
83. NAS, GD 55/34; Stevenson and Wood, *Scottish Heraldic Seals*, iii, p. 575.
84. NAS, GD 55/75; Stevenson and Wood, *Scottish Heraldic Seals*, ii, p. 311.
85. For a still earlier seal, see DCD, Misc. Ch. no. 722; Stevenson and Wood, *Scottish Heraldic Seals*, iii, p. 630, dated c. 1107–27. T. A. Heslop has suggested, however, that this kind of seal was used primarily to close personal letters, rather than to authenticate a grant. Heslop, 'English seals', pp. 15–16.
86. *Kelso Liber*, nos. 31, 354, 474; *Paisley Reg.*, pp. 176, 232, 233; *Beauly Chrs*, no. 6.
87. *Kelso Liber*, no. 272.
88. NAS, GD 45/13/277, 282; NAS, GD 55/30, 32, 36; Stevenson and Wood, *Scottish Heraldic Seals*, ii, p. 278.
89. There survive no contemporary examples of the seal(s) used by Earl Maoldomhnaich of Lennox, but a nineteenth-century transcript said to be of original medieval deeds (now unfortunately lost) includes a description of these. Both were in the equestrian style, one bearing an image of the lion rampant, the second some other 'arms of gentility'. Glasgow University Library, MS. Gen. 198, fos. 179, 199.
90. Stevenson and Wood, *Scottish Heraldic Seals*, ii, pp. 229, 268, 305, 368; iii, pp. 454, 566, 627.
91. NAS, RH 6/15A; NAS, GD 45/13/279; BL, Harley Ch. 84.C.1; Stevenson and Wood, *Scottish Heraldic Seals*, ii, p. 354.
92. No fewer than ten of his seals survive; Neville, 'Earls of Strathearn', i, 330–1.
93. Stevenson and Wood, *Scottish Heraldic Seals*, ii, pp. 333–4.
94. R. A. McDonald, 'Images of Hebridean lordship in the late twelfth and early thirteenth centuries: the seal of Raonall Mac Sorley', *Scottish Historical Review*, 74 (1995), pp. 129–43.
95. Neville, *Native Lordship*, p. 208.
96. Ibid. pp. 19–21.
97. Oram, *Lordship of Galloway*, pp. 89–90, 103–4.
98. W. M. Aird, 'Northern England or southern Scotland? The Anglo-Scottish border in the eleventh and twelfth centuries and the problem of perspective', in J. C. Appleby and P. Dalton (eds), *Government, Religion and Society in Northern England, 1000–1700* (Stroud, 1997), p. 31; McDonald, 'Images of Hebridean lordship', pp. 137–8.
99. G. W. S. Barrow, *The Kingdom of the Scots: Government, Church and Society from the Eleventh to the Fourteenth Century*, 2nd edn (Edinburgh, 2003), p. 316.
100. R. R. Davies, *Domination and Conquest: The Experience of Ireland, Scotland and Wales, 1100–1300* (Cambridge, 1990), p. 51.
101. C. J. Neville and R. A. McDonald, 'Knights, knighthood and chivalric culture

in Gaelic Scotland, c.1050–1300', *Studies in Medieval and Renaissance History*, 3rd Series, 4 (2007), pp. 83–94.
102. Neville, *Native Lordship*, pp. 44–5. Tristram's seal was affixed to a grant in favour of Inchaffray abbey, dated c. 1208. Dupplin Muniments Perth, *penes* Messrs Condie, Mackenzie and Co., no. 11.
103. None of the three extant acts of Maol Iosa includes a sealing clause. All three, however, survive only as cartulary copies.
104. *Inchaffray Liber*, no. 10; *Lindores Cart.*, no. 28; *Moray Reg.*, no. 80. A similar observation applies to Wales, where the rulers of Gwynedd did not begin to use seals on a regular basis until the early thirteenth century. *Acts of the Welsh Rulers*, ed. Pryce, pp. 86–9.
105. Exceptions include Gille Criosd and Aed the sons of Mael Coluim Mac Neachdainn, who made grants to Inchaffray abbey in 1247 and 1257 respectively. Both are simple devices, the latter non-heraldic. Stevenson and Wood, *Scottish Heraldic Seals*, i, p. 489; *Inchaffray Chrs*, pp. 315–16.
106. Neville, *Native Lordship*, pp. 55–9.
107. *Paisley Reg.*, p. 209. The grant of the church of Rosneath to the Cluniac abbey of Paisley survives only as a cartulary copy, but it includes a clause in which Amhlaibh refers to 'my seal'.
108. *Lennox Cart.*, pp. 83–5; NAS, RH 5/21; NLS, Adv. MS. 15.1.18, no. 27; NAS, GD 24/5/1/1; *Paisley Reg.*, pp. 120–1.
109. C. J. Neville 'Women, charters and land ownership in Scotland, 1150–1350', *Journal of Legal History*, 26 (2005), pp. 37–9. For some examples, see NAS, GD 125/2/2, GD 93/1, GD 198/3.
110. *Paisley Reg.*, pp. 133–4.
111. *Moray Reg.*, no. 80.
112. *Early Scottish Charters prior to A.D. 1153*, ed. A. C. Lawrie (Glasgow, 1905), pp. 126, 392. See also Duncan, 'The earliest Scottish charters', pp. 122–3, and Duncan, 'Yes, the earliest Scottish charters', pp. 6–10.
113. A. Ailes, 'Heraldry in twelfth-century England: the evidence', in D. Williams (ed.), *England in the Twelfth Century: Proceedings of the 1988 Harlaxton Symposium* (Woodbridge, 1990), pp. 1–2. See also Crouch, *Image of Aristocracy*, pp. 226–44, and D. Crouch, 'The historian, lineage and heraldry 1050–1250', in P. Coss and M. Keen (eds), *Heraldry, Pageantry and Social Display in Medieval England* (Woodbridge, 2002), p. 29.
114. Clanchy, *From Memory to Written Record*, pp. 282, 308–17; B. M. Bedos-Rezak, 'Medieval identity: a sign and a concept', *American Historical Review*, 105 (2000), pp. 1488–533; B. Bedos-Rezak, 'Replica: images of identity and the identity of images in prescholastic France', in J. Hamburger and A.-M. Bouché (eds), *The Mind's Eye: Art and Theological Argument in the Middle Ages* (Princeton, 2006), pp. 46–64. See also M. Keen, 'Introduction', in Coss and Keen (eds), *Heraldry, Pageantry and Social Display*, pp. 8–9.
115. NAS, GD 55/97; Stevenson and Wood, *Scottish Heraldic Seals*, iii, p. 600; Laing, *Ancient Scottish Seals*, p. 113, no. 679. The origins of the fess chequy

device are discussed in Crouch, *Image of Aristocracy*, p. 222; Ailes, 'Heraldry in twelfth-century England', p. 6, and A. Ailes, 'The knight, heraldry and armour: the role of recognition and the origins of heraldry', in C. Harper-Bill and R. Harvey (eds), *Medieval Knighthood IV: Papers from the Fifth Strawberry Hill Conference 1990* (Woodbridge, 1992), p. 11.
116. Stevenson and Wood, *Scottish Heraldic Seals*, iii, p. 551; P. D. A. Harvey and A. McGuinness, *A Guide to British Medieval Seals* (London, 1996), p. 45; Henderson, 'Romance and politics', pp. 33–8.
117. Laing, *Ancient Scottish Seals*, p. 23, no. 94; p. 95, no. 551; p. 126, no. 769.
118. *The Chronicle of Melrose from the Cottonian Manuscript, Faustina B. IX in the British Museum*, ed. A. O. Anderson and M. O. Anderson (London, 1936), p. 37; more generally, see Neville and McDonald, 'Knights and knighthood', p. 69.
119. NAS, GD 55/168; Laing, *Ancient Scottish Seals*, p. 138, nos. 830, 831.
120. NAS, GD 55/139; Laing, *Ancient Scottish Seals*, p. 23, no. 95; Stevenson and Wood, *Scottish Heraldic Seals*, ii, p. 233.
121. NAS, GD 55/141; Laing, *Ancient Scottish Seals*, p. 88, no. 504.
122. Laing, *Supplemental Descriptive Catalogue*, pp. 53–4, nos. 308, 313; p. 116, no. 690; p. 142, no. 860. Mar's gem, portrayed on a seal of 1295, was all the more unusual in that it was marked with Arabic characters.
123. Laing, *Ancient Scottish Seals*, p. xx.
124. Clanchy, *From Memory to Written Record*, pp. 16–17; Henderson, 'Romance and politics', 26–7; Heslop, 'English seals', pp. 4, 5.
125. Laing, *Ancient Scottish Seals*, p. 138, nos. 830, 831.
126. See, for example, Edinburgh University Library, Laing Charters, no. 87.
127. *Kelso Liber*, no. 272.
128. Ailes, 'The knight, heraldry and armour', p. 12; Ailes, 'Heraldry in twelfth-century England', pp. 4–5.
129. Stevenson and Wood, *Scottish Heraldic Seals*, ii, pp. 262, 265; Laing, *Ancient Scottish Seals*, p. 53, nos. 283, 284; p. 87, no. 503; p. 101, nos. 593–95.
130. Crouch, 'The historian, lineage and heraldry', pp. 29–37.
131. G. W. S. Barrow, *The Anglo-Norman Era in Scottish History* (Oxford, 1980), p. 7.
132. Ibid. pp. 6–19.
133. N. B. Aitchison, *The Picts and the Scots at War* (Stroud, 2003), pp. 61–2.
134. Neville and McDonald, 'Knights and knighthood', pp. 78–9, 94–9; Ailes, 'The knight, heraldry and armour', pp. 18–19.
135. McAndrew, *Historic Heraldry*, pp. 32–5; B. Platts, *Origins of Heraldry* (London, 1980), pp. 72–3; Henderson, 'Romance and politics', pp. 30–3.
136. Stevenson and Wood, *Scottish Heraldic Seals*, ii, pp. 334–8, 432.
137. Ibid. pp. 262–3; Laing, *Ancient Scottish Seals*, App., p. 220, nos. 1203–4; G. S. C. Swinton, 'Six early charters', *Scottish Historical Review*, 2 (1905), pp. 174–6. The devices used by other members of the higher nobility are reviewed briefly in McAndrew, *Historic Heraldry*, pp. 59–65; their antecedents are discussed in Platt, *Origins of Heraldry*, pp. 63–79, 102.

138. Stevenson and Wood, *Scottish Heraldic Seals*, ii, pp. 380-1; iii, p 520; Laing, *Ancient Scottish Seals*, p. 67, nos. 373-4; pp. 102-3, nos. 607-8. For the origins of the Graham scallops, see Platt, *Origins of Heraldry*, pp. 69-70.
139. Stevenson and Wood, *Scottish Heraldic Seals*, iii, p. 561; Laing, *Ancient Scottish Seals*, p. 77, no. 440; p. 80, no. 458.
140. Stevenson and Wood, *Scottish Heraldic Seals*, ii, p. 233.
141. Swinton, 'Six early charters', 178-9; A. Nisbet, *A System of Heraldry Speculative and Practical*, 2 vols (Edinburgh, 1722-42), i, pp. 244-5.
142. Laing, *Ancient Scottish Seals*, p. 121, no. 736; Laing, *Supplemental Descriptive Catalogue*, p. 147, no. 890.
143. See, for example, Laing, *Supplemental Descriptive Catalogue*, p. 94, no. 555.
144. The arms of several families were displayed in Matthew Paris's later works (1244-59), as well as in the compilations known as Glover's Roll (c. 1253-8) and Walford's Roll (c. 1275). *Aspilogia II: Rolls of Arms temp. Henry III*, ed. T. D. Tremlett and H. S. London, 2 vols (London, 1967), and G.J. Brault (ed.), *Aspilogia III: Rolls of Arms of Edward I (1272-1307)*, ed. G. J. Brault, 2 vols (Woodbridge, 1997).
145. NAS, GD 45/13/277, 282; Stevenson and Wood, *Scottish Heraldic Seals*, ii, p. 278.
146. Stevenson and Wood, *Scottish Heraldic Seals*, ii, p. 229.
147. Stevenson and Wood, *Scottish Heraldic Seals*, iii, p. 625-6; Neville, 'Earls of Strathearn', i, pp. 340-1.
148. *Edward I and the Throne of Scotland, 1290-1296*, ed. E. L. G. Stones and G. G. Simpson, 2 vols (Oxford, 1978), ii, pp. 191, 366-70; G. W. S. Barrow, *Robert Bruce and the Community of the Realm of Scotland* (Edinburgh, 2005), pp. 99-102.
149. See the discussion in V. Glenn, 'The late 13th-century chapter seals of Dunkeld and Oslo cathedrals', *Proceedings of the Society of Antiquaries of Scotland*, 132 (2002), pp. 439-58; M. Hall, 'John of Strathearn and Alan Muschamp: two medieval men of Strathearn and their seal matrices', *Tayside and Fife Archaeological Journal*, 11 (2005), pp. 80-7; and National Museum of Antiquities of Scotland, *Angels, Nobles and Unicorns: Art and Patronage in Medieval Scotland* (Edinburgh, 1982), pp. 45-9.
150. There are many thirteenth-century examples of donors borrowing the seals of their secular or ecclesiastical lords.
151. McAndrew, *Historic Heraldry*, pp. 86-108.
152. Ibid. p. 99.
153. Stevenson, *Heraldry in Scotland*, i, p. 273. More recently, see B. M. Bedos-Rezak, 'Du sujet à l'objet: la formulation identitaire et ses enjeux culturels', in P. von Moos (ed.), *Unverwechselbarkeit: persönliche identität und identifikation in der vormodernen gesellschaft* (Cologne, 2004), pp. 63-83.
154. McAndrew, 'Sigillography', pp. 675, 702, 715, 725, 748.
155. The literature here is considerable, but see Barrow, *Robert Bruce*, passim; R. Nicholson, *Scotland: The Later Middle Ages* (Edinburgh, 1978), pp. 1-68; and F. Watson, 'The enigmatic lion : Scotland, kingship and national identity

in the wars of independence', in D. Broun, R. J. Finlay and M. Lynch (eds), *Image and Identity: The Making and Remaking of Scotland through the Ages* (Edinburgh, 1997), pp. 18–37.
156. McAndrew, 'Sigillography', p. 698.
157. Laing, *Supplemental Descriptive Catalogue*, p. 111, nos. 696, 697.
158. M. A. Hall and D. D. R. Owen, 'A Tristram and Iseult mirror case from Perth: reflections on the production and consumption of romance culture', *Tayside and Fife Archaeological Journal*, 4 (1998), pp. 160–2; Laing, *Supplemental Descriptive Catalogue*, p. 11, no. 48. The images on Arlesay's seal include a hare playing a tambourine and a fox playing a pipe.
159. Gaelic noblemen do not appear in the earliest rolls of arms. The arms of the earls of Fife, Lennox and Strathearn are first mentioned in late thirteenth-century compilations. *Aspilogia III*, ed. Brault, pp. 55–6.
160. F. Verstraten, 'Images of Gaelic lordship in Ireland, c. 1200–c. 1400', in L. Doran and J. Lyttleton (eds), *Lordship in Medieval Ireland: Image and Reality* (Dublin, 2007), pp. 57–71.
161. Bedos-Rezak, 'Replica', pp. 46–53.
162. Bedos-Rezak, 'Medieval identity', pp. 1531, 1492.
163. L. A. J. R. Houwen, 'A Scots translation of a Middle French bestiary', *Studies in Scottish Literature*, 26 (1991), p. 215; Neville and McDonald, 'Knights and knighthood', pp. 99–103.
164. Bedos-Rezak, 'Medieval identity', p. 1507. Only a handful of legends were made up of mottoes rather than personal names. See Stevenson, *Heraldry in Scotland*, i, pp. 207–10.
165. Neville, *Native Lordship*, pp. 217–18; *RRS*, i, p. 87; more generally, see D. Broun, 'Gaelic literacy in eastern Scotland between 1124 and 1249', in Pryce (ed.), *Literacy in Medieval Celtic Societies*, pp. 184, 188, 194–7.
166. Both have published extensively in this area, but see, for example, J. Bannerman, 'The Scots language and the kin-based society, in Thomson (ed.), *Gaelic and Scots in Harmony*, pp. 1–19; D. S. Thomson, 'Gaelic learned orders and *literati* in medieval Scotland', *Scottish Studies*, 12 (1968), pp. 57–78. See also W. MacLeod, *Divided Gaels: Gaelic Cultural Identities in Scotland and Ireland c. 1200–c. 1650* (Oxford, 2004).
167. R. Davies, 'Kinsmen, neighbours and communities in Wales and the western British Isles, c.1100–c. 1400', in P. Stafford, J. Nelson and J. Martindale (eds), *Law, Laity and Solidarities: Essays in Honour of Susan Reynolds* (Manchester, 2001), p. 175 and, for Gaelic concepts of the family more generally, T. Charles-Edwards, *Early Irish and Welsh Kinship* (Oxford, 1993). Many of Charles-Edwards' arguments are wholly appropriate to the Scottish context in the later Middle Ages.
168. C. J. Neville, 'A Celtic enclave in Norman Scotland: Earl Gilbert and the earldom of Strathearn, 1171–1223', in Brotherstone and Ditchburn (eds), *Freedom and Authority*, pp. 86–7; Neville, *Native Lordship*, pp. 44–59; Oram, *Lordship of Galloway*, pp. 191–217; Oram, 'Continuity, adaptation and

integration: the earls and earldom of Mar, c.1150–c.1300', in Boardman and Ross (eds), *Exercise of Power*, pp. 56–60.
169. Neville, 'Earls of Strathearn', i, pp. 385–7.
170. *Inchaffray Chrs*, nos. 26, 46, 57; *Lindores Cart.*, nos. 26, 27, 29, 32; *Arbroath Liber*, i, nos. 86, 87.
171. NAS, GD 24/5/1/1.
172. See the various charter texts assembled in Fraser, *Lennox*, ii.
173. Neville, *Native Lordship*, pp. 69, 71.
174. R. Bartlett, *The Making of Europe: Conquest, Colonization and Cultural Change, 950–1350* (Princeton, 1993), p. 286.
175. *Scone Liber*, no. 86. In the closing years of the thirteenth century, similarly, the widow Elizabeth Bisset noted that her seal 'is not well known or recognised (*publicatus*) within Scotland', and requested that various ecclesiastical and secular lords authenticate her documents with their seals. NAS, GD 93/1, GD 125/2/2. For a late (1332) example of a similar claim by a burgess of Berwick, see NAS, GD 1/967/3.
176. *Life of St Margaret*, ed. Forbes-Leith, pp. 39–40.

PART II

LAND AND PEOPLE

CHAPTER 4

Managing the Strathearn estates: the Muschamp inheritance, 1243–1322

INTRODUCTION

The passage of seven hundred years and more has done little to diminish the importance that scholars attach to the wars of independence in the forging of the Scottish national identity. Robert Bruce's victory at Bannockburn bought the king a precious period of respite from the tribulations of England's armies, and gave him the opportunity to begin the arduous process of rebuilding a realm that was still bitterly divided between noble factions.[1] One of Robert I's earliest undertakings as king was to enact legislation, in a parliament he summoned to Ayr in April 1315, which required that henceforth, all who held land in Scotland must swear allegiance to him as their king and liege lord 'against all other mortals'.[2] His reasons for doing so were justifiable and, given his still precarious hold on the throne, inevitable, but in making it impossible for his subjects to hold land in England, Robert I also brought to an abrupt end a long period of open and easy communication with the neighbouring realm.

The fluidity of the political border line in the period before open war erupted in 1296 has been the subject of much scholarly study. Geoffrey Barrow's examination of the English and continental families who colonised Scotland in the twelfth and thirteenth centuries has shown that the settlement of junior branches of noble families in various parts of the kingdom promoted the steady movement of noble men and women back and forth across the political line that divided the realms.[3] Keith Stringer's comprehensive studies of the lords of Galloway and the families of Vescy and Morville, and his research on the English and Scottish possessions of the great border religious houses have shed invaluable light on the 'range and intimacy of the web of cross-Border ties' that characterised this human traffic.[4] These studies emphasise just how inconsequential the Anglo-Scottish border line could be to the noble families who lived and moved in the cosmopolitan world of the thirteenth century. So, too, does the work of Grant Simpson on Roger de Quincy earl of Winchester and constable of Scotland. To persons of rank and status engaged in the brisk business of shaping strategies for the advancement of their children and grandchildren, the need to distinguish between the realms 'was of little real significance'.[5] The value of potential husbands, wives and in-laws was assessed, weighed and measured according to a host of criteria, of course, but the field of candidates to which parents looked in the context of such planning was wide indeed, stretching the

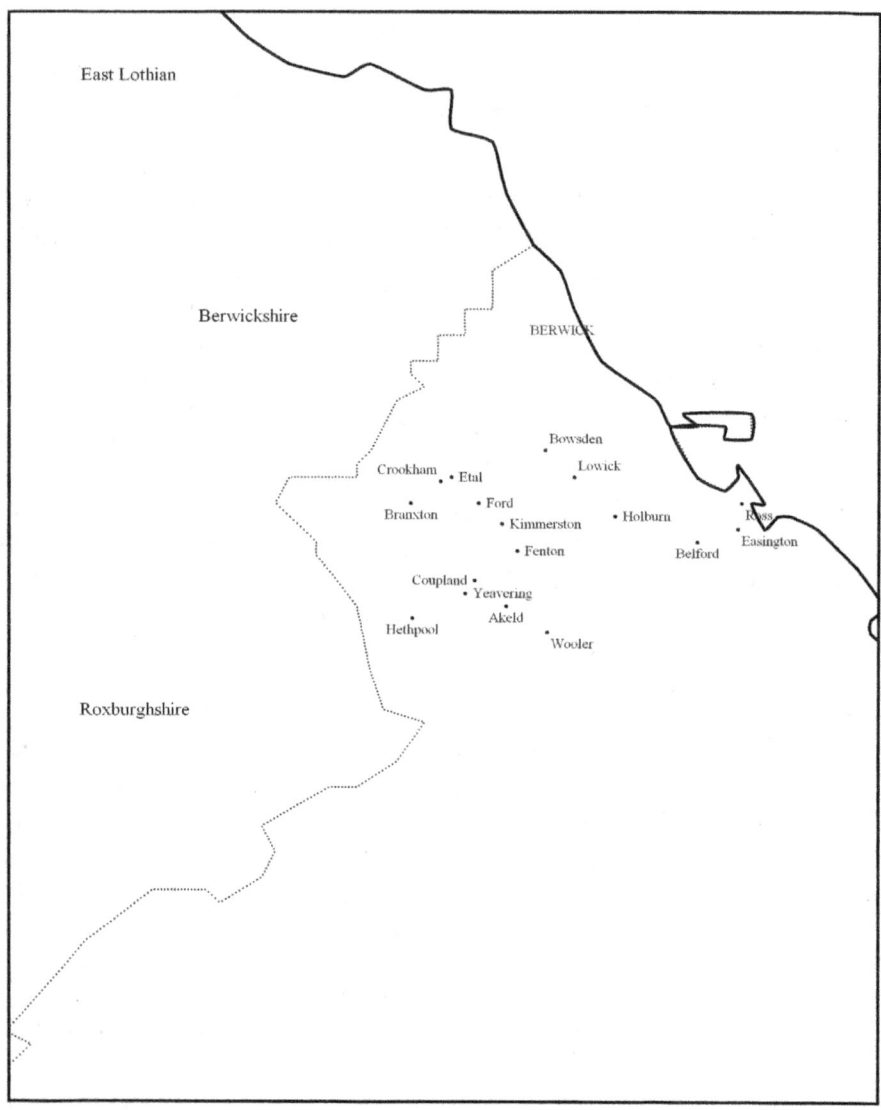

The Strathearn–Muschamp inheritance in the late thirteenth century

length and breadth of the British Isles and even further, across the Channel to the continent.

A casual attitude towards the particulars of national or political allegiance underlay the spectacular success of the Bruce family, whose members controlled two extensive lordships on either side of the Anglo-Scottish border line. They maintained a strong presence in both Yorkshire and Annandale by skilfully deploying their human, financial and political resources at the courts of two kings, but they thrived also because they were careful to balance the temporary eclipse of one branch of the family against the promise of good fortune for the other as new circumstances arose. The Bruces exemplify what Ruth Blakely has called the 'prototype' of a cross-border aristocracy which, until the outbreak of open war in 1296, was able to transcend frontiers.[6] Other examples include the families of the Comyns and the Balliols. The former dominated the Scottish political stage for most of the thirteenth century; the latter successfully negotiated spectacular advancement in both Scotland and England and eventually secured the ultimate prize of the Scottish crown.[7] Bruces, Comyns, Balliols, Vescys, Morvilles and others of their ilk all shared a common perspective in recognising that, like the Anglo-Scottish boundary itself, the line dividing family interest and national allegiance was a fluid, elastic, and eminently amenable to interpretation and manipulation.

Ease of communication and movement between the kingdoms in turn reflected the state of Anglo-Scottish foreign relations. The period between the accession to the Scottish throne of King David I in 1124 and the beginning of the wars of independence has traditionally been portrayed as a period of peaceful relations with England,[8] but it was in fact troubled by bouts of open hostility. Episodes in the later 1130s, the 1170s, 1209-10 and the first years of the reign of Alexander III were particularly serious.[9] In periods of acute tension such as these, the Anglo-Scottish border line acquired new prominence in the lives of noble families, demarcating zones within which political allegiance was at once pressing and potentially damaging. Only the most skilful strategists were able to navigate the perilous shoals that these circumstances generated. Some, like the Foliots and Grimbalds, failed utterly.[10] Others, including Vescys, Bruces, Comyns and Balliols, emerged unscathed from their trials, with their long-term plans for advancement bruised but intact. Generally speaking, in the years between 1124 and 1296 the social, economic and cultural links between the kingdoms were sufficiently homogenous and robust to permit carefully plotted family strategies to survive even the most serious tribulations.[11]

Edward I's conquest of Scotland, on the other hand, represented much more than the temporary eclipse of a long tradition of cross-border lordship.

So, at least, it has traditionally been portrayed by historians. Viewed from a different perspective, however, it becomes apparent that some families managed to survive the dislocation of the wars of independence, if in a much altered state, and to salvage from the wreckage of the conflict a vision of family fortunes that transcended the Anglo-Scottish border line, just as it had been possible to do before 1296. This chapter examines the history of the magnate family of Strathearn and its ties to the barony of Wooler in Northumberland from the middle years of the thirteenth century down to the severance of that link in the opening decades of the fourteenth, and the strategies that successive generations devised in an effort to preserve these English lands. It argues that adopting the perspective which the magnate ranks themselves espoused, one that emphasises the central importance of lineage, makes it possible to assess the impact of the wars of independence on Strathearn fortunes in novel fashion, and to offer new conclusions about the effect of the conflict on the phenomenon of cross-border lordship. Historians of medieval England and Europe more generally have long accepted the notion that the preservation and enhancement of family estates were a central feature of aristocratic life.[12] Similar concerns animated the landholding ranks of Scotland. The wars of independence generated political crises at every level of Scottish society, but nowhere was the uncertainty of these years more acute than among men and women compelled to weigh political allegiance against the prosperity of their kindred. Yet, the Strathearn family managed, in the end, to defy the odds and, with thought and care, to preserve a connection with its English possessions.

The oft-married Earl Malise II of Strathearn (d. 1271) was a typical representative of the mid-thirteenth noblemen who moved easily between Scotland and England. If he did not consider himself altogether 'above, or rather outside, "national considerations"', as did some of his Scottish peers,[13] he was nevertheless more thoroughly involved in the affairs of kingdom than his predecessors had been.[14] Several years before he succeeded his father in 1245, Malise began to make occasional appearances at the court of Alexander II, to stand as witness to the king's *acta*, and surely also to position himself within easy access of the royal patronage that was so vital an avenue of advancement in his time. It was in these early years, in fact, before he succeeded to the earldom of Strathearn, that Malise contracted the first of four marriages, one that would have important consequences for the fortunes of his kindred. Around 1243, he wed Marjory, daughter of Robert de Muschamp, baron of Wooler in Northumberland. The match exemplified the social currency that marriage represented to high-ranking families throughout Britain in the mid-thirteenth century: it was both an opportunity for Muschamp to associate himself on equal terms with an ancient and much respected Gaelic family, and the means for Malise to join the exclusive – and extremely profitable – ranks of the magnates who exercised power and influence on both sides of the Anglo-Scottish border line. The eldest son born of the marriage would inherit two very substantial lordships, and other children would establish new branches of the family, thus perpetuating well into the future the immediate social, financial and political benefits that accrued to their parents' lineages through the match.

The Muschamps in Scotland

In 1243 the links between the Muschamps of Wooler and the Gaelic magnates of Strathearn were not new. Malise's marriage to Marjory, in fact, represented the culmination of a Muschamp association with Scotland that was of considerable age already. Robert de Muschamp's barony was an old one, probably created very soon after the accession of King Henry I.[15] A century later the family had managed to weather a series of childless marriages and an heiress, and an inquest of 1212 returned that the lands were held for the service of four knights. A generation later still another inquest, conducted around the time of Malise's marriage, found that the barony consisted of some twenty-three townships, for which Robert was owed the service of more than five knights.[16] By this time, however, the family had also set down deep roots north of the border. Robert's ancestor, Reginald, was a member of the entourage of Prince David of Cumbria, before the latter's succession to the Scottish throne as David I.[17] That the family had already achieved prominence in cross-border society by the middle years of the twelfth century is apparent in two respects. The first was the readiness of Reginald's heir, his nephew Thomas, to assume his mother Cicely Muschamp's name as a surname in preference to that of his father, Stephen de Bulmer.[18] The other was Thomas's very advantageous marriage. David of Scotland's following was considerable and varied, but his wife's connections with the baronage of Northumberland made a series of personal encounters between the prince and the lord of Wooler highly likely. Whatever the circumstances of Reginald's first meeting with David in the 1120s, the Muschamp attachment to the Scottish royal family proved enduring. Reginald found for his nephew a wife of high standing in the person of King William I's granddaughter, Maud de Vescy.[19] She in turn brought him a permanent stake in the northern kingdom in the shape of a considerable lordship based at Hassington in Berwickshire.

Thomas divided his time between his Northumberland estates and his new possessions in Scotland, for he appears among the witness lists of several charters issued by William I in the opening years of the reign.[20]

Loyalty to – or perhaps wariness of – his wife's Scottish connections probably explains his decision to throw his support behind William's rash decision to go to war against England in 1173. Thomas's precise role in the failed campaigns is difficult to reconstruct. The nineteenth-century historian Edward Bateson posited that there must have been 'some secret understanding' between the lord of Wooler and the king of Scots, one that allowed the latter's army to take the town of Belford, deep in Muschamp territory, in the spring of 1174.[21] No contemporary chronicle source supports that allegation. Benedict of Peterborough noted simply, if with asperity, that Thomas was one of several agents of the 'nefarious treason' committed against the king of England in that year.[22] More certainly, Thomas's involvement in the Scottish assaults saw him forfeit his valuable lands in Northumberland to Odinel de Umfraville, who had fought on the side of Henry II.[23] Thomas remained in Scotland during the period of William's captivity in Normandy, and remained in the Scottish king's following for the duration of his life. He witnessed royal and other *acta* issued at Linlithgow, Crail and Melrose into the early 1180s,[24] though he never abandoned his attempts to regain control of his northern English barony. Restoration of the family's fortunes in England, however, did not occur until Thomas's heir, Robert II de Muschamp, had achieved his age of majority and performed homage to a new king.[25]

The difficulties that beset the Muschamps as a consequence of Thomas's involvement in Angevin family politics reinforced the importance of forging, then maintaining, tenurial ties north of the border. By the time that Robert III succeeded his father, Robert II, around 1208, the family had re-established its good name with the English crown, but it was to be another thirty-five years before its members finally secured immunity from the claims of the powerful Umfraville clan to the barony of Wooler.[26] The Muschamps sought, and found, strong allies in Waldeve and Patrick I, successive earls of Dunbar, wealthy landowners not merely in Lothian, but also in neighbouring Northumberland. The elder Robert is found in the entourage of Earl Patrick in the opening years of the thirteenth century.[27] His son and namesake, Robert III, joined the ranks of other Dunbar associates, such as Bernard de Howden, Gilbert de Home and Alan de Swinton, who moved easily back and forth across the Anglo-Scottish border line in the relatively quiet years of the early reign of Alexander II.[28] Robert III's own charters reveal just how cosmopolitan was this world. In the course of the 1220s he granted portions of his holdings in the township of Hethpool, Northumberland, to the Cistercian monks of Melrose abbey, while simultaneously patronising the Cistercian house of Newminster, near Morpeth.[29] A portion of land in Hassington went to an English tenant; still another became the basis of a marriage portion for Robert III's sister, Gilia, passing to each of her two husbands in turn.³⁰ When she died childless, Robert gave the lands to Master William de Greenlaw, a cleric who had close ties to Muschamp's own lord, the earl of Dunbar.³¹ These grants were all witnessed by the earl, by tenants from Northumberland such as Odinel de Ford, Robert de Akeld, Robert III's uncle, William, and by up-and-coming Scottish landholders, including David de Graham of Mugdock.³² The ease with which English tenants in chief might assign Scottish properties to cross-border associates is apparent in Robert's grant to Melrose abbey, which he dedicated specifically to Henry III and his ancestors, and in the ceremony of sasine in which he infeft his new tenant in Hassington, which he performed in the presence of the English king himself in 1220.

Yet, it was above all to his lands and personal ties in Scotland that Robert de Muschamp was drawn. On several successive occasions in the mid-1240s he failed to appear before justices of the King's Bench at Westminster to answer a plea initiated by one of his own sons-in-law, William de Huntercombe, and he suffered distraint as a consequence of his default.³³ Similar interests kept him north of the border even in the period 1239–41, when Gilbert de Umfraville was attempting to revive the claim to the barony of Wooler that he had inherited from his grandfather, Odinel.³⁴ In the 1240s, however, proximity to the court of the earl of Dunbar offered more exciting prospects for the advancement of Muschamp's family than did England, and Robert's presence in Scotland reflected his determination to take advantage of new circumstances here.

The years of political crisis, 1244–60

The closing years of the reign of Alexander II witnessed considerable upheaval on the Scottish political scene, but also exciting opportunities for ambitious noblemen prepared to take risks. A long-simmering struggle for power between rival factions led, on the one hand, by Walter Comyn earl of Menteith and Patrick II earl of Dunbar and, on the other, Walter and John Bisset and Alan Durward, reached a crisis when the Bissets were exiled from the kingdom and found refuge in England. There, they convinced Henry III that the Comyn-led government was about to conclude an alliance with France and, further, that Henry should demonstrate by forceful action his concern with the state of Scottish affairs. In 1244 Henry III secured from Alexander II a treaty of peace and, from a large group of secular and ecclesiastical barons, sworn undertakings to observe the terms of the agreement.³⁵ At the Bissets' urging he also exacted from Comyn and his ally, the earl of Dunbar, bonds of good behaviour.³⁶

The composition of the factions that emerged during the turmoil of the years 1242–4 has been closely examined from the perspective of Walter Comyn's prominent role in Scottish affairs,[37] but equally significant ties linked Earl Patrick to the forty compurgators who, in the autumn of 1244, became guarantors of his bond. Among the latter was Robert earl of Strathearn, representative of one of the oldest Gaelic lordships north of Forth. In the thick of the Dunbar faction, moreover, there stood Robert de Muschamp, no doubt looking to win political advantage from ongoing events. He proved tremendously successful in doing so when, in or around 1243, he arranged a marriage between the second of his three daughters and Robert of Strathearn's heir, Malise. Less than two years later Malise succeeded to his father's earldom. In the months to come Muschamp was to find that he had hitched his wagon to a rising force on the Scottish political scene.

The marriage represented a notable achievement for Robert de Muschamp. Scholars are accustomed to viewing alliances between Scottish noblemen and English women in the thirteenth century from the point of view of English power politics. To Rees Davies, for example, marriage was 'a subtle instrument of domination',[38] one of several strategies by which the English crown sought to impose a veneer of civilisation over the uncouth Gaels of the British Isles. Similarly, Andrew McDonald has argued that native magnates preferred English wives and actively sought the prospects that association with England offered to 'enhance and promote their status' within the 'confraternity' that was the Anglo-Norman aristocracy of the period.[39] There can be little doubt that Malise of Strathearn acquired a great deal by his marriage to Marjory de Muschamp, including access to rich lands and revenues in Northumberland and a new role as a tenant in chief of the English crown in right of his wife. Not least among the advantages of the match were the prospects that it offered of developing new sources of wealth and patronage for the Strathearn family. The endowment of younger sons with properties acquired by war or conquest was a tried and true strategy among the European nobility of the thirteenth century, and one that had already served the native magnates of Scotland well. Malise's own grandfather, Earl Gille Brigte of Strathearn, had made use of lands that King William had assigned him in the last years of the twelfth century following the suppression of the Mac Uilleim rebellion to establish a son of his second marriage as a wealthy landowner in his own right in Glencarnie, Inverness-shire.[40] The Muschamp marriage offered Malise II the chance to put down new family roots south of the border, and thus to engage in a new phase of estate planning on behalf of the generation that would follow.

The marriage, however, was at least as rewarding to Robert de Muschamp as it was to Malise, if not more so. The family of Strathearn boasted a pedigree that extended deep into the distant past of the Scottish kingdom, further back still than Robert's own ties to Norman England, and upwards into the highest echelons of its magnate ranks. Tradition accorded the earls a prominent role on the political stage in Scotland, access to its wealthiest brides and a meaningful say in the development of royal policy. In 1214, for example, Earl Gille Brigte had performed an important part in the enthronement ceremonies of King Alexander II,[41] and in 1243 his grandson, Muschamp's new son-in-law, could expect to do the same for Alexander's son when the old king eventually died. In 1237 Earl Robert had been one of a group of noblemen who travelled to York to take part in discussions concerning a treaty of peace with England, and had set his seal to the agreements that were generated as a consequence of these diplomatic meetings.[42] Marriage into the family of Strathearn represented, not least, an opportunity to climb the social ladder of the Anglo-Scottish border region. Robert de Muschamp's ties with the earls of Dunbar were strong and close, but however honourable, they were those of a vassal to his lord. The connection created by the marriage of Marjory and Malise placed the lord of Wooler on an equal footing with the greatest magnates in the locality and the kingdom at large. After 1255, moreover, when the political tide shifted again, it gave him access to the innermost circle around the king of Scots.

The factionalism that had seen Henry III become involved in Scottish affairs in 1244 continued through the last years of the reign of Alexander II and well into the opening decade of that of his successor. Alan Durward and his adherents won control of the government through 1249, but until 1258 leadership of the Scottish political scene alternated between the Durward and Comyn parties. Instability in Scotland offered the English king ample opportunity to interfere. After Christmas 1251, moreover, he played the role of an anxious father concerned to ensure the well-being of his daughter Margaret, married to the young Alexander III.[43] In this new capacity, Henry III took steps to exert firm direction over the governance of the realm; first, in 1251 when, after the wedding ceremonies, he agreed to support the return to power of Walter Comyn earl of Menteith; again in 1255 when he once again turned against Comyn; and in the three years that followed, until, finally, in 1258, he assisted in fashioning a compromise between the parties.

Political tension endured as long as it did in large part because both Walter Comyn and Alan Durward were able to draw support from a wide segment of Scottish landed society. At one time or another, the former counted among his adherents a large and very influential kindred, who between them controlled a significant number of the ancient earldoms of the kingdom, as well as important representatives of cross-border families such as Robert de Ros, David de Graham and Nicholas de Soules. Alan Durward, however, could count among his early supporters an equally impressive group, made up of such men as Malcolm earl of Fife, Duncan earl of Carrick, David de Lindsay and cross-border magnate families such as the Bruces and de Vaux.[44] The prizes at stake in the struggle for power were considerable but so, too, were the risks, and in the periods when their rivals were in the ascendancy, both Comyn and Durward, together with their supporters, suffered political marginalisation as well as significant social and financial eclipse. Alan Durward, in particular, learned the hard lessons of political embarrassment at first hand. In the two decades before 1244 Walter Comyn's family had successfully outmanoeuvred his attempts to win title, in turn, to the earldoms of Mar and Atholl. Durward's meteoric rise to prominence that year, accomplished with the aid of Henry III, signalled a new period of prosperity, with a wife in the person of Alexander II's illegitimate daughter, control of the justiciarship of Scotia and, more important still, the powers of patronage inherent in his exalted position.[45] When events turned against him in 1251 and sent him into exile, he lost everything but his wife. Restoration of his influence between September 1255 and October 1257 proved fleeting, and he died in comparative obscurity in 1275.[46]

The trials and tribulations that saw fortune smile alternately, if not always consistently, on Alan Durward and Walter Comyn were not lost on their contemporaries. The earls of Dunbar appear to have weighed carefully the challenges that confronted their family in the tumultuous decade after 1244. Patrick II maintained 'his own political voice' during the period when Walter earl of Menteith controlled the government,[47] allying himself only distantly with the Comyn faction before departing, then dying, on crusade in 1248.[48] Patrick III gambled rather less guardedly with his political prospects. He supported the Comyn-led government established on the occasion of the royal marriage of 1251, but by 1255 had abandoned it in favour of preferment in the entourage of Alan Durward.[49] Thereafter he played a prominent role in directing the business of government in opposition to Walter Comyn. Only after 1260, when he had married into the latter's family, did he once again support openly the kindred of Earl Walter. It was only thereafter, moreover, that he once again took an active part in Scottish affairs.[50]

Like Durward and Comyn, Earls Patrick II and III of Dunbar experienced at close quarters both the promises and the reversals of the tumultuous 1240s and '50s. Malise II of Strathearn proved more circumspect in his actions; accordingly, both he and his adherents weathered the storms of the period more successfully and with greater rewards. Throughout the period after 1251, he took great pains to fashion for himself a reputation as a moderate figure, indebted neither socially nor politically to either of the factions vying for control of the government, attentive above all to the needs of his young king. He proved remarkably successful at treading such a middle ground. In 1254, for example, he appeared alongside members of the Comyn-dominated royal court to witness a grant in favour of Dunfermline abbey,[51] at almost exactly the same time as Alan Durward (then in exile) was performing military service in his stead on King Henry's expedition to Gascony.[52] The following year, when Henry III oversaw the replacement of Walter Comyn's governing party with a more amenable group headed by Durward, Malise of Strathearn again positioned himself to reap the benefits of Henry's actions. He was one of four earls and twelve lay barons, 'beloved friends' all, assigned to govern Scotland and to safeguard the young king and his wife against their 'enemies' and 'gainsayers' for a period of seven years, until Alexander should reach the age of majority.[53] In the months that followed Durward's return to power Malise worked hard to establish his merit in the eyes of King Henry III. His efforts once again paid off, for in the summer of 1258 Henry asked him specifically to watch over and care for Margaret. The earl's reply to the king's request is a model of diplomatic writing, combining in equal measure obsequiousness, diffidence, shrewdness and authority.[54]

The compromise that brought an end to factionalism at the Scottish court in 1258 signalled another turning point in Earl Malise's career, and a fresh opportunity for him to shape circumstances to his benefit. By November 1258 Henry III had been forced to surrender control of his own government into the hands of a baronial reform movement.[55] In Scotland, Earl Walter Comyn had died, and Alexander III was showing signs of his readiness to assume personal responsibility for the conduct of his affairs.[56] No longer required to play the role of tutor on a political stage still dominated by the squabbling remnants of the Comyn and Durward factions, Malise of Strathearn found it expedient to place himself beyond the reach of either group and of any lingering animosities regarding his conduct during the previous decade. In the early summer of 1259 he was in Cahors, Gascony, negotiating a loan, where he remained until the following year.[57]

The course that Earl Malise II steered through the political crises of the years 1244–58 was masterfully designed and skilfully managed. His return from the continent to the still-fraught atmosphere of court politics was planned with equal care. In 1260, when bitter dissension erupted over succession to the earldom of Menteith, he sided openly with the late earl's nephew, John, only to agree, equally quickly, to the compromise that allowed Walter Stewart to assume the title in right of his wife.[58] At the same time, he assumed anew his role as special guardian of Queen Margaret, agreeing to work with a baronial council while arrangements were made for the birth of her first child.[59]

Strathearn lordship in England, 1243–67

To the modern observer, Malise of Strathearn's manoeuvrings might appear erratic, a response to the earl's inability, or a reflection of his unwillingness, to stake out a clear position in a period when the turmoil generated by Alexander III's minority saw other magnates commit themselves wholeheartedly to one or the other of the baronial parties struggling to provide the kingdom with direction. The Scottish chroniclers who wrote about the events of the 1240s and '50s from a near-contemporary perspective vary in their assessments of the men who played prominent roles in perpetuating the factionalism of the time. The author of the *Melrose Chronicle* was generally hostile to Durward and his party; by contrast, the cleric responsible for compiling the first part of the text now known as the *Gesta Annalia II* blamed the disunity on the flawed leadership of Walter Comyn, whom he described as an ambitious, disaffected nobleman who led the kingdom astray.[60] Neither, disappointingly, offered any opinion about Malise of Strathearn's wisdom in choosing to tread the middle ground.

Yet, wisdom it was. If, from one perspective, Malise of Strathearn appears a self-serving, vacillating character, from another his behaviour projects a different image. To many of his fellow magnates at least, the choices he made were honourable. So, at least, is the impression that arises from an examination of the charters that he issued in the 1260s, which were attested by a variety of men drawn from what had been both the Comyn and Durward parties.[61] The earl's contemporaries understood more clearly than do many modern observers that court politics constituted only one of an array of concerns that preoccupied members of the kingdom's magnate ranks; they were aware, moreover, that noblemen who permitted 'national' affairs to overshadow the well-being of their own families engaged in a dangerous game of chance with unpredictable and potentially disastrous consequences. When he criticised Walter earl of Menteith and his adherents for acting 'as if they were kings',[62] the author of the *Gesta Annalia II* was above all taking them to task for what he perceived as unbridled ambition. The Comyn family's rise to pre-eminence in the thirteenth century had been nothing short of spectacular, even if, after the death of Walter in 1258, their prospects for continued advancement were by no means assured. The chronicler's censure notwithstanding, the Comyns exemplified the self-interest that all noble families acknowledged as the foundation of their kindreds' prosperity.

The same self-interest that moved the Comyns to act as if 'they reigned over the people' dictated the political choices of Earl Malise.[63] The speed with which the composition of the Scottish court changed in the decade and a half after 1244 must, on occasion, have appeared bewildering. When Henry III ordered an English army to muster at Newcastle in the summer of 1244 and made known his intention to march against the Scots, the earl of Strathearn found himself in a very uncomfortable dilemma. He was, in right of his wife of less than a year, a tenant in chief of the English crown for a substantial property in the barony of Wooler, and thus legally bound to contribute arms and men to Henry's army. His father-in-law, Robert III de Muschamp, was likewise a tenant in chief, but also the sworn man of Earl Patrick II of Dunbar, who was at the time supporting Walter Comyn's alleged intrigues with Louis IX of France.[64] In 1244, then, Malise had good reason to adopt a position that would neither threaten his English possessions nor reflect adversely on his wife's very wealthy father. (Robert de Muschamp himself considered it appropriate to tread carefully. He remained north of the border even as he was being named a respondent in a civil suit at Westminster, and even as he organised a muster of his own tenants at Henry's command.)[65] Earl Malise's readiness to join a group of subscribers to a bond of good behaviour on behalf of the earl of Dunbar accomplished both aims simultaneously. A decade later, when he sent Alan Durward to perform the foreign military service that he owed in respect of his English properties, Malise took another calculated risk. Members of the governing Comyn party were likely to view with disapproval any rapprochement with the exiled leader, but the earl's continued presence in Scotland served as a powerful statement in support of the earl of Menteith's authority.

Malise's was a difficult balancing act, but one that ultimately bore fruit. In 1250, probably over the course of the summer, [66] Robert III de Muschamp died, to be remembered fondly by Matthew Paris as 'a man of great repute in the northern parts of England'.[67] He was buried not in the parish church of Wooler, which his family had patronised for generations, but rather at Melrose abbey, deep in Scottish territory and, in 1250, still closely associated with the earl of Dunbar.[68] Malise's recent political manoeuvrings ensured him a smooth entry into his wife's inheritance. As one of three coheiresses, Marjory succeeded to a very generous legacy indeed, and as early as October of that year, as arrangements were being made to assign Robert de Muschamp's widow her dower, Malise travelled to England to perform homage for the third part of the barony of Wooler.[69] A near-contemporary extent valued the portion of that third held in chief at £58 14s 5 1/2d, a sum that no thirteenth-century Scottish earl would have considered negligible.[70]

In the months after October 1250 events in Scotland kept Malise preoccupied north of the border. In the spring of 1254, however, the preservation of his English properties once again claimed his undivided attention. This year, in fact, marked a significant turning point in the earl's English interests, and ultimately required that he consider afresh the plans he had so carefully laid for his immediate family members with respect to those lands. When Robert de Muschamp died, his holdings were divided among three co-heiresses. One was his granddaughter Isabel, then about eleven years old, the daughter of his eldest daughter Cicely and Odinel de Ford. Both Cicely and her husband predeceased the lord of Wooler. Isabel shared her portion of the Muschamp inheritance with her mother's two sisters, Marjory, the wife of Malise of Strathearn and Isabel, wife of Sir William de Huntercombe. The younger Isabel died childless in 1254, aged only fifteen.[71] So, too, however, did Countess Marjory. Isabel's third of the barony was therefore divided evenly between the countess's two heiresses and her aunt, Isabel de Huntercombe.[72] The children of Malise and his wife, Muriel and Marjory (the latter known later as Mary), were young, the elder born around 1245, the younger around 1249. The earl could therefore expect to reap the benefits of a long and profitable guardianship over the girls. Within less than a year of his wife's death he petitioned, and paid, the princely sum of £100 in gold for, their wardship and marriage.[73]

The changes wrought to Malise's personal circumstances in England go some way towards explaining the sustained efforts he made to tread a middle ground in his public life in Scotland. Between 1243 and 1254 his status as a tenant in chief of the English crown had required that he contribute financially to Henry III's military expeditions. In 1253, for example, he rendered £10 to the king's escheator in aid of the expedition to Gascony.[74] Another demand for military service in 1254 proved potentially embarrassing and, as noted above, prompted Malise to make the risky decision to send Alan Durward in his stead. In the spring of 1258 there came another command, this one to travel to Chester with a Northumberland levy, for service against the Welsh rebel Llewellyn.[75] On each of these occasions Malise must have considered the timing of Henry's orders at best awkward, and at worst deeply troublesome. After 1254, however, another factor began to loom equally large in the earl's personal considerations. This was the well-being, indeed, the very survival, of his own lineage. Marjory de Muschamp had borne him two daughters but as yet no son, and the future disposition of the earl's vast Scottish patrimony would remain uncertain until and unless he fathered an heir.

In 1257, three years after his wife's death, Malise took steps to remedy this problem by marrying Maud, the daughter of Gilbert earl of Caithness and

Orkney.⁷⁶ This was an advantageous match, both for the earl and his Scottish king. It enabled Malise to carve out a new sphere of influence in Angus, where he acquired property through his new wife, one that complemented the already strong presence there and in neighbouring Inverness-shire of his kinsman, Gilbert of Glencarnie.⁷⁷ Alexander III himself must have looked favourably on the settlement of a trusted baronial agent in a region of the kingdom that had only recently been the focus of rebellion and disaffection.⁷⁸ Finally, the marriage settled Malise's dynastic concerns, for within a year of the marriage, Maud had given birth to the son he wanted. Almost a century later, their great-grandson would find refuge in the north from a wrathful Edward Balliol and would succeed, if briefly, to the title of earl of Caithness and Orkney.⁷⁹

In 1254, however, Malise's second marriage lay in the future. In the meantime, there were political storms to weather at home in Scotland, but rich prospects to look forward to as the earl exploited his recently deceased wife's Northumberland properties on behalf of his young daughters. As noted above, the Muschamp inheritance was considerable, and Malise reaped the rich rewards that the vigorous economy of the mid-thirteenth century directed into his coffers.⁸⁰ In 1254 the part of the barony of Wooler that he controlled consisted of half of the substantial manor of Wooler itself and its parish church, the advowson of which alone was worth £20 per annum;⁸¹ half portions of the townships of Akeld, Yeavering and Coupland, then held for the service of one knight; of Hethpool, part of which was subinfeudated, but the larger part exploited as demesne; of the township of Cheviot, including its large and profitable chase; of the township of Ford, also exploited as demesne; and of the manors of Fenton, Crookham, Kimmerston, Etal and Holburn, subinfeudated to several noble tenants. There were half shares also of the rich and productive manors of Belford, Easington with its grange and Lowick; of the revenues generated by the hospital of St Mary Magdalene in Wooler; and, finally, the whole of the more modest manor of Branxton. The inquest summoned on the occasion of Robert de Muschamp's death, and the extents that were carried out following the deaths of his daughter and granddaughter reveal just how valuable was Malise's portion of the inheritance, even after Robert's widow had been assigned her dower. Peasants working the arable acreage associated with the vills of Hethpool, Heatherslaw, Lowick, Bowsden and Wooler generated a substantial and steady cash flow, with Bowsden alone returning a fixed annual rent of £2 16s 10d, and the revenues derived from its meadow acreage at an all-time high. The rents and various perquisites raised from the free peasant population similarly reflected the substantial expansion of the economy that had characterised the north-east since the late twelfth century.⁸²

In addition to the cash income derived from the rents and the direct exploitation of the Northumberland estates and their pertinents, Malise enjoyed a host of other profits of lordship. Among the more lucrative were the revenues generated by the exercise of judicial authority over tenants great and small, free and unfree. As titular lord of Wooler, for example, the earl sent bailiffs to the royal assize sessions that convened at Newcastle-upon-Tyne in the spring of 1256, where they claimed a portion of the chattels seized from a convicted felon.[83] There were monies to be made from the detention of suspected misdoers, from the amercements levied for breaches of the assizes of bread and ale over which the lords of Wooler had jurisdiction,[84] as well as from the myriad transgressions committed by peasant tenants, collectively assessed at over £4 per annum in 1250.[85] Finally, Malise derived a steady income from the feudal incidents chargeable to the tenants of all these estates. Robert III de Muschamp had owed the crown the service of four knights for the barony of Wooler, but had drawn scutage for a further two and a half knights' fees from the lands that he had subinfeudated;[86] there were also revenues to be made from the wardships and marriage of these tenants and their heirs. It is small wonder that the other beneficiaries of Muschamp's wealth should have sought so vigorously to augment their share of the estate. In October 1251, for example, Robert III's widow, Isabel, brought a suit of dower against her sons-in-law, claiming a more substantial portion of her former husband's possessions.[87] Following the death of Muschamp's granddaughter, William de Huntercombe, the husband of Marjory's sister, petitioned the king for a meticulous survey of the dead girl's lands, intent on ensuring that he received exactly half of what she had owned.[88]

Malise of Strathearn enjoyed control over his daughters' Northumberland lands by the common law custom known as curtesy.[89] He must have invested in some good legal advice, moreover, for he enjoyed the revenues from his share of the Muschamp inheritance for a very long time. Throughout the 1260s he was still exercising judicial prerogatives through his bailiffs of Wooler; in 1269, although by now married for a fourth time and his first wife little more than a memory, he was still accounting at the Exchequer for the scutage owed from his English possessions.[90] The profits he made during these years not only offset the sums that he owed the English crown as a tenant in chief; they must also have gone some way towards rewarding the risks that he had run in the tense period after his first marriage. Equally important, they provided him with the time during which to consider suitable husbands for his Muschamp daughters. The elder, Muriel, was married around her twenty-first birthday to William earl of Mar, soon after the death in 1267 of Mar's first countess. The match represented a well conceived political strategy, designed to underline once and for all Earl Malise's rapprochement with the Comyn family, with whom William had long been closely associated, and his final rejection of Alan Durward's ambitions. Barely a decade earlier, after all, the latter had tried to claim the earldom of Mar as his own.[91] The marriage also cemented a firm link between two of the oldest and most respected native lordships in the kingdom at next to no cost to the patrimonial lands of Strathearn, which Malise had every intention of passing undiminished to his son and heir, Malise. Muriel outlived her husband by several years; she died without heirs of him in 1291.[92]

For the second of his Muschamp daughters, Mary, Malise chose as husband Sir Nicholas de Graham of Dalkeith. The earl's new son-in-law boasted impeccable social and political pedigrees. William de Graham had come to Scotland from Tynedale at the invitation of David I, and in the 1140s moved freely back and forth across the Anglo-Scottish border in the entourages of both the king and his son, Earl Henry.[93] By the reign of William I the family had acquired lands in Eskdale as well as in Midlothian.[94] Nicholas was a descendant of the senior line of Grahams. In the 1240s his kinsman in the junior line, David, was busy building for himself a reputation as an ambitious 'new' man, acquiring properties from the earls of Lennox, Carrick, Strathearn and Dunbar, as well as from other barons.[95] David's close ties to the Dunbar family saw him become actively involved in the Comyn party's efforts to secure control of the Scottish political scene during the turbulent years between 1244 and 1260.[96] Like the earl of Menteith, he suffered political eclipse in 1255.[97] Nicholas's father, Henry de Graham of Dalkeith, by contrast, was a more cautious man, and more circumspect in his support of the Comyns. He stood as one of the guarantors of the bond that King Henry III compelled the earl of Menteith to swear in the autumn of 1244,[98] but thereafter devoted considerable effort to building a relationship with other members of the Comyn affinity.[99] His marriage to the heiress of Roger Avenel brought him the lordship of Abercorn in Linlithgowshire, as well as Kilbucho and Newlands in Peeblesshire and more lands in Eskdale.[100] Membership in the entourage of the earls of Dunbar enabled him to establish contacts with a number of other noblemen, among them Robert III de Muschamp and Malise II of Strathearn. The marriage that was arranged between Henry's son, Nicholas, and Mary, the daughter of Earl Malise, has all the hallmarks of a carefully constructed alliance among three families anxious to take advantage of the promising opportunities that cross-border lordship offered in the later thirteenth century: for Malise, the establishment of a whole new branch of the family in Northumberland with properties over which he could no longer, by English law, exercise direct control; for Nicholas de Graham, the addition to his already extensive holdings in the

Anglo-Scottish border region of a third of the barony of Wooler to be held in conjunct fee, and new social ties to one of the highest-ranking magnate families in Scotland; for the earls of Dunbar, the strengthening of political and social ties in the wider world of border society. In 1269, with tensions between the realms seemingly a thing of the past, the likelihood that Nicholas would be able to administer his dual lordship with ease appeared very good indeed.

The Muschamp inheritance was valuable to Earl Malise II perhaps most significantly because it enabled him to endow his two daughters generously without seriously compromising the integrity of his Scottish patrimony and the inheritance of his elder son. Considerations such as these were part of the fabric of noble life. To the second of his sons by Maud of Orkney and Caithness, Robert, he gave a small estate in Perthshire,[101] sizeable enough for Robert to establish himself as a modest lord in his own right, but no more.[102] His daughter Cecilia, to whom he granted the lands of Keillor near Fowlis Wester, he married into the Methven family, long-established Perthshire tenants of the earls.[103] The location of Cecilia's tocher, hard by the spiritual centre of the earldom at Inchaffray, was a mark of the esteem in which he held his Methven son-in-law, but the estate lay well beyond the upland heart of the earl's territories. This he was able to pass, virtually intact, to his heir when he died in 1271.[104]

The Muschamp inheritance, 1269–1322

In the years between 1269 and 1296 Nicholas and Mary de Graham enjoyed the social and economic rewards that made cross-border lordship so attractive to the Anglo-Scottish nobility of the later thirteenth century. For a good part of this period they lived in Scotland, content, on more than one occasion, to defend themselves against a series of pleas of novel disseisin at the assize sessions held in Newcastle-upon-Tyne by means of attorneys, one of whom was Mary's kinsman, Stephen de Muschamp of Barmoor.[105] The death of Malise II in 1271 required that Nicholas cultivate ties with the new earl of Strathearn, and physical proximity to the affinity of his brother-in-law Malise III was the surest way to accomplish this aim. Although it is apparent that Nicholas and Mary continued to pay close attention to their English lands – Nicholas, for example, made arrangements to send to Edward I's Exchequer the sum that he was charged for distraint of knighthood – [106] the birth of a son around 1278 or 1279 saw them turn their attention to the all important business of estate planning with respect to the Graham family lands in Scotland.[107]

All noble families knew that provision for the spiritual well-being of the kindred was the foundation of earthly good fortune. Accordingly, one of Nicholas's first acts as a married man was the endowment of the church. Sometime between 1279 and 1285, perhaps soon after the birth of his child, he granted to Melrose abbey the estate of Easington in Northumberland, reserving only the revenues generated by the vicarage of the Virgin Mary there for a period of twenty years.[108] The gift to the house where Mary de Graham's grandfather was buried reaffirmed the long-standing relationship between the abbey and the Muschamp kindred, whose members had a long tradition of endowing the Cistercian house out of their Northumberland properties.[109]

For many years after his marriage to Mary of Strathearn Nicholas enjoyed lucrative revenues from his English lands. His share of the Muschamp inheritance increased significantly in November 1291, when his sister-in-law, Muriel of Mar, died without heirs. Her third of the barony of Wooler passed to her sister Mary and her cousin, Walter de Huntercombe, the son of Isabel and William,[110] thus increasing the Graham interest in the barony to one half. Just a few weeks after Muriel's death, Nicholas and Mary travelled to England to take possession of their new estates.[111] They had pressing reasons to want to appear in person before the king's escheator. In the winter of 1291–2 Edward I had become closely involved in proceedings that would determine the claimant to the Scottish throne, rendered vacant by the death of the Maid of Norway.[112] In May 1291, in a demonstration of political will, Edward had belatedly demanded that Muriel perform homage for the lands that she held in England.[113] Prudence dictated that, in an atmosphere of political uncertainty, Nicholas and his wife make a clear demonstration of their allegiance to the English crown. Muriel's share of the Muschamp inheritance, however, was well worth the effort. It included revenues from the exploitation of demesne, rents, profits of justice and other perquisites in Lowick, Hethpool, Heatherslaw, Belford and Bowsden, collectively worth £52 11s 5d, together with the manor of Ross in the Durham liberty of Islandshire, worth a further £10.[114] As had occurred in 1254, moreover, there was some rancour between the heirs in respect of the equitable division of this portion of the Muschamp inheritance, with Walter de Huntercombe, a thoroughly unpleasant character and a sycophantic servant of the English crown, claiming that his share had been unfairly assessed.[115]

In the years of calm before the storms of 1296, Nicholas and Mary continued to pay careful attention to the business arising from their English estates. Nicholas appeared before royal justices when Edward I's *quo warranto* proceedings were convened in Northumberland in the winter and spring of 1293, when he successfully defended his right to hold assizes of ale throughout his lands, title to free chase in the forest of Cheviot and broad legal jurisdiction over his all his free tenants.[116] Lordship in England, however, meant more to Nicholas de Graham than merely a steady, if considerable, stream of ready income. It also offered him the opportunity to expend the social capital that so effectively bound aspiring noblemen on both sides of the border to their wealthy betters. In the mid-1280s Nicholas and his brother Henry arranged the marriage of their sister Idonea to John de Swinburne, a prominent landowner in his own right in both northern England and southern Scotland.[117] The couple were given the lands of Simonburn in Tynedale, to be held of Nicholas. The names of the attestors to the two charters drafted as a consequence of the marriage bear witness to the intricacy of the social links that bound Scottish families to their branches in Northumberland. They included William and John de Soules; Sir Patrick de Graham, married to the sister of Earl Malise II of Strathearn; and William de Airth, a vassal of both the earl of Lennox and Patrick de Graham in Stirlingshire, and a member of the affinity of the Comyns, lords in Tynedale.[118]

Records of the English Chancery and Exchequer closely record the movements of Nicholas and Mary throughout these years. Above all, they attest the ease with which they and nobles like them continued to travel back and forth between the kingdoms in the months preceding the eruption of open conflict in 1296. Nicholas stood as an auditor for Bruce in November 1292 as the discussions that became known as the Great Cause were drawing to a conclusion,[119] just as he must have been preparing to leave for England to appear before justices acting on commissions of *quo warranto*. From the vantage point of the Grahams even the momentous events of the spring and summer months of 1296 did not spell disaster. Although Edward I scored political points by seizing Nicholas's Scottish lands in May 1296 as he marched triumphantly around the kingdom,[120] these were restored to him as soon as he had performed homage at Berwick in September,[121] and he escaped the fate of some of his Graham kinsmen, who were considered too close to the leading Scottish rebels to be allowed to roam free in the months after Edward had left Scotland.[122] The king knew that he had much to lose by alienating northern English landholders like Nicholas and Mary de Graham unnecessarily; Nicholas, for his part, had a great deal to gain by remaining in Edward's favour. In the lay subsidy inquest undertaken in 1296, for example, Graham's Hethpool and Heatherslaw tenants alone were assessed at £48 16s 2d and £19 1s 9d.[123] Such sums must have served as salutary reminders of the prosperity of the Northumberland estates that he controlled. The king, however, was watching him closely. In May 1297, before he left for Flanders, Edward wrote to a handful of border magnates, inviting them to join the expedition, among them Nicholas de Graham.[124]

Many of the Scots who agreed did so as a consequence of their capture at Dunbar in 1296 and in return for their release from prison.[125] Graham did not. For several months he proved uncannily successful at playing a dangerous game of chance with his English overlord, moving with relative ease across the border line, overseeing in person the direction of affairs in the barony of Wooler, and all the while assuring Edward of his allegiance.[126]

In many respects the Scottish risings of 1297 marked a more important turning point than did Edward's easily accomplished conquest of the previous year. They saw a number of magnates, among them Graham's brother-in-law, Earl Malise III of Strathearn, launch open challenges to English overlordship.[127] As hundreds of other landholders became aware, the rebellion required that Graham decide once and for all on which side to commit his allegiance. In defiance of Edward I, he chose the cause of Scottish independence, and from 1297 until his death nine years later it was primarily his landed possessions north of the border that he sought to protect and preserve on behalf of his heir, John.

For many cross-border noblemen, support for the Scottish cause spelled political, social and economic ruin in England, but after 1297 the grim determination of the patriots to oppose foreign domination in turn opened up opportunities to take advantage of the constant shifts in the tide of the war. The most famous of such opportunists was Robert Bruce earl of Carrick, whose ambitions to win the Scottish throne historians have long debated, but whose actions were motivated above all by a deep and abiding obligation to his kindred, past and future, to preserve his patrimonial lands.[128] Nicholas de Graham's decisions were born of a similar blend of self-interest and patriotism. He supported the Scottish rebels for several years after the outbreak of rebellion in 1297, and as a consequence suffered forfeiture of his lands in both kingdoms. The Northumberland properties were granted en bloc to Isabel widow of John de Vescy, a family whose members had been long-time neighbours and one-time allies of the Muschamp family, and to whom the Grahams were related by marriage.[129] The estates in Scotland went to various beneficiaries, among them the 'pragmatist' Patrick IV earl of Dunbar, who remained a staunch adherent of the English throughout the war.[130] Nicholas Graham was still being treated as a rebel in December 1303, when Edward I ordered the presentation of a new master to the hospital of St Mary Magdalene in Wooler, which lay 'in the king's hands by the forfeiture of Nicholas de Graham'.[131]

The events of the following spring, however, signalled to Nicholas the extent to which the future of his family's fortunes in Scotland, as well as the secure possession of his English estates, had become dependent on the good will of the English crown. Fiona Watson has remarked shrewdly that although historians will never really know the motivations of the patriots who submitted to Edward following the reconquest of Scotland in 1304, there can be little doubt that many 'saw themselves now standing between a rock and a very hard place'.[132] Nicholas de Graham was such a man. In March of that year, together with a large number of his fellow Scots, he performed homage and swore allegiance to the crown of England. In equally perceptive fashion, Watson has argued that in 1304, despite his victory, Edward I was shrewd enough to appreciate the lessons that a decade of Scottish opposition had taught him. Among the more important of these were the deep and abiding importance that Scottish landholders attached to their estates, and the overwhelming preoccupation with the notions of lineage and kindred that animated their political choices. In the settlement of Scottish affairs that followed the submissions of 1304, then, Edward was careful to restore their possessions in both kingdoms to a significant number of former Scottish rebels, great and small.[133] Nicholas de Graham benefited from this magnanimity. He was back in possession of the barony of Dalkeith as early as 23 March and, a mere two months later, of most of the lands in Northumberland and Durham that he held with his wife.[134] The process of restoration did not everywhere proceed smoothly, nor did all of the king's newly reconciled subjects resume full control over the estates, revenues and privileges that had been theirs before the war. Nicholas de Graham experienced problems in his attempts to recoup his losses both in England and Scotland. The patronage of the church of Wooler that he and his wife had long enjoyed, a rich source of ready cash, was not returned to the couple. Despite sustained efforts to regain control of the church it remained for many years in the king's hands, perhaps as a costly reminder to the Grahams of the price of disavowing their allegiance to the English crown.[135] Mary was able to recover the advowson only in 1311, and only after King Edward II had agreed to return it to her by special licence.[136] Nicholas also experienced difficulty securing fresh possession of lands in Easington, which had been seized by Patrick IV of Dunbar at the beginning of the war. The earl had been a staunch supporter of the English, and Nicholas's efforts to sue him for recovery proved ineffectual. At his death in 1306, he had still not been able to regain possession of the estate.[137]

In Scotland, Nicholas de Graham suffered still further reverses. His opponent this time was the abbot of Melrose, himself anxious to take advantage of Edward I's policy of rewarding the loyalty of Scottish landholders with the judicious dispensation of patronage and favour. The estates and revenues in dispute in 1304 lay at Westerker, in upper Eskdale where, in the mid-twelfth century, the monks had acquired valuable properties by the gift of Roger Avenel.[138] The original grant had reserved valuable forest and pasturage rights to the Avenel family, and in 1304 Nicholas de Graham and his son John were in turn laying claim to the profits they generated. For several generations the monks' efforts to wrest these privileges from their benefactors' descendants had been frustrated, but conditions in Scotland were now ripe for the renewal of the abbot's designs on Westerker. Nicholas himself may have precipitated a revival of the dispute when, on one occasion, he chased some of the monastery's servants from the lands and unlawfully detained others. So, at least, the abbot complained when he presented a petition to the English parliament in 1305 and requested that Edward defend the 'right and franchises' of his church.[139] It has been suggested that Grahams 'had perhaps been using the political disturbances of the time to reassert their ancestral rights' in Eskdale.[140] If so, the strategy proved ineffectual, and the litigation was ongoing and as yet unresolved in the late spring of 1306, when Nicholas died.

The difficulties that Nicholas and Mary de Graham confronted in the years between 1296 and 1306 were replicated the length and breadth of Scotland, when members of the landed aristocracy from Moray to East Lothian grappled with conflicting questions of fealty, national allegiance and family interest. While some players in the political storms – notably Nicholas's brother-in-law, Malise III of Strathearn – had more to lose than others,[141] landowners great and small were keenly aware that the well-being of their families' fortunes was inextricably linked to the political choices that they made. Perhaps nowhere was the dilemma felt more acutely than among the ranks of the noblemen whose ancestral properties lay hard by the Anglo-Scottish border.[142] Nicholas de Graham died just weeks after Robert Bruce had publicly and dramatically staked his claim to the throne of Scotland, and was spared the dilemma of having to decide whether or not to support Bruce in his new role, but surviving evidence suggests that in the period leading up to his death he and his wife set about attempting to salvage what they could of their substantial cross-border lordships in the midst of deepening political crisis. Mary settled in England, where for the remainder of her life she managed the English properties in dutiful obedience to Edward I and his agents. Their son John remained in Scotland, where he concentrated on preserving the Graham patrimony as well on pursuing the ongoing litigation with Melrose abbey.

The plan proved to be a sound strategy. The post-mortem inquest into Nicholas's holdings in Northumberland confirmed that he and Mary had held their half of the barony of Wooler in conjunct fee. By mid-June Mary had duly performed homage and taken secure possession of her lands.[143] Edward I and, after him, Edward II, recognised that they had much to lose by alienating the loyalty of a tenant in chief who still maintained such close ties to the Scottish rebels. Although Mary was required to send the quota of knights owing from her lands to the English army that campaigned in Scotland in 1310–11,[144] the crown allowed her repeatedly to delay paying the hefty sum of £50 that she owed in relief for her share of her sister Muriel's inheritance. It was not, in fact, until the early autumn of 1314, after Scottish forces had soundly defeated Edward II's army at Bannockburn, that the English king turned his wrath on Mary de Graham. News of the presence at the battle of her son John brought a peremptory demand for payment of the relief.[145] Thereafter, Nicholas's widow appears to have made only muted attempts to maintain her ties with Scotland, preferring a quiet life in the fealty of King Edward. The sale of her interests in the vills of Belford and Ross soon after 1314 offset the payment of relief that the crown had demanded of her; it may also have been precipitated by the severe dislocation to the northern English economy that marked the second decade of the fourteenth century.[146] In 1320 Mary divested herself also of the land of Hassington in Berwickshire that had for generations represented the Muschamp stake in Scotland. Her beneficiary, ironically, was Patrick V of Dunbar.[147] The wars of independence effectively destroyed the centuries-old tenurial links between the Muschamp family and the kingdom of Scotland. Mary's grant to Earl Patrick severed equally venerable social ties.[148] She died a very old woman in October 1322, far from Strathearn, and no longer in communication with the family that she had left behind in 1306.

Conclusion

Like many of his compatriots, Nicholas and Mary's son, John de Graham, sought by every means possible to preserve his Scottish lands during the political crisis of the wars of independence. Although his father had endorsed the Bruce claim to the Scottish throne at the time of the Great Cause, by the opening decade of the new century John had joined his Graham kinsmen, Patrick and David, in support of the guardianship of John Comyn lord of Badenoch,[149] and he was at Strathord on 9 February 1304, when Comyn and a handful of John Balliol's adherents made their formal submission to Edward I.[150] For many Scottish landholders the choice of allegiance after Bruce's seizure of the throne represented little more than the flying of 'flags of convenience', to be hoisted or lowered as circumstances dictated.[151] Concern for his personal freedom, dismay at Robert I's act of sacrilege and, not least, news of Bruce's arrest of his uncle, Earl Malise III of Strathearn,[152] all mitigated against John de Graham's open support for the patriotic cause. Throughout 1307 he was still, nominally at least, in the allegiance of the English crown, charged in the summer with assisting Aymer de

Valence to guard the castles of Ayr and Turnberry against Bruce's marauding, and in the early winter with maintaining the peace within Scotland during Edward's absence abroad.[153]

John's loyalty won him Edward's recognition of title to the Graham estates in Scotland, but the king's support counted for little in the ongoing dispute with Melrose abbey over the lands of Westerker in Eskdale. The abbot was a skilled opponent, prepared to exert as much pressure as required to put into effect the ruling of the parliament of 1305 which had offered the monks a favourable outcome to their claims. As early as the summer of 1308, and certainly by the following spring, Graham had given up his fight and relinquished all but a handful of the lordly prerogatives associated with the estate. Soon thereafter the litigation itself became moot, for he renounced his fealty to Edward II in order to join the forces of King Robert I.[154] Bruce's subsequent championing of the abbot's claims must have rankled, but by then Graham had become fully committed to the Scottish patriotic cause. Forfeiture of the barony of Dalkeith at the command of Edward II just days before Bannockburn had little permanent effect on his fortunes,[155] and he spent the years between 1314 and his death in 1337 in the firm allegiance of the Bruce family.

After Bannockburn, of course, any claims that John de Graham might have entertained to his mother's Northumberland estates vanished, even if his family's connections with the earls of Strathearn remained close and strong.[156] Mary herself had realised that her lands would not pass to him, and in the years preceding her death had made arrangements to disperse her share of the barony of Wooler among a handful of northern noblemen, among them the Yorkshire knight, Sir Nicholas de Meynell.[157] By 1322, moreover, John had committed himself wholly to the cause of Scottish independence,[158] and must surely have considered the notion of cross-border lordship as a vestige of an era now long past. Thanks in large part to his father Nicholas's skilful navigation through the troubled political waters of the wars of independence, however, his family none the less managed to enjoy the benefits of dual allegiance for a much longer period than did most other Anglo-Scottish magnates.

Notes

1. G. W. S. Barrow, *Robert Bruce and the Community of the Realm of Scotland* (Edinburgh, 2005), pp. 341–404; A. Grant, *Independence and Nationhood: Scotland, 1306–1469* (London, 1984), pp. 3–31.
2. *The Records of the Parliaments of Scotland to 1707*, ed. K. M. Brown et al. (St Andrews, 2007), www.rps.ac.uk, 1315/1 (date accessed: 15 March 2008).

3. G. W. S. Barrow, *The Anglo-Norman Era in Scottish History* (Oxford, 1980).
4. K. J. Stringer, 'Nobility and identity in medieval Britain and Ireland: the de Vescy family, c. 1120–1314', in B. Smith (ed.), *Britain and Ireland 900–1300: Insular Responses to Medieval European Change* (Cambridge, 1999), p. 224; K. J. Stringer, 'Identities in thirteenth-century England: frontier society in the far north', in C. Björn, A. Grant and K. J. Stringer (eds), *Social and Political Identities in Western History* (Copenhagen, 1994), pp. 52–6, 66. See also N. M. Webb, 'Settlement and integration: the establishment of an aristocracy in Scotland (1124–1214)', in J. Gillingham (ed.), *Anglo-Norman Studies XXV: Proceedings of the Battle Conference 2002* (Woodbridge, 2003), pp. 227–38, which discusses the links among families of non-baronial rank; and, for a review of tenurial ties between Melrose abbey and its Anglo-Scottish benefactors, *The Chronicle of Melrose Abbey: A Stratigraphic Edition, Vol. 1, Introduction and Facsimile Edition*, ed. D. Broun and J. Harrison (Woodbridge, 2007), pp. 1–4.
5. K. Stringer, 'The early lords of Lauderdale, Dryburgh abbey and St. Andrews priory at Northampton', in K. J. Stringer (ed.), *Essays on the Nobility of Medieval Scotland* (Edinburgh, 1985), p. 44. See also Stringer, 'Identities in thirteenth-century England', p. 32.
6. R. M. Blakely, *The Brus Family in England and Scotland, 1100–1295* (Woodbridge, 2005).
7. A. Young, *Robert the Bruce's Rivals: The Comyns, 1212–1314* (East Linton, 1997); A. Beam, *The Balliol Dynasty, 1210–1364* (East Linton, 2008).
8. W. Ferguson, *Scotland's Relations with England: A Survey to 1707* (Edinburgh, 1977), pp. 20–2.
9. K. J. Stringer, *The Reign of Stephen: Kingship, Warfare and Government in Twelfth-century England* (London, 1993), pp. 28–48; A. A. M. Duncan, *Scotland: The Making of the Kingdom* (Edinburgh, 1975), pp. 216–55, 560–74.
10. *RRS*, i, pp. 100–1.
11. Stringer, 'Identities in thirteenth-century England', pp. 39–41; J. Green, 'Aristocratic loyalties on the northern frontier of England, c.1100–1174', in D. Williams (ed.), *England in the Twelfth Century: Proceedings of the 1988 Harlaxton Symposium* (Woodbridge, 1990), pp. 97–100.
12. The literature here is considerable, but for a comprehensive discussion, see S. Waugh, *The Lordship of England: Royal Wardships and Marriage in English Society and Politics, 1217–1327* (Princeton, 1988), esp. pp. 15–63.
13. Blakely, *The Brus Family*, p. 2.
14. C. J. Neville, *Native Lordship in Medieval Scotland: The Earldoms of Strathearn and Lennox, c. 1140–1365* (Dublin, 2005), pp. 23–5.
15. I. J. Sanders, *English Baronies: A Study of their Origin and Descent, 1086–1327* (Oxford, 1960), p. 100; W. P. Hedley, *Northumberland Families*, 2 vols (Newcastle-upon-Tyne, 1968–70), i, pp. 37–8; A. M. Oliver, 'The family of Muschamp, barons of Wooler', *Archaeologia Aeliana*, 4th Series, 14 (1937), pp. 243–6; W. E. Kapelle, *The Norman Conquest of the North: The Region*

and its Transformation (London, 1979), p. 211; R. Lomas, *County of Conflict: Northumberland from Conquest to Civil War* (East Linton, 1996), pp. 22–3.

16. *Liber feodorum: The Book of Fees commonly called Testa de Nevill*, ed. H. C. Maxwell-Lyte, 3 vols (London, 1920–31), i, p. 200; ii, pp. 1119–20, 1128–9. The second inquest was returned into Exchequer pursuant to a writ of Henry III dated December 1242.
17. *Glasgow Reg.*, no. 1; *Charters of David I*, no. 14.
18. Hedley, *Northumberland Families*, i, pp. 37–8.
19. Ibid. p. 39.
20. *RRS*, ii, nos. 126, 135; possibly also nos. 147, 174, 175.
21. Northumberland County History Committee, *A History of Northumberland*, 15 vols (Newcastle-upon-Tyne, 1893–1940), i, p. 373.
22. *Gesta regis Henrici secundi Benedicti abbatis*, ed. W. Stubbs, 2 vols (London, 1867), i, p. 48.
23. *Chronica magistri Rogeri de Houedene*, ed. W. Stubbs, 4 vols (London, 1868–71), ii, p. 60; Hedley, *Northumberland Families*, i, p. 38; *CDS*, i, nos. 142, 175, 184; J. C. Holt, *The Northerners: A Study in the Reign of King John* (Oxford, 1961), pp. 83, 203.
24. *RRS*, ii, nos. 201, 208; *Melrose Liber*, no. *166.
25. *The Great Roll of the Pipe for the Thirty-first Year of the Reign of King Henry the Second. A.D. 1184–1185*, ed. J. H. Round (London, 1913), p. 11; *The Great Roll of the Pipe for the Thirty-second Year of the Reign of King Henry the Second, A.D. 1185–1186*, ed. J. H. Round (London, 1914), p. 21; *The Great Roll of the Pipe for the Sixth Year of the Reign of King Richard the First, Michaelmas 1194*, ed. D. M. Stenton (London, 1928), p. 133.
26. *Northumberland Pleas from De Banco Rolls 20–37 (5–8 Edward I)*, ed. A. H. Thompson (Durham, 1950), pp. 89, 119; *Feet of Fines, Northumberland and Durham*, ed. A. M. Oliver and C. Johnson, 2 vols (Durham, 1931), i, no. 101.
27. Durham, Dean and Chapter Muniments (DCD) Misc. Ch. 764; J. C. Hodgson, *A History of Northumberland in Three Parts*, 3 vols in 7 (Newcastle-upon-Tyne, 1820–40), II, ii, p. 345.
28. *Melrose Liber*, nos. 279, 283, 284.
29. Ibid. nos. 305, 306; *Chartularium abbathiae de novo monasterio: ordinis Cisterciensis, fundatae anno M.C.XXXVII*, ed. J. T. Fowler (Durham, 1878), p. 80.
30. *Patent Rolls of the Reign of Henry III, 1225–32*, ed. H. C. Maxwell-Lyte, 6 vols (London, 1893–1913), p. 382; *Close Rolls of the Reign of Henry III, 1227–31*, ed. H. C. Maxwell-Lyte, 14 vols (London, 1902–38), p. 508. Gilia married, first, Nicholas de Edgetoft, then William de Laundells, lord of nearby Hownam.
31. *Melrose Liber*, nos. 232, 233; *APS*, i, pp. 408–10; D. E. R. Watt, *A Biographical Dictionary of Scottish Graduates to A.D. 1410* (Oxford, 1977), pp. 242–3; G. F. Black, *The Surnames of Scotland: Their Origin, Meaning and History* (New York, 1946; repr. Edinburgh, 1993), p. 326.
32. William was the younger brother of Robert III's father, Robert II.

33. *Northumberland Pleas*, ed. Thompson, p. 141.
34. See text at note 23 above.
35. *Matthæi Parisiensis, monachi sancti Albani, chronica majora*, ed. H. R. Luard, 7 vols (London, 1872–83), iv, pp. 359, 379–85; Young, *Robert the Bruce's Rivals*, pp. 41–6; Duncan, *Making of the Kingdom*, pp. 535–7.
36. TNA, C 47/22/5/10, 11.
37. Young, *Robert the Bruce's Rivals*, pp. 46–7.
38. R. R. Davies, *Domination and Conquest: The Experience of Ireland, Scotland and Wales, 1100–1300* (Cambridge, 1990), p. 53.
39. R. A. McDonald, 'Matrimonial politics and core-periphery interactions in twelfth- and early thirteenth-century Scotland', *Journal of Medieval History*, 21 (1995), p. 237. See also Stringer, 'Identities in thirteenth-century England', p. 39.
40. Neville, *Native Lordship*, p. 47; A. Ross, 'The lords and lordship of Glencarnie', in S. Boardman and A. Ross (eds), *The Exercise of Power in Medieval Scotland, c. 1200–1500* (Dublin, 2003), p. 162.
41. *Chron. Fordun*, i, p. 280.
42. *Foedera*, I, i, p. 234.
43. Matthew Paris, *Chron. majora*, ed. Luard, v, pp. 501–2, 504–7; Young, *Robert the Bruce's Rivals*, pp. 50–9; Duncan, *Making of the Kingdom*, pp. 560–74.
44. A. Young, 'The political role of Walter Comyn, earl of Menteith, during the minority of Alexander III of Scotland', in Stringer (ed.), *Essays on the Nobility*, pp. 132, 134–7, 139–42; M. H. Hammond, '*Hostiarii regis Scotie*: the Durward family in the thirteenth century', in Boardman and Ross (eds), *Exercise of Power*, pp. 132–3.
45. Hammond, '*Hostiarii regis Scotie*', pp. 124–30.
46. *Scotichronicon*, v, pp. 402–3.
47. A. J. Macdonald, 'Kings of the wild frontier? The earls of Dunbar or March, c.1070–1435', in Boardman and Ross (eds), *Exercise of Power*, p. 145.
48. *Chronicon de Lanercost*, ed. J. Stevenson (Glasgow, 1839), p. 54; Matthew Paris, *Chron. majora*, ed. Luard, v, p. 41.
49. Young, *Robert the Bruce's Rivals*, p. 55; D. E. R. Watt, 'The minority of Alexander III of Scotland', *Transactions of the Royal Historical Society*, 5th Series, 21 (1971), p. 13.
50. Young, *Robert the Bruce's Rivals*, pp. 55–6; Duncan, *Making of the Kingdom*, pp. 565, 567; *Chronicle of Melrose*, ed. A. O. Anderson and M. O. Anderson (London, 1936), p. 112; *Anglo-Scottish Relations 1174–1328: Some Selected Documents*, ed. E. L. G. Stones (Oxford, 1965), pp. 60–9; *The Original Chronicle of Andrew of Wyntoun*, ed. F. J. Amours, 6 vols (Edinburgh, 1903–14), v, pp. 236–7; J. Anderson, '"Marjorie" Comyn or Dunbar', *Scottish Historical Review*, 1 (1904), pp. 228–31; A. Young, 'Noble families and political factions in the reign of Alexander III', in N. Reid (ed.), *Scotland in the Reign of Alexander III* (Edinburgh, 1990), p. 11.

51. *Dunfermline Reg.*, no. 309.
52. *CDS*, i, nos. 1956, 1984–5; *Chron. Melrose*, ed. Anderson and Anderson, p. 111; F. M. Powicke, *King Henry III and the Lord Edward*, 2 vols (Oxford, 1947), i, pp. 231–4.
53. *Foedera*, I, i, pp. 326, 329; Watt, 'The minority of Alexander III', pp. 13–14.
54. TNA, SC 1/5/50; *Facsimiles of the National Manuscripts of Scotland*, ed. H. James, 3 vols (London, 1867–71), i, no. 66.
55. M. Powicke, *The Thirteenth Century, 1216–1307*, 2nd edn (Oxford, 1991), pp. 134–40.
56. Duncan, *Making of the Kingdom*, p. 576.
57. TNA, C 66/73, m. 10; E 368/34, m. 29.
58. *Chron. Fordun*, i, pp. 298–9; Young, *Robert the Bruce's Rivals*, pp. 74–5; Duncan, *Making of the Kingdom*, p. 583; *Calendar of Entries in the Papal Registers relating to Great Britain and Ireland (Regesta Romanorum pontificum). Papal Letters*, ed. W. H. Bliss et al., 14 vols (London, 1893–1960), i, p. 408; Watt, 'The minority of Alexander III', pp. 22–3.
59. *Foedera*, I, i, p. 402.
60. *Chron. Melrose*, ed. Anderson and Anderson, pp. 90–1, 109–16; *Chron. Fordun*, i, pp. 296–9.
61. *Moray Reg.*, App., no. 12; NAS, GD 220/1/A1/3/3, 4; *Inchaffray Chrs*, App., no. 5; *Morton Reg.*, ii, no. 6. See also Northumberland Record Office, ZSW/1/1/16, a charter of Alexander III, witnessed by, among others, Patrick III earl of Dunbar and Malise II earl of Strathearn.
62. *Chron. Fordun*, i, p. 297.
63. Ibid. p. 298.
64. Duncan, *Making of the Kingdom*, p. 535.
65. *Northumberland Pleas*, ed. Thompson, p. 141.
66. *CIPM, 1236–72*, no. 202.
67. Matthew Paris, *Chron. majora*, ed. Luard, v, p. 174.
68. *Chron. Melrose*, ed. Anderson and Anderson, p. 109; Oliver, 'The family of Muschamp', pp. 256–7.
69. *Close Rolls, 1247–51*, pp. 325–26; *Excerpta è rotulis finium in turri londinensi asservatis, Henrico tertio rege, A.D. 1216–72*, ed. C. Roberts, 2 vols (London, 1835–36), ii, p. 90; TNA, E 372/94 m. 18d; TNA, E 372/95 m. 11d.
70. *CIPM, 1236–72*, no. 202; see also no. 341.
71. Ibid. no. 202.
72. Ibid. no. 341; *Excerpta è rotulis finium, 1216–72*, ed. Roberts, ii, p. 207.
73. *Excerpta è rotulis finium, 1246–72*, ii, p. 209; *CPR, 1247–58*, p. 411.
74. *CDS*, i, no. 1904.
75. *Close Rolls, 1256–59*, p. 299.
76. *Inchaffray Chrs*, no 86.
77. In 1256 Gilbert had acquired land in Mar by the gift of Alan Durward. Alasdair Ross has suggested that the grant represented a reward for the earl's 'recent political flexibility', but it is relevant also to note that the marriage to

Countess Maud created new ties to her Comyn relations. See Fraser, *Grant*, iii, no. 6; Ross, 'The lords and lordship of Glencarnie', p. 165.

78. R. A. McDonald, *Outlaws of Medieval Scotland: Challenges to the Canmore Kings, 1058–1266* (East Linton, 2003), pp. 107–10; B. Crawford, 'The earldom of Caithness and the kingdom of Scotland, 1150–1266', in Stringer (ed.), *Essays on the Nobility*, pp. 36–7.
79. C. J. Neville, 'The earls of Strathearn from the twelfth to the mid-fourteenth century, with an edition of their written acts', 2 vols, unpublished PhD dissertation (University of Aberdeen, 1983), i, pp. 112, 147, 150.
80. For details of what follows, see the descriptions of the barony of Wooler and its pertinents in Northumberland County History Committee, *History of Northumberland*, i, pp. 109, 214, 229–30, 241, 252–4, 271–3, 306–26, 373–81, 395, 427–30; xi, pp. 332, 369, 436, 440, 442–3; xiv, pp. 96–102, 117–21, 127, 137–8, 325.
81. *CIPM, 1236–72*, no. 202.
82. See here generally E. Miller, 'Patterns of settlement: northern England', in H. E. Hallam (ed.), *The Agrarian History of England and Wales, Vol. II: 1042–1350* (Cambridge, 1988), pp. 247–56, and C. Dyer, *Standards of Living in the Later Middle Ages: Social Change in England, c. 1200–1520* (Cambridge, 1989).
83. TNA, JUST 1/652, m. 13d.
84. *Placita de quo warranto, temporibus Edw. I. II. & III.*, ed. W. Illingworth (London, 1818), p. 601.
85. TNA, E 372/106, m. 7; TNA, E 368/42 m. 17; *CIPM, 1236–72*, no. 202.
86. Northumberland County History Committee, *History of Northumberland*, xi, 306.
87. TNA, KB 26/145, m. 11d; *Close Rolls, 1247–51*, pp. 441, 450, 472.
88. *CIPM, 1236–72*, no, 216; Northumberland County History Committee, *History of Northumberland*, xi, p. 309. For scutage payments made in 1257, 1259, 1261 and 1262, see Hodgson, *History of Northumberland*, III, iii, pp. 251, 257, 263, 271.
89. Bracton, Henricus de, *De legibus et consuetudinibus Angliae*, ed. S. F. Thorne, 4 vols (Cambridge, MA, 1968–77), ii, pp. 258–9; iv, pp. 360–1.
90. Hodgson, *History of Northumberland*, III, iii, pp. 251, 257, 263–4, 271–2, 281–2.
91. J. B. Paul, *The Scots Peerage*, 9 vols (Edinburgh, 1904–14), v, p. 576; R. D. Oram, 'Continuity, adaptation and integration: the earls and earldom of Mar, c.1150–c.1300', in Boardman and Ross (eds), *Exercise of Power*, pp. 61–2; Hammond, '*Hostiarii regis Scotie*', p. 132. William's first wife had been Elizabeth, daughter of William Comyn earl of Buchan.
92. *Documents Illustrative of the History of Scotland from the Death of King Alexander the Third to the Accession of Robert Bruce*, ed. J. Stevenson, 2 vols (Edinburgh, 1870), i, p. 229; *CCR, 1288–96*, p. 169; *CFR, 1272–1307*, p. 298; *CIPM, 1272–91*, no. 823.

93. *Charters of David I*, nos. 68, 69, 87, 116, 139, 147, 216; Duncan, *Making of the Kingdom*, p. 137.
94. *RRS*, ii, no. 125. See Barrow's reservations about the version of the family's early history offered in *The Scots Peerage*. *RRS*, ii, pp. 204–5.
95. Neville, *Native Lordship*, p. 56; Duncan, *Making of the Kingdom*, pp. 562–3; M. Brown, 'Earldom and kindred: the Lennox and its earls, 1200–1458', in Boardman and Ross (eds), *Exercise of Power*, p. 210.
96. *Foedera*, I, i, p. 257; TNA, C 47/22/12/14; NAS, RH 5/29; Young, *Robert the Bruce's Rivals*, pp. 52, 69.
97. *CPR, 1247–58*, p. 426; *Anglo-Scottish Relations*, ed. Stones, pp. 62–3.
98. TNA, C 47/22/5/11.
99. Young, *Robert the Bruce's Rivals*, pp. 46–7 See also *APS*, i, 408–9, for Henry's presence at a royal court convened in Berwick presided over by Earl Patrick II of Dunbar.
100. *Scots Peerage*, vi, p. 194.
101. *CDS*, ii, no. 823, p. 200.
102. *Inchaffray Liber*, App., no. 17; *Coupar Angus Chrs*, i, no. 86.
103. *Morton Reg.*, ii, no. 6. See also *Morton Reg.* i, nos. 78, 110.
104. For a discussion of the earls' policy of infefting tenants, see Neville, *Native Lordship*, pp. 45–54.
105. TNA, JUST 1/643, m. 10; *Three Early Assize Rolls for the County of Northumberland, saec. XIII*, ed. W. Page (Durham, 1891), p. 301.
106. Hodgson, *History of Northumberland*, i, p. 295.
107. In 1306 a post-mortem jury reported that John de Graham was 'aged twenty-eight years'. *CIPM, 1301–07*, no. 364.
108. *Melrose Liber*, ii, App., nos. 18, 19.
109. R. Fawcett and R. Oram, *Melrose Abbey* (Stroud, 2004), pp. 241–2.
110. Stevenson, *Documents*, i, p. 258; *CIPM, 1272–91*, no. 823. William de Huntercombe had died c. 1271.
111. Stevenson, *Documents*, i, p. 267; *CFR, 1272–1307*, p. 301.
112. For a recent discussion of the events of 1291–92, see A. A. M. Duncan, *The Kingship of the Scots, 842–1292* (Edinburgh, 2002), pp. 197–209.
113. Stevenson, *Documents*, i, p. 229; *CCR, 1288–96*, p. 169; *CFR, 1292–1307*, p. 298.
114. Stevenson, *Documents*, i, p. 258; Northumberland County History Committee, *History of Northumberland*, i, pp. 373–4, 378; xi, pp. 109, 253, 273, 311–13, 429–30; xiv, pp. 100, 119–20.
115. *CDS*, i, nos. 2599, 2618; *CDS*, ii. no. 323; Northumberland County History Committee, *History of Northumberland*, xi, p. 254. For a brief account of Walter de Huntercombe's service to the English crown during the Scottish wars, see C. H. Hunter Blair, 'Northern knights at Falkirk, 1298', *Archaeologia Aeliana*, 4th Series, 25 (1947), pp. 85–6.
116. Hodgson, *History of Northumberland*, III, i, pp. 181–2, 197; *Placita de quo warranto*, ed. Illingworth, pp. 229, 601.

117. Hodgson, *History of Northumberland*, II, ii, p. 250; See also Northumberland Record Office, ZSW/1/1/30. For Swinburne interests in Tynedale, see the old, but still useful, M. F. Moore, *The Lands of the Scottish Kings in England* (London, 1915), pp. 41–7.
118. Neville, 'The earls of Strathearn', i, p. 84; J. G. Smith, *The Parish of Strathblane and its Inhabitants from Early Times: A Chapter of Lennox History* (Glasgow, 1886), p. 130, n. 5; Moore, *Lands of the Scottish Kings*, p. 41; NAS, GD 220/2/37, 38, 39; *CDS*, i, no. 2155.
119. *Edward I and the Throne of Scotland, 1290–1296*, ed. E. L. G. Stones and G. G. Simpson, 2 vols (Oxford, 1978), ii, p. 220.
120. Stevenson, *Documents*, ii, pp. 40, 46, 49.
121. *CDS*, ii, no. 823.
122. Ibid. no. 742; *Chron. Fordun*, i, p. 325.
123. *The Northumberland Lay Subsidy Roll of 1296*, ed. C. M. Fraser (Newcastle-upon-Tyne, 1968), nos. 281, 298. For other assessments, see nos. 107, 286, 293, 308, 311.
124. *CCR, 1296–1302*, pp. 80–1.
125. N. B. Lewis, 'The English forces in Flanders, August–November 1297', in R. W. Hunt, W. A. Pantin and R. W. Southern (eds), *Studies in Medieval History presented to Frederick Maurice Powicke* (Oxford, 1969), p. 313.
126. See, for example, TNA, E 145/59/27.
127. Malise III's movements during the war are reviewed in detail in Neville, 'Political allegiance', pp. 138–41.
128. Discussions of Bruce's political decisions after 1297 are numerous, but see especially, A. A. M. Duncan, 'The community of the realm of Scotland and Robert Bruce: a review', *Scottish Historical Review*, 45 (1966), p. 199; E. L. G. Stones, 'The submission of Robert Bruce to Edward I, c. 1301–1302', *Scottish Historical Review*, 34 (1955), p. 126; Barrow, *Robert Bruce*, p. 159.
129. *CPR, 1292–1301*, pp. 513, 577. Robert III de Muschamp's grandfather, Thomas, had married Maud, the daughter of William de Vescy of Alnwick. Hedley, *Northumberland Families*, i, p. 39. For the Vescys' activities during the wars of Scottish independence, see Stringer, 'Nobility and identity', pp. 199–239.
130. TNA, C 47/22/6/47; Macdonald, 'Kings of the wild frontier?', pp. 153–4.
131. *CPR, 1301–07*, p. 100.
132. F. Watson, *Under the Hammer: Edward I and Scotland, 1286–1307* (East Linton, 1998), p. 193.
133. Barrow, *Robert Bruce*, pp. 173–4; Watson, *Under the Hammer*, pp. 200–07.
134. TNA, SC 1/61/12; *CDS*, ii, no. 1481; *CCR, 1302–07*, p. 138.
135. *CDS*, ii, no. 1847; *CDS*, iii, no. 38; *The Register of William Greenfield Lord Archbishop of York, 1306–1315*, ed. A. H. Thompson, 5 vols (Durham, 1931–40), iv, no. 2001.
136. *Registrum Palatinum Dunelmense: The Register of Richard de Kellawe, Lord Palatine and Bishop of Durham, 1311–16*, ed. T. D. Hardy, 4 vols (London,

1873–8), iv, pp. 108–10; Hodgson, *History of Northumberland*, III, ii, pp. 354–8.
137. TNA, C 47/22/6/47.
138. The dispute is discussed at length in Fawcett and Oram, *Melrose Abbey*, pp. 36, 226–8, where the authors, however, mistakenly refer to the lands of Hassendean, rather than Hassington.
139. TNA, E 145/59/10/462.
140. Fawcett and Oram, *Melrose Abbey*, p. 227.
141. C. J. Neville, 'The political allegiance of the earls of Strathearn during the war of independence', *Scottish Historical Review*, 65 (1986), pp. 133–53.
142. See here Barrow, *Robert Bruce*, pp. 249–50.
143. *CCR, 1302–07*, p. 392; TNA, C 81/1772.
144. TNA, E 159/84, m. 32d.
145. TNA, E 368/85, m. 16d.
146. Northumberland County History Committee, *History of Northumberland*, i, p. 380; TNA, DURH 3/2, fo. 4; I. Kershaw, 'The great famine and agrarian crisis in England 1315–1322', *Past & Present*, 59 (1973), pp. 6–50; Miller, 'Northern England', pp. 258–9.
147. *RRS*, v, no. 444.
148. A Robert de Muschamp 'of the county of Edinburgh' and Thomas de Muschamp of Lanarkshire performed homage to Edward I at Berwick in 1296, and Alan de Muschamp was active in the affinity of Earl Malise III of Strathearn in the closing years of the thirteenth century, but the name disappears from Scottish record thereafter. *CDS*, ii no. 823, pp. 193, 201, 206; M. Hall, 'John of Strathearn and Alan Muschamp: two medieval men of Strathearn and their seal matrices', *Tayside and Fife Archaeological Journal*, 11 (2005), pp. 80–7.
149. Barrow, *Robert Bruce*, pp. 140–1. Both Grahams suffered deep losses as a consequence of this support. See *Documents and Records Illustrating the History of Scotland*, ed. F. Palgrave (London, 1937), pp. 276, 278, 284, 310, 353–4, 356.
150. *CDS*, ii, no. 1741.
151. M. H. Brown, '*Scoti Anglicati*: Scots in Plantagenet allegiance during the fourteenth century', in A. King and M. A. Penman (eds), *England and Scotland in the Fourteenth Century: New Perspectives* (Woodbridge, 2007), p. 103; see also the same author's 'War, allegiance, and community in the Anglo-Scottish marches: Teviotdale in the fourteenth century', *Northern History*, 41 (2004), pp. 229.
152. Neville, 'Political allegiance', pp. 142–6.
153. *CDS*, ii, no. 1961; Barrow, *Robert Bruce*, pp. 221–2; *CCR, 1307–13*, p. 48.
154. *Melrose Liber*, nos. 376–84; *RRS*, v, nos. 110, 122. For a discussion of the litigation, see ibid. pp. 395, 630–1.
155. *CDS*, iii, no. 361.
156. See, for example, charters of John de Graham lord of Abercorn dated c.

1320, witnessed by Malise IV of Strathearn; *The Binns papers, 1320–1864*, ed. J. Dalyell and J. Beveridge (Edinburgh, 1938), nos. 1–5.
157. Northumberland County History Committee, *History of Northumberland*, i, p. 380; xi, pp. 109, 230, 253, 273, 313, 429; xiv, p. 100.
158. His seal, for example, was one of those appended to the Declaration of Arbroath. *The Declaration of Arbroath*, ed. J. Fergusson (Edinburgh, 1970), p. 4.

CHAPTER 5

Peasants, servitude and unfreedom in Scotland, 1100–1350

In the summer of 1278, in an act of piety that will have earned him the admiration of his noble contemporaries, Sir John Comyn of Badenoch made a gift to the Augustinian abbey of Inchaffray of the person of Gille Crìosd Roth ('Ruath, the red-haired'?) son of Gille Ethueny and his future progeny, in perpetuity.[1] The grant was important to the abbey because the canons were engaged at this time in an extensive reorganisation of their estates and a comprehensive building programme, and the manpower that Gille Crìosd and his children represented was much in demand.[2] The gift is also noteworthy because, like other landholders in this part of Strathearn, Sir John was struggling to maintain steady profits in the midst of economic instability. In the later thirteenth century the aristocracy of Scotland was feeling the effects of a rapidly expanding rural economy and of a countryside deeply affected by climatic and environmental fluctuation. It was a generous lord indeed – and an increasingly rare one – who was willing to part with peasant labour in a period when it was at such a premium.

In 1278 the grant and sale of unfree persons, almost always with their progeny, had a venerable history in Scotland. Scholars have long been aware of the existence in the thirteenth-century kingdom of a stratum of landless labourers whose ability to move unfettered about the medieval countryside, to create independent family units, or to establish themselves in trade or rural occupations was severely circumscribed by custom, tradition or law, or some combination of these three. They are equally well aware that, by the end of the fourteenth century, rather suddenly, serfdom 'seems completely to have disappeared'.[3] The reasons for its demise were many and varied. Some were the consequences of long-standing features of the Scottish rural scene. Often cited in this context are the existence in the northern kingdom of a mixed pastoral and agrarian economy, as well as the relatively limited spread of a manorial system on the typical Anglo-Norman model, both of which necessitated a smaller workforce than was the case in the densely populated south of England. Other reasons were the results of more recent developments, notably the easing of pressure on available labour resources in some parts of the kingdom in the midst of war with England and periodic visitations of the plague, which worked to the advantage of a peasantry now able to command better working conditions and higher living standards.[4] The survival of a handful of estate surveys has enabled historians to recreate with some confidence the stages by which the peasants of later medieval Scotland were able to achieve their 'march' towards freedom. Professor Duncan's meticulous study of the extents of Kelso abbey and Coldingham priory, dated to 1290 and c. 1298 respectively,[5] enabled him to conclude with some confidence that already at the turn of the fourteenth century 'personal servility and labour services were much on the wane'.[6] Professor Nicholson's examination of a rental compiled for the lord of Dalkeith in 1376–7 has shown how, less than a century later, rural people in eastern Scotland were taking advantage of the 'considerable opportunities for economic and social advancement' that the post-plague years had generated.[7] There exists, then, general agreement among scholars that by c. 1350 the peasants of Scotland had experienced a dramatic transformation in economic circumstances, which in turn led to significant change in their personal and legal status.

There is, by contrast, little consensus about the ways in which people of the lowest ranks of society experienced unfreedom and servility in the years before conditions improved in the fourteenth century, and therefore scope for an examination of extant record materials relating to the earlier medieval peasantry. How common, for example, was Sir John Comyn's grant of 1278 to Inchaffray abbey? What were the effects of actions like his on people such as Gille Crìosd Roth and his children? What role did the crown, in its capacity as a judicial and legislative authority, play in creating, then perpetuating, the conditions that favoured unfreedom? The uneven nature of extant source materials from the period before 1350 has made it difficult for historians to assess the extent of the trade in human beings in Scotland, and few have ventured much comment on the subject beyond remarking that the rural economy of the kingdom in the high Middle Ages rested on the services of 'tillers of the soil' whose status approximated that of slavery.[8] This chapter examines evidence relating to the peasantry of Scotland from the central medieval period to the mid-fourteenth century. It revisits extant charter texts and other written records that scholars have already examined, and some of its arguments echo the findings of previous studies. It seeks primarily, however, to understand the ways in which the changing economic, political and social landscapes that characterised the 'Anglo-Norman era' affected people of low social rank, especially those of Gaelic ethnicity. Although a close comparison between Scotland and its Irish neighbour in particular can be problematic, the argument is made here that the conditions that led to the transformation of the social and legal status of a broad spectrum of the indigenous population in Ireland after 1171 were in many respects similar to those that affected the peasants in the course of the 'feudalisation' or Europeanisation of Scotland. There are, in short, strong parallels between the experiences of the Irish and Scottish peasantry; the Irish evidence, much more plentiful than that relating to Scotland, offers a useful model by which to examine conditions in Scotland.

Slavery in medieval Scotland

A recent survey of the kingdom in the high Middle Ages repeats the widely held opinion that 'Scotland in 1100 most certainly knew slavery',[9] that is, a category of persons who had no legal competence or any capacity to move about in unrestricted fashion. Written records composed on the English side of the Anglo-Scottish border line confirm this view. Chronicle accounts that describe Scottish incursions of the period leave little doubt, moreover, that English observers regarded this kind of traffic in human beings as utterly barbaric. Symeon of Durham, for example, accused Mael Coluim III of conducting slave raids under the guise of campaigns of territorial expansion, and wrote of the awful fate that awaited the people whom the king took back to Scotland as booty.[10] Later in the twelfth century John of Hexham penned a diatribe against the Gallovidians who fought in the army that David I led into northern England in 1138. These, he charged, indiscriminately slaughtered the men they caught, sparing their widows and daughters in order to carry them off into ignominious slavery.[11] The chronicler further underscored the savagery of the Gaels when he noted their refusal to emulate King David's Christian charity in restoring captives to their freedom.[12]

While commentators such as Symeon of Durham, John of Hexham and others portrayed the seizure and maltreatment of English subjects as the actions of an uncivilised race, their attitudes in respect of enslavement in general were rather more ambiguous. This was no doubt because the rulers of pre-Conquest England were themselves still struggling to abolish slavery.[13] Thus, the biographer of Mael Coluim III's sainted wife, Margaret, for example, made much of the queen's efforts to discover the identity of English prisoners of war the length and breadth of her realm so that she might purchase their freedom,[14] but he had remarkably little to say about the indigenous Gaels who shared their fate. There are, in fact, indications that in twelfth-century Scotland, the reforming church had made few, if any, inroads against the keeping of slaves, especially those of Gaelic origin. Although legend had it that St Ninian of Whithorn (d. c. 432) had abolished the trade in human beings throughout the kingdom, the vigorousness of Scottish contacts with the Dublin-based slave trade is well attested as late as the 1170s,[15] as are the sale and export of Gaels to the Scandinavian realms.[16] Moreover, the clerics who immortalised Scottish saints in carefully crafted hagiographies themselves betrayed a tacit acceptance of, or at least a notable indifference towards, the ownership of slaves. Ailred of Rievaulx's casual mention of the rape of a 'servant girl' by a nobleman of Strathclyde in a story about Ninian's powers of perception is surely an oblique reference to an assault done by a master upon a slave;[17] less veiled is the laconic recounting by the author of a fragmentary life of Kentigern of the treatment that, in the saint's day, was meted out to women found guilty of fornication. According to this writer, the law prescribed one penalty for noblewomen and another, designed specifically to humiliate, for a slave girl.[18] Jocelyn of Furness's *vita* of Kentigern, composed around 1180, retells at great length the miracles attributed to the saint, but although these were many and varied, they did not, apparently, include the freeing of enslaved persons.

Historians quite appropriately regard hagiographical source materials as problematic, but the impression that the eleventh- and twelfth-century *vitae* convey of a tolerance of the enslavement of native Gaels finds echoes in other kinds of written evidence. Some years ago Professor Barrow drew attention to the reference in documents dating to the reigns of Kings David I and Malcolm IV to persons known variously as *cumelache*, *cumelagas* or *cum lawes*, and *cumherbas* or *cum herbes*, and to the etymological link between these terms and the old Irish words *cumal* and *comarba*, signifying, respectively, 'bondswoman or female slave' and 'hereditary servile tenant'.[19] He noted also the tendency of thirteenth-century clerks to translate these terms into Latin with the less offensive *fugitivi*, 'runaway serfs or slaves', and implied that the disappearance of the Gaelic words from written record was coincident with the last stages of widespread slavery in the kingdom. The term *cumelache* and its variants did become obsolete: they are last used in Scotland in documents dating from the earliest years of the reign of William I.[20] As discussed below, however, the reasons for the disappearance of the terms may have had more to do with a change in terminology than a real shift in societal attitudes towards unfree persons. The words were dropped from Irish usage too, around the year 1100.[21] The decline of the conditions associated with slavery in Ireland, however, once portrayed as an achievement of the Anglo-Norman settlers, was in reality a much more gradual process altogether, and in many places more apparent than real well into the late Middle Ages. The pejorative terms used to identify slaves may have fallen into disuse, but the *biataigh* who were their successors in the Lordship lacked the status and dignity of personhood, just as had their enslaved predecessors. Irish scholars have examined in great detail the process by which slaves and persons of low status were transformed into the betaghry. Many of their findings are highly relevant in the Scottish context.

Unfreedom in Ireland to c. 1350

Well into the eleventh century, Irish society drew clear distinctions among persons of low status, some of whom had few or no rights at law. The so-called 'base clients' of early Ireland lived an onerous existence, owing extensive labour services to their lords, but in the eyes of the law they were free, and able to leave the lord's property at will. The *fuídir*, the *bothach* and the *senchleíthe*, by contrast, were only semi-free, their ability to move about the countryside closely hedged about by lordly claims to their persons, their children and their labour. At the very bottom of the social scale was the slave (*cumal*, female; *mug*, male), who enjoyed neither rights nor protection at law.[22] Historians have duly acknowledged the influence of the Christian church in discouraging the ownership of slaves, but they have emphasised also the continuing importance of the trade in human beings to the political ambitions of the rival factions who fought for control of Ireland and to the highly structured rural economy of the high medieval period, both of which played an important role in perpetuating the existence of an unfree underclass.[23]

Gerald of Wales and others of his ilk may have credited the English with effecting a 'civilising' influence on the Gaels of his day,[24] but the legacy of the slaving past in Ireland was enduring, and the chronicler's own comments reveal that, like so many of his contemporaries, he was much more alarmed at the prospect that English people might fall under the yoke of slavery than he was at the lot of unfree men and women of Irish descent. The establishment of the Lordship of Ireland saw incoming noblemen restructure the rural economy. Although scholars now reject as both simplistic and anachronistic the portrayal of the years after 1171 as a period that witnessed the introduction of ready-made 'manorial organisation and feudal law' identical to that of England,[25] there is general agreement that the transformation of the rural landscape had a profound impact on the social and legal status, as well as the material well-being, of the indigenous peasantry.[26] Some native landowners were able to secure favourable terms from the new nobility which enabled them to hold land as free tenants. As one scholar has aptly noted, '[t]he giving of a charter ... implied a recognition of the legal status of the recipient (and of his heirs after him)'.[27] These fortunate few stood on an equal footing with incoming English tenants. Below them were ranged burgesses, farmers, gavillers and cottars, still recognised at law as free, but owing a variety of rents or labour services, or both, to a lord, and restricted in their ability to move off the manor.[28] Irish estate rentals show that the servile obligations and the rents paid by the free tenants might vary widely from manor to manor, but common to all are the relatively favourable conditions under which such peasants lived.[29]

The estate surveys make it clear, however, that a great many native Irish proved unable to secure either the free status or the better living conditions that these more fortunate tenants enjoyed. Here again, recent scholarship has tended to treat as overly simplistic the view put forward by Edmund Curtis early last century that incoming noblemen indiscriminately lumped into the ranks of the new betaghry not merely peasants who had, before 1171, been considered and treated at Irish law as unfree, but also untold numbers of 'semi-free or quite free tenants'. The same fate, he argued, had befallen the poor people of England after 1066, 'when numerous "socmen" and "thegns" were depressed into little better than villein status'.[30] Yet, historians acknowledge that Curtis was essentially accurate, first, in his identification of the betaghry as of predominantly native Irish descent, and second, in his conclusion that the *biataigh* of the Lordship came to include not merely hereditary serfs, but also 'typical Irish commoners', persons of low status who had been free before the coming of the English.[31] Irish society in the Lordship, moreover, was not static, and over the course of the thirteenth century, owing to the regular partitioning of peasant holdings among children, the betaghry came to include men and women whose parents or grandparents had formerly been legally free, even prosperous, commoners.[32] There must also, during the thirteenth century at least, have been a steady supply of new recruits into the betaghry from the ranks of the poorest English and Welsh gavillers and cottars.

If Irish historians have hotly debated the origins of the servile tenants of the Lordship, there is more consensus among them about the ways in which Gaelic men and women experienced unfreedom. The betaghs performed an essential function in the economy of newly established manors as the chief source of labour on the demesne, just as did the villeins of post-Conquest England. Rentals of the manors of Lisronagh, Swords and Finglas, as well as of the estates belonging to the bishops of Cloyne, reveal that they carried out the heavy work of ploughing, tilling, reaping and stacking sheaves, as well as other tasks such as carting, digging ditches and peat, cutting trees for fuel and grinding corn. They paid a rent to the lord for the lands that they held, initially rendered in kind, but also, by the late thirteenth century, in coin. They could own no chattels of their own,[33] and were liable to pay both merchet and heriot, the former for a bond woman to marry off the estate, the second a fine by an unfree man's family surrendered on the occasion of his death. Although conditions after 1200 generally worked to the advantage of the betaghs by increasing the average size of individual holdings and improving material conditions in the countryside,[34] the English law of the settlers treated them as the property of their lords. Accordingly, their owners might give them away or sell them, with or without their holdings. The high value placed on betagh labour in the economic climate of thirteenth-century Ireland is apparent in the grants of their persons, together with that of their children, which pious landlords made to the church. One such gift, dated, c. 1235, assigned to the priory of All Saints near Dublin the person of Reginald Mackelegan, together with three of his kinsmen and others of his *nacio*, a group that must have represented a welcome addition to the monastery's workforce.[35] The value of betagh labour is reflected even more clearly in the alacrity with which the English enacted legislation designed to protect landowners' claims to their unfree tenants. The treaty of Windsor of 1175 made provision for the pursuit and seizure of betaghs – called *nativi* in this context – who attempted to flee their estates.[36] The writs that in England enabled lords to sue for recovery of fugitive villeins were in operation in Ireland as early as 1204, and appear to have been widely used throughout the thirteenth century.[37] As in England, moreover, unfreedom had a significance that was not merely legal. It entailed, for a considerable segment of the Gaelic population, a daily existence that was regulated at every turn, strictly limited and closely supervised.

In Ireland, as elsewhere, however, the weight of local custom acted as a check to the arbitrary exercise of lordly power and authority. The scholars who have examined surviving rentals and extents are near unanimous in finding that betagh lands lay in compact units, set apart from other portions of the manor, and that serfs worked these in family groups.[38] Charter texts suggest that children were only seldom separated from their parents. The prevalence of native Gaels among the ranks of the unfree on manors the length and breadth of the Lordship meant that in most places, members of a kindred group were able to communicate among themselves in their own language, and to form familial and other relationships with people who shared common cultural references. Collectively, these features of manorial life must have gone some way towards encouraging the betagh community to forge a genuine, if hardscrabble, sense of local cohesion. A peasant labour force, moreover, that was perpetually hungry, ill and overworked was bound to be unhappy, its members liable to take flight at any opportunity. These factors, combined with an ongoing need for able-bodied manpower as the manorial economy expanded (especially on ecclesiastical estates), mitigated against the lords' attempts to work their peasants too hard or to charge exorbitant rents. Finally, some cold comfort may have been provided the betaghs by the knowledge that their lowly status was not the exclusive preserve of the indigenous Gaels. Thirteenth- and fourteenth-century records reveal that the fragmentation of estates over several generations may have had proven as impoverishing to poor tenants of English or Welsh descent as it was to natives.[39]

Beyond the boundaries of the Lordship, in the Gaelicised portions of the island the disruptions that accompanied the English settlement of Ireland had only a limited effect on the ways in which rural society functioned and unfree peasants lived much as they had for centuries. A mid-fourteenth-century survey of the estates of Cloyne describes in detail the broad-ranging authority that the bishop continued to exercise over the persons and property of the peasants described as *ascripti glebae*.[40] The survey is in many respects unique and it is of late date, but the conditions on episcopal manors that it describes are believed to have prevailed in 'most of the dioceses of Ireland' in the period before the establishment of the Lordship.[41] The world of the unfree who worked the lands of secular noblemen is more poorly documented, but the legal status of this segment of the Irish peasantry does not appear to have differed much from that of the *ascripti*.[42] Much as it had done before 1170, native law continued to recognise as unfree the children born to thirled parents, as well as those who lost their title to personal freedom as a consequence of legal judgments. The Cloyne survey is notable for its allusion to groups of serfs who were related by blood, like the O Monganes of Balymacstrony and the O Karnys of the town.[43] In Gaelicised Ireland, it would appear, the early medieval concept of 'servile clans' was still current well into the late Middle Ages.[44]

The Unfree in Scotland to c. 1350

The legal, social and economic developments that transformed the slaves of early medieval Ireland into the betaghs of the Lordship had many parallels in Scotland during the 'Anglo-Norman era' and beyond, though there were also some notable differences between the realms. In Scotland, as in Ireland, the attitude of the church towards the enslavement of Christian peoples had important implications for the legal status, if not the material conditions, of persons of low rank. The aspiration of Mael Coluim III and his successors to align themselves wholeheartedly with the tenets of the reforming papacy have been comprehensively examined by historians; they included the establishment (or re-establishment) of the episcopal structure of the *ecclesia Scoticana*, the introduction to the kingdom of new European monastic orders, the steady replacement of the Céli Dé communities of hermits and priests with religious houses that were more acceptable to the advocates of reform and, more generally, a concerted effort to 'rub off all tarnish of barbarity' that soiled their royal persons.[45] English chroniclers were particularly anxious to rehabilitate the reputation of the Scottish monarchy after 1124, when the youngest of the sons of Mael Coluim and Margaret, David, a good friend and the brother-in-law of Henry I, succeeded to the throne. This endeavour is apparent in their efforts to distinguish the young ruler's honourable behaviour in the campaigns of 1138 from the savage conduct of his Gallovidian recruits; it is detectable also in John of Hexham's account of David's anxiety, in the summer of the same year, to restore to freedom the captives he had taken in war.[46] In staging this act in an elaborate ceremony conducted at the door of Carlisle cathedral, the chronicler deliberately evoked manumission ceremonies then current in England, the purpose of which was to endow the act of emancipating serfs – persons who, like captives of war, had no freedom – with a quasi-religious dignity.[47] The exemplary nature of David's actions was, in this sense, very much in keeping with the king's avowed intention to 'civilise' the rude people of Scotland whom God had entrusted to his care.

As was the case elsewhere in the British Isles, however, slavery as a distinct legal category may have been abolished in Scotland at the behest of an enlightened ruler, but the personal and social disabilities associated with the lack of freedom endured well beyond David's reign. They did so, moreover, for many of the same reasons as they did in Ireland. In the century or so after 1124 significant portions of the kingdom were colonised by a new aristocracy, invited by the crown to come from England and northern France and to settle on highly advantageous terms. Much as would occur in Ireland a generation and more later, the incoming noblemen sought to recreate on new soil a manorial economy modeled on that which had been the basis of their families' prosperity in their homelands.[48] As part and parcel of this process they introduced new concepts about how to generate wealth on their estates and clear notions about the 'sharp distinction' between free and unfree persons.[49] As they did in Ireland (and Wales), incoming lords brought some settlers with them to Scotland,[50] but most confidently expected that they could adapt the indigenous social structure to their own uses. The consequence of such an attitude was the assimilation, within the ranks of the thirled peasantry, of a substantial number of tenants who had previously enjoyed some rights and privileges at law. The rapidity with which the new lordships took root in the landscape of Scotland, chiefly south of Forth, moreover, suggests that the settlers successfully translated their ambitions into action.

As occurred a little later in Ireland, a few elements of the native population were able to negotiate favourable arrangements with the incoming aristocracy which enabled them to function much as they had before the twelfth century, as free, independent farmers. Such, for example, were Robert son of Maccus, who obtained from the king (or had confirmed to him) land in Roxburghshire; Yothre Mac Gilhys, who got land in the newly settled region of Moray; and Thurstan son of Osulf, who was granted half a ploughgate in Ednam.[51] In Angus, in the first half of the thirteenth century, the freemen Fearchar Macholf and Cinaed Mac Gillechiar held land in return for rents payable to the monks of Coupar Angus;[52] Gille Thomas Mac Alef controlled a much larger half davach at Kingoldrum.[53] Two native tenants by the name of Gille Magu (Gille Machoi?) Mac Aldie and Gille Crìosd Kide similarly retained possession of their tenements under the new lordship of Kelso abbey,[54] and recent research on the twelfth-century settlement of the parish and barony of Lesmahagow has shown that a handful of native landholders managed to survive relatively unscathed the influx of Flemish colonisers.[55] As in Ireland, then, some native landholders sought written charters attesting their title to land, perceiving these 'as a mechanism for securing or ensuring permanence of possession or use'.[56] Many more free tenants did not receive such title, but their continued status as free persons of consequence may be deduced from the frequency with which, the length and breadth of the kingdom, the crown and members of the new aristocracy called upon men of native descent to bear reliable witness at inquests of various kinds. The settlement of quarrels involving disputed estate boundaries, the appropriation of parish revenues for the endowment of new monasteries, the identification of the lawful heir to a disputed inheritance: all were aspects of the reorganisation of the Scottish landscape that newly settled ecclesiastical and secular lords undertook in the opening decades of the 'Anglo-Norman era', and all were accomplished with the willing cooperation of local landholders anxious to preserve rank and status. Thus, in 1200, a perambulation of the marches of an estate near Peebles brought together a 'melting pot' of recognitors that included landed men of both Cumbric and Gaelic descent from the locality.[57] The testing clauses of charters offer equally sure evidence of the survival, in the newly settled regions, of an order of free tenants, fulfilling their obligation to perform suit of court and, more generally, to bear witness to noble acts. The solemn ceremonies that marked the foundation of a Cistercian house at Melrose abbey in the reign of David I, for example, were attended not only by the cream of the new nobility of the border region, but also by a group of local native worthies described as 'the men of those parts', including Ulfkil son of Æthelstan, Osulf son of Uhtred, Maccus son of Undweyn, and others.[58] The texts of hundreds of royal, ecclesiastical and secular charters also attest the presence, throughout the kingdom, of native persons of modest but legally acknowledged rank and status. Royal and baronial deeds of the late twelfth century addressed the 'thanes and drengs' of the Merse and Lothian,[59] and a community of similar tenants mixed freely with their new Flemish lords in Clydesdale.[60] David I, Malcolm IV and William I occasionally invoked in their documents references to free persons of French, English, Scottish and, sometimes, Gallovidian descent, all of whom, presumably, they considered deserving of inclusion within the general category of *probi homines* of the kingdom.[61] Barrow's comment that the addresses employed in the charters of David I and his son, Earl Henry, have much to reveal about the 'remarkable cross-section of twelfth-century Scottish society' is not merely apt,[62] it serves as a salutary reminder of the fact that some landholders, at least, were able to weather the disruptions that accompanied the influx of foreign aristocrats without catastrophic loss of rank, status or privilege.

The agreements forged between newcomers and natives sometimes required that newly infeft local men hold their land in return for performing military service – Yothre Mac Gilhys, for example, owed serjeanty service in the king's army. Other than the additional obligation to render suit of court, however, more often than not the conditions under which such 'promoted natives'[63] held their estates were not materially or substantially different than those under which their ancestors had lived and worked. Some families, moreover, managed not merely to cling to respectability amidst the changing tenurial conditions of the twelfth century, but to prosper. The descendants of a freeholder settled on the Kelso abbey lands of Fincurrock in the late twelfth century were still in possession of the property a generation and more later.[64] The extant deeds relating to the priory of Coldingham tell the story of a villein of Prendergast, Berwickshire, who was able to abandon his state of bondage to become a burgess of Berwick.[65]

The changing tenurial environment of the new twelfth-century lordships of lowland Scotland made it imperative that promoted natives such as Yothre Mac Gilhys set their new relationships on a legal footing, and secure on behalf of future generations a permanent record of their status as free tenants. As noted, some did so by obtaining charters of infeftment of their lords, and it is highly likely that in Scotland, as in Ireland, many more of these charters were written than the small number of surviving deeds would suggest.[66] A similar concern to anchor themselves firmly among the ranks of the landholding elite is apparent, albeit later, in the territorial lordships that remained under the control of native earls. The fortuitous survival of a handful of documents from the Lennox of Earl Maoldomhnaich (d. c. 1250) sheds valuable light on the otherwise sparsely documented world of Scottish Gaeldom in the early thirteenth century, and in particular on the ways in which indigenous landholders in these parts of the kingdom, too, scrambled for position and privilege in a period of political and social change. A series of written *acta* issued under the authority of the earl established Maurice (Muirchertach?) son of Gilleasbuig Galbraith; Gille Mícheil, Gille Martain and Gille Condad, the sons of Gille Mícheil; Maoldomhnaich and Gille Moire of Luss; and the earl's own brothers, Amhlaibh and Gille Críosd, as feu tenants. All made sure that their charters confirmed them in free and heritable possession of their estates, quit of all obligations save that of rendering the rounds of cheese that were the traditional contribution of the province's landed freeholders to the king's army.[67] Some of these men in turn entrenched their sons' rights by seeking from their lord confirmation of these arrangements.[68] Absolon son of Mac Beatha's charter of the island of Clarinch in Loch Lomond is of especial interest, in that it specified that he was to hold his land of the earl 'free and quit of any secular or servile dues'.[69] As Alexander Grant has shown with respect to their counterparts in nearby Lesmahagow, these men were aware that the terms laid out in their written charters played a crucial role in identifying rank and status and, ultimately, in determining their place in the tenurial hierarchy of the lordship.[70] Above all, they competed not only for tenure in 'feu and heritage', but also for freedom from the obligation to pay merchet for their daughters, a privilege that set them apart from the masses of the servile.

The impression of some continuity in tenurial conditions at the upper level of rural society that the Lennox documents reveals is discernible also in records relating to the lordship of Galloway. Here, too, some promoted natives successfully secured recognition by the ruling family of their status as independent, if minor, landowners, compelled now to render ancient obligations 'dressed up in new clothes',[71] but still occupying an important place among the privileged ranks of the free tenantry. The great lords of the region were themselves aware of the need to distinguish some of their followers from the rabble. The great variety of business associated with the tenure, conveyance and inheritance of land in which they were involved could not have been conducted without recourse to the local experience vested in such men and the familiarity with native custom to which they might bear witness. In the 1240s, for example, the claims of the monks of Paisley to the estates and revenues associated with the church of Kilpatrick would not have been vindicated without the testimony of native worthies, whose knowledge of the history of the ancient holy site was unrivalled;[72] neither would Patrick of Blantyre have succeeded in securing title to his late father's estates in 1263 without the support of the findings of a jury of Gaelic neighbours whose status gave their opinions weight and their decisions trustworthiness.[73] The native men – and women – who attended the lordly court of Malcolm earl of Atholl in the late twelfth century to witness his *acta* suggest that this magnate family still attracted a large following of native tenants,[74] as did that of the earls of Fife, the most 'feudalised' of the kingdom's Gaelic noblemen.[75]

If the upheavals that marked the establishment of new lordships in Scotland after 1124 had a dislocating effect on the ranks of some independent freeholders, they had more dire consequences still for the lowliest members of the peasant population. Here, as in Ireland, incoming lords were anxious to transform the small, scattered estates of their new homeland into profit-generating fermtouns. Contemporary charters, it is true, 'fall short of being a comprehensive source for peasant liabilities and dues, their classification, origin and relative importance',[76] but these sources none the less offer a wealth of information about the social and personal disabilities associated with legal unfreedom in this period of transition, and there is no mistaking the increasing clarity with which contemporary observers identified, and distinguished from other rural workers, persons who were bound to the land.

Just as some native landholders secured for themselves a firm, if modest, position on the lowest rungs of landholding tenantry, so did some unfree persons turn the upheavals that accompanied the settlement of aristocratic newcomers to their advantage. Glimpses of their efforts are few, but instructive. Towards the end of the twelfth century the monasteries of lowland Scotland experienced a period of rapid expansion, establishing new touns the length and breadth of their substantial holdings. Economic urgency lay behind the decision of some abbots to raise a handful of formerly thirled men to the status of free tenants. In this fashion, Osbert, once a bondman, became the 'liege man' of the monks of Kelso, charged with paying them a rent of 8s per annum for a ploughgate at Midlem, as well as with performing several days of boon work every year.[77] Soon thereafter, the prior of Coldingham likewise granted legal freedom to one Haldan and all his heirs, on condition that the new tenant remain on the land and agree to farm twenty nearby acres.[78] Documenting the manumission of unfree persons in the twelfth- and thirteenth-century kingdom is an exercise fraught with difficulty; few monastic administrators thought to record such business transactions on parchment rolls as carefully as did, for example, successive priors of Durham.[79] Extant charter texts, however, like those that transformed the fortunes of Osbert and Haldan, suggest that the reorganisation of the rural economy which incoming aristocrats, and perhaps especially the new religious houses, undertook from c. 1124 onwards generated at least some opportunity for upward movement among the ranks of the indigenous peasantry. Here again, it is highly likely that the survival of a mere handful of written sources conceals considerable activity on the ground. The wording of a later fourteenth-century royal charter granting his freedom to a man bound to the lands of Tannadyce echoes that found in hundreds of similar documents from England in the thirteenth, its formulaic phrases and enrolment in chancery indicative of a practice that was by then routine.[80]

Osbert and Haldan, however, were the exception rather than the rule, and in the middle decades of the twelfth century many more peasants experienced at first hand the harsh consequences of legal unfreedom. Soon after his accession to the throne, in a mix of pious sentiment and pragmatism, David I granted to the abbey that his parents had founded at Dunfermline 'my own men Ragewin, Gillephadruig and Ulchil'.[81] The king's charter was but the first in a long line of similar grants of persons, some made under royal authority, others at the behest of noblemen anxious to supply the new monastic houses of the realm not merely with the estates, parish revenues, mills and other resources that would become the basis of the immense wealth of the Scottish church, but also with the manpower needed to realise a steady income from these properties. Before the end of the twelfth century, the monks of Jedburgh, Kelso and Dryburgh were welcoming similar gifts from local magnates, native and newcomer,[82] and in the opening decade of the thirteenth the Benedictines of Coldingham were accepting thirled labourers as payment for undischarged debts.[83] Simple grants such as these, in which a donor transferred ownership of a named person and his kindred, continued unabated until the end of the thirteenth century, from Berwickshire northwards into the region beyond Forth. Sir John Comyn's grant to Inchaffray of the serf Gille Crìosd Roth in 1278 was but a late manifestation of this kind of transaction. Lordly action need not, moreover, explain the unhappy fate of all such people. Grant's suggestion that some Scottish peasants lost their freedom because they were 'oppressed by their own class' is particularly apt in the context of the changing agricultural economy of the 'Anglo-Norman era'.[84]

Already in the late twelfth century landlords ecclesiastical and secular were demonstrating a growing preoccupation with the adequate provision of peasant labour for their estates. Their concern is apparent in the increasingly elaborate terminology of charters of endowment and infeftment. Just as the recipients of lordly favour sought to ensure that the deeds they commissioned included specific mention of all the natural resources, land- and water-based, real and potential, associated with their new estates, so did they insist that increasingly lengthy lists of appurtenances identify also the human resources that were indispensable to the full exploitation of their lands. Thus, in 1162 the canons of Dryburgh made sure that Hugh de Morville's gift of a half a carucate at Newtonhall included the 'men of the place';[85] so, too, did the monks of Lindores insist that a charter of Earl David of Huntingdon giving them estates in Garioch assign them title to the properties 'together with the men who dwell on those estates and their issue'.[86] Hugh Giffard's new lordship at Fintry in Angus, a reward from Earl David, consisted not merely of land, but also of 'all the *nativi* dwelling there'.[87] It was only with their labour that Gifford could hope to transform this wild and uncultivated part of Tayside into a going concern.

Few landholders were more assiduous in this regard than the great monasteries of lowland Scotland. In the confirmations of their vast holdings that the heads of these houses began regularly to solicit from the crown after 1150, it is rare not to find a clause making mention, as did those of Malcolm IV to Kelso, William I to Holyrood, and Alexander II to Dunfermline, of the monks' firm claims to the serfs who lived on their lands.[88] By 1237 clauses such as the one found in a grant by Sir Thomas de Aunay in favour of Melrose abbey indicate how thoroughly had the transfer of ownership over persons and the association between land and its attendant workforce become customary in the business of conveyance. Aunay's charter gifted to the monks a bloc of estates in Dumfriesshire, 'with all their pertinents and whatever is found within the bounds of these lands, including men'.[89] Forty years later, the abbot of Dunfermline was still insisting that the resources associated with an estate counted 'all the men and cottars living there, with all their issue'.[90] By the late thirteenth century such attention to detail was already becoming obsolete: by then, donors and beneficiaries alike took for granted that the appurtenances attached to lands everywhere included some of the men, women and children – those of no legal status – who lived there.

The steadily expanding rural economy of the period between roughly 1150 and 1300 had an important effect on the development of the early stages of a Scottish law of property with respect to unfree persons. The half century that followed the creation of new secular lordships and the endowment of new religious houses after the accession of David I, it has been said, 'profoundly affected, indeed may be said to have determined, the feudal landscape of Scotland'.[91] It also generated a heavy demand for peasant labour among lords anxious to turn their new acres into productive ventures. Gifts such as those of King David to Dunfermline or David of Huntingdon to Lindores, cited above, provided much needed manpower, and it is to this early period that the majority of extant charters recording the grant of named serfs belong. The carving out of new fields, the erection of farm buildings, the digging of mill ponds were tasks that required hard labour, and it is in this period, too, that the services that peasants performed first became specifically tied to grants, sales or other transfers of landed property. A late-twelfth-century document records the bishop of Moray's lease to Duncan earl of Fife of an extensive bloc of territory in Stratha'an. The former retained the right to collect all revenues arising from the courts convened on the estates, but he was forced to surrender to Earl Duncan possession of the many *nativi* resident there.[92] Around the same time Richard de Morville became involved in a dispute with Henry de St Clair over the persons of two bondsmen and their respective issue. Morville resigned his claim to them, but stipulated that if St Clair should ever relinquish title to the men, they must return to his service, and his alone.[93] The king himself was involved in the scramble to secure and protect claims to thirled labourers. William I, for example, lost possession of several neyfs and their children when the abbot of Scone successfully brought suit against him.[94] In 1206 a protracted disagreement between the priory of St Andrews and a local lord over rights to the kirktoun of Arbuthnott involved not merely title to the revenues arising from the estate, but, equally important, control over the unfree peasants who occupied it.[95] Wherever ambitious lords sought to develop new land they looked now also to establish and preserve their hold over their *nativi*. Their opponents, when bested, tended to be sore losers. On two occasions the abbot of Scone and the prior of St Andrews reluctantly parted with neyfs and their children only after obtaining from them undertakings to pay annual tributes in recognition of their once-servile status.[96] The neyf Osbert who, thanks to the generosity of the abbot of Kelso, clawed his way into the ranks of the free was nevertheless obligated to provide his new master with boon work and plough service every year.[97]

The brieve of neyfty and its antecendents

In Ireland stiff competition among landlords for control over the labour of an unfree peasantry led to the introduction of the English writ of naifty as early as the reign of King John.[98] The earliest texts of its Scottish equivalent appear in the early fourteenth-century treatise *Regiam Majestatem* in a discussion of how *nativi* might argue their freedom,[99] and in the near-contemporary register of brieves known as *Formulary E*, which reproduced a royal precept for determining the status of a man claimed by a lord as his property.[100] As with the case of perambulation, however, there is abundant evidence that long before the reign of Robert I landlords had at their disposal a regular process for proving title to unfree persons in royal and baronial courts of law. The origins of the Scottish brieve of neyfty lie in the conditions created by the settlement in the twelfth century of a new aristocracy determined to exert firm control over an existing native peasant labour force. In its earliest form, the brieve appears as a precept issued by the king, which either extended comprehensive royal protection over the property of litigants (including their serfs) or compelled observance of a prohibition against the unjust detention of unfree persons said to belong to a complainant.[101] To the first category belong, for example, confirmations by David I and Malcolm IV to the abbeys of Dunfermline and Scone of all their possessions and privileges, including title to any unfree man who might seek to escape thirldom to the monasteries' lands.[102] Royal acts of protection and confirmation, however, did not always prove effective, and in Scotland, as in Ireland, the efforts of lords to protect their access to peasant labour were beset with problems. Within a decade of receiving its charter of foundation, the monks of Dunfermline were seeking the king's assistance in securing the return of 'fugitive', that is, runaway, neyfs; David responded by setting his seal to a brieve ordering landowners throughout the Lothian region to restore these persons to the abbey, presumably under pain of heavy penalty.[103] Secular landholders, too, found in the exercise of royal authority a powerful and effective tool. One of Dunfermline's neighbours, the woman Levif, obtained a brieve from the king, which enabled her to search for and seize runaway neyfs and to initiate proceedings against those who gave them shelter.[104]

The practice of seeking royal brieves became more frequent in the next reign, and was well established by the closing years of the twelfth century. Thus, Malcolm IV and William I issued written precepts commanding the restitution of their fugitive serfs on behalf of the abbots of Dunfermline, Holyrood and Scone, as well as at the behest of the church of Restenneth in Angus.[105] Such orders were implicit, moreover, in royal confirmations such as those granted in favour of the monks of Kelso in 1159 and 1166, which extended a general protection over all the abbey's possessions and threatened legal sanction against those who would despoil the church of any of its goods.[106] The power of the secular arm to enforce monastic privileges was not lost on contemporary observers. Thus, the Benedictines of Coldingham obtained from their patron, Earl Patrick I of Dunbar, a mandate that commanded his steward to assist them in their ongoing efforts to regain control over serfs who attempted to flee their estates in the Merse.[107]

As occurred in Ireland, the servile population of Scotland took advantage of the widespread upheavals that accompanied the establishment of new aristocratic lordships to flee their surroundings and escape bondage. In Scotland, as in Ireland, moreover, landlords religious and secular became steadily more preoccupied with the problem of runaway neyfs. The identity of the *cumelache*, *cumelawe* and *cumherba* who appear in twelfth-century documents has much preoccupied historians, as has the etymology of the terms used to describe them, but there is no longer any reason to doubt that these were 'servile tenants in Gaelic guise',[108] thirled to estates that belonged to the church. These too, it would appear, were liable to take advantage of the tenurial changes of the period by attempting flight. For this reason they, and other persons designated more specifically as *fugitivi* were the subjects of the new brieves discussed above, in which David I, Malcolm IV and William I assumed responsibility for assisting the heads of the new religious houses to reclaim these valuable assets from would-be depredators.[109] The focus of scholarly discussion on the origins of the *cumal*-stem words, on the relationship between *cumelache* and *fugitivi* and on the earliest brieves concerning neyfty has meant that few historians have considered what else the terms reveal about the nature of the encounter between newcomers and the native Gaels in the twelfth century. If, as Barrow ventured, the words *cumelache, cumelaga* and *cum lawe* are all derived from a female noun, while the roots of *cumherba* lie in the masculine *comarba*, then the distinction that scribes make between the terms may well have been deliberate. Landlords, it would appear, were as preoccupied with the problems posed by runaway women as they were with the flight of the latter's fathers, brothers and sons, and perhaps even more so. Beyond the essential domestic tasks that servile women performed within monastic precincts, in the wider context of the agrarian economy their status as mothers must have made lords regard them as increasingly valuable sources of labour with every new child born. Surviving charters suggest that kings and barons were especially reluctant to give away their female neyfs; they reveal more certainly that lords pursued runaway women as tenaciously as they did fugitive men. Around the year 1200 the Gaelic *cumal*-words were becoming obsolete, a reflection, probably, of the prejudice that saw Latin-trained scribes purge other Gaelic terms from the vocabulary of charter texts. The gender-neutral word *fugitivi* that replaced them has had the effect of obscuring from modern eyes the continuing reality of a law of unfree persons that regarded women as possessions in some respects even more valuable than their male kindred.

Like the *cumelache*, the scolocs of twelfth- and thirteenth-century charters were native Gaels and, like them, tied to church lands (*ascripti glebae*) and indigenous to the region that had once been the kingdom of Alba.[110] The chronicler Reginald of Durham believed that the term originated in the distant Pictish past;[111] instead, it represented another borrowing from Old Irish.[112] As in Ireland, unfreedom lay heavily on them. The peasants resident on the church lands at Inverkeilor owed their lords substantial food rents.[113] The inquest held on the estates of the bishop of St Andrews at Arbuthnott in 1206 shows that a 'multitude' of scolocs performed a wide variety of heavy labour services throughout the agricultural year.[114] More onerous still was the obligation to provide hospitality (conveth, wayting) to the bishop or his agents whenever the latter chose. The onus of furnishing such guests with the appropriate 'necessaries' of food and drink must have represented a severe drain on the scolocs' limited resources. It was perhaps for this reason that one of them, Gilleanndreis the One-footed, proved recalcitrant in rendering his dues[115] and more certainly why the bishop sometimes forgave his people the obligation.[116]

In the thirteenth century the king's chancery was kept busy issuing brieves of protection or ordering the return of *fugitivi* to their owners, first as a matter of course on behalf of the great monastic establishments, but then at the request of smaller houses, such as those at Inchaffray, Pluscarden and Coupar Angus, anxious to prevent the dissipation of their more limited resources.[117] Royal assizes of 1214 and 1230, the first aimed at regulating agricultural activity in the countryside, the second the lordly right of replegiation, alluded to the challenges that disobedient neyfs posed to their owners' economic well-being.[118] Another threatened with heavy fines and other penalties any lord who refused to surrender a neyf who had been adjudged the possession of another man.[119] The earliest compilation of the customs that governed legal procedures in the Anglo-Scottish border lands, drafted in 1249, made specific provision for the capture of Scottish serfs who tried to win their freedom by fleeing into England,[120] and initially at least, tribunals held in the marches proved responsive to the efforts of lords to recover such offenders.[121] Similarly, the customs and practices described in the so-called *Laws of the Four Burghs* portray the early towns of the kingdom as havens for fugitive bondsmen.[122] The *Assise Regis Willelmi*, which includes material datable to the thirteenth century and earlier, also discusses procedures for the capture of fugitive neyfs in royal courts of law.[123]

The records of central government offer instructive glimpses of increasing lordly preoccupation with the control of servile labour as the thirteenth century wore on. The texts of dozens of contemporary charters confirm the impression of a resource that, in the midst of an expanding economy, was growing more scarce and a great deal more valuable. Some of these documents record disputes about control over specific *nativi* and their labour; others relate in minute detail the transfer of landed estates together with all their human and natural assets. All reveal the extent to which the acquisition of men of unfree status, their wives and their children had become an intrinsic feature of the transfer of property. Early in the reign of Alexander II, the restoration of royal power in the province of Moray following the suppression of the rising of Gilleasbuig Mac Uilleim brought to prominence a number of magnates, among them Walter Comyn and Gille Brigte, youngest son of the earl of Strathearn.[124] The erection of new lordships brought some of these men into conflict with the bishop of Moray, and created something of a scramble for control over the local *nativi*, whose labour was essential to the transformation of the land into profitable ventures. A dispute between Comyn and Bishop Andrew over rights to the royal cain in Badenoch, for example, was settled satisfactorily only when the parties agreed to divide ownership of several neyf families.[125] The bishop drove an equally hard bargain when he made arrangements for Gille Brigte to hold the half davach of Glencarnie when he reserved to himself 'all the native men of the said land'.[126]

In 1225 Bishop Walter of Glasgow purchased a brieve of neyfty against a local landholder, successfully claiming ownership of four men and their families.[127] A generation later, the abbot of Lindores likewise made sure that the estate he had been awarded in a dispute with Norman de Leslie counted among its assets the person of 'John son of Malind and all his issue', though Leslie did manage to claim as his own members of the serf's kindred.[128] King Alexander III's chancery clerks continued to issue royal brieves authorising landholders, secular and religious, to pursue runaway neyfs 'wherever they may find them' and prohibiting further depredations of this kind.[129] Likewise, parties involved in the exchange or purchase of property still sought to ensure that their charters of infeftment make specific mention of the *nativi* associated with their lands. In a deed issued in his favour, for example, Alexander de Montfort took care to note that title to a small estate in Athelstaneford, East Lothian, included the three bondsmen who lived there.[130] In imitation of royal example, magnates such as Malise earl of Strathearn granted their tenants leave to search for fugitive serfs within their own territories, and threatened with lordly sanctions anyone who tried to prevent their recovery.[131] Bishop Matthew Crambeth of Dunkeld so valued his *nativi* that in the settlement of Scottish affairs following Edward I's victory in 1304 he asked that letters directed to the sheriffs of Scotland include in their remit power to effect the seizure of 'the private neyfs taken from him' during the recent disturbances.[132] He was urging nothing less than the expansion of the sheriff's regular jurisdiction into an area that Edward's predecessors on the Scottish throne had considered their prerogative.[133]

By 1304, of course, possession of a servile peasant population meant a great deal more to landlords than the ready availability of a workforce. The vast projects of reclamation aimed at creating arable land from wood, waste and marsh and the laying out of fields, meadow and pasture that the incoming aristocracy had initiated in the twelfth century had, in the course of the thirteenth, transformed the nature of aristocratic power in Scotland. Lordship came to mean more than merely dominion over the natural and human resources of an estate; in the brisk economic environment of the period after 1200 it had acquired also, perhaps primarily, a fiscal dimension. This development in turn had a profound effect on the rural population of the kingdom. Neyfs acquired liabilities by virtue of their unfree status at law, becoming assets that appreciated just as did most other commodities. Aristocratic coffers benefited especially richly from the jurisdiction that lords exercised over the persons of their *nativi*, and from the control of the latter's movements on and off the land. Even more than the labour of their serfs, then, lords prized the lucrative renders of merchet and heriot that in Scotland, as elsewhere, were the traditional marks of unfreedom. These prerogatives, together with amercements and forfeitures levied for unlawful behaviour, were the basis of a considerable proportion of aristocratic revenues, and in the thirteenth century they appreciated steadily. The records of Coldingham priory, which are especially plentiful for this period, bear witness to a lively market in land and peasant labour services among the monks' many free tenants, but also a marked tendency on the part of the prior to reserve to his own coffers the monies realised by his unfree workers' renders in merchet and heriot.[134] Well into the fourteenth century, landlords great and small imitated the practice of the monks of Coldingham by maintaining firm control over the fiscal liabilities not merely of neyfs,[135] but, more valuable still, over the portions of their estates designated as bondage lands or bondlands.[136] Well into the fourteenth century these continued to be associated with services the performance of which obviated the need to expend cash on hired labour.

Duncan's masterful – and still unrivalled – survey of the thirteenth-century countryside has shown convincingly that changes to the Scottish economy worked to the benefit of the great mass of the peasantry, not least in creating, then sustaining, conditions that were much less harsh than those under which English villeins toiled.[137] These developments notwithstanding, the legal liabilities associated with lack of status at law remained both very real and very harsh, and in the thirteenth century notions about the lowly status of unfree persons hardened. Contemporary opinion held that *nativi* and persons of 'foul kyn' could not stand as surety in any legal cause, but must place their trust in their lord to act on their behalf. Legal practice also proscribed their participation in judicial duels and cases taken to arbitration, though servile tenants were expected to attend summonses to the royal host. Still another assize stated bluntly that 'a thryll man may haf nan heritage', and severely limited the circumstances under which children born of an unfree mother might succeed to property.[138] Lawyers maintained that bondmen could own no chattels,[139] though as was the case in Ireland among the *betagii*, this was a highly impractical tenet and widely ignored in practice.[140] Many of the legal liabilities that were the subject of royal legislation were probably more honoured in the breach than in their observance. Collectively, however, they attest the fundamental division that

Scottish society, and the legal customs that regulated it, drew between free and unfree persons. When, under Robert I, lawyers set about drafting the earliest extant formularies of Scottish brieves, they sought to create 'manuals of instruction' intended for use in the royal and baronial courts of their day, and they drew freely on practices that had long obtained in the kingdom.[141] The brieve of neyfty, borrowed from the English treatise known as *Glanvill*, was among them, and the procedure for recovering title to unfree persons as it appeared in *Regiam Majestatem* remained in operation for many years thereafter.[142] The ongoing resolution of questions relating to the legal status of *nativi* as matters most appropriately treated within the purview of royal acts of protection underscores the 'royally focussed' nature of Scottish legal procedure.[143] For their part, landlords were amenable to this state of affairs, because the brieve of neyfty was a highly effective legal tool for enforcing control over the serfs who constituted a large segment of their tenantry.

And enforce it they did. Around 1332 the monks of Dunfermline compiled detailed genealogies of a group of neyfs thirled to abbey estates, an act intended simultaneously to establish at law the servile status of each man and his family lest they seek to claim their freedom, and to safeguard the monks' own titles against would-be encroachers.[144] Abbot Alexander was well aware, it would seem, that confronted with the first kind of challenge, one of the tests of a lord's security was the ability to prove descent from servile stock.[145] His expertise served him well a little later on, when he made use of the brieve of neyfty to prove ownership of the neyf Adam son of Causantin and Adam's two sons against the earl of Fife.[146] Concern for the integrity of the servile population of a sitting tenant was again in evidence when King Robert I allowed Maria, the widow of Edmund Comyn of Kilbride, to settle in the thanage of Formartine in Aberdeenshire, as long as she did not claim as her own the *nativi* already resident there.[147]

Historians have become accustomed to citing an action initiated by Bishop Alexander of Moray in 1364 as 'the last recorded legal suit' for the recovery of a runaway serf in Scotland,[148] and it is certainly the case that thereafter the brieve 'fell into desuetude' largely because the heavy demand for labour services that had been so prominent a feature of estate management in the twelfth and thirteenth centuries had all but disappeared.[149] The demise of the legal category of unfree persons has been quite correctly celebrated as representing a significant improvement in the conditions of the late medieval peasantry, even if most unfree men and women were incapable of appreciating it. In 1318, for example, it is highly doubtful that the half dozen poor men who lost title to a series of tiny holdings in Berwickshire when these were granted as a single tenement to an enterprising landholder were in any better position to oppose their lord's will than had been the serfs Osulf and his son Walter when, more than a century earlier, Robert de Prendergast sold them to the prior of Coldingham.[150] The Berwickshire cottars may well have agreed with their fellows, the 'king's husbandmen', who in 1305 complained in parliament about the precariousness of their existence.[151] They were, none the less, legally free, able to move about the countryside as they chose, and able to aspire to the rank of husbandmen by amassing tenements of their own. Osulf and his ilk were not. Until the closing years of the fourteenth century the legal distinction between free and unfree persons marked a profound and enduring cleavage within the ranks of the rural population.

The experience of unfreedom in Scotland to c. 1350

If surviving source materials make it possible to trace the early history of the Scottish law of property as it affected unfree persons, understanding the lived experience of the lowest levels of the peasantry is a much more challenging task. Scribal practice in Anglo-Norman Ireland was consistent in its identification of the lowest sorts of peasants with the Gaels of the island: it referred to them more or less interchangeably as *nativi*, *Hibernici* or, as noted above, *betagii*, a Latinisation of the Irish term *biataigh*.[152] Throughout the period between 1124 and c. 1350, Scottish scribes used the generic terms *nativi*, which historians have traditionally translated as neyfs, *servi* or *bondi*. The words were no less pejorative than *Hibernici*, but they served the useful purpose of distinguishing persons bound by law and custom to the soil from the *liberi tenentes*, *husbandi*, *homines rustici* and *cotarii* who comprised the free population of the countryside. In Scotland, moreover, lack of status at law affected a more diverse ethnic group; as the cartularies of the great monastic houses of the south attest, it consisted of a significant number of Anglians and persons of Anglo-Scandinavian descent. As in Ireland, however, the transformation of the Scottish countryside that saw a great mass of the peasantry lose its legal freedom affected above all the Gaelic-speaking peoples. In Scotland, as in Ireland, then, the medieval peasant experience was shaped as much by ethnic and racial, as by social, mores.

While some newly endowed noblemen may have brought land-hungry peasants with them, most counted on being able to exploit the resident population and the existing social structure to suit their own needs. They found in the Scottish countryside a large supply of unfree persons tied, like the *betagii*, to the soil. Charters such as those that record King William's gift of the neyf Gillaindreis Mac Suthern and his progeny to Dunfermline abbey, Richard de Morville's grant of Gille Mícheil and his kindred to Henry de St Clair, and Earl David of Huntingdon's quitclaim to the earl of Mar of all rights over the person of Gille Crìosd son of Gille Conghal all bear witness to the harsh reality of the encounter between European lords and many of the common Gaelic folk of the kingdom in the 'Anglo-Norman era'.[153]

The episcopal inquest held at Arbuthnott in 1206 also reveals that the austere existence of the scolocs of Scotland, like that of the *betagii* of Ireland, was mitigated by the weight of custom, which offered them security of tenure on episcopal lands from one generation through the next. Evidence from ecclesiastical charter chests elsewhere suggests that this was indeed the case. In 1265 title to the scolocs resident at Ellon passed to the earl of Buchan when he leased a tract of arable from the bishop of St Andrews, but the earl had to promise that at the expiry of the agreement the land and its occupants would revert intact to their owner.[154] The genealogies compiled on behalf of the monks of Dunfermline in 1332 attest the presence of multiple generations of scolocs on specific estates, as do references to 'scoloc lands' at Redgorton and Muthill in Strathearn, and Ellon and Fetteresso in Aberdeenshire.[155] Place names such as Scollowland (Fife), Scolilands (Dumfriesshire) and Scollatisland (Mar) bear witness to the association between these peasants and the lands they occupied over the course of several generations.[156] In the changeable economy of the thirteenth century, however, even security of tenure might prove ephemeral. Like all neyfs, scolocs were considered the property of their lords and tied to the lords' lands; they were thus at the mercy of aristocratic business decisions. When the bishop of St Andrews placed a new tenant in possession of the kirktoun of Arbuthnott, the latter 'removed altogether' the poor families living there so that he might put their few acres to the plough.[157] In 1222 the prior of St Andrews leased the person of Gille Moire, a scoloc resident at Tarland in Aberdeenshire, to the earl of Mar for a period of several years. He did not relinquish altogether his claim to the children of Gille Moire, noting that at the expiry of the arrangement he intended to settle them on some other part of his estate.[158] The *nativi* who lived under ecclesiastical lordship had little reason to consider themselves more fortunate than those whose lives were under the control of secular magnates.

The resilience of the conditions that perpetuated legal unfreedom on ecclesiastical lands has much to reveal about the paradoxical nature of the Scottish church in the twelfth and thirteenth centuries. Contemporaries at home and abroad praised the efforts of reform-minded bishops and monks to eradicate the barbarous customs of the native Gaels and to enforce strict observance on the part of lay persons and clerics alike of the sacraments, rites and rituals of Rome; they wrote at great length, too, of the achievement of the Mac Malcolm rulers in bringing enlightenment and 'civilisation' to the kingdom. The supporters of reform subjected a great many of the traditions of the old church to careful scrutiny, and found much there to criticise and ultimately to reject. They saw little reason, however, to change the way in which the old church had conducted the business of estate management. Practices that sanctioned the exploitation of an unfree peasantry were too deeply ingrained among clerical magnates to be dislodged easily. When it came, then, the high medieval reform movement profoundly transformed the structure and the spiritual fabric of the Scottish church, but it touched hardly at all the material circumstances of the poorest Gaels who laboured on its behalf.

The entrenchment of a new aristocracy within the landscape in the century and a half after 1124 effected significant changes to the material circumstances under which the poorest people lived and worked. A fortunate few weathered changes in lordship thanks to the kindness of their masters. When in 1199, for example, the bishop of Dunblane resolved a dispute with the hospital of Brackley in England over title to the lands belonging to the church of Findo Gask, he agreed to allow the brethrens' 'liege man', Colmán, to remain there and promised to treat him 'in kindly fashion'.[159] The monks of Scone likewise permitted a man who maintained a toft on a newly acquired estate to stay on site and to continue to use the common pasture to which he had enjoyed access before the land changed hands.[160] A grant of Walter son of Alan to the monks of Melrose conveyed lands in southern Ayrshire which his father had previously given to the priest Alan. The latter remained in possession of them, now as a *conversus* of the abbey.[161] When William de Beauvoir made a gift of a small plot of arable to the monks of May priory, he stipulated that sasine must await the death of his widow, who held a portion of it, and of his servant Ralph, who held another.[162] Colmán and his fellows, however, represented the fortunate few. In many, if not most, parts of the kingdom, by the late twelfth century minor landholders who were not beneficiaries of written charters 'would have counted as unfree peasants, irrespective of their families' previous status'.[163] For such persons, the consequence of lordly acts that carved new davachs, half davachs, carucates, oxgangs and ploughgates the length and breadth of the kingdom was an existence that was much more closely regulated than it had been before. Thousands, no doubt, sank into the obscurity of unfreedom that Curtis described in the wake of the establishment of the Lordship of Ireland.[164] Many must also have suffered wholesale expropriation. What happened, for example, to the smallholders Marnoch the forester and Pàdruig the shepherd and his son when, around 1200, the few acres on which they earned a modest living were divided between the abbot of Cambuskenneth and Sir Richard de Bickerton?[165] When Helen de Morville gave away some of her dower lands in Lauderdale, including the tofts and crofts on which Liulf and his wife Gledewis dwelt?[166] Towards the end of the reign of William I, Earl David of Huntingdon created a new feu in Garioch for Hugh le Bret out of tenements that had been in the hands of a group of native smallholders.[167] One of them, Abraham the mair, may have survived the dislocation thanks to the honourable status of his position among the native population, but his fellows disappear altogether from written sources. A Gaelic tenant named Archibald was likewise dismissed from his little plot in the vicinity of Spyny after the bishop of Moray settled a dispute with a new neighbour. The latter agreed to supply the bishop with six men to assist at the autumn harvest, one of them presumably the now landless Archibald.[168] When Richard Germin quitclaimed to the hospital of Soutra the toft and croft in which Simon son of Gille Brigte lived and worked,[169] the latter can have had few choices: leave his home and suffer whatever fate lay in store for the landless poor, or offer his services to the new lord in the hope of remaining on the estate. A Gaelic peasant named Cinaed Mac Gillechiar likewise faced an uncertain future when Ness, the king's physician, made a gift to the monks of Coupar Angus of the land on which he dwelt.[170]

Medieval charter materials seldom permit anything more than speculation about the lot of men like Simon and Cinaed, but other sources attest the precariousness that troubled the lives of the poorest peasants in the thirteenth century. Assizes attributed to the reign of David I, if more certainly of much later date, nevertheless claimed as customary the maxim that 'a free man may lose his freedom', and further, that if he relinquished it of his own accord, 'he shall never recover it'.[171] As was the case in Ireland, moreover, the ranks of lowly men and women who were the objects of gifts and sales were augmented by persons who sank into their midst for reasons other than unfree birth. Then as now, the benefits of a buoyant economy were not shared equally by all, and the inability to render the services associated with a free tenement brought calamity to many modest families. The thirteenth-century records of Coldingham priory reveal just how easily the downward slide into servility might occur. The widow Sybil had to surrender her few acres into the prior's hands when, owing to the default of a cottar she had employed, she proved unable to discharge the debts that her father had accumulated.[172] In the 1190s 'great necessity' drove Henry and Robert de Prendergast, once prosperous husbandmen, to sell several of their *nativi*; the family's hardships, moreover, continued into the next generation.[173] The stewards of aristocratic estates throughout the realm were shrewd businessmen, ever vigilant in promoting their employers' interests at the expense of poor smallholders. The Coldingham evidence, it has been said, offers a bleak reminder of the 'costs of unfreedom to the serf' on the lands that belonged to the Benedictines,[174] but the comment might equally validly be applied to other regions of the kingdom. Thus, in 1234, the Lennox smallholder Dùghall and his wife fell into difficult financial times and, 'unable to meet our debts without selling or otherwise alienating our heritage', agreed to surrender title to their lands to the abbot of Paisley in return for a much smaller holding and an annual rent in grain.[175] In mid-century Lennox, Christina daughter of Colin Mac Gille Crìosd and her son Alexander came to an arrangement with the local laird, assigning him sasine of family land on the Leven Water in return for a very modest payment of six cows and a chalder of flour.[176] When disaster struck another Paisley tenant, Alan the carpenter had to sell his holding at Auldingilston; he received in return a small sum of money, but just enough to clear his debts and to lift his family out of destitution.[177] The small tragedies that befell people like Christina and Alan must have driven many others to surrender their free status in return for the security and the necessities of life that even the most demanding landlords were grudgingly prepared to offer their neyfs. In the late thirteenth century, for example, in return for their varied labour services on the demesne lands of Coldingham at Fishwick the prior's *bondi* received a steady ration of cheese, bread, fish and ale.[178] For a while at least, the scolocs of Arbuthnott enjoyed security of tenure, but the neyfs who toiled alongside them were not so fortunate, and were expropriated when a new laird decided to expand the production of his arable.[179]

The secular laws that were so prejudicial to persons of unfree status had their counterpart in the spiritual realm. The reformed church of the twelfth and thirteenth centuries taught that its salvific message applied to all and sundry irrespective of race, gender or social rank, and its sermons, *exempla* and hagiographies featured peasants as frequently as they did noblemen. Churchmen were adamant, too that the obligation to pay teinds lay equally on all Scottish Christians irrespective of rank.[180] Meaningful participation in the clerical life, however, was really open only to persons of free status. A passage in *Regiam Majestatem* stated the church's stance on the matter unequivocally when it noted that 'servile status is not consistent with the holding of holy orders', and explored in some detail the problems that arose when a bondman took the vows of a monk without the knowledge or permission of his lord.[181] The treatise dealt with a conundrum that, already in the fourteenth century, had long troubled clerics. As early as 1195 Pope Celestine III had ruled that the Tironensians of Scotland might accept as postulants any clerk or layman who wished to 'fly from the world to the monastic life', a privilege that his successor, Innocent III, was willing to confirm, yet both bulls specifically exempted persons of unfree status.[182] That the rule was not always observed is apparent, however, in the continued debate about servile ordinands that was still preoccupying royal and ecclesiastical lawyers more than a century later. The church's attitude towards unfreedom in Scotland, moreover, was tinged with more than a little moral superiority. Although scholars have argued in support of the 'harmonious' nature of cross-cultural encounters in many parts of the kingdom in the twelfth and thirteenth centuries,[183] evidence of the mistrust with which reforming clerics regarded the old orders of Céli Dé and the contempt in which they held native religious and devotional practices is equally compelling.[184] Stated simply, the clerical reform agenda encouraged members of the revitalised church to draw sharp contrasts between the civilised mores of contemporary Europe and the benighted customs of the indigenous culture of the British Isles. The determination of the new ecclesiastical hierarchy to promote reform and renewal perpetuated the marginalisation of the poorest and weakest members of the native Gaelic population.

Irish estate surveys show that the *betagii* of the medieval lordship lived and worked in family units, their holdings usually grouped together on their lords' estates so that they might make most efficient use of scarce ploughteams. Similar arrangements appear to have been in place on Scottish estates, for example on the Kelso lands at Sprouston, where several little cottages lay together 'at the far end of the toun',[185] and at Coldingham, Swinwood and West Renton, where bondlands were also clustered.[186] Twelfth- and thirteenth-century charters make mention of the *terrae rusticorum* farmed on the estates of Scone abbey,[187] of the bondmen's carucates at Crailing and Smailholm,[188] of cottars' acres at Inchyra, Errol, Athelstaneford and Beath,[189] and of bondland near Caskieben.[190] In the fourteenth century, references to *bondagia* and bondlands throughout the kingdom are frequent in extant charters, suggesting that such divisions of territory were by then well established and widely known features of the arable and pastoral landscapes both north and south of Forth. As in Ireland, moreover, the compact nature of the holdings worked by unfree people had important implications for their daily existence. Scottish scribes did not employ the term *nacio*, as did their Irish counterparts,[191] to refer to the kindred of the *nativi* who were the objects of lordly grants and sales, but it was a rare charter indeed that transferred title of a serf to a new owner without referring also to his *sequela*, and often to members of his more extended kindred. The neyf genealogies compiled for the monks of Dunfermline show that unfreedom was a condition transmitted from one generation to the next. Many families must have been incapable of amassing even the modest payments that would allow daughters to leave the estate, and the entrenchment within local custom of the obligation to render merchet and heriot effectively denied opportunities for emancipation to countless others. And yet, onerous as they were, conditions such as these must have created a rough-and-ready sense of community and cohesion among the lowliest of a lord's tenants comparable to that of the Irish betaghs and, on occasion, opportunities for shared enterprise. A document of 1320 in which the abbot of Dunfermline granted manumission to a group of Gaelic neyfs in return for the render of an ox for the abbey's plough or 4s bears witness to the exercise of collective efforts on the part of several neighbouring families to organise their labour and opportunities for poor people to pool their modest resources in pursuit of the coveted prize of legal freedom.[192] The records of the royal chancery, too, show that brieves of neyfty sometimes worked to the advantage of the king's least privileged subjects. In 1319 the Aberdeenshire serf Adam son of Adam, for example, mounted a successful defence against his lord's attempt to treat him as an unfree person. A royal court ruled that Adam and his children 'may henceforth move around our kingdom wherever and whenever they wish'.[193] In rare instances, appeals to their lords' humanity might secure favourable treatment in otherwise intolerable conditions. Another Dunfermline deed describes in quite astonishing detail the demands of some lowly farm labourers, one of which was that the abbot provide them, in cases of illness or senility, with the care and sustenance that decency and 'human affection' prescribed.[194]

Conclusion

Several years ago, the historian Kenneth Nicholls reminded his readers of the harsh realities that attended the legal distinction between free and unfree people in Ireland, and criticised the tendency of scholars to minimise the social and economic disabilities that were so integral a feature of the betaghs' existence.[195] Historians of the Scottish medieval peasantry would do well to heed his cautionary remarks. While it is undoubtedly the case that *nativi ascripti* were a dying breed in the late fourteenth century and that there were now more avenues by which poor folk might rise into the ranks of the small tenantry, recent scholarship has tended to endow the march of the Scottish neyf towards freedom with over-optimistic inevitability. While few contemporaries were naïve enough to believe the laconic statement of the author of the *Regiam Majestatem* that 'bondage originated in the drunkenness of Noah',[196] the stigma of legal unfreedom still mattered in 1364, when the bishop of Moray considered it worth the trouble and expense to purchase a royal brieve that would permit him to challenge the claims to free status of his tenants, Robert, Naomhín and Domnall. It mattered even more to the three men, who failed to prove their case.[197] For much of the period before 1364 legal, social and economic conditions were harsh for the *nativi* of Scotland. The faint mark that so many thousands of unfree persons left in extant record materials bears eloquent, if largely silent, witness to the marginal position that they occupied in the agrarian world of the kingdom in the 'Anglo-Norman era'. The buoyant economy of the years after 1124 created unfettered opportunities for enterprising commoners to prosper in both town and countryside, and generated the wealth of written documents that has allowed historians to study the ways in which Scottish people shaped their fortunes in this new world. The ability to move about the kingdom, the prospect of finding a suitable marriage partner, the hope of dying unencumbered, however, were privileges accorded only to individuals whom the early common law of Scotland recognised as free. Until the end of the fourteenth century, untold numbers of their lesser fellows never had such choices.

Notes

1. *Inchaffray Chrs*, no. 109.
2. C. J. Neville, *Native Lordship in Medieval Scotland: The Earldoms of Strathearn and Lennox, c. 1140-1365* (Dublin, 2005), p. 82; G. Ewart, 'Inchaffray abbey, Perth & Kinross: excavation and research, 1987', *Proceedings of the Society of Antiquaries of Scotland*, 126 (1996), p. 513.
3. D. Ditchburn and A. J. Macdonald, 'Medieval Scotland, 1100-1560', in R. A. Houston and W. W. J. Knox (eds), *The New Penguin History of Scotland: From the Earliest Times to the Present Day* (London, 2001), p. 135.
4. Ibid. pp. 134-9; I. D. Whyte, 'Rural society and economy', in B. Harris and A. R. MacDonald (eds), *Scotland: The Making and Unmaking of the Nation, c. 1100-1707, Vol. I: The Scottish Nation: Origins to c. 1500* (Dundee, 2006), pp. 167-8; T. C. Smout, *A History of the Scottish People, 1560-1830*, 2nd edn (London, 1970), pp. 40-1; M. Lynch, *Scotland: A New History* (London, 1992), p. 60.
5. *Kelso Liber*, ii, pp. 455-73; *Coldingham Priory. The Correspondence, Inventories, Account Rolls and Law Proceedings of the Priory of Coldingham*, ed. J. Raine (Durham, 1841), pp. lxxxv-civ.
6. A. A. M. Duncan, *Scotland: The Making of the Kingdom* (Edinburgh, 1975), p. 348 and, more generally, pp. 326-48.
7. R. Nicholson, *Scotland: The Later Middle Ages* (Edinburgh, 1978), p. 263. The rental is found in *Morton Reg.*, i, pp. xlvii-lxxvi.
8. I. D. Whyte, *Scotland Before the Industrial Revolution: An Economic and Social History, c. 1050-c. 1750* (London, 1995), p. 10. See also the reference to 'a rural proletariat which figures in no charter', Duncan, *Making of the Kingdom*, p. 346.
9. Ditchburn and Macdonald, 'Medieval Scotland', p. 134. See also D. M. Walker, *The Legal History of Scotland, Vol. I: The Beginnings to A.D. 1286* (Edinburgh, 1988), p. 29.

10. *Symeonis monachi opera omnia*, ed. T. Arnold, 2 vols (London, 1882–5), ii, p. 192. See also *The Peterborough Chronicle, 1070–1154*, 2nd edn, ed. C. Clark (Oxford, 1970), p. 6. The raids are discussed briefly in W. E. Kapelle, *The Norman Conquest of the North: The Region and its Transformation* (London, 1979), pp. 90, 92, 99, 124.
11. *Symeonis monachi opera omnia*, ed. Arnold, ii, p. 290. English attitudes towards Scottish attacks carried out in this period are expertly discussed in M. Strickland, *War and Chivalry: The Conduct and Perception of War in England and Normandy, 1066–1217* (Cambridge, 1996), pp. 313–17, and in J. Gillingham, 'Conquering the barbarians: war and chivalry in twelfth-century Britain', *Haskins Society Journal*, 4 (1993), pp. 67–84.
12. *Symeonis monachi opera omnia*, ed. Arnold, ii, p. 298.
13. D. A. E. Pelteret, *Slavery in Early Medieval England: From the Reign of Alfred to the Twelfth Century* (Woodbridge, 1995); D. A. E. Pelteret, 'Slave raiding and slave trading in early England', *Anglo-Saxon England*, 9 (1981), pp. 99–114.
14. *Life of St. Margaret Queen of Scotland by Turgot Bishop of St Andrews*, ed. W. Forbes-Leith (Edinburgh, 1884), p. 57.
15. B. T. Hudson, *Irish Sea Studies, 900–1200* (Dublin, 2006), p. 31; Pelteret, 'Slave raiding and slave trading', pp. 99–114; P. Holm, 'The slave trade of Dublin, IX to XIIIth century', *Peritia*, 5 (1989), pp. 342–3.
16. B. E. Crawford, *Scandinavian Scotland* (Leicester, 1987), pp. 210–11.
17. *Lives of S. Ninian and S. Kentigern*, ed. A. P. Forbes (Edinburgh, 1874), p. 145.
18. Ibid. p. 237.
19. *RRS*, i, pp. 62–3. More recently, see *Dictionary of the Older Scottish Tongue*, ed. W. A. Craigie et al., 12 vols (Oxford, 1937–2002), i, p. 770. See also below, pp. 163–4.
20. *RRS*, ii, nos. 25, 30, 31.
21. Holm, 'The slave trade of Dublin', p. 339n.
22. F. Kelly, *A Guide to Early Irish Law* (Dublin, 1998), pp. 29–36; *Críth Gablach*, ed. D. A. Binchy (Dublin, 1979), pp. 78, 81–2, 93, 105; T. Charles-Edwards, *Early Irish and Welsh Kinship* (Oxford, 1993), pp. 467–8.
23. Holm, 'The slave trade of Dublin', pp. 317–45; Kelly, *Guide to Early Irish Law*, pp. 95–6; F. Kelly, *Early Irish Farming* (Dublin, 2000), pp. 423–31; K. W. Nicholls, 'Anglo-French Ireland and after', *Peritia*, 1 (1982), pp. 377–81; G. J. Hand, *English Law in Ireland, 1290–1304* (Cambridge, 1967), pp. 193–4.
24. *Expugnatio Hibernica: The Conquest of Ireland*, ed. A. B. Brian and F. X. Martin (Dublin, 1978), pp. 70–1, and, more generally, Holm, 'The slave trade of Dublin', pp. 339–40.
25. E. Curtis, 'The rental of the manor of Lisronagh, 1333 and notes on "betagh" tenure in medieval Ireland', *Proceedings of the Royal Irish Academy*, 43C (1936), p. 63.
26. K. Down, 'Colonial society and economy', in A. Cosgrove (ed.), *A New History*

of Ireland. Vol. II: Medieval Ireland, 1169–1534 (Oxford, 1993), pp. 444–5, 457–8; J. Otway-Ruthven, 'The character of Norman settlement in Ireland', *Historical Studies*, 5 (1965), p. 77; G. Mac Niocaill, 'The origins of the *betagh*', *Irish Jurist*, New Series, 1 (1966), p. 297.

27. Nicholls, 'Anglo-French Ireland and after', p. 375.
28. Down, 'Colonial society', pp. 455–6; J. Otway-Ruthven, 'The organization of Anglo-Irish agriculture in the middle ages', *Journal of the Royal Society of Antiquaries of Ireland*, 4th Series, 81 (1951), pp. 11–12; Hand, *English Law in Ireland*, pp. 196–7.
29. For a summary of the peasant holdings on a number of manors, see J. Otway-Ruthven, *A History of Medieval Ireland*, 2nd edn (New York, 1980), pp. 113–15; J. Lydon, *Ireland in the Later Middle Ages* (Dublin, 1973), pp. 4–7; J. Mills, 'Tenants and agriculture near Dublin in the fourteenth century', *Proceedings of the Royal Society of Antiquaries of Ireland*, 5th Series, 1 (1890), pp. 55–6; and *The Pipe Roll of Cloyne*, ed. P. MacCotter and K. Nicholls (Midleton, 1996), passim.
30. Curtis, 'Rental of the manor of Lisronagh', p. 64.
31. L. Price, 'The origin of the word *betagius*', *Eríu*, 20 (1966), p. 187; Mac Niocaill, 'The origins of the betagh', pp. 297–8; Down, 'Colonial society', pp. 455–8; Hand, *English Law in Ireland*, pp. 190–3; J. Lydon, *The Lordship of Ireland in the Middle Ages* (Toronto, 1972), p. 85.
32. Nicholls, 'Anglo-French Ireland and after', pp. 379–81; Down, 'Colonial society', p. 458.
33. *Calendar of Documents relating to Ireland, preserved in Her Majesty's Public Record Office . . . 1171[–1307]*, ed. H. S. Sweetman, 5 vols (London, 1875–86), ii, no. 717, printed in full in *Registrum prioratum omnium sanctorum iuxta Dublin*, ed. R. Butler (Dublin, 1845), pp. 129–31. This had clearly changed by the late thirteenth century; see *Calendar of Documents relating to Ireland*, ed. Sweetman, iv, p. 2, no. 4; p. 13, no. 21; p. 127, no. 279; p. 378, no. 825; and *Calendar of the Justiciary Rolls or Proceedings in the Court of the Justiciar of Ireland preserved in the Public Record Office of Ireland. XXIII. to XXXI. Years of Edward I*, ed. J. Mills (Dublin 1905), pp. 30–1, 254, 352.
34. Down, 'Colonial society', pp. 457–8; Otway-Ruthven. 'The organization of Anglo-Irish agriculture', p. 12; Mills, 'Tenants and agriculture near Dublin', pp. 56–7.
35. *Registrum prioratum omnium sanctorum*, ed. Butler, no. 53. Reginald's ancestors had been gifted to the priory c. 1166 by Diarmait king of Leinster; ibid. no. 49. Other grants of serf families are noted in Curtis, 'Rental of the manor of Lisronagh', pp. 66–7, and Mills, 'Tenants and agriculture near Dublin', p. 58.
36. *Irish Historical Documents*, ed. E. Curtis and R. B. McDowell (London, 1943), p. 23.
37. Hand, *English Law in Ireland*, pp. 1–2, 196; *Calendar of Documents relating to Ireland*, ed. Sweetman, i, no. 236. For a late thirteenth-century example, see *Calendar of Documents relating to Ireland*, ed. Sweetman, iii, p. 309, no. 622.

38. Down, 'Colonial society', p. 458; Otway-Ruthven, 'The organization of Anglo-Irish agriculture', p. 12; *Calendar of Documents relating to Ireland*, ed. Sweetman, i, no. 3203; iii, no. 459; iv, no. 551; v, nos. 167, 617, 657, 659, 670.
39. Down, 'Colonial society', p. 458; K. Nicholls, *Gaelic and Gaelicised Ireland in the Middle Ages* (Dublin, 1972), pp. 70–1. See also the case of an Irishman of Scandinavian descent whose circumstances threatened to 'reduce him to servitude', *Calendar of Justiciary Rolls, XXIII. to XXXI. Edward I*, ed. Mills, p. 59.
40. *Pipe Roll of Cloyne*, ed. MacCotter and Nicholls, passim.
41. J. Otway-Ruthven, 'The native Irish and English law in medieval Ireland', *Irish Historical Studies* 7 (1950), p. 9; Hand, *English Law in Ireland*, pp. 193–6; Mac Niocaill, 'The origins of the *betagh*', pp. 292–3.
42. *Calendar of Documents relating to Ireland*, ed. Sweetman, i, no. 3203; iii, no. 459; iv, no. 551.
43. *Pipe Roll of Cloyne*, ed. MacCotter and Nicholls, pp. 18–19, 86–7.
44. Otway-Ruthven, *A History of Medieval Ireland*, p. 112; Mills, 'Tenants and agriculture near Dublin', p. 58; C. Doherty, 'Some aspects of hagiography as a source for Irish economic history', *Peritia*, 1 (1982), p. 319.
45. William of Malmesbury, *Gesta regum Anglorum*, ed. W. Stubbs, 2 vols (London, 1887–9), ii, p. 447. The allusion was to King David I; for Queen's Margaret's efforts to educate her husband and his noblemen in the ways of civility, see *Life of St. Margaret*, ed. Forbes-Leith, pp. 38–52.
46. *Symeonis monachi opera omnia*, ed. Arnold, ii, p. 298.
47. For the manumission ceremonies, see Pelteret, *Slavery in Early Medieval England*, p. 151.
48. R. Bartlett, *The Making of Europe: Conquest, Colonization and Cultural Change, 950–1350* (Princeton, 1993), p. 306.
49. Mac Niocaill, 'The origins of the *betagh*', p. 298.
50. R. R. Davies, *The First English Empire: Power and Identities in the British Isles, 1093–1343* (Oxford, 2000), pp. 148, 153.
51. *RRS*, ii, nos. 422, 589; *Melrose Liber*, no. 239.
52. *Coupar Angus Chrs*, i, nos. 39, 52.
53. *Arbroath Liber*, no. 305.
54. *Kelso Liber*, no. 110.
55. A. Grant, 'Lordship and society in twelfth-century Clydesdale', in H. Pryce and J. L. Watts (eds.), *Power and Identity in the Middle Ages: Essays in Memory of Rees Davies* (Oxford, 2007), pp. 120–2. A similar process has been traced in Anglo-Norman Glamorgan: M. Griffiths, 'Native society on the Anglo-Norman frontier: the evidence of the Margam charters', *Welsh History Review*, 14 (1988), pp. 199, 214.
56. W. Davies, 'Charter-writing and its uses in medieval Celtic societies', in H. Pryce (ed.), *Literacy in Medieval Celtic Societies* (Cambridge, 1998), p. 104.
57. *Glasgow Reg.*, no. 104; G. W. S. Barrow, *The Anglo-Norman Era in Scottish History* (Oxford, 1980), p. 34.

58. *Charters of David I*, no. 111.
59. Ibid. no. 10; *Coldstream Chrs*, nos. 8, 11.
60. Grant, 'Lordship and society', pp. 121-2.
61. *Charters of David I*, nos. 4, 14, 16, 41, 44, 53, 57, 58, 66, 71, 85-9, 97, 98, 120, 151, 153n, 161, 162, 167, 171, 177, 180, 185, 192-4, 205, 210, 216; *RRS*, i, nos. 105, 114, 115, 117, 120, 131, 133, 136, 149, 154, 155, 161, 172, 173, 184, 190, 198, 209, 210, 224, 225, 226, 228, 235, 239, 240, 243, 247, 256, 258, 260; *RRS*, ii, nos. 27, 39, 46, 48, 61, 74, 75, 78, 80, 81-3, 96, 100, 116, 140, 144, 179, 218.
62. *Charters of David I*, no. 14.
63. The expression is found in A. Grant, 'Centuries of Scottish feudalism?', unpublished paper presented to the Conference of Scottish Medievalists, January 2003. I am grateful to Dr Grant for permission to cite this paper.
64. *Kelso Liber*, nos. 108, 109, 114.
65. J. Raine, *The History and Antiquities of North Durham* (London, 1852), App., nos. 330-32, 335, discussed in Duncan, *Making of the Kingdom*, pp. 331-2.
66. Nicholls, 'Anglo-French Ireland and after', p. 375.
67. *Lennox Cart.*, pp. 19-20, 25-7, 92; Fraser, *Lennox*, ii, nos. 204, 207; Royal Faculty of Procurators, Hill Collection of Manuscripts, Macfarlane Muniments, ii, no. 3.
68. See, for example, the grant of Gille Mícheil son of Edulf to his son Mael Coluim in *Lennox Cart.*, pp. 83-4.
69. Fraser, *Lennox*, ii, no. 4.
70. Grant, 'Lordship and society', p. 122.
71. R. Oram, *The Lordship of Galloway* (Edinburgh, 2000), p. 200 and, more generally, pp. 191-217.
72. *Paisley Reg.*, pp. 166-8.
73. NAS, RH 5/45.
74. *St Andrews Liber*, pp. 245-6.
75. See, for example, ibid. pp. 241-4; Barrow, *Anglo-Norman Era*, pp. 84-7.
76. K. J. Stringer, *Earl David of Huntingdon, 1152-1219: A Study in Anglo-Scottish History* (Edinburgh, 1985), p. 63.
77. *Kelso Liber*, nos. 117, 470.
78. Durham, Dean and Chapter Muniments (DCD), Misc. Ch. 966.
79. DCD, Loc. XXVIII, no. 1, a roll of manumissions dating from the time of Priors Thomas de Melsanby, Bertram de Middleton and Hugh de Darlington, with a fragment of a roll of 1318. The plentiful manumission records of this period compiled in English monasteries are discussed in detail in Pelteret, *Slavery in Early Medieval England*, pp. 140-55.
80. *Registrum magni sigilli regum Scottorum*, ed. J. M. Thomson et al., 11 vols (Edinburgh, 1882-1914), i, no. 345, App., nos. 1117, 1611. See also Hugh de Giffard's manumission of the bondman Richard Soylard in NAS, GD 28/17, summarised in *Calendar of Writs preserved at Yester House, 1166-1503*, ed. C. C. H. Harvey and J. Macleod (Edinburgh, 1930), no. 17.
81. *Charters of David I*, no. 36.

82. *RRS*, ii, no. 62, *Kelso Liber*, no. 128; *Dryburgh Liber*, App., no. 1.
83. DCD, Misc. Ch. 982.
84. A. Grant, 'To the medieval foundations', *Scottish Historical Review*, 73 (1994), p. 18.
85. *Dryburgh Liber*, no. 201.
86. *Lindores Cart.*, no. 4.
87. NAS, GD 28/4; Stringer, *Earl David*, p. 234, no. 27.
88. *RRS*, i, no. 131; *RRS*, ii, no. 39; *Dunfermline Reg.*, no. 74.
89. *Melrose Liber*, no. 206. For another example, dated 1258 x 1271, see NAS, GD 45/27/3036.
90. *Dunfermline Reg.*, no. 86.
91. Barrow, *Anglo-Norman Era*, p. 64.
92. *Moray Reg.*, no. 16.
93. *APS*, i, p. 94.
94. *RRS*, ii, nos. 15, 353.
95. *Miscellany of the Spalding Club, vol. V* (Aberdeen, 1852), pp. 210–13, discussed in Duncan, *Making of the Kingdom*, p. 330.
96. *Scone Liber*, no. 84; NLS, Adv. MS. 15.1.18, no. 27.
97. *Kelso Liber*, nos. 117, 470.
98. *Calendar of Documents relating to Ireland*, ed. Sweetman, i, no. 236.
99. *Regiam Majestatem and Quoniam Attachiamenta*, ed. T. M. Cooper (Edinburgh, 1947), pp. 111–17.
100. *Formulary E: Scottish Letters and Brieves, 1286–1424*, ed. A. A. M. Duncan (Glasgow, 1976), p. 12; *The Register of Brieves as contained in the Ayr MS., the Bute MS. and Quoniam Attachiamenta*, ed. T. M. Cooper (Edinburgh, 1946), p. 36, no. 5. See also the brieves recorded later in the fourteenth century, in *Quoniam Attachiamenta*, ed. T. D. Fergus (Edinburgh, 1996), pp. 231–7.
101. H. L. MacQueen, *Common Law and Feudal Society in Medieval Scotland* (Edinburgh, 1993), pp. 122–9; H. L. MacQueen, 'Pleadable brieves, pleading and the development of Scots law', *Law and History Review*, 4 (1986), pp. 402–22; A. Harding, 'The medieval brieves of protection and the development of the common law', *Juridical Review*, New Series, 11 (1966), pp. 115–49.
102. *Charters of David I*, nos. 172, 225; *RRS*, i, nos. 118, 243.
103. *Charters of David I*, no. 20.
104. Ibid. no. 142.
105. *RRS*, i, nos. 118, 192, 195, 243; *RRS*, ii, nos. 25, 39, 163, 336.
106. *RRS*, i, no. 131; *RRS*, ii, no. 63.
107. Raine, *North Durham*, App., no. 121.
108. Duncan, *Making of the Kingdom*, p. 328; *RRS*, i, pp. 62–4; *Dictionary of the Older Scottish Tongue*, ed. Craigie, i, p. 770.
109. *Charters of David I*, nos. 20, 172; *RRS*, i, nos. 118, 195; *RRS*, ii, nos. 25, 30, 31.
110. *Regiam Majestatem*, ed. Cooper, p. 113.
111. *Reginaldi monachi Dunelmensis libellus de admirandis beati Cuthberti*

virtutibus, ed. J. Raine (Durham, 1835), p. 179; the relevant passage reads *qui Pictorum lingue scollofthes cognominantur.*
112. *Contributions to a Dictionary of the Irish Language, Fascicule S,* gen. ed. E. G. Quin (Dublin, 1939), p. 101; Mills, 'Tenants and agriculture near Dublin', p. 57; Doherty, 'Some aspects of hagiography', p. 314.
113. *Arbroath Liber,* i, no. 56.
114. *Miscellany of the Spalding Club, vol. V,* pp. 211–13 and, more generally, Duncan, *Making of the Kingdom,* pp. 340–4.
115. Duncan, *Making of the Kingdom,* p. 330.
116. *Miscellany of the Spalding Club, vol. V,* p. 213.
117. *Kelso Liber,* nos. 15, 394, 399; *Inchaffray Chrs,* no. 53; S. R. MacPhail, *History of the Religious House of Pluscarden* (Edinburgh, 1881), pp. 204–6; *Rental Book of the Cistercian Abbey of Cupar-Angus,* ed. C. Rogers, 2 vols (Edinburgh, 1879–80), i, p. 326.
118. *APS,* i, pp. 397, 399.
119. Ibid. p. 381.
120. G. Neilson (ed.), 'The march laws', in *Stair Society Miscellany, vol. I* (Edinburgh, 1971), pp. 17–18.
121. TNA, C 145/13/21 and, more generally, C. J. Neville, *Violence, Custom and Law: The Anglo-Scottish Border Lands in the Later Middle Ages* (Edinburgh, 1998), pp. 7–8.
122. *APS,* i, pp. 335, 350, 681. The dating of this compilation is discussed in H. L. MacQueen and W. J. Windram, 'Laws and courts in the burghs', in M. Lynch, M. Spearman and G. Stell (eds), *The Scottish Medieval Town* (Edinburgh, 1988), pp. 209–12.
123. *APS,* i, p. 381; MacQueen, *Common Law and Feudal Society,* pp. 87–9.
124. G. W. S. Barrow, 'Badenoch and Strathspey, 1130–1312. 1. Secular and political', *Northern Scotland,* 8 (1988), pp. 1–7.
125. *Moray Reg.,* no. 76.
126. Fraser, *Grant,* iii, no. 5.
127. *Glasgow Reg.,* no. 129.
128. *Lindores Cart.,* no. 84.
129. See, for example, *Midlothian Chrs,* p. 35; *Dunfermline Reg.,* no. 81.
130. *Laing Chrs,* no. 7. See also a grant of Alexander III to William earl of Mar of the land of Tillicoultry 'with all the neyfs who lived there' under the former owner, NAS, GD 124/1/513.
131. *Inchaffray Chrs,* App. no. 5.
132. TNA, E39/100/132B.
133. Harding, 'Medieval brieves of protection', p. 125; see also P. Hyams, *Kings, Lords and Peasants in Medieval England: The Common Law of Villeinage in the Twelfth and Thirteenth Centuries* (Oxford, 1980), pp. 229n, 232–3.
134. Duncan, *Making of the Kingdom,* pp. 336–7; DCD, Misc. Ch. nos. 858, 860–8. 982; *Facsimiles of the National Manuscripts of Scotland,* ed. H. James, 3 vols (London, 1867–71), i, no. 54.

135. The examples here are numerous, but for references to the reservations of such incidents, see *Kelso Liber*, nos. 104, 109; *Historical Manuscripts Commission Report on the Manuscripts of Colonel David Milne Holme of Wedderburn Castle* (London, 1902), pp. 223-4; *Miscellany of the Spalding Club, vol. V*, p. 211. See also Alan of Galloway's reservation of the fiscal renders payable by the men of the land of Fairslie in a grant to Alan de Ros, NLS, Adv. MS. 15.1.18, fo. 75.
136. *Aberdeen-Banff Collections*, p. 298; *Lindores Cart.*, nos. 116, 117; *Midlothian Chrs*, pp. 38-9; Duncan, *Making of the Kingdom*, pp. 343, 345; and, for examples to c. 1350, *RMS*, i, no. 18; App. i, nos. 29, 66, 68; App. ii, no. 1073.
137. Duncan, *Making of the Kingdom*, pp. 326-48.
138. *APS*, i, pp. 398-401; *Regiam Majestatem*, ed. Cooper, pp. 106-7, 114-15.
139. *Regiam Majestatem*, ed. Cooper, pp. 114-15.
140. The *betagii* were similarly barred from owning any property, but the justiciary rolls make it clear that they did, in fact, amass both money and movable goods. See, for example, *Calendar of Justiciary Rolls, XXIII. to XXXI. Edward I*, ed. Mills, pp. 30-1, 254, 352. A mandate of King Malcolm IV mentions the possessions of *rustici*; assizes of Alexander II and Alexander III specified the payment of a cow and sheep from neyfs who refused to pay teind, to attend the king's army, or to observe the laws of the forest. *RRS*, ii, no. 281; *APS*, i, pp. 397, 691.
141. A. A. M. Duncan, '*Regiam Majestatem*: a reconsideration', *Juridical Review*, New Series, 6 (1961), pp. 199-217; A. Harding, '*Regiam Majestatem* amongst medieval law books', *Juridical Review*, New Series, 29 (1984), pp. 109-11; *Formulary E*, ed. Duncan, pp. 1-2, 12; *Quoniam Attachiamenta*, ed. Fergus, pp. 60-4, 106-7; *Register of Brieves*, ed. Cooper, p. 36.
142. *RRS*, i, p. 62; *Regiam Majestatem*, ed. Cooper, pp. 111-13; Harding, 'Brieves of protection', pp. 127-42; Hyams, *Kings, Lords and Peasants*, pp. 231-2.
143. J. Hudson, 'Legal aspects of charter diplomatic in the twelfth century: a comparative approach', *Anglo-Norman Studies*, 25 (2003), p. 134.
144. *Dunfermline Reg.*, nos. 325-31, edited in S. Taylor, 'Babbet and bridin pudding or polyglot Fife in the middle ages', *Nomina*, 17 (1994), pp. 113-16.
145. *Regiam Majestatem*, ed. Cooper, pp. 111-12.
146. *Dunfermline Reg.*, no. 379.
147. NLS, Adv. MS. 34.2.1b, fo. 139.
148. *Moray Reg.*, no. 143; See, for example, Nicholson, *The Later Middle Ages*, p. 109; Ditchburn and Macdonald, 'Medieval Scotland', p. 135.
149. MacQueen, *Common Law and Feudal Society*, p. 127.
150. Edinburgh University Library, Laing Charters, no, 69; DCD, Misc. Ch. 865.
151. *Memoranda de Parliamento, 1305*, ed. F. W. Maitland (London, 1893), p. 230.
152. Price, 'The origin of the word *betagius*', pp. 187-90.
153. *RRS*, ii, no. 164; *APS*, i, p. 94; BL, Harl. Ch. 83 C.24.
154. *Aberdeen-Banff Collections*, pp. 311-12.

155. *Dunfermline Reg.*, nos. 332–35; *Lindores Cart.*, nos. 32–34. There were still men referred to as scolocs at Ellon in 1387; *Aberdeen-Banff Collections*, pp. 310–1.
156. J. Robertson, 'On scholastic offices in the Scottish church in the twelfth and thirteenth centuries', in *Miscellany of the Spalding Club, vol. V*, App. to the Preface, p. 67.
157. *Miscellany of the Spalding Club, vol. V*, pp. 211–13.
158. NLS, Adv. MS. 15.1.18, no. 27.
159. *Inchaffray Chrs*, App. no. 4. For other examples, see Grant, 'To the medieval foundations', p. 19.
160. NAS, RH 6/40.
161. *Melrose Liber*, no. 74.
162. *May Records*, no. 25.
163. Grant, 'Lordship and society', p. 122.
164. Curtis, 'Rental of the manor of Lisronagh', p. 64.
165. *Cambuskenneth Reg.*, nos. 81–4.
166. K. Stringer, 'The early lords of Lauderdale, Dryburgh abbey and St. Andrew's priory, Northampton', in K. J. Stringer (ed.), *Essays on the Nobility of Medieval Scotland* (Edinburgh, 1985), p. 66.
167. *Lindores Cart.*, no. 129.
168. *Moray Reg.*, no. 27.
169. *Midlothian Chrs*, p. 26.
170. NAS, GD 83/3. For similar examples, see DCD Misc. Ch. 938; *Lindores Cart.*, no. 18; Fraser, *Annandale*, i, no. 3.
171. *APS*, i, p. 319.
172. DCD, Misc. Ch. 894, 900, 912.
173. DCD, Misc. Ch. 860, 864, 865, 868, and see other examples at nos. 862, 982.
174. J. Donnelly, 'The lands of Coldingham priory, 1100–1300' (1989), p. 166.
175. *Paisley Reg.*, pp. 178–80.
176. Fraser, *Lennox*, ii, no. 20.
177. *Paisley Reg.*, p. 58.
178. *Coldingham Priory*, ed. Raine, p. lxxxvii.
179. *Miscellany of the Spalding Club, vol. V*, pp. 212–13.
180. *Statutes of the Scottish Church*, ed. D. Patrick (Edinburgh, 1907), p. 23.
181. *Regiam Majestatem*, ed. Cooper, pp. 116–17.
182. *Lindores Cart.*, nos. 93, 94.
183. K. Stringer, 'Reform monasticism and Celtic Scotland: Galloway c.1140–c.1240', in E. J. Cowan and R. A. McDonald (eds), *Alba: Celtic Scotland in the Medieval Era* (East Linton, 2000), p. 153; A. McDonald, 'Scoto-Norse kings and the reformed religious orders: patterns of monastic patronage in twelfth-century Galloway and Argyll', *Albion*, 27 (1995), pp. 201–2, 218; A. Young, 'The earls and earldom of Buchan in the thirteenth century', in A. Grant and K. J. Stringer (eds), *Medieval Scotland: Crown, Lordship and Community – Essays presented to G. W. S. Barrow* (Edinburgh, 1993), pp. 185–6; M. O.

Anderson, 'The Celtic church in Kinrimund', *Innes Review*, 25 (1974), pp. 67–76; Barrow, *Kingdom of the Scots*, pp. 187–202.
184. See the discussion in Neville, *Native Lordship*, pp. 162–84.
185. *Kelso Liber*, p. 457.
186. *Coldingham Correspondence*, ed. Raine, pp. xcv, xcviii.
187. *Scone Liber*, no. 21.
188. *Midlothian Chrs*, pp. 38–9.
189. NAS, RH 6/40; BL, MS. Harl. 4693, fos. 34v–35r; *Laing Chrs*, no. 7; *Dunfermline Reg.*, no. 86.
190. *Lindores Cart.*, nos. 116, 117.
191. *Registrum prioratum omnium sanctorum*, ed. Butler, no. 53.
192. *Dunfermline Reg.*, no. 302.
193. *RMS*, i, App., no. 67. For similar challenges dating from the reign of David II, see W. Robertson, *An Index, drawn up around the year 1629, of many records of charters, granted by the different sovereigns of Scotland between the years 1309 and 1413* (Edinburgh, 1798), p. 47, no. 22; p. 66, no. 22; p. 89, no. 249.
194. *Dunfermline Reg.*, no. 354.
195. Nicholls, *Gaelic and Gaelicised Ireland*, p. 70.
196. *Regiam Majestatem*, ed. Cooper, p. 118.
197. *Moray Reg.*, no. 143.

Chapter 6

The social space of Scottish lordship: finding friendship in written source materials, 1100–1400

A recent historiographical trend has seen scholars explore the myriad 'spaces' within which medieval people interacted on a daily basis. Although now considerable in range and scope, their studies share much common ground in conceptualising space as a multiplicity of sites, real and imagined, in which individuals asserted meaningful control over their persons, the material world around them and the people with whom they came into contact. The ground-breaking work of the French sociologist and philosopher, Henri Lefebvre, in reshaping the notion of space, broadly understood, as a locus of power, authority and influence has quite justifiably been hailed as liberating the study of the past from historiographical traditions that once severely restricted the questions that scholars might ask of extant source materials.[1] His re-imagination of societal relations as the interaction of a triad of perceived, conceived and lived spaces has in turn encouraged medievalists to explore the past from the paradigms of architectural, urban, theatrical, ideological and cultural space, to name but a few.

Just as it has in the field of western history generally, Lefebvre's work has promising implications for the study of medieval history, especially in the contexts of family and social discourse. His re-conceptualisation of the European past has found welcome application in the study of friendship in the medieval period. A large, and still growing, body of scholarly work on ties of affection has examined in novel fashion the expression of Christian, spiritual, political and poetic friendship. *Amicitia* in the medieval context, it suggests, drew heavily, though not exclusively, on ancient, especially Ciceronian, concepts of mutual accord, respect and goodwill, and its language borrowed heavily from the literary models of antiquity.[2] In the twelfth century, in particular, there developed among the schoolmen who populated the monastic and episcopal offices of the reformed church a 'fascination with friendship',[3] which generated a very considerable body of writing. One of the consequences of this new interest was that friendship acquired new dimension as a 'public activity', and the terminology associated with it expressed a pragmatism and utility that the ancients would hardly have recognised.[4] Understanding medieval *amicitia*, Gerd Althoff has claimed, means above all grasping the notion of friendship as 'the exercise of political power'.[5] Viewed from this perspective, friendship becomes both a tool ('razor sharp', according to Margaret Mullett) with which to comprehend how noblemen, secular and ecclesiastical, negotiated relationships with the persons with whom they came into contact,[6] and a process eminently suited to scholarly examination. The final chapter of this book explores ways in which Lefebvre's triad of perceived, conceived and lived spaces may be applied to the study of social space in Scotland in the two and a half centuries after 1150, and in particular to notions of friendship as they appear in extant charter materials and other written sources from this period. The dangers associated with close study of charter texts are many and varied, and the challenges that these record sources present to the historian have been amply illustrated in the preceding chapters of this work. For all their problems, though, charters, indentures of agreement and other documents related to the conveyance of land remain a crucial source of written information for the study of the period between 1150 and 1400 in Scotland. Used judiciously, they offer rare and precious glimpses of both the breadth and the boundaries of the social space that delineated the mental world of the landholding ranks, and of the ways in which Scottish noblemen conceived of friends and expressed friendship.

The noblemen – and women – of twelfth- and thirteenth-century Scotland were generous patrons of their immediate and extended families, of their tenants and clients, and perhaps most famously of the monks, nuns, priests and friars dedicated to the service of God. The latter were careful, for the most part, to record the grants and gifts that they received in charters, indentures, chirographs and other kinds of written title deeds, and although the formal Latin style that scribes employed discouraged excesses of editorial expression, the texts of these documents still allowed plenty of scope for references to bonds of amity and friendship. Collectively, such allusions paint a picture of a complex series of interconnected, overlapping personal relationships that illustrate in compelling fashion Brian McGuire's observation that friendship as a category of analysis 'is not a static phenomenon but an expression of human binding that varies according to circumstance'.[7] Supplemented with references from other contemporary documents, including chronicles and diplomatic letters, they reveal that while the kingdom of Scotland may have occupied a peripheral space in the western European world, it was closely in touch with intellectual developments there.

The term 'friend' (*amicus*) and its cognates, then, were already being deployed in a host of new philosophical, spiritual, political and literary contexts when written documents first became popular in Scotland. The charters of the medieval kingdom, like those of nearby England, 'are a rich source for the language of friendship'.[8] In both parts of the British Isles the words were sometimes employed purely as rhetorical flourish, but on occasion scribes made specific allusion to *amici* in order to emphasise special ties of affection or affinity between and among persons. In the years both before and immediately after he succeeded to the throne, for example, David I regularly addressed his charters to his friends, sometimes identifying them specifically as *Francis et Anglis et Scotis*, sometimes linking them in fellowship with his 'barons and men'.[9] It was not, in fact, until the middle of his reign that friends began to disappear from clauses of address in royal documents, and that the phrase *omnibus probis hominibus suis* became 'the standard general address for Scottish royal acts'.[10] Perhaps in imitation of the early practice of royal clerks, in the twelfth century scribes in the employ of secular and ecclesiastical barons also demonstrated a readiness to include friends among the persons addressed in the *inscriptiones* of written deeds. They may well have done so at the behest of the noblemen who commissioned their work. Earls Waldeve and Patrick I of Dunbar, for example, addressed their 'friends and men' in grants issued in favour of the priory of Coldstream, of which they were especially important patrons;[11] Robert II Bruce of Annandale and his son William likewise included their *amici* in charters that bestowed land and fishing privileges on two secular tenants.[12] Richard de Morville, Walter son of Alan, Richard de Melville, Reginald Prat, Earl David of Huntingdon: all considered it appropriate to link friends with the good (*boni*) and worthy (*probi*) men of their lordships as suitable recipients of magnatial greetings.[13] Long after the king's clerks had rejected the familiarity implicit in the terminology of friendship in favour of more formal assertions of dignity and status appropriate to the sovereign authority of the Scottish crown, scribes elsewhere in the realm continued to accept that *amici* might merit a place in address clauses. It is true that such persons never maintained centre stage there; after 1200 the diplomatic customs and practices in use in the royal writing office began to exert a notable influence over those of scribes elsewhere in the realm. By 1250, friends had been all but banished from the opening words of Scottish charters.

Where they do appear, then, references to friends in address clauses merit scrutiny.[14] As Keith Stringer has noted, some of these may have been intended to invoke a 'spirit of chivalrous fellowship' among the people gathered to witness the acts of a great lord,[15] and it is perhaps in this light that, when he acknowledged the coming of age of a new tenant by confirming the latter's title to the family estate, Earl Maoldomhnaich of Lennox (d. c. 1250) assembled the chief men of his lordship and addressed them in welcoming fashion as 'all his friends and men'.[16] In contexts such as this terms of friendship were freighted with significance. Another deed of Maoldomhnaich announced to 'all his friends and men' the earl's gift of valuable fishing rights to the monks of Paisley.[17] The awarding of tocher lands to his sister and her new husband offered another, equally suitable, occasion on which to make special mention of *amici*.[18] The earl's near contemporaries, Earls Gille Brigte and Robert of Strathearn, even more frequently addressed their 'friends and men' or their 'friends and worthy men' when they made public their acts of lordly generosity.[19] As in Lennox, special ceremonies here, too, were designed to bring the good men of the earldom into especially close partnership with the ruling kindred. Thus, in 1220, for example, in his capacity as heir to his father's vast territories and his exalted status as mormaer, Robert undertook a formal confirmation of Gille Brigte's grants to the Austin priory of Inchaffray. He did so before a large assembly of the chief men of the region, whom he addressed as his 'dear friends'; the canons he referred to as his 'most special friends'.[20] References such as these may reflect no more than editorial licence on the part of the individual scribes charged with drafting documents for Maoldomhnaich and Gille Brigte; after all, the informality characteristic of diplomatic practice well into the thirteenth century made it possible for clerks in episcopal and baronial employ to choose from a variety of styles in all aspects of their record writing.[21] It is, none the less, significant that the charters in which Gille Brigte specifically identifies friends were drafted by more than a single scribe, and, moreover, that such familiarity should have begun to wane in the mid-thirteenth century. After c. 1250, the baronial household of Strathearn, like others across the kingdom more generally, grew increasingly sophisticated, and scribes now more consistently aligned their writing practices with models then current among royal clerks. The disappearance of friends from address clauses, therefore, is symptomatic of the spreading influence of the king's chancery where, as indicated above, the term did not remain in regular use after 1150. Women donors in Scotland, it might be noted, do not appear to have been any more likely to refer to *amici* or *amicae* in the opening clauses of their written charters. There are examples of such addresses in documents drafted as far apart as Buchan, Fife and Moray,[22] but these reveal no suggestive patterns.

If donors' friends were generally ushered out of all but a handful of address clauses, they none the less continued to occupy an important place in the mental world of the Scottish nobility. The setting of baronial and ecclesiastical courts offered especially rich venues for landholders and their scribes to note bonds of *amicitia* and to give open expression to the varied notions of friendship that were gaining currency among the *literati* of western Europe. In the 1170s, for example, Eschina the wife of Walter son of Alan I made a gift of land in Mow to the Cluniac monks of Paisley. She did so on behalf of the souls of many people, including King Henry II of England, kings of Scotland living and dead, members of the royal family of Scotland, her deceased daughter and other members of her family, but also, more generously, those of 'all my friends'.[23] In the elaborate charter that they issued in 1198 on the occasion of the foundation of a house of Austin canons at Inchaffray, Earl Gille Brigte and Countess Maud of Strathearn commemorated not only their own souls and those of their kindred, past, present and future, but also, more comprehensively, those 'of all our friends'.[24] Two and a half generations later the clerk who recorded William de Abernethy's gift of an annuity to the Premonstratensian monks of Dryburgh carefully noted the donor's dedication of his grant to a host of intimates, including 'ancestors, successors, friends and family'.[25] Clauses of commemoration and remembrance, it has been shown, accomplished an array of purposes in the social and religious spaces of medieval Scotland, chief among them the forging of a spiritual fellowship between donors and the persons with whom they associated themselves in the act of giving. The link bespoke affection not only in the here and now, but for eternity.[26] Membership in such exclusive affinities was most often reserved to members of the donor's kindred, and the readiness of people like Eschina, Gille Brigte, Maud and William to extend this special status to friends was both unusual and noteworthy.

In Scotland, ceremonies of religious endowment generated highly charged spiritual and emotional spaces within which to express and to record *amicitia*. Across the length and breadth of the kingdom, however, from the mid-twelfth century onwards, charter materials became equally important vehicles for affirming the close association between courts of law and acts of friendship. By the end of the reign of King David I in 1153, clerical scribes were demonstrating a new sensitivity to the language of friendship and a shrewd appreciation of its appropriateness in the environment of court-based dispute resolution. There can be little doubt that changes in charter terminology represent in part Scottish exemplars of a tremendous growth in ecclesiastical law and the spread of canonical procedure, both of which are apparent in the law courts of western Europe more generally at this time. In Scotland, as elsewhere, this process saw lay practices 'sucked into the procedural orbit of the Church'.[27] Legal innovation, for example, is apparent in the introduction to the kingdom of the practice of recording settlements in writing, in the form of indentures, chirographs and final concords. Models for these, borrowed from the papal chancery, were introduced to Scotland directly from Rome by papal legates and papal judges-delegate, as well as via England.[28] The new European emphasis on *amicitia* as 'pragmatic activity' found fertile ground in which to flourish in the northern kingdom,[29] and these kinds of record materials are redolent of the language of friendship.

Scottish clerical scribes were quick to adopt the convention of referring to written settlements by the terms *amicabilis concordia* or *amicabilis compositio*. Editorial licence sometimes allowed for more imaginative or elaborate references, for example to agreements and compromises 'made amicably' between parties,[30] or 'in friendly fashion and charitably'.[31] Other records mention a composition effected in a 'friendly and consensual way';[32] an 'amicable and final concord';[33] a compromise that reached an 'amicable conclusion';[34] disputes 'amicably resolved and ended', or 'amicably agreed'.[35] The terminology of friendship found in these documents often establishes a direct link between the conclusion of enmity and the re-establishment of peace,[36] and, as is the case in England and on the continent, with sentiments of charity and love.[37] Allusions such as these represent more than rhetorical flourish. Words of friendship had a powerful resonance within the milieux of medieval courts of law, and the *literati* of medieval Scotland quite consciously imbued them with the multilayered meanings of friendship familiar to them as a relationship that joined the temporal and the earthly to the eternal and the divine. Yet it was not only in sacred space that friendship flourished. In 1213 the solemnity of a courtroom decision to alter the descent of the earldom of Menteith demanded nothing less than the drafting of an 'amicable concord', duly accomplished after an elaborate ceremony performed before some of the greatest magnates in the realm.[38]

Arbitration represented only one of several procedural options available to litigants in the royal, ecclesiastical and baronial courts of the thirteenth century,[39] but records relating to settlements reached by arbitration and mediation (styled *compositiones, concordiae, ordinationes*) are especially rich and varied in their references to friendship. In 1221 a dispute concerning the patronage of the church of Gullane came before a tribunal at the urging of 'friends of God' from both sides;[40] a year later, the 'common friends' of contending parties once again brought the disputants together for mediation before 'good men' (*boni homines*).[41] The texts of final concords and amicable compositions frequently bear witness to the active role of friends in providing counsel in the highly charged atmosphere of the court. Thus, at Arbroath over the course of the later thirteenth and the early fourteenth centuries disagreements ranging from the location of estate boundaries to the obligation to pay teinds came to a satisfactory conclusion thanks to the 'counsel of friends of both parties'.[42] At Lindores a consensus achieved thanks to the timely intervention of 'friendly mediators' led the disputants to set their seals to a final concord; on another occasion, a quarrel over title to land claimed by the monks ended after members of the assembled court heard – and wisely heeded – the mediation of *amici* who were present.[43]

Friendly advice and counsel were not always proffered from both sides in a dispute, and scribes were careful to note instances in which the *amici* of either complainant or respondent played the deciding role in bringing closure to a case. In the mid-thirteenth century, for example, Walter son of Turpin was persuaded to come to a settlement with the abbot of Arbroath 'after taking counsel with his friends'.[44] Around 1205 William de Valognes accepted the counsel of his friends and abandoned altogether his claim to land in East Lothian to the monks of Newbattle.[45] A case determined before the justiciar of Lothian saw the respondent do the same after his *amici* had advised him of the wisdom of surrender.[46] Still again, in 1283 Earl Malise of Strathearn agreed to place his trust in the prudent counsel of his 'friends and men' in litigation concerning the payment of rents and cain.[47]

The text of the amicable concord to which Malise set his seal leaves little doubt, however, that the earl accepted the advice of his friends with bad grace. His ill humour arose from the obligation to pay second teinds to the abbey of Inchaffray, and his reluctance to acknowledge his debts serves as a salutary reminder, if any were needed, that the language of amity and affection that runs through the texts of so many indentures, concords and chirographs sometimes disguises the rancour that might trouble relations between lords and their beneficiaries. Nowhere is such an appreciation more relevant than in the environment of the vigorous economy of twelfth- and thirteenth-century Scotland, where lords secular and ecclesiastical were engaged in stiff competition for control over the rich revenues of the kingdom's resources and the reformed church had yet to lay out clearly the boundaries of its jurisdiction in matters related to the payment of teinds and appointments to parish churches.[48] A great deal of tension between the ecclesiastical and the secular authorities underlies, for example, the words of friendship found in a series of *compositiones* arranged by Bishop Andrew in the course of his tenure of the bishopric of Moray (1222–42), copies of which a clerk later entered into the cathedral's cartulary.[49] The bishop's relations with his tenants and neighbours were often fractious, a reflection in part of the disorder endemic to the region in the early thirteenth century,[50] but a consequence also of the efforts of the spiritual leaders of Moray to secure adequate funding for their see. The language of *amicitia* that permeates so many of the indentures of Bishop Andrew's time stands in considerable contrast to the acrimony that troubled his episcopate, and only thinly disguises a grim determination on his part to assert ecclesiastical privilege in the face of vigorous opposition from his secular neighbours.

The influence of friends in the venue of the courtroom is most frequently attested in the context of arbitration and mediation but it is evident in several other circumstances, too. Records generated in the resolution of criminal causes reveal the extent to which felons depended on the assistance of friends to help them restore their good name. Thus, in 1334, a thief taken in possession of stolen animals looked to his *amici* to help him redeem a heavy fine.[51] Incidents of feud in later medieval Scotland generated bitter enmity not only between an offender and his victim, but also between the kindred of both parties. Extant documents therefore accord friends almost as prominent a role in the re-establishment of good relations after open animosity as they do the local magnates and heads of kindred involved. The feud that erupted between the Drummond and Menteith families around 1360, for example, was settled only when the former agreed to make amends to two Menteith brothers, as well as 'members of their kin, their friends, their tenants and their adherents'.[52]

Landholders interested in attracting new tenants or in making provision for their souls alienated land, its appurtenances and its income only after thorough and lengthy discussions with persons who had a stake of some kind in the property at issue. The dispositive clauses of charter texts sometimes mention that donors made grants only after securing the consent of family members, especially heirs.[53] More unusually, such clauses sometimes reveal the active participation of friends in the important business of estate management and inheritance planning. In the later 1180s, for example, William de Somerville noted that a grant to the bishop of Glasgow had been made only after he had taken the advice of both family members and friends.[54] Malcolm son of Malcolm confirmed a gift that his grandfather had made to Cambuskenneth abbey 'with the counsel and advice of my kinsmen and friends'.[55] A young nobleman in early thirteenth-century Fife dutifully consulted all his relatives and *amici*, including his uncle and overlord, before alienating in perpetuity a small portion of his estate.[56] The Lennox knight Sir Ralph Noble promised to care for the minor heirs of a favoured tenant by ensuring that only the latter's 'closest friends' would be given custody of the children.[57] Specific mention of the kindred was both an implicit and an explicit statement that the persons so named would not attempt in future to challenge the validity of the grant. Lordly acts accomplished with the added endorsement of friendly assent or consent, however, were of a special nature. They created strong bonds of fictive kinship, by extending membership within the exclusive circle of the family to a select few who were not related by blood, thereby joining them with the donor and his all his *parentes* in the public performance of giving. The marriage of Gaelic notions of fictive kinship and European ideas of special spiritual friendship is strikingly demonstrated in a handful of deeds from early thirteenth-century Renfrew and Argyll, where the monks of Paisley received generous gifts of land from the kindred of the Scoto-Norse lord Somhairle, ruler of Argyll and Kintyre.[58] Its members may have felt a particular affinity for the priory (later abbey) because the monks were reputed to have cared for Somhairle's body after his death in battle in 1164.[59] Raonall, Domhnall and Oengus each in turn identified himself as the priory's *verus frater et amicus*, and each earnestly enjoined his friends and kinsmen to show favour to the house. The monks themselves bestowed 'special friend' status on two other local noblemen,[60] though notably not on other contemporary benefactors, the aggressive and litigious kindred of the earls of Lennox.[61]

Transactions involving the sale and lease of property were as weighty in the urban environment of medieval Scotland as they were in the countryside. In the thirteenth century already, the purchase and alienation of land were closely regulated by burgh custom. A charter in which the widow of a burgess of Perth agreed to surrender her claim to a tenement twice mentions the common counsel that her husbands and friends had given her, first in its dispositive, then in its sealing clauses.[62] Burgh custom held that burgesses who wished to alienate their tenements must first offer these to their relatives;[63] a deed of later that century, however, adds that a Glasgow burgess also extended this favour to his *amici*.[64] References such as these confirm what historians have long known about the importance of neighbourly cooperation and consensus in the conduct of everyday business in the towns of medieval Scotland.[65]

The presence of friends at ceremonies of conveyance and endowment and the crucial role that friendship played in the curial setting reveal that the social space of the thirteenth-century landholding nobility was inclusive, its boundaries at once flexible, accommodating and comprehensive. It suggests also that there is considerable scope, in the study of medieval Scottish lordship, for a consideration of ties of affection above and beyond those of the kindred. Much the same might be said of the fourteenth, when friends retained their valuable roles as advisors to their lords in the business of gifting and granting,[66] donors continued to think it appropriate to commemorate the souls of their *amici* present and future,[67] lords still occasionally addressed them in charters,[68] and a chancery clerk considered appropriate to record as routine in a royal brieve the kinsmen and *amici* of a man accused of homicide.[69] Friends likewise remained instrumental in bringing litigating parties together and in arranging amicable concords and agreements;[70] at Paisley, a scribe was already referring to such persons as *amicabiles compositores*.[71] Significant change to twelfth-century conceptualisations of *amicitia* did not in fact occur in Scotland until well into the fifteenth, when bonds of manrent and the ties of fictive kinship that they forged cast the language of friendship in a series of new conceptual frameworks.[72] Something of the flavour implicit in the forging of alliances based on political friendship, however, is apparent already in the late thirteenth, in the 'amicable agreement' that Robert Bruce made with Count Florence of Holland in 1292. Here, the issue at stake was nothing less than control over the realm of Scotland itself.[73]

Throughout the period 1150–1400 scribes in the employ of baronial houses demonstrated a keen awareness of the special role that friends might play in the complicated world of personal alliance and national politics. That they managed to do so despite the increasingly fossilised structure of charter phraseology reveals how important they believed such *amici* to be. Anyone who has spent any time reading Scottish charter materials will recall that, almost from the moment that such documents were introduced into the kingdom in the twelfth century, donors bestowed grants of land, privilege and income on beneficiaries who were almost universally accorded the status of *dilecti fideli*. Scribal practice in such matters certainly did not change thereafter, but the clerics who drafted written instruments sometimes managed to break the bonds of convention and to identify the recipients of baronial favour with greater imagination and perhaps more accuracy. Thus, around 1250, in a charter that he issued in favour of the Hospitallers, Simon son of Simon of Kinnear also mentioned his *amicus specialissimus*, Hugh de Kilmany.[74] A century later, John Graham lord of Abercorn made a grant of land to his 'beloved friend', Lady Agnes de Munford. He was, perhaps, already positioning himself within the social space of the powerful Douglas clan, one of whose members Agnes would marry before too long.[75] The lengthy text of a tack dated October 1361 notes that one of the two parties involved in a dispute over title to land in Angus agreed to settle when he recognised that the mediator who had offered his services 'was a friend, and that he should avoid getting a reputation for ingratitude' with such a powerful lord.[76] In 1385 Andrew Mercer, merchant, burgess of Perth and lord of Meikleour in Strathearn, arbitrated a dispute between Robert Stewart earl of Fife and Menteith and one of Stewart's tenants. He added to the notarised copy of the resulting agreement a brief comment about his role in bringing the parties together into 'tendyr frenschepe'.[77] Appropriately, an indenture of 1360 that recorded the conclusion of a bitter feud between the supporters of John Drummond and members of the Menteith of Rusky family repeatedly equated the influence of *amici* with that of kindred.[78]

In written instruments of the twelfth and thirteenth centuries friends are sometimes as conspicuous by their absence as they are by their presence. In 1128, for example, Earl Causantin of Fife summoned into his presence all the great men of his province in order to settle a bitter argument over title to the lands of Kirkness which had arisen between the canons of St Andrews and the nobleman Robert de Burgundy. As has been noted on more than one occasion in this volume, the event is noteworthy in several respects; here, its interest lies in the careful note that one observer kept of the 'great multitude' of people who answered the earl's call. Anyone who mattered in contemporary Fife was present that day: among them the *iudex*, several comital officials, members of the provincial army, tenants long resident in the region, even an 'old and venerable man', but, apparently, nary a friend of either earl or prior.[79] In their foundation charter to Inchaffray abbey Gille Brigte of Strathearn and his wife Maud explicitly linked the weal of their souls to that of their friends, but they were highly unusual in doing so, and the foundation charters of other Scottish monastic houses, where these have survived or can reasonably be recovered, make scant allowance for the role of *amici*. By contrast, *probi homines* appear in their thousands in the charter texts that constitute the documentary evidence for the topics examined in this book. They were the people whom donors addressed in ceremonies that celebrated acts of largesse; they were the men who obediently gathered at the command of their king or lord to divulge what they knew about the antecedents of an estate, the age of an heir, the boundaries of a ploughed field, the authenticity of a piece of parchment or a waxen seal. 'Worthy men' also acted in their hundreds as jurors and recognitors and offered their opinions about the crimes, misdemeanours and trespasses of their fellows; they sat in judgment when they supported or rejected claims to free status by the peasants who worked the kingdom's fields. *Boni et probi homini* populate the households of great lords in the guise of members of the kindred or tenants of considerable or lesser stature, and as hangers on or birds of passage visiting halls and fortified castles only temporarily. Many played an important role as advisors when their lords convened courts in order to conduct public ceremonies of grant, sale, purchase, quitclaim and lease, and clerical scribes carefully recorded their names in the witness clauses of charters and other written deeds.[80] As the several chapters of this book have shown, the 'good and worthy men' of Scotland are ubiquitous in the source materials that survive from the period between 1150 and 1400.

Yet, friends, too, managed to make their presence felt, even in the laconic terminology of later medieval instruments of conveyance. That they did so at all reveals much about the mental world of the clerical writers of the time. By the closing years of the fourteenth century, clerical scribes were thoroughly acquainted with the full range of meaning that literate men all over the medieval west associated with *amicitia*. They had also, however, acquired a generations-old familiarity with the customs and mores peculiar to the culture of the Gàidhealtachd, and had developed the skills required to accommodate native Scottish particularism within the Latin tradition of charter writing. The few examples that follow are of a varied nature, but collectively they illustrate the ways in which scribes absorbed, internalised and expressed notions of friendship that drew on the cultures of both Gaels and Europeans. In the twelfth century, notably, scribes trained in the Latin tradition came into immediate contact with the rich tradition of gift giving and hospitality that enabled Gaelic noblemen throughout the British Isles to 'increase their ever-widening circle of friends and retainers, allies and vassals'.[81] An awareness of the unusual nature of the early thirteenth-century Strathearn household, for example, is apparent in the scribal practice there of including in charter witness lists not only the names of the earls' chief tenants, but alongside them wives, sons, daughters, uncles and brothers and individuals like Gille Crìosd the Gael and Richard the son of Lugán, whom they dubbed in especially intimate fashion the earl's *socius* and 'my knight', respectively.[82] The commingling of native and European notions of friendship is discernible in a host of other contexts associated with record keeping, perhaps most notably in seal usage,[83] but also in the readiness of vassals to endow their children with the personal names of their magnate friends.[84]

Twelfth-century English chroniclers recognised in the Scottish royal household the kind of *amici* with whom schoolmen all over Europe would have been familiar. Aelred of Rievaulx, who knew more than most about the subject,[85] described the 'old friendship' (*antiqua amicitia*) that King David I shared with Robert I Bruce.[86] Jordan Fantosme's account of William I's ill fated attempts to annex Northumberland described a similar kind of affection between the king and Sir Roger de Mowbray, and juxtaposed it with William's threat to deny the status of royal *ami* to his opponent, Sir Robert de Vaux.[87] Friendship forged and tested in the thick of war was an important theme of chronicle writing in Scotland in the later thirteenth and the fourteenth centuries. The casual reference by the author of the chronicle now known as *Gesta Annalia II* to the 'true' friendship between Robert I and the earl of Gloucester was later picked up by John Barbour. His poem, *The Bruce*, described the close 'frendschip' that bound the king to a handful of fortunate men, chief among them Sir James Douglas.[88] The understanding of *amicitia* as 'public activity', discussed at the beginning of this chapter, was familiar in the mid-thirteenth century, and had already found expression in diplomatic meetings arranged between envoys representing the crowns of Scotland and England.[89] The author of a formulary of legal brieves and other royal precepts dated c. 1330 used the word in this sense when he included it in his recital of a typical royal commission for negotiating peace with an enemy nation.[90] *Amicitia* of this kind was enacted publicly when King

Henry III of England extended his favour and protection to a select group of noblemen whom he charged with governing Scotland during the minority of Alexander III.[91] The magnates who enjoyed such special attention were in no doubt about what Henry's friendship – or its revocation – meant. Neither were the Guardians when, in March 1288, they addressed Edmund of Cornwall as their *amicus*.[92] After 1296 no landholder of any rank could fail to grasp the divide that separated the political *amici* from Scottish *inimici* in the diplomatic correspondence that issued from the English chancery.[93] In the opening decades of the struggle for independence Scottish intellectuals drew widely on the writings of European philosophers when they sought to escape the onerous burden of English political 'friendship'.[94] As Maurice Powicke pointed out many years ago, the lengthy deliberations of the Great Cause exposed a broad spectrum of Scottish noblemen and intellectuals to contemporary interpretations of natural and Roman law.[95] It was in this context that the author of the poem now known as *Liber Extravagans*, written at the turn of the fourteenth century, appealed to 'friends of the law' in his own attempt to defend Scottish independence.[96]

Between 1150 and 1400 the *literati* of medieval Scotland developed a thorough grasp of the conceptual complexity of *amicitia*, and they deployed the language of friendship with precision whenever they considered it most appropriate, most evocative, most powerful. Recent studies of the manuscript formerly known as the *Chronicle of Melrose* have even made it possible to glimpse the process by which *amicitia* in its new European guise first found its way into the Cistercian annalistic tradition in the kingdom. Entries under the years 1177 and 1185 record, respectively, the deaths of two of the abbey's generous patrons, Walter son of Alan I and Robert Avenel; both were written c. 1200. The monks responsible for compiling this part of the chronicle referred to each of the benefactors as a *familiaris* of Melrose.[97] A generation later, the continuator of this early material had abandoned – as old fashioned? – that term in favour of the more up-to-date *amicus* in his notice of the death of another patron, Patrick I of Dunbar.[98] Other references to friendship in the chronicle, although infrequent, employ the latter.[99] Might the newer terminology have gained currency at Melrose in particular by means of the mortuary rolls that the abbots received on a regular basis and via the 'Cistercian newsnet' that kept its monks in regular contact with developments in England and the continent?[100]

In 1985 Jenny Wormald's study of bonds of manrent led her to suggest that until well into the fifteenth century, friendship 'still carried a clear connotation of kinship'.[101] Yet the evidence examined here suggests that long before this, the social space of the landholding nobility, perceptual, conceptual and lived, was by no means defined merely, or only, by membership in a real or fictive kindred. Its boundaries were fluid enough to accommodate other bonds of affection and a broader category of personal relationship. The formulaic terminology of deeds of conveyance will always make it difficult to reconstruct in thoroughly reliable fashion the social landscape in which noble men and women interacted in the Middle Ages. Yet, this brief study has shown that even these most intransigent of record materials have a great deal to offer the historian of Scottish medieval friendship.

Notes

1. B. A. Hanawalt and M. Kobialka (eds), 'Introduction', in *Medieval Practices of Space* (Minneapolis, 2000), p. ix; H. Lefebvre, *The Production of Space*, trans. D. Nicholson-Smith (Oxford, 1991).
2. J. McEvoy, 'The theory of friendship in the Latin middle ages: hermeneutics, contextualisation and the transmission and reception of ancient texts and ideas, from c.A.D. 350 to c.1500', in J. Haseldine (ed.), *Friendship in Medieval Europe* (Stroud, 1999), pp. 3–44; J. McEvoy, 'Ultimate goods: happiness, friendship, and bliss', in A. S. McGrade (ed.), *The Cambridge Companion to Medieval Philosophy* (Cambridge, 2003), p. 271; Y. Hirata, 'John of Salisbury, Gerard Pucelle and *amicitia*', in Haseldine (ed.), *Friendship in Medieval Europe*, p. 153; J. M. Ziolkowski, 'Twelfth-century understandings and adaptations of ancient friendship', in A. Welkenhuysen, H. Braet and W. Verbecke (eds), *Mediaeval Antiquity* (Louvain, 1995), pp. 59–81; R. Hyatte, *The Arts of Friendship: The Idealization of Friendship in Medieval and Early Renaissance Literature* (Leiden, 1994), pp. 47–86.
3. Ziolkowski, 'Twelfth-century understandings', p. 60.
4. J. McLoughlin, '*Amicitia* in practice: John of Salisbury (c.1120–1180) and his circle', in D. Williams (ed.), *England in the Twelfth Century: Proceedings of the 1988 Harlaxton Symposium* (Woodbridge, 1990), pp. 165–80; J. Haseldine, 'Understanding the language of *amicitia*. The friendship circle of Peter of Celle (c.1115–1183)', *Journal of Medieval History*, 20 (1994), p. 240; J. Haseldine, 'Friendship and rivalry: the role of *amicitia* in twelfth-century monastic relations', *Journal of Ecclesiastical History*, 44 (1993), p. 393.
5. G. Althoff, 'Friendship and political order', in Haseldine (ed.), *Friendship in Medieval Europe*, p. 91.
6. M. Mullett, 'Power, relations and networks in medieval Europe', *Revue belge de philologie et d'histoire/Belgisch tijdschrift voor filologie en geschiedenis*, 83 (2005), pp. 256–9; Althoff, 'Friendship and political order', p. 93; Haseldine, 'Understanding the language of *amicitia*', pp. 258–60.
7. B. P. McGuire, *Friendship and Community: The Monastic Experience, 350–1250* (Kalamazoo, 1988), p. xiii.
8. J. Barrow, 'Friends and friendship in Anglo-Saxon charters' in Haseldine

(ed.), *Friendship in Medieval Europe*, p. 106. For the twelfth century; see J. Meddings, 'Friendship among the aristocracy in Anglo-Norman England', in C. Harper-Bill (ed.), *Anglo-Norman Studies, XXII: Proceedings of the Battle Conference, 1999* (Woodbridge, 2000), pp. 187–204.

9. *Charters of David I*, nos. 4, 14, 16, 23, 25, 28, 166. David's son Henry also addressed his friends, but exclusively in deeds issued in favour of English or French beneficiaries; ibid. nos. 60, 61, 63, 64, 74, 129.
10. G. W. S. Barrow, '*Omnibus probis hominibus [suis]*: the Scottish royal general address (*inscriptio*), c.1126–1847', in T. Kölzer et al. (eds), *De litteris, manuscriptis, inscriptionibus . . .* (Vienna, 2007), p. 59; *RRS*, i, p. 73; *RRS*, ii, pp. 76–7.
11. *Coldstream Chrs*, nos. 7, 26.
12. Fraser, *Annandale*, i, nos. 1, 2.
13. *Panmure Reg.*, ii, p. 69; *Paisley Reg.*, p. 48; Fraser, *Melville*, iii, nos. 4, 8; K. J. Stringer, *Earl David of Huntingdon, 1152-1219: A Study in Anglo-Scottish History* (Edinburgh, 1985), pp. 227 (nos. 2, 13), 232 (no. 23), 234–5 (nos. 27–8), 262 (no. 69), 268 (no. 79). For other early examples, see *Dunfermline Reg.*, nos. 158, 159, 162.
14. For some examples from different parts of the kingdom, see *Dryburgh Liber*, nos. 68, 92, 150, 155, 225; *Arbroath Liber*, i, nos. 35, 37, 56, 58, 63, 70, 80, 89, 93, 94, 206; *Cambuskenneth Reg.*, nos. 71, 86; *Scone Liber*, nos. 58, 84; *Lindores Cart.*, no. 85; *Moray Reg.*, no. 95; *Glasgow Reg.*, nos. 45, 46, 87; *Aberdeen Reg.*, i, p. 14; ii, p. 268; *Morton Reg.*, ii, no. 5; *Paisley Reg.*, pp. 20, 88, 90; Fraser, *Lennox*, ii, no. 1.
15. K. J Stringer, 'The charters of David earl of Huntingdon and lord of Garioch: a study in Anglo-Scottish diplomatic', in K. J. Stringer (ed.), *Essays on the Nobility of Medieval Scotland* (Edinburgh, 1985), p. 82.
16. *Lennox Cart.*, p. 34.
17. *Paisley Reg.*, p. 216. For an example from early thirteenth-century Moray, see Fraser, *Sutherland*, iii, no. 1.
18. Fraser, *Lennox*, ii, App., no. 202. See also no. 204 and no. 205, a charter of Mael Coluim son of Maoldomhnaich that also uses the term *amici* in the address clause.
19. *Inchaffray Liber*, nos. 18, 27; App., nos. 2, 3; *Inchaffray Chrs*, nos. 4, 5, 9, 11, 12, 28, 34, 43, 44.
20. *Inchaffray Chrs*, no. 41; *Inchaffray Liber*, no. 16.
21. G. W. S. Barrow, 'The Scots charter', in G. W. S. Barrow, *Scotland and its Neighbours in the Middle Ages* (London, 1992), pp. 156–8.
22. *Arbroath Liber*, i, no. 132; *Scone Liber*, no. 96; *Moray Reg.*, nos. 106, 107
23. *Paisley Reg.*, p. 74.
24. *Inchaffray Chrs*, no. 9.
25. *Dryburgh Liber*, no. 175.
26. C. J. Neville, 'Women, charters and land ownership in Scotland, 1150–1350', *Journal of Legal History*, 26 (2005), pp. 27–30; E. Jamroziak, 'Making friends

beyond the grave: Melrose abbey and its lay burials in the thirteenth century', *Cîteaux: commentarii Cistercienses*, 56 (2005), pp. 326–31.

27. P. Wormald, 'Charters, law and the settlement of disputes in Anglo-Saxon England', in W. Davies and P. Fouracre (eds), *The Settlement of Disputes in Early Medieval Europe* (Cambridge, 1986), p. 162; J. A. Brundage, *Medieval Canon Law* (New York, 1995), pp. 48–69, 120–53; H. L. MacQueen, 'Canon law, custom and legislation: law in the reign of Alexander II', in R. D. Oram (ed.), *The Reign of Alexander II, 1214–49* (Leiden, 2005), pp. 222–42.
28. Wormald, 'Charters, law and the settlement of disputes', p. 162; see also the entry in the Glossary, p. 270.
29. McLoughlin, '*Amicitia* in practice', pp. 167, 174.
30. *Dryburgh Liber*, no. 269; *Kinloss Records*, p. 116; *Paisley Reg.*, pp. 323–7; *Brechin Reg.*, ii, no. ccxii; *Dunfermline Reg.*, nos. 212–15, 219; *Coupar Angus Chrs*, i, no. 32; *North Berwick Carte*, no. 17.
31. *Dryburgh Liber*, no. 192. For an 'amicable composition and special agreement' dated 1272 x 1282, see *Inchaffray Chrs*, no. 111.
32. *Moray Reg.*, no. 3.
33. *Arbroath Liber*, i, no. 366.
34. *Glasgow Reg.*, no. 143.
35. *Moray Reg.*, no. 39; *Kelso Liber*, no. 181.
36. See, for example, *Dryburgh Liber*, no. 192; *Cambuskenneth Reg.*, no. 118; *May Records*, no. 39.
37. Haseldine, 'Understanding the language of *amicitia*', p. 254; M. T. Clanchy, 'Law and love in the middle ages', in J. Bossy (ed.), *Disputes and Settlements: Law and Human Relations in the West* (Cambridge, 1983), pp. 47–67.
38. Fraser, *Menteith*, ii, p. 214; *CPR, 1258–66*, p. 176.
39. P. C. Ferguson, *Medieval Papal Representatives in Scotland: Legates, Nuncios, and Judges-delegate, 1125–1286* (Edinburgh, 1997), pp. 177–8, 182–5; see also table at pp. 209–68.
40. *Dryburgh Liber*, no. 36. Friends, it has been noted, were 'ideal mediators' in dispute resolution; Althoff, 'Friendship and political order', p. 96.
41. *Dryburgh Liber*, no. 84.
42. *Arbroath Liber*, i, nos. 230, 331.
43. *Lindores Cart.*, nos. 96, 57. See also BL, Harl. Ch. 52 B.16; *Glasgow Reg.*, nos. 127, 140, 147; *Inchcolm Chrs*, no. 19; *Inchaffray Chrs*, no. 111; *Dunfermline Reg.*, nos. 222, 223, 227.
44. *Arbroath Liber*, i, no. 306; see also ibid. no. 366.
45. *Newbattle Reg.*, no. 119.
46. *Glasgow Reg.*, no. 126.
47. *Inchaffray Chrs*, no. 113.
48. Duncan, *Scotland: The Making of the Kingdom* (Edinburgh, 1975), p. 289; G. W. S. Barrow, 'Badenoch and Strathspey, 1130–1312: 2. The church', *Northern Scotland*, 9 (1989), pp. 1–2; MacQueen, 'Canon law, custom and legislation, pp. 236–7; Ferguson, *Medieval Papal Representatives*, p. 189.

49. NLS, Adv. MS. 34.4.10, fos. 15r–v, 18r–21v, 24v, 26r, 28v–29r, 39r–41r–v, 42v–43r; *Moray Reg.*, nos. 27, 28, 31, 35, 39, 74, 77, 83, 87, 88, 94, 120. The observations that follow are based on an examination of the MS cartulary, following the reservations discussed in A. Ross, 'The Bannatyne Club and the publication of Scottish ecclesiastical cartularies', *Scottish Historical Review*, 85 (2006), pp. 217–23. See also another teind dispute in which Bishop Andrew was involved, this time with Kinloss abbey, in *Kinloss Records*, pp. 116–19.
50. G. W. S. Barrow, 'Badenoch and Strathspey, 1130–1312: 1. Secular and political', *Northern Scotland*, 8 (1988), pp. 4–6; R. A. McDonald, *Outlaws of Medieval Scotland: Challenges to the Canmore Kings, 1058–1266* (East Linton, 2003), pp. 45–7.
51. *Exch. Rolls*, i, p. 436.
52. NAS, GD 160/11/1, discussed in S. Boardman, *The Early Stewart Kings: Robert II and Robert III 1371–1406* (Edinburgh, 1996), p. 16.
53. See, for example, *Holyrood Liber*, no. 11; *Kelso Liber*, no. 52; *Cupar Angus Rental*, i, p. 342; NAS, RH 1/6/15; NAS, RH 6/68; NAS, GD 212, Box 10, Coldstream, nos. 21–3; NAS, GD 160/112/2; NLS, Adv. MS. 15.1.18, no. 45; W. W. Scott (ed.), 'Eight thirteenth-century texts', *Scottish History Society Miscellany, vol. XIII* (Edinburgh, 2004), Text 3.
54. *Glasgow Reg.*, no. 52. For similar examples from the twelfth and early thirteenth centuries, see *Paisley Reg.*, pp. 50, 231; Fraser, *Menteith*, ii, pp. 209–10; *Dunfermline Reg.*, no. 179; *Coupar Angus Chrs*, i, no. 30. The participation of members of the kindred in acts of conveyance in contemporary Wales is discussed in M. Griffiths, 'Native society on the Anglo-Norman frontier: the evidence of the Margam charters', *Welsh History Review*, 14 (1988), pp. 200–1, 212–13.
55. *Cambuskenneth Reg.*, no. 194.
56. *Lindores Cart.*, no. 71.
57. Fraser, *Menteith*, ii, pp. 207–8.
58. *Paisley Reg.*, pp. 125–7.
59. A. McDonald, 'Scoto-Norse kings and the reformed religious orders: patterns of monastic patronage in twelfth-century Galloway and Argyll', *Albion*, 27 (1995), p. 212.
60. *Paisley Reg.*, pp. 77–8.
61. C. J. Neville, *Native Lordship in Medieval Scotland: The Earldoms of Strathearn and Lennox, c. 1140–1365* (Dublin, 2005), pp. 138–41.
62. *Scone Liber*, no. 96.
63. *Leges quatuor burgorum*, ch. 42, in *APS*, i, pp. 340–1.
64. *Glasgow Reg.*, no. 236. For other thirteenth-century examples from Glasgow, see *Paisley Reg.*, pp. 382, 385.
65. E. Ewan, 'The community of the burgh in the fourteenth century', in M. Lynch, M. Spearman and G. P. Stell (eds), *The Scottish Medieval Town* (Edinburgh, 1988), pp. 228–44; E. Ewan, *Townlife in Fourteenth-century*

Scotland (Edinburgh, 1991); H. L. MacQueen and W. J. Windram, 'Laws and courts in the burgh', in Lynch, Spearman and Stell (eds), *The Scottish Medieval Town*, pp. 208-27; Duncan, *Making of the Kingdom*, pp. 496-8.

66. *Crossraguel Chrs*, no. 20; *Arbroath Liber*, ii, nos. 27, 29; *Cambuskenneth Reg.*, no. 105; *Moray Reg.*, no. 161; *Paisley Reg.*, pp. 224-6; *Inchaffray Chrs*, no. 135.
67. *Brechin Reg.*, i, no. 13; *Morton Reg.*, ii, no. 176.
68. *Moray Reg.*, no. 154; *Lennox Cart.*, p. 49.
69. *Formulary E: Scottish Letters and Brieves, 1286-1424*, ed. A. A. M. Duncan (Glasgow, 1976), p. 24, dating to 1330 or shortly before.
70. *Brechin Reg.*, ii, no. ccxv; *Cambuskenneth Reg.*, nos. 149, 185, 199; *Moray Reg.*, no. 137 and p. 474, no. 22; *Glasgow Reg.*, no. 255; *Aberdeen Reg.*, i, p. 8; ii, pp. 283, 285; *Paisley Reg.*, p. 47; *Coupar Angus Chrs*, i, no. 96; Fraser, *Sutherland*, iii, no. 11.
71. *Paisley Reg.*, pp. 28, 44, 46, 146. This designation became standard after 1400.
72. J. Wormald, *Lords and Men in Scotland: Bonds of Manrent, 1442-1603* (Edinburgh, 1985); J. Wormald, 'The blood feud in early modern Scotland', in Bossy (ed.), *Disputes and Settlements*, pp. 117-19. See also the recent discussion in A. Cathcart, *Kinship and Clientage: Highland Clanship in Scotland, 1451-1609* (Leiden, 2006), pp. 126-8. The linking of kinsmen and friends in the brieve mentioned above in n. 69 is significant here.
73. *Edward I and the Throne of Scotland, 1290-1296*, ed. E. L .G. Stones and G. G. Simpson, 2 vols (Oxford, 1978), ii, p. 162. The document printed here was almost certainly a forgery, written long after its purported date, but its late thirteenth-century provenance is not in doubt. See G. G. Simpson, 'The claim of Florence, Count of Holland, to the Scottish throne, 1291-2', *Scottish Historical Review*, 36 (1957), pp. 120-22.
74. *Balmerino Liber*, no. 16.
75. *Morton Reg.*, ii, no. 54; J. B. Paul, *The Scots Peerage*, 9 vols (Edinburgh, 1904-14), vi, pp. 196, 342-3.
76. *Panmure Reg.*, ii, p. 174.
77. Fraser, *Menteith*, ii, pp. 261-2. For another reference to Robert Stewart's 'tenderness', see ibid. p. 252.
78. Fraser, *Menteith*, ii, pp. 239-46, discussed Fraser, *Menteith*, i, pp. 109-14.
79. *St Andrews Liber*, pp. 117-18.
80. G. W. S. Barrow, 'Witnesses and the attestation of formal documents in Scotland, twelfth-thirteenth centuries', *Journal of Legal History*, 16 (1995), pp. 1-20.
81. C. M. O'Sullivan, *Hospitality in Medieval Ireland, 900-1500* (Dublin, 2004), p. 110.
82. *Inchaffray Chrs*, nos. 3-5, 9, 11-14, 19, 55; C. J. Neville, 'A Celtic enclave in Norman Scotland: Earl Gilbert and the earldom of Strathearn, 1171-1223', in T. Brotherstone and D. Ditchburn (eds), *Freedom and Authority: Scotland*

c. 1050–c. 1650 – Historical and Historiographical Essays presented to Grant G. Simpson (East Linton, 2000), pp. 81–91; Neville, *Native Lordship*, p. 48.
83. See above, Chapter 3.
84. Such borrowings occurred in twelfth-century Lennox and Strathearn, as they did in Wales and Ireland. Neville, *Native lordship*, pp. 110–11; M. Hammond, 'Ethnicity, personal names and the nature of Scottish Europeanization', in B. K. U. Weiler et al. (eds), *Thirteenth Century England, XI: Proceedings of the Gregynog Conference, 2003* (Woodbridge, 2007), pp. 85–92; F. S. Suppe, 'Roger of Powys, Henry II's Anglo-Welsh middleman, and his lineage', *Welsh History Review*, 21 (2002), pp. 5–6; F. Verstraten, 'Naming practices among the Irish secular nobility in the high middle ages', *Journal of Medieval History*, 32 (2006), pp. 47–52.
85. Aelred's ideas about friendship are discussed in McGuire, *Friendship and Community*, pp. 296–338; Aelred of Rievaulx, *Spiritual Friendship*, ed. and trans. M. E. Laker (Kalamazoo, 1977), pp. 15–40; and E. Freeman, *Narratives of a New Order: Cistercian Historical Writing in England, 1150-1220* (Turnhout, 2002), pp. 68–9, 84–5.
86. Aelred of Rievaulx, *Relatio de standardo*, in *Chronicles of the Reigns of Stephen, Henry II and Richard I*, ed. R. Howlett, 4 vols (London, 1884–9), iii, p. 192.
87. *Jordan Fantosme's Chronicle*, ed. R. C. Johnston (Oxford, 1981), pp. 100, 112.
88. *Chron. Fordun*, i, p. 339; J. Barbour, *The Bruce*, ed. A. A. M. Duncan (Edinburgh, 1977), pp. 87, 769.
89. Matthew Paris, for example, noted that the treaty of York of 1237 was preceded by 'friendly discussions' between the parties. *Matthæi Parisiensis, monachi sancti Albani, chronica majora*, ed. H. R. Luard, 7 vols (London, 1872–83), iii, p. 414.
90. *Formulary E*, ed. Duncan, pp. 41–2.
91. *Foedera*, I, i, pp. 326, 331. See also the letter of King William I's son, Robert de London, sent to Hubert de Burgh in 1220, in which Robert addresses the chancellor as his 'respected lord and dearest friend', in *Royal and Historical Letters Illustrative of the Reign of Henry III*, ed. W. W. Shirley (London, 1862–6), i, no. 140.
92. *Documents Illustrative of the History of Scotland from the Death of King Alexander the Third to the Accession of Robert Bruce*, ed. J. Stevenson, 2 vols (Edinburgh, 1870), I, p. 49.
93. See, for example, *Rot. Scot.*, i, pp. 136, 219, 472, 518, 543, 567–8, 730. See also *Documents Illustrative of the History of Scotland*, ed. Stevenson, ii, p. 370, for Edward I's juxtaposition of the position of England's friends and enemies.
94. A. Broadie, 'John Duns Scotus and the idea of independence', in E. J. Cowan (ed.), *The Wallace Book* (Edinburgh, 2007), pp. 77–8.
95. F. M. Powicke, *The Thirteenth Century, 1216-1307*, 2nd edn (Oxford, 1991), pp. 610–11.

96. *Scotichronicon*, ix, p. 83.
97. *The Chronicle of Melrose from the Cottonian Manuscript, Faustina B. IX, in the British Museum*, ed. A. O. Anderson and M. O. Anderson (London, 1936), pp. 42, 45.
98. Ibid. p. 82. For the dating of the various accretions to the original annals, see *The Chronicle of Melrose Abbey: A Stratigraphic Edition, Vol. 1, Introduction and Facsimile Edition*, ed. D. Broun and J. Harrison (Woodbridge, 2007), pp. 9, 48–55, and A. A. M. Duncan, 'Sources and uses of the chronicle of Melrose, 1167–1297', in S. Taylor (ed)., *Kings, Clerics and Chronicles in Scotland, 500–1297: Essays in Honour of Margaret Ogilvie Anderson on the Occasion of her Ninetieth Birthday* (Dublin, 2000), pp. 147–76.
99. *Chronicle of Melrose*, ed. Anderson and Anderson, pp. 84, 112.
100. Broun and Harrison, *Chronicle of Melrose Abbey*, p. 26; Duncan, 'Sources and uses', p. 161.
101. Wormald, *Lords and Men*, p. 86.

Conclusion

In a ground-breaking study that explored the construction of national identities in the Middle Ages the late Rees Davies drew attention to the existence of a plurality of conceptual frontiers within the British Isles. Each represented a space where the 'political cultures, values and processes' of an indigenous Gaelic population confronted those of English and European aristocrats.[1] The boundaries limning these frontiers, he showed, were at times hotly contested, but everywhere they changed over the course of the three centuries after 1050 as a consequence of close contact between these peoples. The story of that interaction, the telling of which earned Davies widespread admiration, was one of accommodation and acculturation, of the establishment of a successful and productive *modus vivendi*.[2] Davies was quick, none the less, to liken the cultural divide that distinguished natives and newcomers to a shifting tide rather than a yawning gulf. The aptness of the metaphor is readily apparent in the history of the Gaelic language over the duration of the 'Anglo-Norman era' and its immediate aftermath. In 1050 the Gaelic-speaking population vastly outnumbered that of the incoming settlers, but already by 1250 lords like Malise II earl of Strathearn, Maoldomhnaich earl of Lennox and Duncan earl of Carrick had all been forced to acquire competence in the language of a royal court now dominated by noblemen of English, French and Flemish descent. By 1400, moreover, the Inglis of lowland Scotland had so thoroughly triumphed over the Gàedil of the highlands that the chronicler John of Fordun could refer to the spoken word as the trait that most obviously distinguished the civility and peacefulness of the former region from the barbarity and rudeness of the latter.[3] Yet, as the work of Davies and several other scholars has demonstrated, the process by which Inglis displaced Gaelic was by and large peaceful.[4]

The several chapters in this book have revealed much about other contexts in which Gaels and Europeans in Scotland first ventured into each other's conceptual frontiers and the means by which they effected a shift in the boundary lines of each other's worlds. Some of the encounters saw contest and conflict: long after the erection of new lordships in Moray, for example, noblemen loyal to the Mac Malcolm rulers had to deal with the efforts of a displaced and deeply disgruntled aristocracy reluctant to surrender its

CONCLUSION

authority in the region.[5] Likewise, settlers in the south-west competed for authority, often bitterly, with the descendants of the once dominant native dynasty of Feargus of Galloway.[6] Moray and Galloway, however, were exceptional. In most other regions of the kingdom, and in virtually all encounters in which the issues at stake were something other than territory and the exercise of power, relations between Gaels and Europeans were less antagonistic and the process of transculturation more fruitful. In 1150 the cultural touchstones of the Anglo-Norman aristocrat Walter FitzAlan were manifestly unlike those that animated the activities of his near neighbour, Maol Iosa of Strathearn.[7] As the studies above have shown, however, close interaction between their descendants effaced many of those differences. In the generations that followed the deaths of Walter and Maol Iosa, each of the ethnic groups they represented found in the customs, mores and practices of the other much to attract it, so that by 1400 the aristocratic culture of Scotland owed as much to its Gaelic as it did to its European antecedents.

The pace at which this process of hybridisation took place varied according to circumstances, although the 'tides' sometimes shifted discernibly under the impetus of one or the other culture. Thus, the adoption of written instruments as the normal medium for preserving the memory of acts of conveyance occurred almost everywhere in the kingdom after 1150 when European norms associated with record keeping prevailed over the native preference for entrusting the memory of deeds done and actions taken to oral recitations and eye-witness recollections. As Chapter 3 has shown, the spread of the concomitant practice of authenticating documents with waxen seals was more measured in part because, initially at least, the idea of reducing complex notions of kindred and lineage to a two-dimensional medium failed to capture the imagination of Gaelic landholders. That said, by the mid-fourteenth century men and women of consequence throughout the kingdom had come to regard the probative value of seals as virtually unassailable. In a discussion of valid proofs, for example, the text of a mid-fourteenth century assize recalled the liability that had befallen Malise V of Strathearn in the 1330s, when he had foolishly left his seal in the possession of a treacherous follower: the earl lost title to his patrimony.[8] A decade later, by contrast, when he was led off to captivity in England, William Bisset took care to entrust his seal to his mother, who subsequently used it to authenticate agreements on behalf of her son.[9]

As yet another of the chapters in this book has demonstrated, deeply rooted views about personal status among the native population survived relatively unscathed the establishment of a new aristocracy on Scottish soil in the late twelfth and the thirteenth centuries. Legal unfreedom persisted in large part because the incomers found a place within the structure of the

English-style manorial economy they brought with them for a class of men and women to whom Gaelic custom had historically denied rights at law. So, too, were they willing (if not always happy) to accommodate the social aspirations of men of local consequence described in Chapter 5 as 'promoted natives'.[10] By the turn of the fourteenth century, and more certainly as a consequence of the shock that war with England wrought on the kingdom after 1296, many of the linguistic, cultural and political reference points that had once distinguished natives from newcomers were fast becoming obsolete. As Chapter 4 has argued, the single-mindedness that drove both Malise II of Strathearn and his son-in-law Nicholas de Graham to protect title to their estates at all costs was a shared appreciation of the close link between land and family that transcended each man's ethnic background. In a different way, the study of friendship offered in Chapter 6 reveals that Scottish understandings of *amicitia* were informed by both Gaelic and European notions of affinity, affection and alliance.

Perhaps nowhere was the boundary between the customs of the native Gaels and those of the settlers at once more resilient and more porous than in the realm of law. Nowhere, more certainly, is the ebb and flow of competing ideas and traditions that characterised the years between 1150 and 1400 more compellingly illustrated. In the first part of this period incoming aristocrats confronted a legal system that was in most respects alien to that which they had known in England or the continent, a body of law redolent of precepts and practices that they must have considered at least outdated and at worst barbaric. In 1150, for example, the beheading of hand-having thieves and the resolution of disputes by recourse to judicial combat were fast becoming vestigial in all but the most remote reaches of England, but they were still – and they remained – deeply entrenched in Scottish procedure.[11] In the fourteenth century scribes trained in the most up-to-date chancery practices of England and Europe still struggled to cope with terms such as *ranscauth*, *haymhald* and the 'law of Clan MacDuff' and the special rules that they prescribed in Scottish courts of law, including payment in kine rather than coin.[12] Two centuries later, finally, James VI's legal expert Sir John Skene thought it timely to draft a handbook that identified and explained such arcana to his professional brethren.[13] Still again, the many customs and practices associated with the feud and its pacification – letters of slains and remission, assythment, judicial exile – must have struck incoming aristocrats as challenging obstacles to the style of lordly governance for which the vigorous legal reforms of Angevin-era England had prepared them. None the less they adopted them readily enough, just as they did the wide-ranging powers of mediation and arbitration with which these conventions endowed them within their territories.

CONCLUSION

And yet, as Frederic Maitland long ago opined (and the work of his commentators has since confirmed) there was much in twelfth-century Scotland that the settlers found familiar, and a host of conditions that made it possible for them to shape the law to their advantage.[14] The most fundamental, but also the most important, of these was the social, political and economic status that all magnates associated with the possession of land, and the power over men and women that it placed in the hands of aristocratic landholders. As Chapter 1 has shown, after 1150 baronial courts quickly became principal venues for the exercise of lordship the length and breadth of Scotland, much like the assemblies of the mormaers of old had been before the reign of David I. The cohesion of native Gaelic communities offered a ready-made medium through which to give expression to the English institution of the visnet, and juries composed of the *probi homines* drawn from the locality were everywhere rapidly put to work conducting inquests into matters as varied as confirming the age of a dead man's heir, assessing property for the purpose of warrandice and determining the guilt or innocence of an accused felon.[15] As Chapter 2 has argued, the cooperation of native and newcomer was crucial to the all-important business of estate creation: simply put, the carving out of new holdings would not have proceeded as smoothly as it did if the newcomers had not been prepared to give the indigenous Gaels a voice in the restructuring of the rural landscape.

Historians have long acknowledged the debt that the common law of later medieval Scotland owed its English antecedents. The best of recent scholarship acknowledges the extent to which Scottish litigants rejected English practice where this threatened to dislocate too starkly conditions that obtained on the ground. Thus, while William I no doubt 'borrowed shamelessly' from his contemporary Henry II when he formulated some of his assizes,[16] neither he nor his royal successors were willing to reject Gaelic customs out of hand in 'slavish' deference to English sophistication.[17] The process of hybridisation that in the years between 1150 and 1400 transformed the aristocracy of Scotland, the laws by which they governed and the kind of lordship that they exercised over people were the consequence of a rich reciprocal exchange between the cultures of the Gàidhealtachd and Europe in which each of the components was instrumental.

NOTES

1. R. R. Davies, *The First English Empire: Power and Identities in the British Isles, 1093–1343* (Oxford, 2000), p. 92.
2. R. R. Davies, *Domination and Conquest: The Experience of Ireland, Scotland and Wales, 1100–1300* (Cambridge, 1990), p. 62. Other scholars have since taken up

use of the term: see, for example, D. Broun, 'Anglo-French acculturation and the Irish element in Scottish identity', in B. Smith (ed.), *Britain and Ireland, 900–1300: Insular Responses to Medieval European Change* (Cambridge, 1999), p. 152; D. Broun, 'Gaelic literacy in eastern Scotland between 1124 and 1249', in H. Pryce (ed.), *Literacy in Medieval Celtic Societies* (Cambridge, 1998), pp. 185, 198.

3. *Chron. Fordun*, i, p. 38.
4. G. W. S. Barrow, 'The lost Gàidhealtachd of medieval Scotland', in G. W. S. Barrow, *Scotland and its Neighbours in the Middle Ages* (London, 1992), pp. 105–26; Broun, 'Gaelic literacy', pp. 183–201; D. D. Murison, 'Linguistic relationships in medieval Scotland', in G. W. S. Barrow (ed.), *The Scottish Tradition: Essays in Honour of Ronald Gordon Cant* (Edinburgh, 1974), pp. 71–83; H. L. MacQueen, 'Linguistic communities in medieval Scots law', in C. W. Brooks and M. Lobban (eds), *Communities and Courts in Britain, 1150–1900* (London, 1997), pp. 13–23.
5. See here B. E. Crawford, 'The earldom of Caithness and the kingdom of Scotland, 1150–1266', in K. J. Stringer (ed.), *Essays on the Nobility of Medieval Scotland* (Edinburgh, 1985), pp. 25–43 and R. D. Oram, 'David I and the Scottish conquest and colonisation of Moray', *Northern Scotland*, 19 (1999), pp. 1–19.
6. K. J. Stringer, 'Periphery and core in thirteenth-century Scotland: Alan, son of Roland, lord of Galloway and constable of Scotland', in A. Grant and K. J. Stringer (eds), *Medieval Scotland: Crown, Lordship and Community – Essays presented to G. W. S. Barrow* (Edinburgh, 1993), pp. 82–113; K. J. Stringer, 'Acts of lordship: the records of the lords of Galloway to 1234', in T. Brotherstone and D. Ditchburn (eds), *Freedom and Authority: Scotland c. 1050–c. 1650: Historical and Historiographical Essays presented to Grant G. Simpson* (East Linton, 2000), pp. 203–34; R. Oram, *The Lordship of Galloway* (Edinburgh, 2000); R. Oram, 'Fergus, Galloway and the Scots', in R. D. Oram and G. Stell (eds), *Galloway: Land and Lordship* (Edinburgh, 1991), pp. 117–30; R. D. Oram, 'A family business?: colonization and settlement in twelfth- and thirteenth-century Galloway', *Scottish Historical Review*, 72 (1993), pp. 111–45.
7. For FitzAlan, see G. W. S. Barrow, *The Kingdom of the Scots: Government, Church and Society from the Eleventh to the Fourteenth Century*, 2nd edn (Edinburgh, 2003), p. 314; for Strathearn, see C. J. Neville, *Native Lordship in Medieval Scotland: The Earldoms of Strathearn and Lennox, c. 1140–1365* (Dublin, 2005), pp. 14, 17–19.
8. *APS*, i, p. 736; C. J. Neville, 'The political allegiance of the earls of Strathearn during the war of independence', *Scottish Historical Review*, 65 (1986), pp. 143–51.
9. *Dunfermline Reg.*, nos. 382, 383.
10. See above, p. 157.
11. C. J. Neville, *Violence, Custom and Law: The Anglo-Scottish Border Lands in the Later Middle Ages* (Edinburgh, 1998), p. 7; *Wigtownshire Chrs*, p. xxviii;

Glasgow Reg., i, no. 110; *Melrose Liber*, nos. 175, 325; 'Miscellaneous monastic charters', ed. D. E. Easson, *Scottish History Society Miscellany, vol. VIII* (Edinburgh, 1951), pp. 809; J. Raine, *The History and Antiquities of North Durham* (London, 1852), App., nos. 397, 398; *Exch. Rolls*, i, pp. 4, 17, 442; BL, Add MS 24703, fos. 28v–29r.

12. *RMS*, ii, no. 187; Barrow, *The Scottish Tradition: Essays in Honour of Ronald Gordon Cant*, p. 125; *Exch. Rolls*, i, p. 436; *Quoniam Attachiamenta*, ed. T. D. Fergus (Edinburgh, 1996), pp. 135, 207; *Inchaffray Chrs*, App. to Preface, no. 34; J. Bannerman, J., 'MacDuff of Fife', in A. Grant and K. J. Stringer (eds), *Medieval Scotland: Crown, Lordship and Community – Essays presented to G. W. S. Barrow* (Edinburgh, 1993), p. 38. For some examples of fines, forfeitures, amercements and reparations paid in kine, see *Historiae Dunelmensis scriptores tres: Gaufridus de Coldingham, Robertus de Graystanes, et Willelmus de Chambre*, ed. J. Raine (Durham, 1839), i, App., pp. lv–lvi; *Exch. Rolls*, i, pp. 5, 6, 8, 17, 19–20, 49–50, 154; *Aberdeen-Banff Collections*, p. 523; *Documents Illustrative of the History of Scotland from the Death of King Alexander the Third to the Accession of Robert Bruce*, ed. J. Stevenson, 2 vols (Edinburgh, 1870), i, p. 408; *CDS*, v, no. 366.
13. J. Skene, *De significatione verborum* (Edinburgh, 1597).
14. F. Pollock and F. W. Maitland, *The History of English Law Before the Time of Edward I*, 2 vols, 2nd edn (Cambridge, 1968), i, p. 222; G. W. S. Barrow, *The Anglo-Norman Era in Scottish History* (Oxford, 1980), p. 164; J. Hudson, 'Legal aspects of charter diplomatic in the twelfth century: a comparative approach', *Anglo-Norman Studies*, 25 (2003), p. 132. More generally, see H. L. MacQueen, *Common Law and Feudal Society in Medieval Scotland* (Edinburgh, 1993).
15. For some examples of each, see NAS, RH 2/2/13, no. 10a, RH 5/45, RH 5/29; *Highland Papers*, ed. J. R. N. MacPhail, 4 vols (Edinburgh, 1914–34), ii, pp. 125–9; *Arbroath Liber*, i, no. 231.
16. Davies, *First English Empire*, p. 160.
17. H. L. MacQueen, 'Tears of a legal historian: Scottish feudalism and the *ius commune*', *Juridical Review*, New Series (no vol.) (2003), p. 13.

Bibliography

Manuscript sources

Blair Atholl
Muniments of the Duke of Atholl

Durham
Muniments of the Dean and Chapter, Durham Cathedral (DCD)
   Loc. XXVIII
   Miscellaneous Charters
   Specialia

Edinburgh
Edinburgh University Library
Laing Charters

National Archives of Scotland
GD1/54 Haddington documents and miscellaneous papers
GD 1/88 Title deeds to lands in Stirlingshire, the Lennox, Cromarty, Fife and Forfar
GD 1/828 Title deeds to lands of Cloquat, Alyth Parish, Perthshire
GD 1/940 Charter by the earl of Moray
GD 1/967 Renton of Lamberton Charters, etc.
GD 1/1155 Baillie of Coulterallers
GD 1/1386 Charters relating to North Berwick and Thuristoun, East Lothian
GD 24 Stirling Home Drummond Moray of Abercairny
GD 28 Papers of the Marquis of Tweeddale (Yester)
GD 40 Papers of the Kerr family, Marquises of Lothian (Lothian Muniments)
GD 45 Papers of the Maule family, Earls of Dalhousie
GD 55 Charters of the Abbey of Melrose
GD 82 Makgill, Viscounts Oxfuird, General Series
GD 83 Papers of the Ramsay family of Bamff, Perthshire
GD 84 Papers of the Mackay family, Lords Reay
GD 93 Papers of the Munro family of Foulis
GD 124 Papers of the Erskine family, Earls of Mar and Kellie
GD 125 Papers of the family of Rose of Kilravock
GD 160 Papers of the Drummond family, Earls of Perth (Drummond Castle Papers)

GD 198 Papers of the Haldane family of Gleneagles, Perthshire
GD 203 Lindsay papers
GD 212 Maitland Thomson notebooks
GD 220 Papers of the Graham family, Dukes of Montrose (Montrose Muniments)
GD 254 Papers of the Lindsay family of Dowhill
PA 5 Manuscript Collections of early Scottish laws
RH 1 Miscellaneous Transcripts
RH 2/2/13, Cosmo Innes's Transcripts, vol. 1
RH 5 Documents Transferred from Public Record Office, London
RH 6 Register House charters, 1st series

National Library of Scotland
Acc. 9769 Crawford papers
Adv. Charters
Adv. MS. 15.1.18
Adv. MS. 22.2.14
Adv. MS. 29.4.2(x)
Adv. MS. 33.2.32
Adv. MS. 34.1.3A
Adv. MS. 34.2.1b
Adv. MS. 34.4.3
Adv. MS. 34.4.10

Scottish Catholic Archives
MS JB 1, no. 3, Liber Ruber Ecclesiae

Glasgow
Glasgow University Library
General Manuscripts

Royal Faculty of Procurators
Hill Collection of MSS, Macfarlane Muniments

London
British Library
Add MS 24703
Add MS 33245
Cotton Charters, xviii
Lord Frederick Campbell Charters, xxx
Harley Charters
Harley Manuscript 4693

The National Archives
C 47 Chancery: Miscellanea
C 66 Chancery and Supreme Court of Judicature: Patent Rolls
C 81 Chancery: Warrants for the Great Seal, Series I
C 145 Chancery: Miscellaneous Inquisitions
DL 25 Duchy of Lancaster: Deeds, Series L
DURH 3 Palatinate of Durham: Chancery Court: Cursitor's Records
E 39 Exchequer: Treasury of Receipt: Scottish Documents
E 101 King's Remembrancer: Accounts Various
E 145 Exchequer: King's Remembrancer: Extents etc. (Excise)
E 159 Exchequer: King's Remembrancer: Memoranda Rolls and Enrolment Books
E 368 Exchequer: Lord Treasurer's Remembrancer: Memoranda Rolls
E 372 Exchequer: Pipe Office: Pipe Rolls
JUST 1 Justices in Eyre, of Assize, of Oyer and Terminer, and of the Peace, etc.: Rolls and Files
KB 26 Court of Common Pleas and King's Bench, and Justices Itinerant: Early Plea and Essoin Rolls
SC 1 Special Collections: Ancient Correspondence of the Chancery and the Exchequer
SC 8 Special Collections: Ancient Petitions

Perth
Messrs Condie, Mackenzie and Co., Kinnoull Trustees' Muniments

Woodhorn
Northumberland Record Office
Swinburne (Capheaton) Estate Papers, ZSW/1/1/16

Printed primary sources

APS, i; *Acts of the Parliaments of Scotland*, ed. T. Thomson and C. Innes, 12 vols (Edinburgh, 1814–75).
Aberdeen-Banff Antiquities; Illustrations of the Topography and Antiquities of the Shires of Aberdeen and Banff, ed. J. Robertson and G. Grub, 4 vols (Edinburgh, 1843).
Aberdeen-Banff Collections; Collections for a History of the Shires of Aberdeen and Banff, ed. J. Robertson and G. Grub, 5 vols (Aberdeen, 1843–69).
Aberdeen Reg.; Registrum episcopatus Aberdonensis, ed. C. Innes, 2 vols (Edinburgh, 1845).
The Acts of the Welsh Rulers, 1120–1283, ed. H. Pryce (Cardiff, 2005).
Aelred of Rievaulx, *Relatio de standardo*, in R. Howlett (ed.), *Chronicles of the Reigns of Stephen, Henry II and Richard I*, 4 vols (London, 1884–9).
Aelred of Rievaulx, *Spiritual Friendship*, ed. and trans. M. E. Laker (Kalamazoo, 1977).

BIBLIOGRAPHY

Anglo-Scottish Relations 1174–1328: Some Selected Documents, ed. E. L. G. Stones (Oxford, 1965).

Arbroath Liber; Liber s. Thome de Aberbrothoc, ed. C. Innes and P. Chalmers, 2 vols (Edinburgh, 1848–56).

Aspilogia II: Rolls of Arms temp. Henry III, ed. T. D. Tremlett and H. S. London, 2 vols (London, 1967).

Aspilogia III: Rolls of Arms of Edward I (1272–1307), ed. G. J. Brault, 2 vols (Woodbridge, 1997).

Balmerino Liber; Liber sancte Marie de Balmorinach, ed. W. B. D. D. Turnbull (Edinburgh, 1841).

Barbour, J., *The Bruce*, ed. A. A. M. Duncan (Edinburgh, 1997).

Bateson, M., 'The Scottish king's household and other fragments, from a fourteenth century manuscript in the library of Corpus Christi College, Cambridge', *Scottish History Society Miscellany*, vol. II (Edinburgh, 1904), pp. 3–43.

Beauly Chrs; The Charters of the Priory of Beauly, ed. E. C. Batten (London, 1977).

The Binns Papers 1320–1864, ed. J. Dalyell and J. Beveridge (Edinburgh, 1938).

Birch, W. de G., *Catalogue of Seals in the Department of Manuscripts in the British Museum*, 6 vols (London, 1887–1900).

Bracton, Henricus de, *De legibus et consuetudinibus Angliae*, ed. S. F. Thorne, 4 vols (Cambridge, MA, 1968–77).

CCR; Calendar of the Close Rolls preserved in the Public Record Office. Edward I, 5 vols (London, 1900–8).

CDS; Calendar of Documents relating to Scotland preserved in Her Majesty's Public Record Office, London, ed. J. Bain, G. G. Simpson and R. L. G. Stones, 5 vols (Edinburgh, 1881–8, 1986).

CFR; Calendar of the Fine Rolls preserved in the Public Record Office, ed. H. C. Maxwell-Lyte, 22 vols (London, 1911–62).

CIPM; Calendar of Inquisitions Post Mortem and Other Analogous Documents preserved in the Public Record Office, ed. H. C. Maxwell-Lyte, 17 vols (London, 1898–1955).

CPR; Calendar of the Patent Rolls preserved in the Public Record Office, Edward I, 4 vols (London, 1893–1901)

CPR; Calendar of the Patent Rolls preserved in the Public Record Office, Henry III, 5 vols (London, 1906–13).

Calendar of Documents relating to Ireland preserved in Her Majesty's Public Record Office . . . 1171[–1307], ed. H. S. Sweetman, 5 vols (London, 1875–86).

Calendar of Entries in the Papal Registers relating to Great Britain and Ireland (Regesta Romanorum pontificum): Papal Letters, ed. W. H. Bliss et al., 14 vols (London, 1893–1960).

Calendar of the Justiciary Rolls or Proceedings in the Court of the Justiciar of Ireland preserved in the Public Record Office of Ireland. XXIII. to XXXI. Years of Edward I, ed. J. Mills (Dublin, 1905).

Calendar of Writs preserved at Yester House 1166–1503, ed. C. C. H. Harvey and J. Macleod (Edinburgh, 1930).

Cambuskenneth Reg.; Registrum monasterii s. Marie de Cambuskenneth, ed. W. Fraser (Edinburgh, 1872).
Charters of David I; The Charters of David I: The Written Acts of David I King of Scots, 1124–53, and of his Son Henry, Earl of Northumberland, 1139–52, ed. G. W. S. Barrow (Woodbridge, 1999).
Chartularium abbathiae de novo monasterio: ordinis Cisterciensis, fundatae anno M.C.XXXVII, ed. J. T. Fowler (Durham, 1878).
Chron. Fordun; Joannis de Fordun Chronica gentis Scotorum, ed. W. F. Skene, 2 vols (Edinburgh, 1871–2).
Chronica magistri Rogeri de Houedene, ed. W. Stubbs, 4 vols (London, 1868–71).
The Chronicle of Melrose Abbey: A Stratigraphic Edition, Vol. 1, Introduction and Facsimile Edition, ed. D. Broun and J. Harrison (Woodbridge, 2007).
The Chronicle of Melrose from the Cottonian Manuscript, Faustina B. IX, in the British Museum, ed. A. O. Anderson and M. O. Anderson (London, 1936).
Chronicles of the Picts, Chronicles of the Scots, and Other Early Memorials of Scottish History, ed. W. F. Skene (Edinburgh, 1867).
Close Rolls of the Reign of Henry III, ed. H. C. Maxwell-Lyte, 14 vols (London, 1902–38).
Coldstream Chrs; Chartulary of the Cistercian Priory of Coldstream, ed. C. Rogers (London, 1879).
Cooper, T. M., *Select Scottish Cases of the Thirteenth Century* (Edinburgh, 1914).
The Correspondence, Inventories, Account Rolls and Law Proceedings of the Priory of Coldingham, ed. J. Raine (Durham, 1841).
Coupar Angus Chrs; Charters of the Abbey of Coupar Angus, ed. D. E. Easson, 2 vols (Edinburgh, 1947).
Críth Gablach, ed. D. A. Binchy (Dublin, 1979).
Crossraguel Chrs; Charters of the Abbey of Crossraguel, ed. F. C. H. Blair, 2 vols (Edinburgh, 1886).
The Declaration of Arbroath, ed. J. Fergusson (Edinburgh, 1970).
Documents Illustrative of the History of Scotland from the Death of King Alexander the Third to the Accession of Robert Bruce, ed. J. Stevenson, 2 vols (Edinburgh, 1870).
Documents and Records Illustrating the History of Scotland, ed. F. Palgrave (London, 1937).
Dryburgh Liber; Liber s. Marie de Dryburgh, ed. J. Spottiswoode (Edinburgh, 1847).
Dunfermline Reg.; Registrum de Dunfermelyn, ed. C. Innes (Edinburgh, 1842).
Early Scottish Charters Prior to A.D. 1153, ed. A. C. Lawrie (Glasgow, 1905).
Edward I and the Throne of Scotland, 1290–1296, ed. E. L .G. Stones and G. G. Simpson, 2 vols (Oxford, 1978).
Excerpta è rotulis finium in turri Londinensi asservatis, Henrico tertio rege, A.D. 1216–72, ed. C. Roberts, 2 vols (London, 1835–6).
Exch. Rolls; Rotuli scaccarii regum Scotorum. The Exchequer Rolls of Scotland, ed. J. Stuart et al., 23 vols (Edinburgh, 1878–1908).

BIBLIOGRAPHY

Expugnatio Hibernica: The Conquest of Ireland, ed. A. B. Brian and F. X. Martin (Dublin, 1978).
Facsimiles of the National Manuscripts of Scotland, ed. H. James, 3 vols (London, 1867–71).
Feet of Fines, Northumberland and Durham, ed. A. M. Oliver and C. Johnson, 2 vols (Durham, 1931).
Foedera; Foedera, conventiones, literae et cuiuscunque generis acta publica . . ., ed. T. Rymer, 4 vols in 7 (London, 1816–69).
Formulary E: Scottish Letters and Brieves, 1286–1424, ed. A. A. M. Duncan (Glasgow, 1976).
Formulary of Old Scots Legal Documents, ed. P. Gouldesbrough (Edinburgh, 1985).
Fraser, *Annandale*; Fraser, W., *The Annandale Family Book of the Johnstones, Earls and Marquises of Annandale*, 2 vols (Edinburgh, 1894).
Fraser, *Carlaverock*; Fraser, W., *The Book of Carlaverock*, 2 vols (Edinburgh, 1873).
Fraser, *Colquhoun*; Fraser, W., *The Chiefs of Colquhoun and their Country*, 2 vols (Edinburgh, 1869).
Fraser, *Douglas*; Fraser, W., *The Douglas Book*, 4 vols (Edinburgh, 1885).
Fraser, *Grandtully*; Fraser, W., *The Red Book of Grandtully*, 2 vols (Edinburgh, 1868).
Fraser, *Grant*; Fraser, W., *The Chiefs of Grant*, 3 vols (Edinburgh, 1883).
Fraser, *Lennox*; Fraser, W., *The Lennox*, 2 vols (Edinburgh, 1874).
Fraser, *Melville*; Fraser, W., *The Melvilles, Earls of Melville and the Leslies, Earls of Leven*, 3 vols (Edinburgh, 1890).
Fraser, *Menteith*; Fraser, W., *The Red Book of Menteith*, 2 vols (Edinburgh, 1880).
Fraser, *Sutherland*; Fraser, William, *The Sutherland Book*, 3 vols (Edinburgh, 1892).
Gesta regis Henrici secundi Benedicti abbatis, ed. W. Stubbs, 2 vols (London, 1867).
Glasgow Reg.; Registrum episcopatus Glasguensis, ed. C. Innes, 2 vols (Edinburgh, 1843).
The Great Roll of the Pipe for the Sixth Year of the Reign of King Richard the First, Michaelmas 1194, ed. D. M. Stenton (London, 1928).
The Great Roll of the Pipe for the Thirty-first Year of the Reign of King Henry the Second. A.D. 1184–1185, ed. J. H. Round (London, 1913).
The Great Roll of the Pipe for the Thirty-second Year of the Reign of King Henry the Second, A.D. 1185–1186, ed. J. H. Round (London, 1914).
Highland Papers, ed. J. R. N. MacPhail, 4 vols (Edinburgh, 1914–34).
Historiae Dunelmensis scriptores tres: Gaufridus de Coldingham, Robertus de Graystanes, et Willelmus de Chambre, ed. J. Raine (Durham, 1839).
Holyrood Liber; Liber cartarum Sancte Crucis, ed. C. Innes (Edinburgh, 1840).
Inchaffray Chrs; Charters, Bulls and Other Documents relating to the Abbey of Inchaffray, ed. W. A. Lindsay, J. Dowden and J. M. Thomson (Edinburgh, 1908).
Inchaffray Liber; Liber insule missarum, ed. C. Innes (Edinburgh, 1847).

Inchcolm Chrs; Charters of the Abbey of Inchcolm, ed. D. E. Easson and A. Macdonald (Edinburgh, 1938).
Irish Historical Documents, ed. E. Curtis and R. B. McDowell (London, 1943).
Irish Royal Charters: Texts and Contexts, ed. M. T. Flanagan (Oxford, 2005).
Jordan Fantosme's Chronicle, ed. R. C. Johnston (Oxford, 1981).
Kelso Liber; Liber s. Marie de Calchou, ed. C. Innes (Edinburgh, 1846).
Kinloss Records; Records of the Monastery of Kinloss, ed J. Stuart (Edinburgh, 1872).
Laing Chrs; Calendar of the Laing Charters, A.D. 854–1837, ed. J. Anderson (Edinburgh, 1899).
Laing, H., *Descriptive Catalogue of Impressions from Ancient Scottish Seals* (Edinburgh, 1850).
Laing, H., *Supplemental Descriptive Catalogue of Ancient Scottish Seals, Royal, Baronial, Ecclesiastical, and Municipal, embracing the period from A.D. 1150 to the Eighteenth Century* (Edinburgh, 1866).
Lennox Cart.; Cartularium comitatus de Levenax, ed. J. Dennistoun (Edinburgh, 1833).
Liber feodorum: The Book of Fees commonly called Testa de Nevill, ed. H. C. Maxwell-Lyte, 3 vols (London, 1920–31).
Life of St. Margaret Queen of Scotland by Turgot Bishop of St Andrews, ed. W. Forbes-Leith (Edinburgh, 1884).
Lindores Cart.; Chartulary of the Abbey of Lindores, ed. J. Dowden (Edinburgh, 1903).
Lives of S. Ninian and S. Kentigern, ed. A. P. Forbes (Edinburgh, 1874).
Matthew Paris; Matthæi Parisiensis, monachi sancti Albani, chronica majora, ed. H. R. Luard, 7 vols (London, 1872–83).
May Records; Records of the Priory of the Isle of May, ed. J. Stuart (Edinburgh, 1868).
Melrose Liber; Liber sancte Marie de Melros, ed. C. Innes, 2 vols (Edinburgh, 1837).
Memoranda de Parliamento, 1305, ed. F. W. Maitland (London, 1893).
Midlothian Chrs; Registrum domus de Soltre, necnon ecclesie collegiate S. Trinitatis prope Edinburgh, . . . Charters of the Hospital of Soltre, of Trinity College, Edinburgh, and Other Collegiate Churches in Mid-Lothian, ed. D. Laing (Edinburgh, 1861).
'Miscellaneous monastic charters', ed. D. E. Easson, *Scottish History Society Miscellany*, vol. VIII (Edinburgh, 1951), pp. 1–16.
Miscellany of the Spalding Club, ed. J. Stuart, 5 vols (Aberdeen, 1841–52).
Moray Reg.; Registrum episcopatus Moraviensis e pluribus codicibus consarcinatum circa A.D. MCC, ed. C. Innes (Edinburgh, 1837).
Morton Reg.; Registrum honoris de Morton, ed. T. Thomson, A. Macdonald and C. Innes, 2 vols (Edinburgh, 1853).
Neilson, G. (ed.), 'The March Laws', in *Stair Society Miscellany*, vol. I (Edinburgh, 1971), pp. 15–24.
Newbattle Reg.; Registrum s. Marie de Neubotle abbacie Cisterciensis beate virginis de Neubotle chartarium vetus, 1140–1528, ed. C. Innes (Edinburgh, 1849).
North Berwick Carte; Carte monialium de Northberwic, ed. C. Innes (Edinburgh, 1847).

The Northumberland Lay Subsidy Roll of 1296, ed. C.M. Fraser (Newcastle-upon-Tyne, 1968).
Northumberland Pleas from De Banco Rolls 20–37 (5–8 Edward I), ed. A. H. Thompson (Durham, 1950).
The Original Chronicle of Andrew of Wyntoun, ed. F. J. Amours, 6 vols (Edinburgh, 1903–14).
Paisley Reg.; Registrum monasterii de Passelet, ed. C. Innes (Glasgow, 1832).
Panmure Reg.; Registrum de Panmure, ed. H. Maule (Edinburgh, 1874).
Patent Rolls of the Reign of Henry III, ed. H. C. Maxwell-Lyte, 6 vols (London, 1893–1913).
The Peterborough Chronicle 1070–1154, ed. C. Clark, 2nd edn (Oxford, 1970).
The Pipe Roll of Cloyne, ed. P. MacCotter and K. Nicholls (Midleton, 1996).
Placita de quo warranto, temporibus Edw. I. II. & III., ed. W. Illingworth (London, 1818).
Quoniam Attachiamenta, ed. T. D. Fergus (Edinburgh, 1996).
RMS; Registrum magni sigilli regum Scottorum, ed. J. M. Thomson et al., 11 vols (Edinburgh, 1882–1914).
RRS, i; The Acts of Malcolm IV King of Scots, 1153–1154, Regesta Regum Scottorum, vol. I, ed. G. W. S. Barrow (Edinburgh, 1960).
RRS, ii; The Acts of William I King of Scots, 1165–1214, Regesta Regum Scottorum, vol. II, ed. G. W. S. Barrow (Edinburgh, 1971).
RRS, v; The Acts of Robert I King of Scots, 1306–1329, Regesta Regum Scottorum, vol. V, ed. A. A. M. Duncan (Edinburgh, 1988).
The Records of the Parliaments of Scotland to 1707, ed. K. M. Brown et al. (St Andrews, 2007), www.rps.ac.uk.
Regiam Majestatem and Quoniam Attachiamenta, ed. T. M. Cooper (Edinburgh, 1947).
Reginaldi monachi Dunelmensis libellus de admirandis beati Cuthberti virtutibus, ed. J. Raine (Durham, 1835).
The Register of Brieves as contained in the Ayr MS., the Bute MS. and Quoniam Attachiamenta, ed. T. M. Cooper (Edinburgh, 1946).
The Register of William Greenfield Lord Archbishop of York, 1306–1315, ed. A. H. Thompson, 5 vols (Durham, 1931–40).
Registrum episcopatus Brechinensis, 2 vols (Edinburgh, 1856).
Registrum palatinum Dunelmense: The Register of Richard de Kellawe, Lord Palatine and Bishop of Durham, 1311–16, ed. T. D. Hardy, 4 vols (London, 1873–78).
Registrum prioratum omnium sanctorum iuxta Dublin, ed. R. Butler (Dublin, 1845).
Rental Book of the Cistercian Abbey of Cupar-Angus, ed. C. Rogers, 2 vols (Edinburgh, 1879–80).
Robertson, W., *An Index, drawn up around the year 1629, of many records of charters, granted by the different sovereigns of Scotland between the years 1309 and 1413* (Edinburgh, 1798).

Rot. Scot.; *Rotuli Scotiae in turri Londoniensi et in domo capitulari Westmonasteriensi asservati*, ed. D. MacPherson et al., 2 vols (London, 1814–19).
Royal Commission on the Ancient and Historical Monuments of Scotland, *Eleventh Report with Inventory of Monuments and Construction in the Counties of Fife, Kinross and Clackmannan* (Edinburgh, 1933).
Royal and Historical Letters Illustrative of the Reign of Henry III, ed. W. W. Shirley, 2 vols (London, 1862–6).
Scone Liber; *Liber ecclesie de Scon*, ed. C. Innes (Edinburgh, 1843).
Scotichronicon; *Scotichronicon by Walter Bower in Latin and English*, gen. ed. D. E. R. Watt, 9 vols (Aberdeen, 1987–97).
Scott, W. W. (ed.), 'Eight thirteenth-century texts', *Scottish History Society Miscellany, vol. XIII* (Edinburgh, 2004), pp. 1–41.
Selectus diplomatum et numismatum Scotiae thesaurus, ed. J. Anderson (Edinburgh, 1739).
The Sheriff Court Book of Fife, 1515–1522, ed. W. C. Dickinson (Edinburgh, 1928).
Skene, J., *De significatione verborum* (Edinburgh, 1597).
St Andrews Liber; *Liber cartarum prioratus sancti Andree in Scotia*, ed. T. Thomson (Edinburgh, 1841).
Statutes of the Scottish Church, ed. D. Patrick (Edinburgh, 1907).
Stevenson, J. H. and M. Wood, *Scottish Heraldic Seals: Royal, Official, Ecclesiastical, Collegiate, Burghal, Personal*, 3 vols (Glasgow, 1940).
Swinton, G. S. C., 'Six Early Charters', *Scottish Historical Review* 2 (1905), pp. 173–80.
Symeonis monachi opera omnia, ed. T. Arnold, 2 vols (London, 1882–5).
Three Early Assize Rolls for the County of Northumberland, saec. XIII, ed. W. Page (Durham, 1891).
Tractatus de legibus et consuetudinibus Angliae qui Glanvilla vocatur, ed. G. D. G. Hall (London, 1965).
The Triumph Tree, ed. T. O. Clancy (Edinburgh, 1998).
Vetera monumenta Hibernorum et Scotorum historiam illustrantia, ed. A. Theiner (Rome, 1864), no. 335.
Watt, D. E. R., *A Biographical Dictionary of Scottish Graduates to A.D. 1410* (Oxford, 1977).
Wigtownshire Chrs; *Wigtownshire Charters*, ed. R. C. Reid (Edinburgh, 1960).
William of Malmesbury, *Gesta regum Anglorum*, ed. W. Stubbs, 2 vols (London, 1887–9).

Secondary sources

Ailes, A., 'Heraldry in twelfth-century England: the evidence', in D. Williams (ed.), *England in the Twelfth Century: Proceedings of the 1988 Harlaxton Symposium* (Woodbridge, 1990), pp. 1–16.
Ailes, A., 'The knight, heraldry and armour: the role of recognition and the origins of heraldry', in C. Harper-Bill and R. Harvey (eds), *Medieval Knighthood IV:*

BIBLIOGRAPHY

Papers from the Fifth Strawberry Hill Conference 1990 (Woodbridge, 1992), pp. 1–21.

Aird, W. M., 'Northern England or southern Scotland? The Anglo-Scottish border in the eleventh and twelfth centuries and the problem of perspective', in J. C. Appleby and P. Dalton (eds), *Government, Religion and Society in Northern England, 1000–1700* (Stroud, 1997), pp. 27–39.

Aitchison, N. B., *The Picts and the Scots at War* (Stroud, 2003).

Alexander, A., 'Perambulations and boundary descriptions', in H. E. J. Le Patourel, M. H. Long and M. F. Pickles (eds), *Yorkshire Boundaries* (Leeds, 1993), pp. 39–51.

Althoff, G., 'Friendship and political order', in J. Haseldine (ed.), *Friendship in Medieval Europe* (Stroud, 1999), pp. 91–105.

Anderson, J., '"Marjorie" Comyn or Dunbar', *Scottish Historical Review*, 1 (1904), pp. 228–31.

Anderson, M. O., 'The Celtic church in Kinrimund', *Innes Review*, 25 (1974), pp. 67–76.

Arlinghaus, F.-J., M. Ostermann, O. Plessow and G. Tscherpel (eds), *Transforming the Medieval World: Uses of Pragmatic Literacy in the Middle Ages* (Turnhout, 2006).

Bannerman, J., 'The king's poet and the inauguration of Alexander III', *Scottish Historical Review*, 68 (1989), pp. 120–49.

Bannerman, J., 'Literacy in the highlands', in I. B. Cowan and D. Shaw (eds), *The Renaissance and Reformation in Scotland: Essays in Honour of Gordon Donaldson* (Edinburgh, 1983), pp. 214–35.

Bannerman, J., 'The lordship of the Isles', in J. M. Brown (ed.), *Scottish Society in the Fifteenth Century* (London, 1977), pp. 209–40.

Bannerman, J., 'MacDuff of Fife', in A. Grant and K. J. Stringer (eds), *Medieval Scotland: Crown, Lordship and Community – Essays presented to G. W. S. Barrow* (Edinburgh, 1993), pp. 20–38.

Bannerman, J., 'The Scots language and the kin-based society', in D. S. Thomson (ed.), *Gaelic and Scots in Harmony: Proceedings of the Second International Conference on the Languages of Scotland (University of Glasgow, 1988)* (Glasgow, 1988), pp. 1–19.

Barrow, G. W. S., *The Anglo-Norman Era in Scottish History* (Oxford, 1980).

Barrow, G. W. S., 'The army of Alexander III's Scotland', in N. H. Reid (ed.), *Scotland in the Reign of Alexander III, 1249–1286* (Edinburgh, 1990), pp. 132–47.

Barrow, G. W. S., 'Badenoch and Strathspey, 1130–1312. 1. Secular and political', *Northern Scotland*, 8 (1988), pp. 1–7.

Barrow, G. W. S., 'Badenoch and Strathspey, 1130–1312. 2. The church', *Northern Scotland*, 9 (1989), pp. 1–16.

Barrow, G. W. S., 'The earls of Fife in the 12th century', *Proceedings of the Society of Antiquaries of Scotland*, 87 (1955), pp. 51–62.

Barrow, G. W. S., 'The early charters of the family of Kinninmonth of that ilk', in D. A. Bullough and R. L. Storey (eds), *The Study of Medieval Records: Essays in Honour of Kathleen Major* (Oxford, 1971), pp. 107–31.

Barrow, G. W. S., *The Kingdom of the Scots: Government, Church and Society from the Eleventh to the Fourteenth Century*, 2nd edn (Edinburgh, 2003).
Barrow, G. W. S., *Kingship and Unity: Scotland, 1000–1306*, 2nd edn (Edinburgh, 2003).
Barrow, G. W. S., 'The lost Gàidhealtachd of medieval Scotland', in G. W. S. Barrow, *Scotland and its Neighbours in the Middle Ages* (London, 1992), pp. 105–26.
Barrow, G. W. S., '*Omnibus probis hominibus [suis]*: the Scottish royal general address (*inscriptio*), c.1126–1847', in T. Kölzer, F.-A. Bornschlegel, C. Friedl and G. Vogeler (eds), *De litteris, manuscriptis, inscriptionibus* (Vienna, 2007), pp. 57–66.
Barrow, G. W. S., 'The pattern of lordship and feudal settlement in Cumbria', *Journal of Medieval History*, 1 (1975), pp. 117–38.
Barrow, G. W. S., 'Popular courts', in G. W. S. Barrow, *Scotland and its Neighbours in the Middle Ages* (London, 1992), pp. 217–45.
Barrow, G. W. S., 'Pre-feudal Scotland: shires and thanes', in G. W. S. Barrow, *The Kingdom of the Scots: Government, Church and Society from the Eleventh to the Fourteenth Century*, 2nd edn (Edinburgh, 2003), pp. 7–56.
Barrow, G. W. S., *Robert Bruce and the Community of the Realm of Scotland*, 4th edn (Edinburgh, 2005).
Barrow, G. W. S., *Scotland and its Neighbours in the Middle Ages* (London, 1992).
Barrow, G. W. S., 'The Scots charter', in G. W. S. Barrow, *Scotland and its Neighbours in the Middle Ages* (London, 1992), pp. 91–104.
G. W. S. Barrow (ed.), *The Scottish Tradition: Essays in Honour of Ronald Gordon Cant* (Edinburgh, 1974).
Barrow, G. W. S., 'A twelfth century Newbattle document', *Scottish Historical Review*, 30 (1951), pp. 41–9.
Barrow, G. W. S., 'Witnesses and the attestation of formal documents in Scotland, twelfth–thirteenth centuries', *Journal of Legal History*, 16 (1995), pp. 1–20.
Barrow, J., 'Friends and friendship in Anglo-Saxon charters' in J. Haseldine (ed.), *Friendship in Medieval Europe* (Stroud, 1999), pp. 106–23.
Bartlett, R., *The Making of Europe: Conquest, Colonization and Cultural Change, 950–1350* (Princeton, 1993).
Bartlett, R., 'Medieval and modern concepts of race and ethnicity', *Journal of Medieval and Early Modern Studies*, 31 (2001), pp. 39–56.
Beam, A., *The Balliol Dynasty, 1210–1364* (East Linton, 2008).
Bedos-Rezak, B. M., 'Du sujet à l'objet: la formulation identitaire et ses enjeux culturels', in P. von Moos (ed.), *Unverwechselbarkeit: persönliche identität und identifikation in der vormodernen gesellschaft* (Cologne, 2004), pp. 63–83.
Bedos-Rezak, B., 'The king enthroned, a new theme in Anglo-Saxon royal iconography: the seal of Edward the Confessor and its political implications', in B. M. Bedos-Rezak, *Form and Order in Medieval France: Studies in Social and Quantitative Sigillography* (Aldershot, 2003), Article IV.
Bedos-Rezak, B. M., 'Medieval identity: a sign and a concept', *American Historical Review*, 105 (2000), pp. 1488–533.

Bedos-Rezak, B., 'Medieval seals and the structure of chivalric society', in H. Chickering and T. H. Seller (eds), *The Study of Chivalry: Resources and Approaches* (Kalamazoo, 1988), pp. 313–72.

Bedos-Rezak, B., 'Replica: images of identity and the identity of images in prescholastic France', in J. E. Hamburger and A.-M. Bouché (eds), *The Mind's Eye: Art and Theological Argument in the Middle Ages* (Princeton, 2006), pp. 46–64.

Black, G. F., *The Surnames of Scotland: Their Origin, Meaning and History* (New York, 1946, repr. Edinburgh, 1993).

Blair, C. H. Hunter, 'Northern knights at Falkirk, 1298', *Archaeologia Aeliana*, 4th Series, 25 (1947), pp. 68–114.

Blakely, R. M., *The Brus Family in England and Scotland, 1100–1295* (Woodbridge, 2005).

Bloch, M., 'Introduction', in M. Bloch (ed.), *Political Language and Oratory in Traditional Societies* (London, 1975), pp. 1–28.

Boardman, S., *The Campbells, 1250–1513* (Edinburgh, 2006).

Boardman, S., 'The Campbells and charter lordship in medieval Argyll', in S. Boardman and A. Ross (eds), *The Exercise of Power in Medieval Scotland, c. 1200–1500* (Dublin, 2003), pp. 95–117.

Boardman, S., *The Early Stewart Kings: Robert II and Robert III, 1371–1406* (Edinburgh, 1996).

Boardman, S. and A. Ross (eds), *The Exercise of Power in Medieval Scotland, c. 1200–1500* (Dublin, 2003).

Brand, P., *Kings, Barons and Justices: The Making and Enforcement of Legislation in Thirteenth-century England* (Cambridge, 2003).

Brand, P. (ed.), 'Parliament of autumn 1305, text and translation', in C. Given-Wilson, P. Brand, A. Curry, R. E. Horrow, G. Martin, W. M. Ormord and J. R. S. Phillips (eds), *The Parliament Rolls of Medieval England*. CD-ROM (Leicester, 2005).

Briggs, C. F., 'Literacy, reading and writing in the medieval west', *Journal of Medieval History*, 26 (2000), pp. 397–420.

Britnell, R. (ed.), *Pragmatic Literacy, East and West, 1200–1330* (Woodbridge, 1997).

Broadie, A., 'John Duns Scotus and the idea of independence', in E. J. Cowan (ed.), *The Wallace Book* (Edinburgh, 2007), pp. 77–85.

Brotherstone, T. and D. Ditchburn (eds), *Freedom and Authority: Scotland c. 1050–c. 1650: Historical and Historiographical Essays presented to Grant G. Simpson* (East Linton, 2000).

Broun, D., 'Anglo-French acculturation and the Irish element in Scottish identity', in B. Smith (ed.), *Britain and Ireland, 900–1300: Insular Responses to Medieval European Change* (Cambridge, 1999), pp. 135–53.

Broun, D., *The Charters of Gaelic Scotland and Ireland in the Early and Central Middle Ages* (Cambridge, 1995).

Broun, D., 'Gaelic literacy in eastern Scotland between 1124 and 1249', in H. Pryce (ed.), *Literacy in Medieval Celtic Societies* (Cambridge, 1998), pp. 183–201.

Broun, D., *The Irish Identity of the Kingdom of the Scots* (Woodbridge, 1999).
Broun, D., 'The property records in the Book of Deer as a source for early Scottish society', in K. Forsyth (ed.), *Studies on the Book of Deer* (Dublin, 2008), pp. 309–60.
Broun, D., *Scottish Independence and the Idea of Britain from the Picts to Alexander III* (Edinburgh, 2007).
Broun, D., 'The writing of charters in Scotland and Ireland in the twelfth century', in K. Heidecker (ed.), *Charters and the Use of the Written Word in Medieval Society* (Turnhout, 2000), pp. 113–32.
Brown, M., 'Earldom and kindred: the Lennox and its earls, 1200–1458', in S. Boardman and A. Ross (eds), *The Exercise of Power in Medieval Scotland, c. 1200–1500* (Dublin, 2003), pp. 201–24.
Brown, M., 'Scotland tamed? Kings and magnates in late medieval Scotland: a review of recent work', *Innes Review*, 45 (1994), pp. 120–6.
Brown, M. H., '*Scoti Anglicati*: Scots in Plantagenet allegiance during the fourteenth century', in A. King and M. A. Penman (eds), *England and Scotland in the Fourteenth Century: New Perspectives* (Woodbridge, 2007), pp. 94–115.
Brown, M., 'War, allegiance, and community in the Anglo-Scottish marches: Teviotdale in the fourteenth century', *Northern History*, 41 (2004), pp. 219–38.
Brundage, J. A., *Medieval Canon Law* (New York, 1995).
Burnett, C. J. and M. D. Dennis, *Scotland's Heraldic Heritage: The Lion Rejoicing* (Edinburgh, 1997).
Caldwell, D. H., 'Finlaggan, Islay – stones and inauguration ceremonies', in R. Welander, D. J. Breeze and T. O. Clancy (eds), *The Stone of Destiny: Artefact and Icon* (Edinburgh, 2003), pp. 61–75.
Campbell, C., *The Scots Roll: A Study of a Fifteenth Century Roll of Arms* (Kinross, 1995).
Cathcart, A., *Kinship and Clientage: Highland Clanship in Scotland, 1451–1609* (Leiden, 2006).
Charles-Edwards, T., *Early Irish and Welsh Kinship* (Oxford, 1993).
Charles-Edwards, T. M., M. E. Owen and P. Russell (eds), *The Welsh King and his Court* (Cardiff, 2000).
Clanchy, M. T., *From Memory to Written Record: England 1066–1307*, 2nd edn (Oxford, 1993).
Clanchy, M. T., 'Law and love in the middle ages', in J. Bossy (ed.), *Disputes and Settlements: Law and Human Relations in the West* (Cambridge, 1983), pp. 47–67.
Contributions to a Dictionary of the Irish Language, Fascicule S, gen. ed. E. G. Quin (Dublin, 1939).
Cooper, T. M., *The Dark Age of Scottish Legal History, 1350–1650* (Glasgow, 1952).
Cooper, T. M., 'The general development of Scots law', in *Introduction to Legal History* (Edinburgh, 1958), p. 5.
Cooper, T. M., 'Melrose abbey *versus* the earl of Dunbar', *Juridical Review*, 55 (1943), pp. 1–8.

Coss, P. and M. Keen (eds), *Heraldry, Pageantry and Social Display in Medieval England* (Woodbridge, 2002).
Cowan, E. J. (ed.), *The Wallace Book* (Edinburgh, 2007).
Cowan, E. J. and R. A. McDonald (eds), *Alba: Celtic Scotland in the Medieval Era* (East Linton, 2000).
Crawford, B. E. (ed.), *Church, Chronicle and Learning in Medieval Scotland: Essays presented to Donald Watt on the Occasion of the Completion of the Publication of Bower's Scotichronicon* (Edinburgh, 1999).
Crawford, B. E., 'The earldom of Caithness and the kingdom of Scotland, 1150–1266', in K. J. Stringer (ed.), *Essays on the Nobility of Medieval Scotland* (Edinburgh, 1985), pp. 25–43.
Crawford, B. E., *Scandinavian Scotland* (Leicester, 1987).
Crouch, D., 'The historian, lineage and heraldry 1050–1250', in P. Coss and M. Keen (eds), *Heraldry, Pageantry and Social Display in Medieval England* (Woodbridge, 2002), pp. 17–37.
Crouch, D., *The Image of Aristocracy in Britain, 1100–1300* (London, 1992).
Curtis, E., 'The rental of the manor of Lisronagh, 1333 and notes on "betagh" tenure in medieval Ireland', *Proceedings of the Royal Irish Academy*, 43C (1936), pp. 41–76.
Davies, R., 'Kinsmen, neighbours and communities in Wales and the western British Isles, c.1100–c.1400', in P. Stafford, J. Nelson and J. Martindale (eds), *Law, Laity and Solidarities: Essays in Honour of Susan Reynolds* (Manchester, 2001), pp. 172–87.
Davies, R. R., 'The administration of law in medieval Wales: the role of the *Ynad Cwmwd (Judex Patrie)*', in T. M. Charles-Edwards, M. E. Owen and D. B. Walters (eds), *Lawyers and Laymen: Studies in the History of Law presented to Professor Dafydd Jenkins on his Seventy-fifth Birthday, Gŵyl Ddewi 1986* (Cardiff, 1986), pp. 258–73.
Davies, R. R., *The Age of Conquest: Wales, 1063–1415* (Oxford, 1991).
Davies, R. R. (ed.), *The British Isles, 1100–1500: Comparisons, Contrasts and Connections* (Edinburgh, 1988).
Davies, R. R. *Domination and Conquest: The Experience of Ireland, Scotland and Wales, 1100–1300* (Cambridge, 1990).
Davies, R. R., *The First English Empire: Power and Identities in the British Isles, 1093–1343* (Oxford, 2000).
Davies, R. R., 'In praise of British history', in R. R. Davies (ed.), *The British Isles, 1100–1500: Comparisons, Contrasts and Connections* (Edinburgh, 1988), pp. 9–25.
Davies, R. R., *Lordship and Society in the March of Wales, 1282–1400* (Oxford, 1978).
Davies, W., 'Charter-writing and its uses in medieval Celtic societies', in H. Pryce (ed.), *Literacy in Medieval Celtic Societies* (Cambridge, 1998) pp. 99–112.
Davies, W., 'Introduction', in W. Davies, G. Halsall and A. Reynolds (eds), *People and Space in the Middle Ages, 300–1300* (Turnhout, 2006), pp. 1–12.

Davies, W., 'Land and power in early medieval Wales', *Past and Present*, 78 (1978), pp. 3–23.
Davies, W., 'Populations, territory and community membership: contrasts and conclusions' in W. Davies, G. Halsall and A. Reynolds (eds), *People and Space in the Middle Ages, 300–1300* (Turnhout, 2006), pp. 295–307.
Davies, W., G. Halsall and A. Reynolds (eds), *People and Space in the Middle Ages, 300–1300* (Turnhout, 2006).
Davis, G. R. C., *Medieval Cartularies of Great Britain* (London, 1958).
Dickinson, W. C., 'The administration of justice in medieval Scotland', *Aberdeen University Review*, 34 (1952), pp. 338–51.
Dickinson, W. C., 'Surdit de sergaunt', *Scottish Historical Review*, 39 (1960), pp. 170–75.
Dictionary of the Older Scottish Tongue, ed. W. A. Craigie et al., 12 vols (Oxford, 1937–2002).
Ditchburn, D. and A. J. Macdonald, 'Medieval Scotland, 1100–1560', in R. A. Houston and W. W. J. Knox (eds), *The New Penguin History of Scotland: From the Earliest Times to the Present Day* (London, 2001), pp. 96–181.
Dodgshon, R. A., *Land and Society in Early Scotland* (Oxford, 1981).
Doherty, C., 'Some aspects of hagiography as a source for Irish economic history', *Peritia*, 1 (1982), pp. 300–28.
Donaldson, G., 'Aspects of early Scottish conveyancing', in P. Gouldesbrough (ed.), *Formulary of Old Scots Legal Documents* (Edinburgh, 1985), pp. 153–86.
Donnelly, J., 'The lands of Coldingham priory, 1100–1300', unpublished PhD dissertation (University of Cambridge, 1989).
Douglas, W., 'Culross abbey and its charters, with notes on a fifteenth-century transumpt', *Proceedings of the Society of Antiquaries of Scotland*, 60 (1925–6), pp. 67–94.
Down, K., 'Colonial society and economy', in A. Cosgrove (ed.), *A New History of Ireland. Vol. II: Medieval Ireland, 1169–1534* (Oxford, 1993), pp. 439–91.
Driscoll, S. T., 'The archaeological context of assembly in early medieval Scotland – Scone and its comparanda', in A. Pantos and S. Semple (eds), *Assembly Places and Practices in Medieval Europe* (Dublin, 2004), pp. 73–94.
Driscoll, S. T., 'Formalising the mechanisms of state power: early Scottish lordship from the ninth to the thirteenth centuries', in S. M. Foster, A. Macinnes and R. MacInnes (eds), *Scottish Power Centres from the Early Middle Ages to the Twentieth Century* (Glasgow, 1998), pp. 33–58.
Driscoll, S. T., 'Govan: an early medieval royal centre on the Clyde', in R. Welander, D. J. Breeze and T. O. Clancy (eds), *The Stone of Destiny: Artefact and Icon* (Edinburgh, 2003), pp. 77–83.
Driscoll, S. T., 'Picts and prehistory: cultural resource management in early medieval Scotland', *World Archaeology*, 30 (1998), pp. 142–58.
Duffy, P. J., D. Edwards and E. FitzPatrick (eds), *Gaelic Ireland c. 1250–c. 1650: Land, Lordship and Settlement* (Dublin, 2001).
Duncan, A. A. M., 'The community of the realm of Scotland and Robert Bruce: a review', *Scottish Historical Review*, 45 (1966), p. 199.

Duncan, A. A. M., 'The earliest Scottish charters', *Scottish Historical Review*, 37 (1958), pp. 103–35.
Duncan, A. A. M., *The Kingship of the Scots, 842–1292* (Edinburgh, 2002).
Duncan, A. A. M., '*Regiam Majestatem*: a reconsideration', *Juridical Review*, New Series, 6 (1961), pp. 199–217.
Duncan, A. A. M., *Scotland: The Making of the Kingdom* (Edinburgh, 1975).
Duncan, A. A. M., 'Sources and uses of the chronicle of Melrose, 1167–1297', in S. Taylor (ed.), *Kings, Clerics and Chronicles in Scotland, 500–1297: Essays in Honour of Margaret Ogilvie Anderson on the Occasion of her Ninetieth Birthday* (Dublin, 2000), pp. 146–85.
Duncan, A. A. M., 'William, son of Alan Wallace: the documents', in E. J. Cowan (ed.), *The Wallace Book* (Edinburgh, 2007), pp. 42–63.
Duncan, A. A. M, 'Yes, the earliest Scottish charters', *Scottish Historical Review*, 78 (1999), pp. 1–38.
Dyer, C., *Standards of Living in the Later Middle Ages: Social Change in England, c. 1200–1520* (Cambridge, 1989).
Ewan, E., 'The community of the burgh in the fourteenth century', in M. Lynch, M. Spearman and G. P. Stell (eds), *The Scottish Medieval Town* (Edinburgh, 1988), pp. 228–44.
Ewan, E., *Townlife in Fourteenth-century Scotland* (Edinburgh, 1991).
Ewart, G., 'Inchaffray abbey, Perth & Kinross: excavation and research, 1987', *Proceedings of the Society of Antiquaries of Scotland*, 126 (1996), pp. 469–516.
Fawcett, R. and R. Oram, *Dryburgh Abbey* (Stroud, 2005).
Fawcett, R. and R. Oram, *Melrose Abbey* (Stroud, 2004).
Ferguson, J., 'The barony in Scotland', *Juridical Review*, 24 (1912–13), pp. 99–121.
Ferguson, P. C., *Medieval Papal Representatives in Scotland: Legates, Nuncios, and Judges-delegate, 1125–1286* (Edinburgh, 1997).
Ferguson, W., *Scotland's Relations with England: A Survey to 1707* (Edinburgh, 1977).
Finnegan, R., *Oral Traditions and the Verbal Arts* (London, 1992).
FitzPatrick, E., *Royal Inauguration in Ireland, c. 1100–c. 1600: A Cultural Landscape* (Woodbridge, 2004).
Flanagan, M.-T., 'The context and uses of the Latin charter in twelfth-century Ireland', in H. Pryce (ed.), *Literacy in Medieval Celtic Societies* (Cambridge, 1998), pp. 113–32.
Flanagan, M.-T., 'Strategies of lordship in pre-Norman and post-Norman Leinster', *Anglo-Norman Studies*, 20 (1997), pp. 107–26.
Forsyth, K., 'The stones of Deer', in K. Forsyth (ed.), *Studies on the Book of Deer* (Dublin, 2008), pp. 398–438.
Forsyth, K. (ed.), *Studies on the Book of Deer* (Dublin, 2008).
Foster, S. M., 'Before Alba: Pictish and Dál Riata power centres from the fifth to the late ninth centuries AD', in S. M. Foster, A. Macinnes and R. MacInnes (eds), *Scottish Power Centres from the Early Middle Ages to the Twentieth Century* (Glasgow, 1998), pp. 1–31.

Foster, S. M., A. Macinnes and R. MacInnes (eds), *Scottish Power Centres from the Early Middle Ages to the Twentieth Century* (Glasgow, 1998).

Frame, R., 'Aristocracies and the political configuration of the British Isles', in R. R. Davies (ed.), *The British Isles, 1100–1500: Comparisons, Contrasts and Connections* (Edinburgh, 1988), pp. 142–59.

Freeman, E., *Narratives of a New Order: Cistercian Historical Writing in England, 1150–1220* (Turnhout, 2002).

Gameson, R., 'The gospels of Margaret of Scotland and the literacy of an eleventh-century queen', in L. Smith and J. H. M. Taylor (eds), *Women and the Book: Assessing the Visual Evidence* (London, 1997), pp. 148–71.

Geertz, C., *The Interpretation of Cultures* (New York, 1973).

Gilbert, J. M., *Hunting and Hunting Reserves in Medieval Scotland* (Edinburgh, 1979).

Gillingham, J., 'Conquering the barbarians: war and chivalry in twelfth-century Britain', *Haskins Society Journal*, 4 (1993), pp. 67–84.

Glenn, V., 'The late 13th-century chapter seals of Dunkeld and Oslo cathedrals', *Proceedings of the Society of Antiquaries of Scotland*, 132 (2002), pp. 439–58.

Grant, A., 'The construction of the early Scottish state', in J. R. Maddicott and D. M. Palliser (eds), *The Medieval State: Essays presented to James Campbell* (London, 2000), pp. 47–71.

Grant, A., 'Crown and nobility in late medieval Britain', in R. Mason (ed.), *Scotland and England, 1286–1815* (Edinburgh, 1987), pp. 34–59.

Grant, A., 'Franchises north of the border: baronies and regalities in medieval Scotland', in M. Prestwich (ed.), *Liberties and Identities in the Medieval British Isles* (Woodbridge, 2008), pp. 155–99.

Grant, A., *Independence and Nationhood: Scotland, 1306–1469* (London, 1984).

Grant, A., 'Lordship and society in twelfth-century Clydesdale', in H. Pryce and J. L. Watts (eds), *Power and Identity in the Middle Ages: Essays in Memory of Rees Davies* (Oxford, 2007), pp. 98–124.

Grant, A., 'Scotland: politics, government and law', in S. H. Rigby (ed.), *A Companion to Britain in the Later Middle Ages* (Oxford, 2003), pp. 283–308.

Grant, A., 'Scotland's "Celtic fringe" in the late middle ages: the MacDonald lords of the Isles and the kingdom of Scotland', in R. R. Davies (ed.), *The British Isles, 1100–1500: Comparisons, Contrasts and Connections* (Edinburgh, 1988), pp. 118–41.

Grant, A., 'Thanes and thanages, from the eleventh to the fourteenth centuries', in A. Grant and K. J. Stringer (eds), *Medieval Scotland: Crown, Lordship and Community – Essays presented to G. W. S. Barrow* (Edinburgh, 1993), pp. 39–81.

Grant, A., 'To the medieval foundations', *Scottish Historical Review*, 73 (1994), pp. 4–24.

Grant, A. and K. J. Stringer (eds), *Medieval Scotland: Crown, Lordship and Community – Essays presented to G. W. S. Barrow* (Edinburgh, 1993).

Grant, A. and K. J. Stringer, *Uniting the Kingdom?: The Making of British History* (London, 1995).

Green, J., 'Aristocratic loyalties on the northern frontier of England, c.1100–1174', in D. Williams (ed.), *England in the Twelfth Century: Proceedings of the 1988 Harlaxton Symposium* (Woodbridge, 1990), pp. 83–100.

Griffiths, M., 'Native society on the Anglo-Norman frontier: the evidence of the Margam charters', *Welsh History Review*, 14 (1988), pp. 179–216.

Hall, M., 'John of Strathearn and Alan Muschamp: two medieval men of Strathearn and their seal matrices', *Tayside and Fife Archaeological Journal*, 11 (2005), pp. 80–7.

Hall, M. A. and D. D. R. Owen, 'A Tristram and Iseult mirror case from Perth: reflections on the production and consumption of romance culture', *Tayside and Fife Archaeological Journal*, 4 (1998), pp. 150–65.

Hammond, M., 'Ethnicity, personal names and the nature of Scottish Europeanization', in B. K. U. Weiler, J. E. Burton, P. R. Schofield and K. Stöber (eds), *Thirteenth Century England, XI: Proceedings of the Gregynog Conference, 2003* (Woodbridge, 2007), pp. 82–94.

Hammond, M., 'Ethnicity and the writing of medieval Scottish historiography', *Scottish Historical Review*, 85 (2006), pp. 1–27.

Hammond, M. H., '*Hostiarii regis Scotie*: the Durward family in the thirteenth century', in S. Boardman and A. Ross (eds), *The Exercise of Power in Medieval Scotland, c. 1200–1500* (Dublin, 2003), pp. 118–38.

Hanawalt, B. A. and M. Kobialka, 'Introduction', in B. A. Hanawalt and M. Kobialka (eds), *Medieval Practices of Space* (Minneapolis, 2000), pp. ix–xviii.

Hand, G. J., *English Law in Ireland 1290–1304* (Cambridge, 1967).

Harding, A., 'The medieval brieves of protection and the development of the common law', *Juridical Review*, New Series, 11 (1966), pp. 115–49.

Harding, A., '*Regiam Majestatem* amongst medieval law books', *Juridical Review*, New Series, 29 (1984), pp. 97–111.

Harvey, P. D. A., 'Personal seals in thirteenth-century England', in I. Wood and G. A. Loud (eds), *Church and Chronicle in the Middle Ages: Essays presented to John Taylor* (London, 1991), pp. 17–27.

Harvey, P. D. A. and A. McGuinness, *A Guide to British Medieval Seals* (London, 1996).

Haseldine, J. (ed.), *Friendship in Medieval Europe* (Stroud, 1999).

Haseldine, J., 'Friendship and rivalry: the role of *amicitia* in twelfth-century monastic relations', *Journal of Ecclesiastical History*, 44 (1993), pp. 390–414.

Haseldine, J., 'Understanding the language of *amicitia*. The friendship circle of Peter of Celle (*c*.1115–1183)', *Journal of Medieval History*, 20 (1994), pp. 237–60.

Hedley, W. P., *Northumberland Families*, 2 vols (Newcastle-upon-Tyne, 1968–70).

Henderson, G. D. S., 'Romance and politics on some medieval English seals', *Art History*, 1 (1978), pp. 26–42.

Herbert, M., 'Charter materials from Kells', in F. O'Mahoney (ed.), *The Book of Kells: Proceedings of a Conference at Trinity College Dublin, 6–9 September 1992* (Aldershot, 1994), pp. 60–77.

Heslop, T. A., 'English seals from the mid-ninth century to 1100', *Journal of the British Archaeological Association*, 133 (1980), pp. 1–16.

Hirata, Y., 'John of Salisbury, Gerard Pucelle and *amicitia*', in J. Haseldine (ed.), *Friendship in Medieval Europe* (Stroud, 1999), pp. 153–65.

Historical Manuscripts Commission Report on the Manuscripts of Colonel David Milne Holme of Wedderburn Castle (London, 1902).

Hodgson, J. C., *A History of Northumberland in Three Parts*, 3 vols in 7 (Newcastle-upon-Tyne, 1820–40).

Holford, M. and K. Stringer, *Border Liberties and Loyalties: North-east England, 1200–1400* (Edinburgh, forthcoming).

Holm, P., 'The slave trade of Dublin, IXth to XIIIth century', *Peritia*, 5 (1989), pp. 317–45.

Holt, J. C., *The Northerners: A Study in the Reign of King John* (Oxford, 1961).

Houwen, L. A. J. R., 'A Scots translation of a Middle French bestiary', *Studies in Scottish Literature*, 26 (1991), pp. 207–17.

Hudson, B. T., *Irish Sea Studies, 900–1200* (Dublin, 2006).

Hudson, J., 'Legal aspects of charter diplomatic in the twelfth century: a comparative approach', *Anglo-Norman Studies*, 25 (2003), pp. 121–38.

Hyams, P., *Kings, Lords and Peasants in Medieval England: The Common Law of Villeinage in the Twelfth and Thirteenth Centuries* (Oxford, 1980).

Hyatte, R., *The Arts of Friendship: The Idealization of Friendship in Medieval and Early Renaissance Literature* (Leiden, 1994).

Innes, T., *Scots Heraldry: A Practical Handbook* (Edinburgh, 1934).

Jackson, K., *The Gaelic Notes in the Book of Deer* (Cambridge, 1972).

Jamroziak, E., 'Making friends beyond the grave: Melrose abbey and its lay burials in the thirteenth century', *Cîteaux: commentarii Cistercienses*, 56 (2005), pp. 323–35.

Johnstone, N., 'Cae Llys, Rhosyr: a court of the princes of Gwynedd', *Studia Celtica*, 33 (1999), pp. 251–95.

Kapelle, W. E., *The Norman Conquest of the North: The Region and its Transformation* (London, 1979).

Keen, M., 'Introduction', in P. Coss and M. Keen (eds), *Heraldry, Pageantry and Social Display in Medieval England* (Woodbridge, 2002), pp. 1–16.

Kelly, F., *Early Irish Farming* (Dublin, 2000).

Kelly, F., *A Guide to Early Irish Law* (Dublin, 1998).

Kelly, S., 'Anglo-Saxon lay society and the written word', in R. McKitterick (ed.), *The Uses of Literacy in Early Medieval Europe* (Cambridge, 1990), pp. 36–62.

Kershaw, I., 'The great famine and agrarian crisis in England 1315–1322', *Past & Present*, 59 (1973), pp. 3–50.

King, A., 'Best of enemies: were the fourteenth-century Anglo-Scottish marches a "frontier society"?', in King, A. and M. A. Penman (eds), *England and Scotland in the Fourteenth Century: New Perspectives* (Woodbridge, 2007), pp. 116–35.

King, A. and M. A. Penman (eds), *England and Scotland in the Fourteenth Century: New Perspectives* (Woodbridge, 2007).

Lefebvre, H., *The Production of Space*, trans. D. Nicholson-Smith (Oxford, 1991).

Lewis, N. B., 'The English forces in Flanders, August–November 1297', in R. W.

Hunt, W. A. Pantin and R. W Southern (eds), *Studies in Medieval History presented to Frederick Powicke* (Oxford, 1969), pp. 310–18.

Lomas, R., *County of Conflict: Northumberland from Conquest to Civil War* (East Linton, 1996).

Lydon, J., *Ireland in the Later Middle Ages* (Dublin, 1973).

Lydon, J., *The Lordship of Ireland in the Middle Ages* (Toronto, 1972).

Lynch, M., *Scotland: A New History* (London, 1992).

Lynch, M., M. Spearman and G. P. Stell (eds), *The Scottish Medieval Town* (Edinburgh, 1988).

Macdonald, A., 'Major early monasteries: some procedural problems for field archaeologists', in D. J. Breeze (ed.), *Studies in Scottish Antiquity presented to Stewart Cruden* (Edinburgh, 1984), pp. 69–86.

Macdonald, A. J., 'Kings of the wild frontier? The earls of Dunbar or March, c.1070–1435', in S. Boardman and A. Ross (eds), *The Exercise of Power in Medieval Scotland, c. 1200–1500* (Dublin, 2003), pp. 139–58.

MacLeod, W., *Divided Gaels: Gaelic Cultural Identities in Scotland and Ireland c. 1200–c. 1650* (Oxford, 2004).

Mac Niocaill, G., 'The origins of the *betagh*', *Irish Jurist*, New Series, 1 (1966), pp. 292–8.

MacPhail, S. R., *History of the Religious House of Pluscarden* (Edinburgh, 1881).

MacQueen, H. L., 'The brieve of right re-visited', in R. Eales and D. Sullivan (eds), *The Political Context of Law: Proceedings of the Seventh British Legal History Conference, Canterbury 1985* (London, 1987), pp. 17–25.

MacQueen, H. L., 'The brieve of right in Scots law', *Journal of Legal History*, 3 (1982), pp. 52–70.

MacQueen, H. L., 'Canon law, custom and legislation: law in the reign of Alexander II', in R. D. Oram (ed.), *The Reign of Alexander II, 1214–49* (Leiden, 2005), pp. 221–51.

MacQueen, H. L., *Common Law and Feudal Society in Medieval Scotland* (Edinburgh, 1993).

MacQueen, H. L., 'Girth: society and the law of sanctuary in Scotland', in J. W. Cairns and O. F. Robinson (eds), *Critical Studies in Ancient Law, Comparative Law and Legal History* (Oxford, 2001), pp. 333–52.

MacQueen, H. L., 'The kin of Kennedy, "kenkynnol" and the common law', in Grant and Stringer (eds), *Medieval Scotland: Crown, Lordship and Community – Essays presented to G. W. S. Barrow* (Edinburgh, 1993) pp. 274–96.

MacQueen, H. L., 'The laws of Galloway: a preliminary survey', in R. D. Oram and G. P. Stell (eds), *Galloway: Land and Lordship* (Edinburgh, 1991), pp. 131–43.

H. L. MacQueen, 'Linguistic communities in medieval Scots law', in C. W. Brooks and M. Lobban (eds), *Communities and Courts in Britain, 1150–1900* (London, 1997), pp. 13–23.

MacQueen, H. L., 'Pleadable brieves, pleading and the development of Scots law', *Law and History Review*, 4 (1986), pp. 402–22.

MacQueen, H. L., 'Scots law under Alexander III', in N. H. Reid (ed.), *Scotland in the Reign of Alexander III, 1249–1286* (Edinburgh, 1990), pp. 74–102.

MacQueen, H. L., 'Some notes on wrang and unlaw', in H. L. MacQueen (ed.), *Stair Society Miscellany Five* (Edinburgh, 2006), pp. 13–26.

MacQueen, H. L., 'Tears of a legal historian: Scottish feudalism and the *ius commune*', *Juridical Review*, New Series (no vol.) (2003), pp. 1–28.

MacQueen, H. L. and W. J. Windram, 'Laws and courts in the burghs', in M. Lynch, M. Spearman and G. P. Stell (eds), *The Scottish Medieval Town* (Edinburgh 1988), pp. 208–27.

McAndrew, B. A., *The Historic Heraldry of Scotland* (Woodbridge, 2006).

McAndrew, B. A., 'The sigillography of the Ragman Roll', *Proceedings of the Society of Antiquaries of Scotland*, 129 (1999), pp. 663–752.

McDonald, A., 'Scoto-Norse kings and the reformed religious orders: patterns of monastic patronage in twelfth-century Galloway and Argyll', *Albion*, 27 (1995), pp. 187–219.

McDonald, R. A., 'Images of Hebridean lordship in the late twelfth and early thirteenth centuries: the seal of Raonall Mac Sorley', *Scottish Historical Review*, 74 (1995), pp. 129–43.

McDonald, R. A., *Manx Kingship in its Irish Sea Setting, 1187–1229: King Ragnvaldr and the Crovan Dynasty* (Dublin, 2007).

McDonald, R. A., 'Matrimonial politics and core-periphery interactions in twelfth- and early thirteenth-century Scotland', *Journal of Medieval History*, 21 (1995), pp. 227–47.

McDonald, R. A., *Outlaws of Medieval Scotland: Challenges to the Canmore Kings, 1058–1266* (East Linton, 2003).

McDonald, R. A., 'Rebels without a cause? The relations of Fergus of Galloway and Somerled of Argyll with the Scottish kings, 1153–1164', in E. J. Cowan and R. A. McDonald (eds), *Alba: Celtic Scotland in the Medieval Era* (East Linton, 2000), pp. 166–87.

McEvoy, J., 'The theory of friendship in the Latin middle ages: hermeneutics, contextualization and the transmission and reception of ancient texts and ideas, from c. A.D. 350 to c.1500', in J. Haseldine (ed.), *Friendship in Medieval Europe* (Stroud, 1999), pp. 3–44.

McEvoy, J., 'Ultimate goods: happiness, friendship, and bliss', in A. S. McGrade (ed.), *The Cambridge Companion to Medieval Philosophy* (Cambridge, 2003), pp. 254–75.

McGuinness, A. F., 'Non-armigerous seals and seal-usage in thirteenth-century England', in P. R. Coss and S. D. Lloyd (eds), *Thirteenth Century England V: Proceedings of the Newcastle upon Tyne Conference 1993* (Woodbridge, 1995), pp. 165–77.

McGuire, B. P., *Friendship and Community: The Monastic Experience, 350–1250* (Kalamazoo, 1988).

McKay, H. and R. F. Wolf, 'Pictland and its symbols stones', in P. O'Neill (ed.), *Exile and Homecoming: Papers from the Fifth Australian Conference of Celtic Studies* (Sydney, 2005), pp. 289–308.

McKechnie, H., *Judicial Process upon Brieves, 1219–1532* (Glasgow, 1956).
McLoughlin, J., '*Amicitia* in practice: John of Salisbury (c.1120–1180) and his circle', in D. Williams (ed.), *England in the Twelfth Century: Proceedings of the 1988 Harlaxton Symposium* (Woodbridge, 1990), pp. 165–80.
Meddings, J., 'Friendship among the aristocracy in Anglo-Norman England', in C. Harper-Bill (ed.), *Anglo-Norman Studies, XXII: Proceedings of the Battle Conference, 1999* (Woodbridge, 2000), pp. 187–204.
Megaw, B., 'Norseman and native in the kingdom of the Isles: a re-assessment of the Manx evidence', *Scottish Studies*, 20 (1976), pp. 1–44.
Miller, E., 'Patterns of settlement: northern England', in H. E. Hallam (ed.), *The Agrarian History of England and Wales, Vol. II: 1042–1350* (Cambridge, 1988), pp. 245–59.
Mills, J., 'Tenants and agriculture near Dublin in the fourteenth century', *Proceedings of the Royal Society of Antiquaries of Ireland*, 5th Series, 1 (1890), pp. 54–63.
Milne, I. R., 'An extent of Carrick in 1260', *Scottish Historical Review*, 34 (1955), pp. 46–9.
Moore, M. F., *The Lands of the Scottish Kings in England* (London, 1915).
Mullett, M., 'Power, relations and networks in medieval Europe', *Revue belge de philologie et d'histoire/Belgisch tijdschrift voor filologie en geschiedenis*, 83 (2005), pp. 255–9.
Murison, D. D., 'Linguistic relationships in medieval Scotland', in G. W. S. Barrow (ed.), *The Scottish Tradition: Essays in Honour of Ronald Gordon Cant* (Edinburgh, 1974), pp. 71–83.
National Museum of Antiquities of Scotland, *Angels, Nobles and Unicorns: Art and Patronage in Medieval Scotland* (Edinburgh, 1982).
Neville, C. J., 'A Celtic enclave in Norman Scotland: Earl Gilbert and the earldom of Strathearn, 1171–1223', in T. Brotherstone and D. Ditchburn (eds), *Freedom and Authority: Scotland c. 1050–c. 1650: Historical and Historiographical Essays presented to Grant G. Simpson* (East Linton, 2000), pp. 75–92.
Neville, C. J., 'Charter writing and the exercise of lordship in thirteenth-century Celtic Scotland', in A. Musson (ed.), *Expectations of the Law in the Middle Ages* (Woodbridge, 2001), pp. 67–89.
Neville, C. J., 'The earls of Strathearn from the twelfth to the mid-fourteenth century, with an edition of their written acts', 2 vols, unpublished PhD dissertation (University of Aberdeen, 1983).
Neville, C. J., 'Finding the family in the charters of medieval Scotland, 1150–1350', in E. Ewan and J. Nugent (eds), *Finding the Family in Medieval and Early Modern Scotland* (Aldershot, 2008), pp. 11–21.
Neville, C. J., 'Native lords and the church in thirteenth-century Strathearn, Scotland', *Journal of Ecclesiastical History*, 53 (2002), pp. 454–75.
Neville, C. J., *Native Lordship in Medieval Scotland: The Earldoms of Strathearn and Lennox, c. 1140–1365* (Dublin, 2005).
Neville, C. J., 'The political allegiance of the earls of Strathearn during the war of independence', *Scottish Historical Review*, 65 (1986), pp. 133–153.

Neville, C. J., *Violence, Custom and Law: The Anglo-Scottish Border Lands in the Later Middle Ages* (Edinburgh, 1998).
Neville, C. J., 'Women, charters and land ownership in Scotland, 1150–1350', *Journal of Legal History*, 26 (2005), pp. 21–45.
Neville, C. and R. A. McDonald, 'Knights, knighthood and chivalric culture in Gaelic Scotland, c.1050–1300', *Studies in Medieval and Renaissance History*, 3rd Series, 4 (2007), pp. 57–106.
Nicholls, K. W., 'Anglo-French Ireland and after', *Peritia*, 1 (1982), pp. 370–403.
Nicholls, K., *Gaelic and Gaelicised Ireland in the Middle Ages* (Dublin, 1972).
Nicholson, R., *Scotland: The Later Middle Ages* (Edinburgh, 1978).
Nicolaisen, W. F. H., 'On Pictish rivers and their confluences', in D. Henry (ed.), *The Worm, the Germ and the Thorn: Pictish and Related Studies presented to Isabel Henderson* (Balgavies, 1997), pp. 113–18.
Nisbet, A., *A System of Heraldry Speculative and Practical*, 2 vols (Edinburgh, 1722–42).
Northumberland County History Committee *A History of Northumberland*, 15 vols (Newcastle-upon-Tyne, 1893–1940).
Oliver, A. M., 'The family of Muschamp, barons of Wooler', *Archaeologia Aeliana*, 4th Series, 14 (1937), pp. 243–57.
Oram, R. 'Fergus, Galloway and the Scots', in R. D. Oram and G. Stell (eds), *Galloway: Land and Lordship* (Edinburgh, 1991), pp. 117–30.
Oram, R., *The Lordship of Galloway* (Edinburgh, 2000).
Oram, R. D., 'Continuity, adaptation and integration: the earls and earldom of Mar, c.1150–c.1300', in S. Boardman and A. Ross (eds), *The Exercise of Power in Medieval Scotland, c. 1200–1500* (Dublin, 2003), pp. 46–66.
Oram, R. D., *David I: The King Who Made Scotland* (Stroud, 2004).
Oram, R. D., 'David I and the Scottish conquest and colonisation of Moray', *Northern Scotland*, 19 (1999), pp. 1–20.
Oram, R. D., 'A family business?: colonization and settlement in twelfth- and thirteenth-century Galloway', *Scottish Historical Review*, 72 (1993), pp. 111–45.
Oram, R. D. (ed.), *The Reign of Alexander II, 1214–49* (Leiden, 2005).
Oram, R. D. 'Scots law under Alexander III', in N. H. Reid (ed.), *Scotland in the Reign of Alexander III, 1249–1286* (Edinburgh, 1990), pp. 92–5.
Oram, R. and G. Stell (eds), *Lordship and Architecture in Medieval and Renaissance Scotland* (Edinburgh, 2005).
O'Sullivan, C. M., *Hospitality in Medieval Ireland, 900–1500* (Dublin, 2004).
Otway-Ruthven, J., 'The character of Norman settlement in Ireland', *Historical Studies*, 5 (1965), pp. 75–84.
Otway-Ruthven, J., *A History of Medieval Ireland*, 2nd edn (New York, 1980).
Otway-Ruthven, J., 'The native Irish and English law in medieval Ireland', *Irish Historical Studies*, 7 (1950), pp. 1–16.
Otway-Ruthven, J., 'The organization of Anglo-Irish agriculture in the middle ages', *Journal of the Royal Society of Antiquaries of Ireland*, 4th Series, 81 (1951), pp. 1–13.

Pantos, A. and S. Semple (eds), *Assembly Places and Practices in Medieval Europe* (Dublin, 2004).
Paul, J. B. (ed.), *The Scots Peerage*, 9 vols (Edinburgh, 1904–14).
Pelteret, D., 'Slave raiding and slave trading in early England', *Anglo-Saxon England*, 9 (1981), pp. 99–114.
Pelteret, D. A. E., *Slavery in Early Medieval England: From the Reign of Alfred to the Twelfth Century* (Woodbridge, 1995).
Penman, M. A., *David II, 1329–71* (East Linton, 2004).
Platts, B., *Origins of Heraldry* (London, 1980).
Pollock, F. and F. W. Maitland, *The History of English Law Before the Time of Edward I*, 2 vols, 2nd edn (Cambridge, 1968).
Powicke, F. M., *King Henry III and the Lord Edward*, 2 vols (Oxford, 1947).
Powicke, F. M., *The Thirteenth Century, 1216–1307*, 2nd edn (Oxford, 1991).
Prestwich, M. (ed.), *Liberties and Identities in the Medieval British Isles* (Woodbridge, 2008).
Price, L., 'The origin of the word *betagius*', *Ériu*, 20 (1966), pp. 185–90.
Pryce, H. (ed.), *Literacy in Medieval Celtic Societies* (Cambridge, 1998).
Raine, J., *The History and Antiquities of North Durham* (London, 1852).
Reid, N. H. (ed.), *Scotland in the Reign of Alexander III, 1249–1286* (Edinburgh, 1990).
Reid, R. R., 'Barony and thanage', *English Historical Review*, 35 (1920), pp. 161–99.
Richens, R., 'Ancient land divisions in the parish of Lesmahagow', *Scottish Geographical Magazine*, 108 (1992), pp. 184–9.
Robertson, J., 'On scholastic offices in the Scottish church in the twelfth and thirteenth centuries', in *Miscellany of the Spalding Club, vol. V* (Aberdeen, 1852), App. to the Preface, pp. 56–77.
Ross, A., 'The Bannatyne Club and the publication of Scottish ecclesiastical cartularies', *Scottish Historical Review*, 85 (2006), pp. 202–30.
Ross, A., 'The lords and lordship of Glencarnie', in S. Boardman and A. Ross (eds), *The Exercise of Power in Medieval Scotland, c. 1200–1500* (Dublin, 2003), pp. 159–74.
Royal Commission on the Ancient and Historical Monuments of Scotland (RCAHMS), CANMORE Database, http://www.rcahms.gov.uk/search.html#canmore.
Rushforth, R., *St. Margaret's Gospel-book: The Favourite Book of an Eleventh-century Queen of Scots* (Oxford, 2007).
Sanders, I. J., *English Baronies: A Study of their Origin and Descent, 1086–1327* (Oxford, 1960).
Schmitt, J.-C., 'The rationale of gestures in the West: third to thirteenth centuries', in J. Bremmer and H. Roodenburg (eds), *A Cultural History of Gesture* (Ithaca, 1991), pp. 59–70.
Schulte, P., M. Mostert and I. van Renswoude (eds), *Strategies of Writing: Studies on Text and Trust in the Middle Ages* (Turnhout, 2008).
Scott, W. W., 'The use of money in Scotland, 1124–1230', *Scottish Historical Review*, 58 (1979), pp. 105–31.

Sellar, W. D. H., 'Celtic law and Scots law: survival and integration', *Scottish Studies*, 29 (1989), pp. 1–27.

Sellar, W. D. H., 'Law and institutions, Gaelic', in M. Lynch (ed.), *The Oxford Companion to Scottish History* (Oxford, 2001), pp. 381–2.

Sharpe, R., 'Dispute settlement in medieval Ireland: a preliminary inquiry', in W. Davies and P. Fouracre (eds), *The Settlement of Disputes in Early Medieval Europe* (Cambridge, 1986), pp. 169–89.

Simms, K., 'Guesting and Feasting in Gaelic Ireland', *Journal of the Royal Society of Antiquaries of Ireland*, 108 (1978), pp. 67–100.

Simpson, G. G., 'The claim of Florence, Count of Holland, to the Scottish throne, 1291–2', *Scottish Historical Review*, 36 (1957), pp. 111–24.

Simpson, G. G., 'The *familia* of Roger de Quincy, earl of Winchester and constable of Scotland', in K. J. Stringer (ed.), *Essays on the Nobility of Medieval Scotland* (Edinburgh, 1985), pp. 102–30.

Simpson, G. G., *Handlist of the Acts of Alexander III, the Guardians, John, 1249–1296* (Edinburgh, 1960).

Simpson, G. G. and B. Webster, 'The archives of the medieval church of Glasgow: an introductory survey', *Bibliotheck*, 3 (1962), pp. 195–201.

Smith, B. (ed.), *Britain and Ireland, 900–1300: Insular Responses to Medieval European Change* (Cambridge, 1999).

Smith, J. G., *The Parish of Strathblane and its Inhabitants from Early Times: A Chapter of Lennox History* (Glasgow, 1886).

Smout, T. C., *A History of the Scottish People, 1560–1830*, 2nd edn (London, 1970).

Stacey, R. C., *Dark Speech: The Performance of Law in Early Ireland* (Philadelphia, 2007).

Stevenson, J. H., *Heraldry in Scotland*, 2 vols (Glasgow, 1914).

Stock, B., *The Implications of Literacy: Written Language and Models of Interpretation in the Eleventh and Twelfth Centuries* (Princeton, 1983).

Stoller, P., *The Taste of Ethnographic Things: The Senses in Anthropology* (Philadelphia, 1989).

Stones, E. L. G., 'The submission of Robert Bruce to Edward I, c.1301–1302', *Scottish Historical Review*, 34 (1955), pp. 122–34.

Street, B. V., *Literacy in Theory and Practice* (Cambridge, 1984).

Strickland, M., *War and Chivalry: The Conduct and Perception of War in England and Normandy, 1066–1217* (Cambridge, 1996).

Stringer, K. J., 'Acts of lordship: the records of the lords of Galloway to 1234', in T. Brotherstone and D. Ditchburn (eds), *Freedom and Authority: Scotland c. 1050–c. 1650: Historical and Historiographical Essays presented to Grant G. Simpson* (East Linton, 2000), pp. 203–34.

Stringer, K. J., 'The charters of David Earl of Huntingdon and lord of Garioch: a study in Anglo-Scottish diplomatic', in K. J. Stringer (ed.), *Essays on the Nobility of Medieval Scotland* (Edinburgh, 1985), pp. 72–101.

Stringer, K. J., *Earl David of Huntingdon, 1152–1219: A Study in Anglo-Scottish History* (Edinburgh, 1985).

BIBLIOGRAPHY

Stringer, K., 'The early lords of Lauderdale, Dryburgh abbey and St. Andrews priory at Northampton', in K. J. Stringer (ed.), *Essays on the Nobility of Medieval Scotland* (Edinburgh, 1985), pp. 44–71.

Stringer, K., 'The emergence of a nation-state, 1100–1300', in J. Wormald (ed.), *Scotland: A History* (Oxford, 2005), pp. 39–76.

Stringer, K. J. (ed.), *Essays on the Nobility of Medieval Scotland* (Edinburgh, 1985).

Stringer, K. J., 'Identities in thirteenth-century England: frontier society in the far north', in C. Björn, A. Grant and K. J. Stringer (eds), *Social and Political Identities in Western History* (Copenhagen, 1994), pp. 28–66.

Stringer, K. J., 'Nobility and identity in medieval Britain and Ireland: the de Vescy family, c.1120–1314', in B. Smith (ed.), *Britain and Ireland 900–1300: Insular Responses to Medieval European Change* (Cambridge, 1999), pp. 199–239.

Stringer, K. J., 'Periphery and core in thirteenth-century Scotland: Alan, son of Roland, lord of Galloway and constable of Scotland', in A. Grant and K. J. Stringer (eds), *Medieval Scotland: Crown, Lordship and Community – Essays presented to G. W. S. Barrow* (Edinburgh, 1993), pp. 82–113.

Stringer, K. J., 'Reform monasticism and Celtic Scotland: Galloway c.1140–c.1240', in E. J. Cowan and R. A. McDonald (eds), *Alba: Celtic Scotland in the Medieval Era* (East Linton, 2000), pp. 127–65.

Stringer, K. J., *The Reign of Stephen: Kingship, Warfare and Government in Twelfth-century England* (London, 1993).

Stringer, K., 'States, liberties and communities in medieval Britain and Ireland (c.1100–1400)', in M. Prestwich (ed.), *Liberties and Identities in the Medieval British Isles* (Woodbridge, 2008), pp. 5–36.

Suppe, F. S., 'Roger of Powys, Henry II's Anglo-Welsh middleman, and his lineage', *Welsh History Review*, 21 (2002), pp. 1–23.

Taylor, S., 'Babbet and bridin pudding or polyglot Fife in the middle ages', *Nomina*, 17 (1994), pp. 99–118.

Taylor, S., 'The coming of the Augustinians to St Andrews and Version B of the St Andrews foundation legend', in S. Taylor (ed.), *Kings, Clerics and Chronicles in Scotland, 500–1297: Essays in Honour of Margaret Ogilvie Anderson on the Occasion of her Ninetieth Birthday* (Dublin, 2000), pp. 115–23.

Taylor, S. and J. M. Henderson, 'The medieval marches of Wester Kinnear, Kilmany parish, Fife', *Tayside and Fife Archaeological Journal*, 4 (1998), pp. 232–47.

Thomson, D. S., 'Gaelic learned orders and *literati* in medieval Scotland', *Scottish Studies*, 12 (1968), pp. 57–78.

Thorne, S. E., 'Livery of seisin', *Law Quarterly Review*, 52 (1936), pp. 345–64.

Verstraten, F., 'Images of Gaelic lordship in Ireland, c. 1200–c. 1400', in L. Doran and J. Lyttleton (eds), *Lordship in Medieval Ireland: Image and Reality* (Dublin, 2007), pp. 47–74.

Verstraten, F., 'Naming practices among the Irish secular nobility in the high middle ages', *Journal of Medieval History*, 32 (2006), pp. 43–53.

Walker, D. M., *The Legal History of Scotland, Vol. I: The Beginnings to A.D. 1286* (Edinburgh, 1988).
Watson, F. J., 'Adapting tradition? The earldom of Strathearn, 1114–1296', in R. Oram and G. Stell (eds), *Lordship and Architecture in Medieval and Renaissance Scotland* (Edinburgh, 2005), pp. 26–43.
Watson, F., 'The enigmatic lion : Scotland, kingship and national identity in the wars of independence', in D. Broun, R. J. Finlay and M. Lynch (eds), *Image and Identity: The Making and Remaking of Scotland through the Ages* (Edinburgh, 1997), pp. 18–37.
Watson, F. J., 'The expression of power in a medieval kingdom: thirteenth-century Scottish castles', in S. Foster, A. Macinnes and R. MacInnes (eds), *Scottish Power Centres from the Early Middle Ages to the Twentieth Century* (Glasgow, 1998), pp. 59–78.
Watson, F., *Under the Hammer: Edward I and Scotland, 1286–1307* (East Linton, 1998).
Watt, D. E. R., 'The minority of Alexander III of Scotland', *Transactions of the Royal Historical Society*, 5th Series, 21 (1971), pp. 1–23.
Waugh, S., *The Lordship of England: Royal Wardships and Marriage in English Society and Politics, 1217–1327* (Princeton, 1988).
Webb, N. M., 'Settlement and integration: the establishment of an aristocracy in Scotland (1124–1214)', in J. Gillingham (ed.), *Anglo-Norman Studies XXV: Proceedings of the Battle Conference 2002* (Woodbridge, 2003), pp. 227–38.
Webster, B., *Scotland from the Eleventh Century to 1603* (Cambridge, 1975).
Welander, R., D. J. Breeze and T. O. Clancy (eds), *The Stone of Destiny: Artefact and Icon* (Edinburgh, 2003).
Whyte, I. D., 'Rural society and economy', in B. Harris and A. R. MacDonald (eds), *Scotland: The Making and Unmaking of the Nation, c. 1100–1707. Vol. I: The Scottish Nation: Origins to c. 1500* (Dundee, 2006), pp. 158–73.
Whyte, I. D., *Scotland Before the Industrial Revolution: An Economic and Social History c. 1050–c. 1750* (London, 1995).
Willock, I. D., *The Origins and Development of the Jury in Scotland* (Edinburgh, 1966).
Winchester, A. L., 'The multiple estate: a framework for the evolution of settlement in Anglo-Saxon and Scandinavian Cumbria', in J. R. Baldwin and I. D. Whyte (eds), *The Scandinavians in Cumbria* (Edinburgh, 1985), pp. 89–101.
Woolgar, C. M., *The Senses in Late Medieval England* (New Haven and London, 2006).
Wormald, J., 'The blood feud in early modern Scotland', in J. Bossy (ed.), *Disputes and Settlements: Law and Human Relations in the West* (Cambridge, 1983), pp. 101–44.
Wormald, J., 'An early modern postscript: the Sandlaw dispute, 1546', in W. Davies and P. Fouracre (eds), *The Settlement of Disputes in Early Medieval Europe* (Cambridge, 1986), pp. 191–205.
Wormald, J., *Lords and Men in Scotland: Bonds of Manrent, 1442–1603* (Edinburgh, 1985).

Wormald, P., 'Charters, law and the settlement of disputes in Anglo-Saxon England', in W. Davies and P. Fouracre (eds), *The Settlement of Disputes in Early Medieval Europe* (Cambridge, 1986), pp. 149–68.
Young, A., 'The earls and earldom of Buchan in the thirteenth century', in A. Grant and K. J. Stringer (eds), *Medieval Scotland: Crown, Lordship and Community – Essays presented to G. W. S. Barrow* (Edinburgh, 1993), pp. 174–203.
Young, A., 'Noble families and political factions in the reign of Alexander III', in N. Reid (ed.), *Scotland in the Reign of Alexander III, 1249–1286* (Edinburgh, 1990), pp. 1–30.
Young, A., 'The political role of Walter Comyn, earl of Menteith, during the minority of Alexander III of Scotland', in K. J. Stringer (ed.), *Essays on the Nobility of Medieval Scotland* (Edinburgh, 1985), pp. 131–49.
Young, A., *Robert the Bruce's Rivals: The Comyns, 1212–1314* (East Linton, 1997).
Young, C. R., *The Royal Forests of Medieval England* (Leicester, 1979).
Ziolkowski, J. M., 'Twelfth-century understandings and adaptations of ancient friendship', in A. Welkenhuysen, H. Braet and W. Verbecke (eds), *Mediaeval Antiquity* (Louvain, 1995), pp. 59–81.

Index

Abercairney, 55
Abercorn
　John de Graham, lord of, 145n, 195
　lordship of, 129
Aberdeen, 26, 78
　castle, 26
Aberdeenshire, 23, 26, 168, 170, 175
Abernethy, William de, 190
Abraham the mair, 172
Absolon, son of Mac Beatha, 158
abthanages, 54, 68n
acres, 49, 51, 53, 55, 60, 70n, 161, 171, 172, 174
Adam, son of Adam, serfs 175
Adam, son of Causantin and his sons, serfs, 168
advowsons, 22, 82, 127, 134, 191
Affrica, daughter of Edgar de Dunscore, 62
Airth
　parish church of, 43
　William de, 132
Akeld (Northumberland)
　Robert de, 119
　township of, 127
Alan, son of Roland *see* Galloway, lords of
Alan the carpenter, 173
Alan the priest, 171
Alba, kingdom of, 2, 3, 20, 73, 164
Alexander I (1107–24), seal of, 85
Alexander II (1214–49), 16, 20, 25, 30, 47, 48, 49, 54, 57, 60, 62, 86, 99, 116, 118, 119, 121, 161, 165, 183n
　daughter of, 122
　mother of *see* Ermengarde
　written deeds of, 57, 116, 161
Alexander III (1249–86), 16, 18, 25, 41, 47, 48, 49, 51, 62, 74, 80, 115, 121, 123, 124, 127, 141n, 166, 182n, 183n, 198
　marriage of, 121–2; *see also* Margaret, wife of Alexander III
　minority of, 119–24, 129, 198
　written deeds of, 80, 123, 141n
All Saints, priory of (Ireland), 153
allegiance, 9–10, 113–16, 131, 133–7
Alneto, Thomas, arms of, 93
Alnwick (Northumberland), 144n
amercements, 128, 167, 211n; *see also* fines
amicitia see friendship
Angevin rulers of England, 3, 4, 13–14, 43, 46, 118, 208; *see also* Henry II, Richard I, John
'Anglo-Norman era', 2, 3, 5, 7, 15, 16, 63, 92, 96, 97, 148, 154, 156, 160, 170, 176, 206

Anglo-Scottish border, 5–6, 48, 91, 102n, 113–15, 116, 118, 129–30, 135, 149, 165
　aristocracy of, 5–6, 113–37, 138n, 156, 208
　laws of, 165
　monasteries of, 113
Angus, 53, 54, 56, 76, 127, 156, 161, 163, 195
　earls of, 15, 23, 86, 98; Mael Coluim, 98, (arms of), 93, (*iudex* of), 57
Angus the *iudex*, 57
animals, stolen, 23, 193; *see also* cows, kine, oxen, sheep
Annandale, 15, 16, 19, 77, 86, 93, 115, 188
　lords of *see* Bruce
appurtenances, 5, 42, 128, 142n, 160, 161, 193
arable land, 47, 50, 51, 53, 54, 60, 61, 127, 166, 170, 171, 173, 174
arbitration, arbitrators, 17, 23, 33n, 48, 67n, 167, 191, 192, 193, 195, 208
Arbroath, 191
　abbey of, 53, 80, 82, 53, 191
　abbot of, 56, 80, 192
　monks of, 54, 70n, 80, 82
Arbuthnott, 162, 164, 170, 173
Archibald, tenant of Garioch, 172
archives
　episcopal, 77
　monastic, 73, 77–8
　royal, 77
Ardlair, 54
Argyll (*Ergadie*), Argyllshire, 9n, 26, 194
　Angus (Oengus) of, 194
　barons of, 22
　bishop of, 15, 89; seal of, 89
　chiefs of, 81
　Donald (Domhnall) of, 194
　Ewan (Eoghan) son of Duncan (Donnchadh) of, 15; Alexander, son of, 30
　jury from, 28
　lords of, 21–2, 88; Somhairle, 87, 194, (seal of), 87, (sons of), 28–9, 87, 194
　see also Campbell family
aristocracy
　Anglo-Norman or English, 26, 53, 55, 58–9, 73–4, 77, 81, 84, 85, 87–8, 89–90, 92, 93, 94, 98, 113, 115, 120, 150, 155, 157, 160, 162, 206–9
　cross border *see* Anglo-Scottish border, aristocracy of
　European, 26, 27, 31, 43, 55, 59, 59–60, 73–4, 77,

240

INDEX

81, 85, 87–8, 90, 92, 93, 95, 96–7, 98, 113, 120, 157, 160, 162, 170, 206–9
  Flemish, 54, 156, 157, 206, 208
  Gaelic, 14, 26, 30–1, 53, 58–60, 73–4, 77, 81, 82, 85, 86–8, 89–90, 93–9, 109n, 129, 157, 158, 160, 206–9; see also Gaeldom, Gaelicised regions, Gàidhealtachd
Arlesay, William de, arms of, 95, 109n
armorial bearings and symbols, 5–6, 72, 84–5, 87, 89–99, 207
Arrochar, 60
ascripti, 154, 164, 175
Ashkirk, 47
Asseby, Peter de, 79–80
assemblies, 15, 18, 19–27, 44, 53, 54, 56–8, 75, 119, 188, 189, 192, 196, 209
assembly sites, 13, 24–7, 38n
assizes
  English, 43, 128, 209
  grand, 43
  of David I, 172
  of King Willliam (*Assise Regis Willelmi*), 62, 165, 209
  'of the land', 63
  petty, 43
  royal, 44, 80, 165, 183n
  Scottish, 44, 62, 165, 167, 183n, 207
assythment, 208
Athelstaneford, 166, 174
Atholl, 25
  breitheamh of, 56
  countess of, Isabella, 22; her sister Farbhlaidh, 22
  earldom of, 122
  earls of, 15, 24; Malcolm, 158; Thomas of Galloway, seal of, 86
  lordly courts of, 22, 158
Auchterarder, thanage of, 57
Auchtergaven, suitor of, 58
Augustinian order, 61, 147, 189, 190
Auldingilston, 173
Aunay, Sir Thomas de, 161
Avenel family, 135
  Robert, 198; seal of, 91
  Roger, 129, 134; seal of, 86
  William, seal of, 86, 91
Avesans, John, arms of, 95
Ayr, 113
  castle of, 137
  forest of, 79
Ayrshire, 86, 171

Badenoch, 22, 136, 147
  lords of see Comyn, John; Comyn, Walter
Balglass, Corrie of, 60
Balliol
  Edward, 127
  family, 9n, 115
  Ingram de, 50–1
  John, 80; see also John, king of Scotland
Balloch, 24
Balmerino, abbey of, 25

Balymacstrony (Ireland), 154
Banff, 47, 78
Bannockburn, battle of, 113, 136, 137
Bara, Gilbert de, 48
  mother of, 48
Barbour, John, 197
Barmoor (Northumberland), 130
Baron's Cairn, 26
barones, 22, 35n
baronies, 15–16, 26, 43
Barrow, Geoffrey, 2, 13, 16, 26, 43, 46, 56, 92, 113, 143n, 150, 157, 164
Bathgate, church of, 43
Bayeux Tapestry, 90
Beath, 174
Beauvoir, William de, 171
  widow and servant of, 171
Belford (Northumberland), 127, 131, 136
Benedictine order, 160, 163, 172
Berkeley, Richenda, daughter of Winfred de, 79
Berwick, 24, 132, 143n, 145n
  burgess of, 110n, 157
Berwickshire, 117, 136, 157, 160, 168, 169
bestiaries, 97
betaghs see Ireland, betaghs of
Bible see gospel books
Bickerton, Richard de, 171
Bidun, Walter de, chancellor of Scotland, 45
Bisset, Elizabeth, seal of, 110n
  John, 119
  Walter, 199
  William, seal of, 207
Blantyre, Patrick of, 158
bondlands, 167, 174
bondmen and bondwomen, 150, 152, 157, 159, 160, 162, 163, 166, 167, 173
bonds
  of friendship, 187, 199
  of good behaviour, 119, 120, 125, 129
  of manrent, 195, 198
boni homines, 188, 191, 196; see also *probi homines*; *fideles homines*
Book of Deer, 42, 78
books, 29, 74; see also gospel books
boon work, 159, 162
bothach, 151
boundary clauses see charters, clauses of
boundary markers, 47, 59–62
bounds, boundaries, 5, 27, 41–64, 156, 191, 196; see also perambulation
Bower, Walter, 1, 2; see also *Scotichronicon*
Bowsden (Northumberland), 127, 131
Brackley, hospital of (Northamptonshire), 171
Branxton (Northumberland), 127
breitheamh, *breitheamhnan*, 13, 17, 56–8
  of Atholl, 56; see also Gille Moire
  of Buchan, 22, 56
  of Fife, 44
  of Lennox, 56; see also Gille Crìosd
  of Strathearn, 56; see also Mac Beatha
  see also *iudex*
Bret, Hugh le, 172

Brice *iudex* of Mearns, 56
Brien, tenant of Henry II, 76
brieves, 4, 13, 17, 51–2, 62, 76, 77, 163, 164, 166, 194, 203n
  formularies of, 17, 162, 168, 197; *see also* Formulary E; Regiam Majestatem
  judicial, 52
  judicial process on, 52
  of division, 66n
  of neyfty (*de nativis*), 58, 162–9, 175
  of perambulation, 5, 41–52, 58, 62, 63, 162
  of protection, 163, 165, 168
  of right, 62
  of terce, 66n
Bruce
  family, 9n, 15, 21, 92, 94, 115, 122, 136, 137; arms of, 93
  Robert I of Annandale, 15, 16, 77, 197; seal of, 86
  Robert II, 188; seal of, 86
  Robert V, 'the Competitor', 132, 133, 195
  William, 19, 188
  see also Robert I, king of Scotland
Buchan, 20, 21, 26, 36n, 61, 189
  breitheamh of, 22, 56
  countesses of, 22; Margaret, 15; Marjory, 56
  earldom of, 22
  earls of, 15, 22, 56, 170; Feargus, 19, 24; William Comyn, 165–5, (seal of), 86
  tenants of, 26
Bulmer, Stephen de, 117; *see also* Muschamp, Thomas
Burgh, Hubert de, chancellor of England, 204n
Burgundy, Sir Robert of, 44, 196

Caddesley, 51
Cahors, 123
cain, 58, 192
Caithness and Orkney, earls of, 86
  Gilbert, 126–7, 141n; Maud, daughter of, 126–7, 130
  Malise V earl of Strathearn, 127
Callendar, William, 58
calumpnie, 23
Cambuskenneth
  abbey, 193
  abbot of, 78, 171
  monks of, 50
Campbell
  Colin 'Iongantach', 28
  family, 81
Campsie, parish of, 57
caput, 25
Caputh, Robert de, 57
Carlisle, 77
  cathedral, 155
Carrick, 19
  Duncan (Donnchadh), son of Gille Brigte lord of, 87–8, 206; mother of, 87; seal of, 86, 93
  earls of, 87–8, 129; Duncan, 122; Gille Brigte, 86, 87–8; Robert Bruce, 133, (seals of), 88
carucates, 50, 160, 171, 174

Caskieben, 174
Castelton, 26
castle guard, 20
castles, 20, 24–5, 29, 76, 196
Castleside, 26
Catter, 26
Celestine III, pope, 46, 173
Céli Dé, 154, 174
  of Kirkness, 42, 44
  of St Serf, 44
cellarers, 54
ceremonies, 5, 14, 18, 24–31, 196
  of conveyance, 30, 75, 194, 207
  of endowment, 42, 194, 196
  of enthronement, 121
  of foundation, 126
  of homage, 29, 30
  of infeftment, 42, 76, 79
  of lease, 196
  of manumission, 155, 179n
  of perambulation, 41–64
  of purchase, 196
  of quitclaim, 22, 79–80, 196
  of resignation, 29
  of sale, 79–80, 119
  see also performance; ritual
chamber, royal, 54
chancellor of Scotland, 45, 52, 77; *see also* Bidun, Walter de
chancery
  episcopal, 77, 78, 83
  European, 208
  monastic, 77, 78
  papal, 190
  royal, 77
  Scottish, 44, 46–7, 51–2, 77, 160, 165, 166, 175, 189, 194, 208; *see also* chapel, royal
chapel, royal, 44–5, 52
charters, 4, 5–6, 7–8, 14, 19, 24, 26, 27–31, 47, 48, 52, 53, 57, 58, 73–83, 86, 89, 95, 98, 99, 116, 123, 124, 132, 148, 151, 158, 165, 166, 169–70, 171, 172, 174, 187, 188, 194, 196–7
  baronial, 157, 189
  clauses of; address, 157, 188–9, 194, 200n; attestation, 79, 98 (*see also* witness lists); boundary, 52–64; commemoration, 190, 194; corroboration, 79, 98; dedication, 190; dispositive, 79, 193, 194; place date, 25; sanction, 74–5, 79; sealing, 84, 98, 194; testing, 55, 56, 156, 196, 197
  ecclesiastical, 156, 170
  episcopal, 52
  forgery of, 80–1, 82, 203n
  loss of, 80–1, 102n
  monastic, 161
  of confirmation, 43, 45, 49, 50, 52, 158, 161, 163, 189
  of endowment, 160
  of excambium, 49
  of foundation, 45, 163, 190, 196
  of infeftment, 14–15, 157, 160, 166

INDEX

of quitclaim, 30, 79–80
of sale, 79–80
royal, 52, 77, 87, 156, 157, 160, 161, 188
secular, 156
surrender of, 80–1
terminology of, 20, 60–1, 77, 79, 160–2, 190, 195, 196, 199
texts of, 17, 24, 42, 43, 48, 55, 62, 78, 79, 85, 148, 156, 157, 161, 164, 165, 187, 196
chattels, 152, 167
Chester, 126
Cheviot (Northumberland), 127
forest of, 127
Cheyne, Sir Reginald, 33n, 51
chirographs, 18, 187, 190, 192
Christina, daughter of Colin Mac Gille Crìosd, 173
Alexander, son of, 173
Chronicle of Melrose, 124, 198
chronicles and chroniclers, 74, 84, 118, 124, 149, 151, 155, 164, 187, 197, 198; *see also* *Chronicle of Melrose*; *Gesta Annalia I* and *II*; *Scotichronicon*
Cistercian order, 48, 53, 118, 131, 156, 198
Clanchy, Michael, 5, 30–1, 75, 78, 81, 89, 90
Clarinch, island of, 158
Clere, Ralph de, signet of, 86
clients, 18, 22, 23, 27, 58–9
Cloyne, bishop of, 152, 154
Cluniac order, 28, 82, 190
Clunie, 29, 30
Clyde river, 73
Clydesdale, 3, 43, 55, 157
Cochno, 82
coin, 23, 77, 99, 208
Coldingham, 174
altar of the church of, 75
monks of, 160, 167
prior of, 159, 167, 169, 172; Thomas, 72–3
priory of, 148, 163, 173
serfs of, 163
written deeds of, 73, 157, 167, 172
Coldstream, priory of, 188
Colmán, of Findo Gask, 171
comarba, 150, 164
comhdhail place names *see* courts, popular
common law
of England, 13–14, 16, 41, 89, 128, 129, 153, 208, 209
of Scotland, 5, 13–14, 16, 17, 22–4, 41–3, 45, 55, 62, 63–4, 81, 83–4, 147–9, 161–9, 172, 176, 208–9
compositions, 192, 194
amicable, 191
compurgation, compurgators, 120
Comyn
Edmond, of Kilbride, Maria, widow of, 168
family, 9n, 15, 21, 22, 94, 115, 121–3, 124–5, 129, 131, 142n
John, 18
John, lord of Badenoch, 136, 147, 148, 160
Richard, 51

Walter, earl of Menteith, 119–20, 121–3, 124, 125, 129
William, 19, 57
William, earl of Buchan, 165–6; seal of, 86
William, of Kilbride, 80
concords
amicable, 191–2, 194
final, 43, 50, 190
confirmations, 24, 44, 50, 51, 52, 62, 79, 89, 163, 189
constable of Scotland, 45, 47, 54, 113–14; *see also* Morville, Richard de; Quincy, Roger de
conveth, 18, 164–5
conveyance, 5, 19, 29, 62–3, 76, 158, 187, 202n, 207
Cooper, Lord, of Culross, 13, 17, 42, 44
Corbet
Patrick, seal of, 86
Robert, seal of, 86
Walter, seal of, 86
Cornwall, Edmund of, 198
cottars, 161, 169, 172, 174
counter-seals, 91; *see also* seals and seal usage
Coupar, 26
Coupar Angus
abbey of, 22, 165
monks of, 49–50, 156, 172
Coupland (Northumberland), 127
courts, *curiae*, 4, 5, 13–40, 191, 193, 194, 196y, 209
baronial, 4, 5, 13, 14, 19, 23, 24, 26, 27, 31, 55, 58, 62, 73, 74, 75, 76, 77, 83, 89, 158, 162, 168, 189, 190, 191, 209
border, 165
ecclesiastical, 31, 189, 191, 192
'feudal', 14–16, 23
'full' (*plena curia*), 19, 21, 24, 30
head, 18, 24
native Gaelic, 14, 23, 27, 28, 31
of Fife and Fothrif, 20
of Fife, Fothrif and Kinross, 23
of western Europe, 13, 78, 190
outdoor, 24–7
popular, 26
royal, 5, 13, 23, 25, 50, 58, 62, 73, 74, 76, 77, 143n, 162, 165, 168, 175, 191, 206
suit of *see* suit of court
venues, 24–7
cows, 23, 173, 183n; *see also* kine
Crail, 118, 174
Crailing, 174
Crambeth, Matthrew, bishop of Dunkeld, 166
Cranston, church of, 79
crime, 15, 23, 28, 84, 193, 196, 209; *see also* homicide; theft, thieves
Cristin, *sector* of Strathardle, 58
Croc, Sir Robert de, seal of, 88
Crookham (Northumberland), 127
crosses, 28, 61–2, 72, 74, 75, 85, 89
Crossraguel, monks of, 30
Cruggelton, 26
crusades, 91, 122

cues
  aural, 28–31, 79
  olfactory, 30
  visual, 28–31, 79, 80
  written, 79
Culross
  abbey of, 53
  monks of, 53, 102n
  shire of, 53–4
cumal 150, 151, 164; *see also cumelache, cumherbas*
Cumberland, 77
Cumbria, 177
  nobility of, 87–8
  prince of *see* David I
cumelache, cumelagas, cum lawes, 150, 163, 164
cumherbas, cum herbes, 150, 163, 164
Curry, Peter de, seal of, 86
curses, cursing, 28–9, 74–5; *see also* charters, clauses of sanction
curtesy of England, 128
custom
  Anglian, 2
  Brittonic, 2
  Burgh, 194
  English, 2, 3, 206–8
  European, 2–4, 5, 21, 27, 30–1, 41–2, 197, 206–8
  Flemish, 2
  French, 2, 206–8
  Gaelic, 2–4, 5, 7, 21, 22, 25, 27–31, 41–2, 46, 56, 158, 197, 208, 209
  Irish, 7
  Norse, 2, 3
cymanfa, 25

D'Aubigny, Sir William, 87
  Maud, daughter of, 87
  Maud de Senlis, wife of, 87
daggers, 31
Dalkeith
  barony of, 129, 134, 137, 148
  Graham family of *see* Graham
davachs, 156, 166, 171
David I (1124–53), 3, 5, 6, 15, 16, 25, 41, 42–3, 44, 45, 46, 47, 49, 54, 55, 56, 73, 74, 76, 77, 78, 85, 87, 115, 117, 129, 149, 150, 155, 156, 157, 160, 161, 163, 164, 172, 179n, 188, 190, 197, 209
  as prince of Cumbria, 53, 75, 117, 188
  Edgar, brother of *see* Edgar of Scotland
  seal of, 85, 163
  serfs of, 160
  son Henry *see* Northumberland, Henry earl of
  written deeds of, 75–6, 150, 157, 160, 163, 188
David II (1329–71), 185n
Davies, Rees, 1, 120, 206
debt, 72, 73, 75, 80, 83–4, 173, 192
Deer, Book of *see* Book of Deer
  monks of, 61
dempsters *see breitheamh, breitheamhnan*; learned orders

Desnes Ioan, 81
Diarmait king of Leinster, 178n
diplomas, 77
dispute settlement, 13–14, 23, 41, 43–52, 53, 55–6, 59, 61, 63–4, 156, 161–2, 165–6, 168, 171, 172, 190, 191, 195, 201n, 202n, 208
distraint 119, 130
Domnall, serf of Moray, 175
Donald (Domnall), son of Somhairle of the isles, 194
Donnchadh the *iudex* of Mearns, 56
Donnchadh the Small or the Younger, 58
doomsmen *see* learned orders
Douglas
  Agnes, wife of John Graham, 195
  family, 195
  Sir James, 197
Doune, 21
Doune of Invernochty, 26
dower, dower lands, 125, 127, 128, 171
drengs, 157
Drummond family, 193
  John, 195
Drumpellier, 43
Dryburgh
  abbey of, 49, 51,79
  abbot of, 51, 79
  monks of, 79
Dublin, 150, 153
Dùghall, smallholder of Lennox, 82–3, 173
Dull, 25
Dumbarton, 47, 60
Dumfries, 28
Dumfriesshire, 86, 161, 170
Dunbar
  battle of, 133
  earls of, 56, 87–8, 93, 119, 121, 122, 129, 130, 188; Gospatrick I, (seal of), 87, (seals of sons of), 87; Patrick I, 51, 118, 119–20, 163, 188, 198, (arms of, 93); Patrick II, 33n, 51, 72–3, 119, 122, 125, 143n, (seal of), 72; Patrick III, 122, 141n; Patrick IV, 133, 134; Patrick V, 136; Waldeve, 118, 188, (written deeds of), 188
  family, 118, 125, 129; arms of, 92, 93; seals of, 91
Dunblane, bishop of, 171
Duncan, Archibald, 7, 148, 167
Duncan II (1093–4), seal of, 85
Dunfermline
  abbey of, 54, 58, 123, 160, 161, 163, 168, 169, 175
  abbot of, 29, 78, 161, 163, 175; Alexander, 168
  chapter house of, 29
  high altar of church of, 29
  lands of, 58, 168
  monks of, 54, 58,161, 163, 168, 170, 171
  neyf genealogies of, 58, 168, 170, 174
  register of, 58
  serfs of, 160, 163, 169
Dunkeld, bishop Matthew of, 166
Dunscore, Edgar de, 62

244

INDEX

Durham, 73, 74
  manumission rolls of, 159, 180n
  monks of, 75
  priors of; Bertram de Middleton, 180n; Hugh de Darlington, 180n; Thomas de Melsanby, 180n
  Reginald of, 164
  Symeon of, 149
  written deeds of, 73, 180n
Durward
  Alan, 19, 119, 121–3, 124, 125, 126, 129, 141n
  family, 81, 121
  Thomas, 81

Earlston, 51
Easington (Northumberland), 127, 131, 134
  vicarage of, 131
East Haven, 49
East Lothian, 54, 56, 63, 73, 84, 86, 135, 166, 192
ecclesia Scoticana, 48, 154
Edgar of Scotland (1097–1107), 75
Edgetoft, Sir Nicholas de, 139n
Edinburgh, 86
  castle, treasury of, 29
  sheriff of, 43
Ednam, 74, 156
Edward I, king of England, 17, 21, 24, 47, 81, 94, 95, 130, 131, 132–7, 166, 204n
Edward II, king of England, 134, 135, 136, 137
Edward the Confessor, king of England, 85
Ellon, 19, 21, 26, 170, 184n
England, 4, 5, 13, 17, 20, 21, 25, 40n, 41, 77, 78, 84, 85, 87–8, 89, 92, 93, 94, 96, 97, 113, 115, 119, 120, 121, 122, 123, 125, 126–37, 147, 149, 153, 155, 165, 171, 188, 190, 191, 197, 204n, 207, 208
  army of, 113, 115, 116, 123, 125, 232–3, 136
  chancery of, 132, 198, 204n, 208; *see also* Burgh, Hubert de
  charters from, 40n, 160, 208
  court of King's Bench of, 119
  curtesy of, 128
  exchequer of, 21, 128, 130, 132, 139n
  justices of, 128
  kings of *see* Edward I; Edward II; Edward the Confessor; Henry I; Henry II; Henry III; John; Richard
  manorial system of, 147, 151–2, 208
  parliament of, 81, 135, 137, 169
  Quo warranto proceedings in, 132
  Scottish treaties with 132, 119, 121, 204n; *see also* York
  villeins of, 191, 193, 198, 204n
  war with, 3, 6–7, 84, 94, 102n, 113–16, 118, 132–7, 148, 166, 197, 198, 208
enmity, 191, 193, 198, 204n
Ergadie see Argyll
Ermengarde, queen of Scotland, 25
Errol, 174
  church of, 25
  Gilbert de Hay, lord of, 33n
escheat, 22, 24, 55, 190

Eskdale, 30, 129, 134–5
estate creation and formation, 22, 43, 48–9, 52, 53–6, 58–9, 60, 63, 209
estate management, 18, 83, 99, 113–17, 148, 168, 171, 172–3, 193, 196
estate surveys *see* extents
Etal (Northumberland), 127
Ettrick, forest of, 46
exchange of land, 54, 77, 79–80, 166
extents, 17, 42, 53, 62, 125, 127, 135, 148, 152, 153, 154, 174

fairs, 26
Fairslie, 183n
Falconer, Robert, arms of, 95
family and family ties, 4, 6, 18, 22, 23, 54, 59–60, 79–80, 81, 85, 87, 92, 96, 97–8, 113–37, 147, 153, 157, 158, 160–1, 162, 164, 166, 167, 168, 169–70, 171, 172, 174–5, 186, 187, 190, 193–4, 195, 196, 202n, 203n, 207, 208; *see also* kinship ties; lineage; *parentes*
Fantosme, Jordan, 76, 84, 197
Farnyhill, le, 26
feasting, 18
Fedale, 57
felony *see* crime; homicide; theft, thieves
Fenton (Northumberland), 127
Fetteresso, 170
feud, 193, 195, 208
'feudal' hosts, 20
'feudalism', notion and institutions of, 14, 19–20, 74, 149, 159, 161
fideles homines, 48, 55, 63
fields, 29, 46, 53, 54, 60, 61, 161, 166, 196
Fife, 20, 21, 23, 25, 26, 27, 29, 35n, 39n, 56, 84, 94, 170, 189, 193, 196
  army of, 21, 196
  earldom of, 15
  earls of, 59, 87, 102n, 159, 168, 196; arms of, 109n; Constantine (Causantín), 21, 25, 195–6; Duncan I (Donnchadh), 15, 87; Duncan II (Donnchadh), justiciar of Scotia, 87, 162, (seal of), 87; Malcolm I (Mael Coluim), 29, 53–4, 87, (seal of), 87; Malcolm II, 29, 122, (seal of), 87; Robert Stewart earl of Fife and Menteith *see* Stewart, Robert
  family of, 87
  iudex of, 196
  jury from, 29
  Mac Duff of, 80
  men of, 26, 44
  tenants in, 55, 196
final concords *see* concords, final
Fincurrock, 157
Findo Gask, church of, 171
Findony, 27
fines, 14, 22, 24, 165, 193, 211n; *see also* amercements
Finlaggan, 26
Fintry, lordship of, 161
Fishwick, 173

245

'Fitheleres Flat', 60
FitzAlan family *see* Stewart
FitzAvelyn, Alan, arms of, 94
Flanders, 96, 132, 156
Foliot family, 115
Ford
　Odinel de, 119, 126; Cicely de Muschamp, wife of, 126
　township of (Northumberland), 127
Fordell
　moor of, 26, 27, 39n
　William, lord of, 3n
Fordun, John of, 2, 206; *see also Gesta Annalia I and II*
forest
　English *see* Cheviot
　lands, 45, 46, 47, 79, 134
　law, 46, 183n
　royal jurisdiction in, 46-7
　see also Ayr, Cheviot, Ettrick, Gala, Gatton, Innerleithen, Leader, Selkirk
forfeiture, 19, 22, 23, 132, 137, 167, 211n
forgery, 80-1, 82, 84
Formartine, 168
formularies *see* brieves, formularies of
Formulary E, 162
Forres, 54
Forth river, 13, 14, 16, 19, 21, 22, 23, 24, 53, 55, 73-4, 77, 82, 94, 99, 120, 155, 160, 174
Fotheringham, Roger de, arms of, 95
Fothrif, 20, 23
Fowlis Wester, 130
France, 5, 45, 91, 119, 125, 155
　King of, 191-2; *see also* Louis IX
friends, 17, 18, 27, 33n, 59, 63, 123, 187, 195, 204n
　advice and counsel of, 191-2, 193-4, 195
　in the curial setting, 189-96
　of felons 193, 194
　political, 195, 197-8
　spiritual, 193-4
friendship, 7-8, 87, 186-99, 208
　as a conceptual tool, 186-7, 195
　as a pragmatic activity, 191
　as public activity, 187, 197
　Christian, 186, 198
　Ciceronian, 186
　European notions of, 197
　Gaelic notions of, 197
　in the curial setting, 189-96
　language of, 186, 188, 190, 191, 192, 195, 198
　political, 186, 197-8
　spiritual, 186, 190
　terminology of, 188, 192, 198
frithalos, 23
fugitivi, 150, 163-6, 168
fuídir, 151
Furness, Jocelyn of, 150
fustum et baculum, 24, 29

Gaeldom, Gaelicised regions, Gàidhealtachd, 2-3, 7, 14, 19, 21, 22, 28, 44, 53, 54-60, 80, 82-3,
86-8, 89, 96-9, 149-50, 156, 157-9, 160, 169-71, 173, 197, 206, 209
Gala, forest of, 46
Galbraith, Maurice, son of Gilleasbuig, 158
Galloway, 2, 20, 26, 81, 87-8, 207
　lords of, 9n, 81, 87-8, 113, 207; Alan son of Roland, 19, 21, 183n; Feargus, 207; written deeds of, 81, 158
　Thomas of, earl of Atholl, seal of, 86
gallows, 15, 60
games, 26
Garioch, 53, 55, 161, 172
　Archibald, tenant of, 172
Gascony, 123, 126; *see also* Cahors
Gatton, forest lands in, 45
gems, 91-2, 107n
Germin, Richard, 172
Gesta Annalia I and II, 2, 124, 197
gesture, 27-9, 75-6
Giffard, Hugh, 161
Gilleanndreis the One-footed, 165
Gille Coluim, tenant of Fife, 56
Gille Condad, son of Gille Mícheil, 158
Gille Críosd, *breitheamh* of Lennox, 56
Gille Críosd, son of Gille Conghal, 170
Gille Críosd the Gael, 197
Gille Martain, son of Gille Mícheil, 158
Gille Mícheil, son of Edulf, 180n
Gille Mícheil, son of Gille Mícheil, 158
Gille Mícheil the bondman, 169
Gille Moire, *breitheamh* of Atholl, 56
Gille Moire, scoloc of Tarland, 170
Gille Moire, tenant of prior of St Andrews, 89
Gillephadruig the serf, 160
Glamorgan, 179n
Glanvill, 83, 168
Glasgow
　bishop of, 21, 193; John, 75; Walter, 166; William Wishart, 83
　burgess of, 194
　cartulary of, 78
　cathedral church of, 47, 76, 78, 83; canons of, 49, 55; cantor of, 56; chancery clerks of, 83; servants of, 83; tenants of, 47
　diocese of, 57
　lands of, 53
　mair of, 58
　Official of, 83
　seal of dean of, 89
Glassary, Gilbert of, 28
Glen Fruin, 60
Glencarnie, 120
　Gilbert I of, 81, 166; seal and *signum* of, 89
　Gilbert II of, 126
Gloucester, earl of, 197
Gorthy, Tristram de, 88
　seal of, 106n
gospel books, 28-9, 31, 39n, 74, 78, 99
governors (*duces*), 21
Gowrie, Carse of, 47
Graham
　arms of, 93

INDEX

David, 122
David de, of Mugdock, 23, 119, 129
family, 93, 129–30, 132, 133, 135, 137
Henry de, of Dalkeith and Abercorn, 129, 143n
John, of Abercorn, 145n, 195; his wife Agnes Douglas, 195
John de, son of Nicholas, 130, 131, 133, 135–7; seal of, 146n
Nicholas de, of Dalkeith, 129–37, 208; Henry de, brother of, 132; Idonea de, sister of, 132; Marjory (Mary) of Strathearn, wife of, 129, 130–7
Patrick de, the elder, 132
Patrick de, the younger, 136
William de, 129
see also Abercorn
Grant, Alexander, 3, 8n, 16, 43, 55, 158, 160, 180n
Great Cause, 81, 94–5, 131, 132, 136, 198
great seal of Scotland, 76–7, 85
Greenlaw, Master William de, 119
Grimbald family, 15
Gruoch, wife of Mac Beatha son of Findlaech, 42
Guardians of Scotland, 51–2, 198
guesting, 18
Gullane, church of, 191
Gwynnedd, rulers of, 76, 106n

Haddington, sheriff of, 45
hagiographies, 74, 150, 173
Hailes
  mill pool of, 50
  parson of, 50
Haldan, bondman of Coldingham, 159, 160
Hassington, 117, 118, 119, 136
Hay, Gilbert de, lord of Errol, 33n
Haymhald, 208
Heatherslaw (Northumberland), 127, 131, 132
Henry, son of David I *see* Northumberland, Henry earl of
Henry I, king of England, 77, 117, 155
Henry II, king of England, 46, 76, 118, 190, 209
Henry III, king of England, 41, 119, 121, 122, 123, 125, 126, 128, 129, 139n, 197
Margaret, daughter of *see* Margaret, wife of Alexander III
heraldic images and symbols, 89–99; *see also* armorial bearings and symbols
heraldry, 84–5
  language of, 90, 96
Herez, William de, arms of, 95
Heriot, 152, 167, 174
hermits, 154
Hethpool (Northumberland), 118, 127, 131, 132
Hexham, John of, 149, 155
Hibernici, 169
hills, hilltops, 26, 29, 57, 59, 80; *see also* moot hills
Holburn (Northumberland), 127
Holland, Florence count of, 81, 195

holy objects *see* gospel books, relics
Holyrood
  abbey of, 43, 50–1, 161
  abbot of, 76, 163
  monks of, 51, 161
  prior of, 49
  serfs of 163
homage, acts of, 24, 29, 30, 125, 131, 132, 134, 135, 145n
Home, Gilbert de, 118
homicide, 194
Horndean, 75
  family, arms of, 93
hospitality, 18, 164–5, 197
Hospitallers, 195
Howden, Bernard de, 118
Hownam (Northumberland), 139n
Hungus, king of Picts, 61, 76
Huntercombe
  Walter de, 131, 143n
  William de, 119, 126, 128, 131; Isabel de Muschamp, wife of, 126, 131
Huntingdon, earls of
  David, 9n, 53, 54, 55, 91, 161, 169–70, 172, 188; written deeds of, 55, 157, 160–1
  John, 50, 51; suitors of, 50; tenants of, 45, 55
husbandmen, 169, 172
hybridity, concept of, 4, 8, 207, 209

identity
  ethnic, 59
  family, 6, 85, 96–9
  individual, 85
  linguistic, 59, 97
  national, 113
illuminated manuscripts, 77
images, imagery, 6, 85, 96–8
inauguration, sites of, 26; *see also* Finlaggan, Tynwald
Inchaffray
  abbey and priory of, 18, 80, 106n, 130, 147, 148, 160, 165, 189, 190, 196
  abbots of, 192; Hugh, 80
  canons of, 18, 19, 55, 60, 61, 80, 189
  foundation charter of, 196
Inchcolm
  abbey of, 28
  canons of, 28, 33n
Inchmartin, Alexander de, 33n
Inchyra, 174
indentures, 5, 8, 17, 73, 187, 190, 192
infeftment, 23, 42, 49, 53, 76, 79
inheritance, 2, 156, 158, 193, 209
Innerleithen, forest of, 47
Innocent III, pope, 173
inquests, 22, 28, 30, 42, 45, 47, 51, 63, 75–6, 117, 127, 132, 135, 139n, 156, 164, 170, 209
Inverkeilor, 164
Inverness-shire, 88, 120, 127
Ireland, 24, 25, 34n, 40n, 75, 76, 148, 157, 162, 163, 164, 167, 169, 172, 174, 204n
  base clientage in, 151

247

Ireland (cont.)
  betaghs of (betagii, biataigh), 150–4, 167, 169, 170, 174, 175, 183n
  English in, 150–1, 152, 154
  estate rentals from, 152–4, 174
  free tenants in, 151, 156
  Gaelicised regions of, 151, 154, 169
  justiciary rolls of, 183n
  law of see law, Irish
  lawbooks of, 24, 27
  Lordship of, 150, 151–4, 171, 174
  native population of, 149, 151–4
  nativi of, 153
  rural economy of, 151–4, 155
  scribes of, 169, 174
  slavery in, 7, 150–1, 154
  villeins of, 7
  Welsh in, 152, 154
  written deeds of, 40n, 150, 153, 156, 157
Islandshire, liberty of (Durham), 13
Isle of Masses see Inchaffray
iudex
  Angus the, 57
  king's, 56
  of Fife, 196
  of Lennox, 83
  of Mearns, 46–7, 56
  see also breitheamh, breitheamhnan; Brice; Donnchadh; Dùghall; Mac Gillerachcah

James VI (1567–1625), 208
Jedburgh, 25
  monks of, 160
jewellery, 91, 95; see also gems; lockets; pendants; rings
John
  son of Malind, 166
  son of Orm, seal of, 86
John, king of England, 46, 162
John, king of Scotland (1292–6), 80, 136
judex see *iudex*
judicial
  combat, 167, 208
  exile, 208
juries, jurors, 4, 22, 29, 41, 42, 47, 54, 56, 158, 196, 209
jurisdiction, 18, 166, 167
  criminal, 14–16, 23
  ecclesiastical, 192
  royal, 46
justice, 5
  baronial, 14–16
  in England, 13–14
  in Europe, 13–14
  in Scotland, 13–14, 23
  mediated, 16
  private, 16
justices, 17, 89
  episcopal, 57
  papal, 57, 78, 79, 82
justiciars, 13, 16, 17, 25, 46–7, 49, 56
  of Lothian, 192
  of Scotia, 54, 57, 87, 122
  see also Comyn, William; Durward, Alan; Fife, Donnchadh II earl of; Lindsay, David de; Strathearn, Gille Brigte earl of

Keillor, 130
Kellie, Maol Muire, thane of, 56
Kelly, 26
Kelso
  abbey of, 46, 67n, 91, 148, 156
  abbot of, 80, 81, 161, 162
  lands of, 157, 174
  monks of, 50, 80, 86, 91
  serfs of, 159, 163
  written deeds of, 77, 81, 161
Kenmore, 24, 26
Kent
  Ralph de, 80; seal of, 88
  Robert de, 50, 80
Kide, Gille Crìosd, 156
Kilbride, 80, 168; see also Comyn, Edmond; Comyn, William
Kilbucho, 129
Kilmany, Hugh de, 194
Kilpatrick, church of, 53, 57, 82, 158
Kimmerston (Northumberland), 127
Kinblethmont, 23, 54
kindred, heads of, 98, 193–4
kine, 208, 211n; see also cows; oxen
king lists, 99
king's chapel see chancery, Scottish
Kinghorn, 51
Kingoldrum, 156
Kinloch, Alan de, arms of, 94
Kinloss, abbey of, 202n
Kinnear, Simon, son of Simon of, 195
Kinninmonth, shire of, 50
Kinross, 23
kinship, fictive, 193–4, 195, 198–9
kinship ties, 87, 92–3, 97–8, 198
Kintore, John de, arms of, 95
Kintyre, 82
Kinveachy, 81; see also Glencarnie, Gilbert I of
Kirkness, 42, 196
knight service, 19–20, 117, 127, 128, 136
knighthood, knights, 56, 72, 88, 90–1
knights' feus, 16, 18, 19–20, 21, 128
Kyle, 86

Lammermuir, 80
Lanark, sheriff of, 43
Lanarkshire, 43
'land of earls', 24, 26, 74, 89, 99
language
  Anglian, 2
  Arabic, 107n
  Brittonic, 2
  English, 2, 59, 63, 206
  Flemish, 2, 59, 206
  French, 2, 59, 63, 206
  Inglis, 206
  Irish Gaelic, 150, 151, 164, 169

INDEX

Latin, 13, 20, 22, 24, 27, 56, 83, 97, 164, 169, 187, 188, 197
  legal, 45
  Norse, 2
  of friendship, 8, 186, 188, 190, 191, 195, 198
  of heraldry, 90, 96
  of seal legends, 72, 97
  of signs, 90, 95
  Scottish Gaelic, 2, 4, 14, 16, 30, 42, 57–8, 59–60, 63, 78, 97, 150, 164, 206
  vernacular, 79
Laon, Anselm of, 96
Largo, 26
Lauderdale, 9n, 48, 171
Laundells, William de, 139n
Laurencekirk, 79
law
  border, 165
  burgh, 165
  ecclesiastical, 173–4, 190
  English *see* common law of England
  European, 59, 89
  forest, 46, 183n
  Irish, 151–4
  of Clan MacDuff, 208
  Roman, 198
  Scottish *see* common law of Scotland
  Scottish Gaelic, 22, 56–9
lawbooks, 24
Laws of the Four Burghs, 165
Leader, forest of, 46
learned orders, 13, 28, 56, 97–8
lease, 48, 161–2, 170, 194, 195
Lebevre, Henri, 186, 187
Leicester, earl of, arms of, 92
Leinster, 76, Diarmait, king of, 178n
Lennox, 19, 22, 26, 40n, 60, 82, 84, 94, 98, 157, 173, 189, 193, 204n
  Amhlaibh, brother of Maoldomhnaich, earl of, 82, 158; seal of, 88, 106n
  breitheamh of, 56
  dean of, 21
  Dùghall, brother of Maoldomhnaich, earl of, 82
  earls of, 15, 24, 56, 59, 129, 132, 194; arms of, 109n; Malcolm I, 21, 30, 33n, 80, (seal of), 86, 94; Malcolm II, 30; Maoldomhnaich, 19, 21, 23, 30, 53, 60, 82, 88, 189, 206, (seal of), 30, 105n, (sister of), 189, (written deeds of), 98, 157–8, 189
  family, 9n, 57, 82, 88–9, 194
  Gille Crìosd, brother of Maoldomhnaich, earl of, 60, 158
  iudex of, 82
  jury from, 30, 89
  Mael Coluim, son of Maoldomhnaich earl of, 19, 180n, 200n
  tenants of, 19, 21, 23, 28, 53, 82–3, 88, 89, 94
  written deeds from, 53, 82, 89, 98
Leslie, Norman de, 166
Lesmahagow, 156, 158
Letham, Ketel de, 56

letters, 5, 56, 72, 73, 105n
  diplomatic, 187
  of remission, 208
  of slains, 208
  patent, 51–2
Leven river, 60, 173
Levif, woman land holder, 163
Liber Extravagans, 198
Lindores, 191
  abbey, 54, 161
  abbot of, 102n, 166
  monks of, 50, 57, 160–1, 192
Lindsay
  David de, justiciar of Lothian, 51, 122
  family, 94
  Simon de, seal of, 91
  William de, seal of, 86
lineage, 27, 92, 98, 116, 117, 126, 134, 207; *see also* family and family ties
Linlithgow, 118
  sheriff of, 43
Linlithgowshire, 129
Lisronagh (Ireland), 152
Lismore, 15
literacy, 30–1, 73–83, 90, 98–9, 100n
  pragmatic, 73
literati, 8, 83, 97, 190, 191, 198
literature
  devotional, 95
  of Gaelic Scotland, 28, 97–9
  romance, 95, 97
litigation, litigants, 23, 26, 41, 42, 48–9, 50, 52, 62, 135, 137, 192
Liulf and wife Gledewis, of Lauderdale, 100n, 172
Llewelyn of Wales, 126
Loch Leven, 44
Loch Lomond, 60, 158
Lochindorb, 19
Lochore
  Constantine of, 29, 80
  David of, 29, 80
  Philip of, 29
lockets, 91
London, Robert de, 204n
  seal of, 86, 91
Longus, Thor, 74–5
Lothian, 118, 157, 163
  justiciar of *see* justiciars
Louis IX, king of France, 125
Lowick (Northumberland), 127, 131
Luke, son of Theobald of Pitlandy, 60
lumnarcas, 21
Luss, 60
  Gille Moire of, 158
  Maoldomhnaich of, 158
  Maurice of, 83

Mac Aeda, Mael Coluim, 76–7
Mac Aldie, Gille Magu, 156
Mac Alef, Gille Thomas, 156
Mac Banhyl', Mac Beatha, 58
Mac Beatha, *breitheamh* of Strathearn, 56

249

Mac Beatha, son of Findlaech, 42
  wife of, 42
Mac Beatha Mac Torphin, 56
Maccus son of Undweyn, 156
MacDuff of Fife, 80; *see also* law of Clan MacDuff
Mac Edolf, Gille Mícheil, 89
  Donnchadh, son of, 89
Mac Gilhys, Yothre, 156, 157
Mac Gillechiar, Cinaed, 156, 172
Mac Gille Martain, Farquhar, 23
Mac Gillerachcah, Boli, *iudex* of Mearns, 56
Macholf, Fearchar, 156
Mackelegan, Reginald, 153
Mackindoyr', Cailean, 58
Mac Malcolm rulers, 3, 29, 45, 47, 73–4, 76, 77, 87, 97, 99, 154, 170, 206
Mac Neachdainn, Gille Críosd and Aed, sons of Mael Coluim, seals of, 106n
MacQueen, Hector, 13, 42, 48
Mac Suibhne, Dùghall, 82
Mac Suthern, Gillaindreis, 169
Mac Uilleim
  family, 78, 100n, 120
  Gilleasbuig, 165
Mael Coluim III *see* Malcolm III
mair
  Abraham the, 172
  of Glasgow, 58
  office of, 13
Malcolm, son of Malcolm, 193
Malcolm III (1057–93), 1, 99, 149, 154, 155, 160, 178n
Malcolm IV (1153–65), 43, 45, 49, 77, 78, 87, 150, 157, 163, 164, 183n
  seal of, 85
  written deeds of, 44, 45, 47, 77, 150, 155, 161, 163, 183n
Man
  isle of, 26
  rulers of, 26; Ragnvald, seal of, 87, 88
Manuel, prioress of, 49
manumission, 155, 159, 160, 175, 179n, 180n; *see also* ceremonies of manumission
Maol Muire, thane of Kellie, 56
Mar, 20, 21, 22, 26, 170
  countess of, Muriel of Strathearn, 128–9, 131
  earldom of, 81, 122, 129
  earls of, 15, 59, 86, 169; seals of, 91, 107n; William, 128–9, 182n; William Comyn, 19
marches *see* bounds, boundaries
marching the bounds *see* perambulation
Margaret, Maid of Norway, 131
Margaret, wife of Alexander III, queen of Scotland, 25, 121, 123, 124
Margaret, wife of Malcolm III, queen of Scotland, 74, 149, 155, 160, 179n
  gospel book of, 29, 74, 78
  her biographer, 99, 149
  see also St Margaret
Marnoch the forester, 171
marriage, 2, 6, 18, 53, 116–17, 120–1, 126, 128, 129, 132, 133. 141n, 176

marriage portion *see* tocher
Marshall, arms of Fergus and John, 95
marshlands, 61, 166
Mauchline, 61
Maule
  Christine, lady of, 33n, 52
  Eschina de, 55
  see also Mow; Stewart, Walter
May, priory of, 43, 171
Mearns, 53
  iudex of, 56
  see also Brice; Donnchadh; Mac Gillerachcah
mediation, mediators, 17, 33n, 48, 191, 193, 19, 201n, 208; *see also* arbitration
Megdubyl, Cailean, 58
Meikleour, Andrew Mercer, lord of, 195
Melginch, parson and church of, 76
Melrose
  abbey of, 25, 28, 45, 46, 80, 86, 91, 118, 119, 131, 135, 136, 198
  abbots of, 79, 134–5, 137, 198; William, 61
  church of, 40n, 125
  clerk of, 28
  conversus of, 171
  estates of, 54
  monks of, 28, 40n, 46, 50, 51, 60, 62, 91, 118, 134, 137, 161, 171, 198
  mortuary rolls of, 198
  servants of, 135
  written deeds of, 33n, 78, 79, 125, 156, 161
Melville
  Philip de, 53
  Richard de, 188
memorials, 47
memory, 3, 29, 58, 62, 63, 74, 207
Menteith, 21
  earldom of, 123, 191
  earls of; Robert Stewart earl of Fife and Menteith, 195, 203n, (seals of), 86; Walter Comyn, 119–20, 121–2, 124, 125, 129; Walter Stewart, 123
  tenants of, 26
Menteith family of Rusky, 193, 195
Mercer, Andrew, burgess of Perth and lord of Meikleour, 195
merchet, 152, 158, 167, 174
Merse, 157, 163
Meschin, Ranulf le, 77
metes *see* bounds, boundaries
Methven family, 130
  lord of *see* Mowbray, Roger de
Meynell, Sir Nicholas de, 137
Midlem, 159
Midlothian, 79, 129
Migvie, 24, 26
military service, 20, 125, 126, 157
miracles, 150
monastic orders, 48, 49, 54, 55, 78, 154, 156, 159, 161, 165, 169; *see also* Augustinian order; Benedictine order; Cistercian order; Cluniac order; Premonstratensian order; Tironensian order

INDEX

Mondynes, 53
Montfort, Alexander de, 166
Moorfoot, 43
  marches of, 45
moors, 26, 27, 39n, 47, 54
moot hills, 26
Moravia, family of
  arms of, 93
  William de, of Tullibardine; arms of, 94-5
Moray, 2, 9n, 55, 76, 84, 135, 156, 165, 189, 192, 200n, 206
  bishop of, 161-2, 165-6, 172, 175; Alexander, 168; Andrew, 89, 192, 202n; register of, 78, 89, 100n, 192, 202n; seal of, 89
  seal of chapter of, 89
mormaers, mormaerships, 2, 3, 4, 15, 16, 20, 22, 23, 53, 56, 58-9, 189, 209
Morpeth (Northumberland), 118
Mortimer, William de, 28
Morville
  family, 15, 92, 113, 115
  Helen de, 171-2
  Hugh de, 160
  Richard de, constable of Scotland, 45, 46, 162, 169, 188; seal of, 86
  William de, seal of, 86
Morwick, Ernulf de, 100n
Mow, 190; see also Maule
Mowbray, Roger de, 26, 197
Mugdock, 119; see also Graham, David de
multiple estates, 2, 54
Munford, Lady Alice de, 195
Murthly
  servant of, 58
  suitor of, 58
Muschamp
  Alan de, 145n
  Cicely, daughter of Robert III, 126
  Cicely, mother of Thomas, 117
  family, 117, 119, 125, 131, 133, 135, 136
  Gilia de, 119; husbands of, 119, 139n
  inheritance, 126-37; see also map on p. 114
  Isabel, daughter of Robert III, 126, 127, 128, 131; see also Huntercombe, William de
  Isabel, granddaughter of Robert III, 126, 127, 128
  Marjory see Strathearn, countesses of
  Reginald de, 117
  Robert II de, baron of Wooler, 118, 139n; William, brother of, 139
  Robert III de, baron of Wooler, 6, 28, 116, 120-1, 125, 126, 127, 128, 129, 131; son-in-law of, 119; widow of, 125, 127, 128; written deeds of, 118; see also Strathearn, Earl Malise II of
  Robert de, of Edinburgh, 145n
  Stephen de, of Barmoor, 130
  Thomas, nephew of Reginald, 117-18, 144n; Maud de Vescy, wife of, 117; see also Bulmer family
  Thomas de, of Lanarkshire, 145n
  William de, 119

musicians see learned orders
Muthill, 170

Naomhín, serf of Moray, 175
nativi, 161, 162, 165, 166, 167, 168, 169, 170, 172, 174, 175; see also neyfs; peasants; serfs
Ness, king's physician, 172
Ness, son of Ness, 60
'New British history', 1-3
Newbattle
  abbey of, 48
  abbot of, 48, 63
  monks of, 33n, 43, 45, 48, 61, 63, 192
  prior of, 49
  written deeds of, 60-1
Newcastle-upon-Tyne, 125, 128, 130
Newlands, 129
Newminster, abbey of (Northumberland), 118
Newtonhall, 160
neyfs, 163, 166, 167, 170, 173, 175, 182n, 183n
  genealogies of, 58, 168, 170, 174
  see also *nativi*; peasants; serfs
neyfty, brieve of see brieves, of neyfty
Nicholas IV, pope, 102n
Nigg, 26
Noble, Sir Ralph, 193
Norman, son of Edulf, 56
Normandy, 96, 118
'Normanisation', 4, 55
Normanville
  John de, 51; father of, 51; grandfather of, 51
North Berwick, nunnery of, 86
Northumberland, 41, 116-17, 118, 120, 126, 127, 128, 129, 131, 132, 133, 134, 137, 197
  Countess Ada of, 45, 65n
  Henry earl of, 45; written deeds of, 45, 200n
  jury of, 41
Norway, Maid of see Margaret
notaries, notarised copies, 72, 195
notifications, 5, 8, 17, 45, 73

O Karny family of Ireland, 154
O Mongane family of Ireland, 154
oath helpers, 24
oaths, 24, 28-9, 52, 56, 62, 74, 76, 79, 82-3, 119; see also compurgation, compurgators
Odo, son of Simon, 50
  son of, 50
óenaig, 25
Oengus, son of Donnchadh, son of Ferchad, land holder in Lennox
  father of, 89
  seal of, 89
Oengus, son of Somhairle of the isles, 194
Oliphant family, arms of, 93
open-air meetings see assembly sites
orality, 75-83, 98-9, 100n
ordeals, 15
ordinationes see concords
Orkney, earl of see Caithness
Osbert, bondman of Kelso, 159, 160, 162
Osulf, serf, and Walter his son, 169

Osulf, son of Uhtred, 156
oxen, 82, 175; see also cows, kine
oxgangs, 171

Pàdruig the shepherd, 171
Paisley
  abbey of, 28, 30, 50, 53, 55, 57, 61-2, 82, 106n, 173, 194; high altar of church of, 82-3
  abbots of, 30, 62, 173; William, 82
  monks of, 50, 53, 61-2, 82, 89, 158, 189, 190, 194
  scribe of, 194

Panmure, 52
papacy, 28, 46, 102n, 154, 173; see also Celestine III; Innocent III; Nicholas IV
  chancery of, 190-1
  envoys from, 54
  judges-delegate of, 57, 78, 79, 82, 191
  legates of, 191
parage, 92
parentes, 193
Paris, Matthew, 108n, 125, 204n
parish churches, 43, 192; see also advowson
parliament of Scotland, 22, 83, 113
pasture, 43, 46, 47, 50, 52, 54, 80, 134-5, 166, 171
patronage, secular, 116, 120, 122, 134
patronage of churches see advowson
peasants
  of England, 127, 167, 169
  of Ireland, 148-9, 151-4, 175
  of Scotland, 147-9, 159-75, 196
  see also nativi; neyfs; serfs
peat bogs, 61
Peebles, 156
Peeblesshire, 56, 129
Peffer, 43
pendants, 91
Penshiels family, arms of, 93
perambulation, 5, 17, 20, 22, 23, 25, 37n, 41-64, 156, 162; see also brieves of perambulation; charters, boundary clauses of
perambulators, 56-60
performance, 27-31, 193
perquisites see profits of lordship
Perth, 23, 99
  Andrew Mercer, burgesses of, 195
  goldsmith of, 99
  widow of a burgess of, 194
Perthshire, 27, 130
  land holders in, 57, 94
Peterborough, Benedict of, 118
Picardy, 96
Picts, 92, 164
  king of, 61, 76
  see also Hungus
'pit and gallows', 15
Pitlandy, Luke, son of Theobald of, 60
plague, 148
plaints, 17
plea rolls, 13, 14
pleas, 17, 119, 130

pleas of the crown see crime
pledges, 74, 82, 167
plough service, 152, 162
ploughgates, 44, 54, 159, 171
Pluscarden, priory of, 165
poets see learned orders
Poitiers, Gilbert of, 96
Pow Water, 61
power centres, 26
Prat, Reginald, 188
precepts, royal 42, 43, 44-5, 47, 48, 49, 51-2, 57, 58, 162, 163, 183n, 197; see also brieves
premicerios, 21
Premonstratensian order, 48, 190
Prendergast, 157
  Henry de, 172
  Robert de, 169, 172
prerogative
  baronial, 23
  lordly, 77
  royal, 48
privy seals, 91
probi homines, 50, 55, 58, 63, 157, 188, 196, 209
profits of lordship, 5, 21, 43, 59, 127-8, 131, 134, 135, 137, 162, 166-7, 183n

quarries, 61
Quincy family, 9n, 92
  arms of, 93
  Robert de, earl of Winchester, constable of Scotland, 48, 113-14
  Saer de; arms of, 92-3; wife of, 92; seal of, 86, 90-1
quitclaim, 21, 26, 29, 30, 77, 78, 79, 80-1, 169-70, 172, 196
Quo warranto proceedings, 131, 132

Ragewin the serf, 160
Ragman Roll, 24, 94
Ramsay, Sir John, 25
rancour, 192; see also enmity
ranscauth, 208
Raonall, son of Somhairle of the isles, 194
rape, 150
recognitions, 17, 47
recognitors, 23, 24, 37n, 41, 49, 50-1, 52, 54, 57, 61-2, 76, 156, 196
Redgorton, 170
Regiam Majestatem, 83-4, 162, 168, 173, 175
relics, 28, 31, 39n, 54, 56, 74
renders, 167
  in animals, 82
  in money, 125, 127
Renfrew, 194
rentals see extents
rents, 23, 131, 156, 159, 192
  cheese, 158
  food, 33n, 152, 164, 173
  money, 125, 127, 128, 152
reparation, 211n
replegiation, 165

INDEX

resignation, 24, 162; *see also fustum et baculum*
Restalrig
  Edward de, seal of, 86
  Thomas de, 50
Restenneth, canons of, 102n
  serfs of the church of, 163
Revel, Henry de, 50
  Richard, son of, 50
Richard, son of Lugán, 197
Richard I, king of England, 46
Riddell family, 79
  arms of, 93
  Hugh, 79; seal of, 79
  Richard, seal of, 79
  William, Isabel, wife of, 28
Rievaulx, Aelred of, 150, 197
rings, 31, 91
ritual, 5, 14, 27–31, 43, 52, 57
rivers, 25, 57, 59–60, 61, 74
Robert, serf of Moray, 175
Robert, son of Fulbert, seal of, 86
Robert, son of Maccus, 156
Robert I (1306–29), 14, 16–17, 41, 113, 135, 136–7, 162, 168, 197
  written deeds of, 52
Robert III (1390–1406), 4
rod and staff, 21; *see also fustum et baculum*
rolls, 47
  justiciary, of Ireland, 183n
  mortualry, 195
  of arms, 94, 109n; Glover's, 108n; Walford's, 108n
  of manumission, 180n
Rome, 170
Ros
  Alan de, 183n
  Robert de, 122
Rosneath, church of, 106n
Ross, earls of, 86
  seals of, 91
Ross (Durham), 131, 136
Roth, Gille Criosd, son of Gille Ethueny, 147, 148, 160
Roxburghshire, 86, 91, 156
Rusky, 195

St Andrews, 22, 25, 29, 61
  bishop of, 164–5, 170
  canons of, 196
  cartulary of, 42, 100n
  foundation legend of, 61, 76
  high altar of church of, 76, 80
  prior of, 29, 49, 50, 162, 170, 196
  priory of, 50; tenants of, 89
  see also Gille Moire
St Clair, Henry de, 162, 169
St Colban, parish church of, 82
St Columba, 28
St Cuthbert, 74–5
St Kentigern, 76, 150
St Margaret of Scotland, 74; *see also* Margaret, wife of Malcolm III
St Mary's church *see* Easington (Northumberland), vicarage of
St Ninian of Whithorn, 149–50
St Serf, church of, 44
St Victor, Hugh of, 96
'sake, soke, toll, team and infangenthief', 15
sale, 79–80, 161, 172, 173, 174, 194, 196
sanctuaries, 61
Sanquhar
  lands of, 61–2
  William de, 61–2; father of, 61–2
sasine, delivery of, 23, 29, 40n, 44–5, 48, 75, 77, 79, 119, 171, 173; *see also* infeftment
satellites, 21
satraps, 21
Scalebroc, Roger de, seal of, 86
Scandinavia, 150, 169, 179n
Scolilands, 170
Scollatisland, 170
Scollowland, 170
scoloc lands, 170
scolocs, 164–5, 170, 173, 184n
Scone, 26
  abbey of, 1613, 174
  abbot of, 162, 163
  monks of, 99, 171
  serfs of, 163, 174
Scotia, 20, 21, 27
  justiciar of *see* justiciars
Scotichronicon, 1
Scotland
  army of, 20, 21, 118, 136, 149, 155, 157, 158, 167, 183n, 196
  law of *see* common law of Scotland
  rural economy of, 21, 48–9, 61, 62–3, 147–9, 159–61, 164–7, 168, 170, 171, 176, 192
'Scottish king's household' (treatise), 52
scribes and clerks, 19, 22, 24, 25, 28, 29, 42, 43, 44, 46–7, 48, 51–2, 56, 58, 82, 164, 165, 166, 169, 174, 175, 187, 188, 189, 190, 191, 192, 194, 196–7, 208
  baronial, 25, 188, 189–90, 195
  episcopal, 78, 188, 189
  Irish, 169, 174
  monastic, 55, 188
  royal, 51–2, 77, 188, 194
sealed instruments, 5–6, 62, 72–3, 192
seals
  armorial, 72, 91–3, 94
  baronial, 80, 84, 85–99
  borrowing, 86, 89, 98, 108n
  burgh, 99
  comital, 86
  counter-seals, 91
  ecclesiastical, 85, 110n
  episcopal, 85, 89
  equestrian, 72, 90–1
  in Gaelic Ireland, 96
  in Wales, 106n
  legends inscribed on, 72, 97, 109n
  matrices, 89, 94, 97, 98
  of common folk, 85

seals (cont.)
  of lesser nobility, 85, 86, 88–9, 91–5
  of men, 84
  of Scottish Gaelic magnates, 86–7, 88–96
  of townspeople, 84, 85
  of women, 84, 89, 110n
  probative value of, 207
  royal, 51–2, 85
  secular, 72, 85–6, 110n
  semiotics implications of, 96–8
  urban, 84
seals and seal usage, 5–6, 51–2, 62, 72–5, 76, 79, 83–99, 192, 196, 197, 207; *see also* gems; great seal; lockets; pendants; privy seals; rings; signets
sector see suitors
Selkirk, forest of, 45
Selkirkshire, 47
senchleíthe, 151
Senlis, Maud de, 87
senses, 27
serfdom
  church's attitude toward, 170–1, 173–4
  in Ireland, 148–9, 151–4, 175
  in Scotland, 7, 147, 154–76
serfs, 147–75
  emancipation of, 155
  families of, 147, 148, 153–4, 159, 160–1, 162, 164, 165–6, 167, 168, 169–70, 171, 172–3, 14–15
  female, 152–3, 164, 165, 167
  legal liabilities of, 167–8, 176
  manumission of, 155
  runaway see *fugitivi*
  see also nativi; neyfs; peasants
sergeants, 20, 23
serjeanty service, 157
sermons, 74, 173
Seton family, arms of, 93
sheep, 23, 183n
sheriffs,13, 16, 17, 43, 45, 46–7, 49, 54, 166
sheriffdoms, 16
shires, 53, 62
sigillography and sign theory, 85, 90, 96–7; *see also* seals and seal usage
signatures, 83
signets, 83, 86; *see also* seals
signum, 89
Simon, son of Gille Brigte, of Soutra, 172
Simonburn (Northumberland), 132
Skene, Sir John, 208
slave raids, 149
slave trade, 150, 151
slavery
  church's attitude toward, 149–50, 151, 154
  in England, 149
  in Ireland, 150, 151–4
  in Scotland, 7, 8, 149–51, 154–5
slaves, runaway *see fugitivi*
Slipperfield, lord of, 51; *see also* Comyn, Richard
Smailholm, 174
smell *see* cues, olfactory

Solet, Robert, arms of, 95
Somerled, tenant of Lennox, 30
  Thomas, son of, 30
Somerville, William de, 193
sorryn, 23
Soules
  John de, 132
  Nicholas de, 18, 22
  William de, 132
sounds, 27
Soutra, hospital of, 172
Soylard, Richard, bondman, 180n
space
  concepts of, 9n, 186–7
  conceptual, 79, 198
  sacred, 191
  social, 17, 59, 186–99
speech, 28–31, 78–9
speech acts, 27–30
Sproull, Walter, arms of, 94
Sprouston, 174
Spyny, 172
Stewart
  Alan son of Walter, 50, 171; seal of, 86, 90–1
  David, 27; *see also* Strathearn, David earl of
  family, 15, 19, 20, 21, 27, 55, 90, 92
  Robert, earl of Fife and Menteith, 195, 203n
  tenants of, 50
  Walter, earl of Menteith, 123
  Walter son of Alan, lord of Strathgryfe, 50, 61, 88, 171, 188, 198, 207; Eschina, wife of, 50, 55, 190; seal of, 86, 90–1; vassals of, 88; *see also* Croc, Sir Robert de; Kent, Robert de
Stirling, 50, 54
  sheriff of, 54
Stirlingshire, 132
Stobo, parish of, 57
Stow, tenants of, 46
Strageath, parish church of, 80
Stratha'an, 162
Strathardle, *sector* of, 58
Strathbrock, 33n
Strathclyde, noblemen of,150
Strathearn, 20, 21, 22, 26, 27, 67n, 94, 126, 129, 130, 136, 147, 170, 195, 204n, 207
  breitheamh of, 56
  countesses of, 128; Iseulte, 55, 98; Marjory, 6, 116, 117, 120, 121, 125, 126, 128; Maud D'Aubigny, 87, 88, 190, 196; Maud of Caithness and Orkney, 126–7, 130, 141n
  courts of, 80
  earldom of, 116
  earls of, 15, 24, 33n, 53, 56, 59, 117, 129, 137, 165; arms of, 93–4, 109n; David Stewart, 27; Ferteth (Ferchad), 88; Gilbert (Gille Brigte), justiciar of Scotia, 19, 87, 98, 120, 121, 189, 190, 196, (Gilbert, son of), 88, 165, *see also* Glencarnie, (Robert, son of), 18, (seal of), 87, 93–4, (tenants of), 88, (wife of) *see* countesses of, (written deeds of), 98; Malise I (Maol Iosa), 106n, 207; Malise

INDEX

II, 6, 7, 117, 120, 121–30, 141n, 166, 206, 208, (arms of), 94, (Cecilia, daughter of), 130, (husband of), 130, *see also* Methven, (Marjory (Mary), daughter of), 126, 128, 129, *see also* Graham, Nicholas de, (Muriel, daughter of), 126, 128–9, 131, *see also* Mar, countesses of, (estates in England), 120–30, (Robert, son of), 130, (sister of), 132, (son-in-law of), 130, *see also* Methven, (written deeds of), 124; Malise III, 6, 7, 20, 21, 80, 129, 130, 133, 135, 136, 192, (arms of), 95, (seal of), 207; Malise IV, 7, 146n; Malise V, earl of Caithness and Orkney, 127; Robert, 116, 120, 121, 189, (arms of), 94, (seal of), 121; Robert Stewart, 195
   family, 7, 9n, 87, 88, 98, 116–37, 189, 197
   Feargus of, 50, 57, 88
   Household of, 197
   Maol Iosa, son of Ferchad of, 88
   tenants of, 21, 55, 98, 130, 198
   written deeds from, 53, 80, 89
Strathgryfe, 19, 88
   Walter son of Alan, lord of *see* Stewart, Walter son of Alan
Strathord, 136
Strathspey, 22, 36n
streams, 59
Stringer, Keith, 2, 6, 55, 113, 188
suit of court, 20, 21, 35n, 50, 89, 156, 157
suitors (*sectores*), 21, 22, 23, 24, 25, 26, 27, 28, 50, 57, 58, 59–60, 80, 89
   of Auchtergaven, 58
   of Murthly, 58
   of Strathardle, 58
sureties *see* pledges
Sutherland, seals of earls of, 86
Swinburne, John de, 132
Swinton, 75, 100n
   Alan de, 118
Swinwood, 174
Swords (Ireland), 152
Sybil, widow of Coldingham, 172
symbolic objects, 27, 76–7

tack *see* lease
Tannadyce, 160
Tarland, 170
Tarves, 56
Tay river, 161
teinds, 43, 183n, 191, 192, 202n
tenant obligations, 20; *see also* castle guard; military service; suit of court
tenants, 18, 22, 24, 27, 44, 54, 55, 59, 76, 96, 155, 157, 168, 173, 188, 192, 193, 196
   Anglian, 54
   Anglo-Norman, 54
   English, 118, 119, 127, 128
   European, 22, 88
   feu, 158
   free, 55–6, 58, 157–8, 167, 169, 175
   Gaelic, 22, 23, 54–9, 60, 81, 82, 83, 88, 89, 98, 155–60, 172

noble, 63
unfree, 167–8
tenure
   free, 21, 57, 158–60
   hereditary, 158
   in baroniam, 15–16
   in feu and heritage, 158
terce, 19; *see also* tocher
terrars, 54
testimony
   of eye-witnesses, 56, 83, 207
   of native Gaels, 56, 57, 158
   oral, 28, 49, 54, 58, 59–60, 63, 78–9, 83, 207
   sworn, 30, 44, 45, 52
thanages, 16, 57, 168; *see also* Auchterarder; Kellie
thanes, 16, 21, 22, 56, 152, 157; *see also* Maol Muire
theft, thieves, 23, 193, 208
Thomas the vicar, 25
Thor, son of Sweyn, seal of, 86
Thurstan, son of Osulf, 156
Tillicoultry, 182n
timber, 83
Tironensian order, 48, 173
tocher, 53, 55, 118–19, 120, 130, 189; *see also* terce
tòiseachean, 16; *see also* thanes
Tom-na-Chaisteal, 26
tournaments, 25, 91, 92
transfer of sasine, 79
Traquair, sheriff of, 45
Tullibardine, Sir William de Moravia of, 94–5
Turgot *see* Margaret, queen of Scotland, biographer of
Turnberry, castle of, 137
Tynedale, liberty of, 41, 129, 132, 144n
Tynwald, 26; *see also* Man

Ulchil the serf, 160
Ulfkil, son of Æthelstan, 156
Umfraville family, 118
   Gilbert de, 119
   Odinel de, 118, 119
unfreedom, 7, 148–9, 171; *see* neyfty; serfdom; slavery
   in Ireland, 151–4, 164, 171
   in Scotland, 149–51, 154–74, 207–8
upland, 54
Urquhart, 19
Urr river, 81
Uviat, David, 48

Valence, Aymer de, 137
valleys, 54, 57, 59
Valognes
   Philip de, 49–50
   William de, 63, 192
vassals, 18, 22, 31, 46, 72, 77, 88, 94, 121, 197
Vaux family, 122
   Sir Robert de, 197
   William de, 48

Vere, Robert de, 40n
Vescy
  Eustace de, 90–1; seal of, 86, 91; written deeds of, 91
  family, 113, 115, 133
  Isabel widow of John de, 133
  Maud de, 144n
  William de, 144
villeinage
  in England, 152, 157, 167
  in Ireland, 151–4
visnet, 209

Wales, 20, 24, 25, 34n, 35n, 75, 76, 155, 179n, 202n
  lawbooks of, 24, 27
  see also Glamorgan, Gwynnedd
Wales, Gerald of, 151
Walter, son of Turpin, 192
Walton, Ness of, 56
wands, 40n
wardrobe, clerk of the, 39n
wardship, 126, 128
Warenne, Ada de, countess of Northumberland, 45, 65n
warrandice, warranty, 62, 209
warrants, 51–2
wayting, 18, 164–5
Wedale, 48
West Reton, 174
West Sands, St Andrews, 25
Westerker, 134–5, 137
western isles (*Ynchgalle*), 2, 21
  Alexander of the, 30
  lords of, 26
  Raonall, son of Somhairle, 28
  see also Argyll, lords of
Westminster, 119, 125
Whithorn, 149
Whitton
  lands of, 91
  Patrick de, seal of, 86
William, son of Bernard, 70n
William I (1165–1214), 15, 43, 44, 46, 47, 48, 49, 50, 54, 55, 62, 78, 79, 87, 88, 91, 94, 97, 117, 118, 120, 129, 157, 162, 163, 164, 172, 197, 204n, 209

granddaughter of, 117
mother of, 55; see also Warenne, Ada de
neyfs of, 162
seal of, 85
written deeds of, 44, 45, 49, 78, 117, 118, 150, 157, 161, 169
Winchester, earl of see Quincy, Roger de
Windsor, treaty of, 153
witness lists, 45, 75, 98, 117, 132, 196, 197; see also charters; clauses of attestation; testing
witnesses, 5, 21, 24, 27, 29, 42, 48, 49, 50, 57, 58, 59–60, 63, 74, 75–6, 78, 87, 116, 141n, 146n, 156, 158–9
women, 25, 63, 73, 84, 158
  as land holders, 55, 163
  as perambulators, 55
  as slaves, 150
  seal usage by, 89
  seals of, 84
  serfs, 152, 161, 164, 167, 172, 208
  written deeds of, 189, 194
woodlands, 46, 54, 166; see also forest
Wooler (Northumberland)
  bailiffs of, 128
  barony of, 6, 116, 117, 118, 119, 121, 125, 127, 128, 130, 131, 133, 135, 137
  hospital of St Mary Magdalene in, 127, 133
  parish church of, 125, 127, 134
  peasant tenants of, 127, 128
  see also Muschamp
writing, 27, 30, 56, 59–60, 73–82
writ of naifty (English), 162
writs, 84, 153, 162; see also brieves
written deeds, written instruments, 27, 28, 30, 58, 59, 63, 73–83, 84, 89, 94, 98–9, 148, 149, 187, 188, 190, 195, 196, 199, 207; see also brieves; charters; chirographs; indentures; letters; notifications; sealed instruments

year books, 13, 14
Yeavering (Northumberland), 127
Yynchgalle, 22; see also Argyll
York, 121
  treaty of, 204n
Yorkshire, 115, 137